Microsoft Access
Inside & Out

Mary Campbell

Microsoft Access
Inside & Out

Osborne **McGraw-Hill**
Berkeley New York St. Louis San Francisco
Auckland Bogotà Hamburg London Madrid
Mexico City Milan Montreal New Delhi Panama City
Paris São Paulo Singapore Sydney
Tokyo Toronto

Osborne **McGraw-Hill**
2600 Tenth Street
Berkeley, California 94710 U.S.A.

For information on translations and book distributors outside of the U.S.A., please write to Osborne **McGraw-Hill** at the above address.

Inside & Out Series

234567890 DOC 99876543

ISBN 0-07-881818-4

Publisher
Kenna S. Wood

Acquisitions Editor
Frances Stack

Associate Editor
Jill Pisoni

Editorial Assistant
Judith Kleppe

Project Editor
Cindy Brown

Copy Editor
Ann Krueger Spivack

Proofreaders
Linda Medoff
Lindy Clinton

Indexer
Richard Shrout

Computer Designer
Patricia Jani Beckwith

Illustrator
Susie Kim

Cover Designer
Mason Fong

Contents at a Glance

Part VII • Appendixes

Contents

Part I • Creating Access Databases

Part II • Queries

Part III • Forms and Reports

15   *Adding OLE Objects to Forms and Reports* **437**

Part IV · Macros

Part V • Network and Administrative Topics

19 Special Considerations for Network Use 535

20 Network Administrator's Guide to Access 545

Part VI • Programming

21 Introduction to Access Basic 575

Part VII · Appendixes

Acknowledgments

I would like to thank Cedar Point Amusement Park/Resort in Sandusky, Ohio for the pictures of the roller coasters in the book. I also appreciate the information they supplied on the 100 years of roller coasters at the park since it provided helpful information on the construction and operation of the coasters. Cedar point has 10 roller coasters, more than any amusement park in the world. Special thanks to Robin Innes of Cedar Point Amusement Park/Resort for his help in getting the material we needed during the park's busy summer season. For more information on park hours for the 1993 season you can call (419) 628-0830.

I would like to thank Gabrielle Lawrence for all her work on the project.

Special thanks to the many individuals at Microsoft who helped with this project especially Erin Carney, Shelly Womac, Marty Taucher, and Monte Slichter.

All of the staff at Osborne played an important role in completing this project. Frances Stack was an important help in securing the needed beta and making arrangements for the special photographs needed for the book. Jill Pisoni was also helpful in coordinating all the pieces of this large project as we worked against tight deadlines. Cindy Brown and all of the other dedicated staff members in the production department at Osborne did an excellent job with the book and helped make this tightly scheduled project as painless as possible.

Introduction

Microsoft is the industry leader in providing application software for the Windows environment. Since they are the developers of Windows itself and have many years of experience with this environment, their leadership position in application software for the Windows platform is not surprising. The new Access data management software has many exciting features that will help it to become the leading Windows data management program.

Access database management software has been many years in development. It is designed for users who want to take full advantage of the Windows environment for their database management tasks while remaining end users and leaving the programming to others. Access supports dynamic data exchange (DDE), the ability to incorporate text and graphics on a screen or report. The product provides a graphical user interface like one you would expect from any leading product in this market. Reports, forms, and queries are easy to design and execute. For individuals with a technical slant, you'll appreciate the macro and programming capabilities of this full-featured product. Access Basic is the programming language supported, which some users may have already mastered by using Quick Basic.

About This Book

Access Inside and Out is designed for every Access user. A new user will probably want to start at the beginning of the book and read the chapters in the first few parts before skipping to specific topics at the end. Intermediate and advanced users will probably want to skip to the exact information that they need to solve the problem at hand.

This book provides the essential information that you will need on each topic. It provides the necessary steps to duplicate complicated actions quickly. The examples are designed to be practical business applications with as much high-interest material as possible. This book has numerous examples that show creative screen and report designs.

How This Book Is Organized

Access Inside and Out is divided into 7 parts, 21 chapters, and 5 appendices. You will find all the major topics and features covered in this material.

Part I introduces you to Basic Features. In Chapter 1 you learn about the new terminology for Access, the database components, and an overview of what the product does. In Chapter 2 you learn how to design an Access database and its associated tables. You learn what field types to use for each type of information that you want to store. In Chapter 3 you learn how to customize the basic tables by changing field properties, relationships, and indexes. In Chapter 4 you learn how to enter and edit data. Chapter 5 shows you how to utilize any data entry investment you have already made as you import and export data.

Part II focuses on queries which are used to answer questions about the database data as you view a subset of the records. In Chapter 6 you learn how to design queries that select data. In Chapter 7 you create more sophisticated queries that access multiple tables, compute query totals, and produce cross tabs.

Part III covers Forms and Reports. In Chapter 8 you learn how to create a custom form with the FormWizard. In Chapter 9 you learn how to create, name, save, and print a basic report. Chapters 10 and 11 cover customizing forms and reports with controls and other settings. In Chapter 12 you learn how to use expressions in reports and forms to compute a field on a form or report or compute totals across records. Chapter 13 focuses on using multiple tables in reports and forms. In Chapter 14 you learn how to use color, 3D, and special effects. Chapter 15 shows you how to use Object Linking and Embedding (OLE) to add pictures, charts, and objects that have been created in other programs such as Microsoft Paintbrush to your forms and reports.

Part IV covers macros which allow you to automate tasks. Chapter 16 introduces you to basic concepts and options. Chapter 17 provides some examples of using macros in forms and reports. Chapter 18 shows you how to create a custom application.

Part V covers network & administrative topics. Chapter 19 covers editing data in a multi-user environment and other special considerations for network users. Chapter 20 is a network administrator's guide for Access covering security settings, backup considerations, and recovery and compaction procedures.

Part VI introduces programming with Access Basic.

Part VII contains all the appendixes for this book.

Conventions Used

Throughout the book, menu selections and dialog box options are shown with underlined letters to indicate which letter you type to activate a menu or make a selection from it.

Although this book is not a tutorial, there are some examples of how to complete data entry. The data to be entered is shown in bold.

When keys are to be pressed in combination they are joined with a hyphen as in CTRL-HOME. Keys to be pressed sequentially one after the other are joined with a comma (,) as in HOME, DOWN ARROW.

PART

I

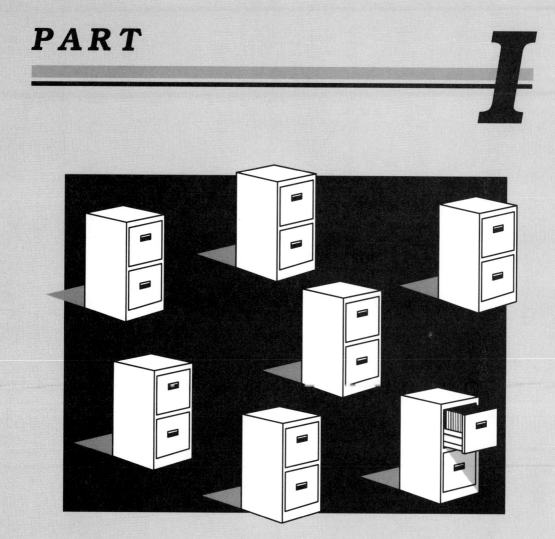

Creating Access Databases

CHAPTER

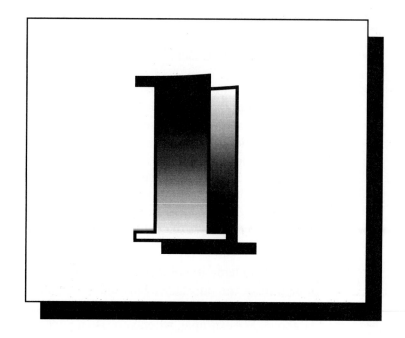

Introduction to Access

Microsoft Access is an exciting new database management system for Windows. It provides standard data management features for data storage and retrieval but uses graphical tools made possible by the Windows environment to make tasks easier to perform.

Microsoft Access' new terminology and wide array of features may seem a little overwhelming at first. This book is designed to put you at ease and explain the terminology and features that you need to be productive immediately even if this is the first database that you have used. This chapter introduces the basic components of the package and provides general instructions that will work in any part of the package.

What Is an Access Database?

Like other database management systems, Access provides a way to store and manage information. Microsoft refers to Access as a *relational database product* since Access allows you to relate data from different sources. Although the package may not meet some other components of a true relational database we will consider it to be such for the purposes of this book. If you are interested in reading more rigorous descriptions of relational databases, look at one of the several college text books available on database management or consult the writings of C.J. Date *Database: A Primer*, or James Martin *Principles of Database Management*.

Access considers both the tables of data that store your information and the supplemental objects that present information and work with it to be part of the database. This differs from standard database system terminology in which only the data itself is considered part of the database. For example, when you use a package such as dBASE IV, you might have an employee database, a client database, and a supplier database. Each of the databases are separate files. You would have additional files in your dBASE directory for reports and forms. With Access you could have all three types of information in one database along with the accompanying reports and forms. All the data and other database objects would all be stored in one file in the same fashion as an R:Base database.

Access stores data in tables that are organized by rows and columns. A database can contain one table or many. Other objects such as reports, forms, queries, macros, and program modules are considered to be part of the database along with the tables. You can have these other objects in the database along with the tables—either including them from the beginning or adding them as you need them.

The basic requirement to having a database is that you have at least one table. All other objects are optional. Storing the related objects in the same file as the table makes it easy to organize everything you need in one place with one filename, which expedites making the crucial backups needed to safeguard your data investments. While this approach means improved relational integrity between database components, it also has some drawbacks—such as lengthier and more difficult data recovery and database optimization.

Since an Access database can contain many tables and other objects it is possible to create one database that will meet the information requirements for an entire company. You can build this database gradually, adding information and reports for various application areas as you have time. You can define relationships between pieces of information in tables.

You can have more than one database in Access. Each database has its own tables and other objects. You can use the move and copy features of this package to move and copy objects from one database to another although you will only work with one database at a time.

As you build more sophisticated systems you will use all the objects that Access supports. For now, a quick look at each component will show you the building blocks that you can use as you create your own databases.

Tables

Tables are tabular arrangements of information. *Columns* represent *fields* of information or one particular piece of information that can be stored for each entity in the table. The *rows* of the table contain the records. A *record* contains one of each field in the database. Although a field can be left blank, each record in the database has the potential for storing information in each field in the table. Figure 1-1 shows some of the fields and records in an Access table.

Generally each major type of information in the database is represented by a table. You might have a Supplier table, a Client table, and an Employee table. It is unlikely that such dissimilar information would be placed together in the same table although this information is all part of the same database.

Other considerations determine how you group data into tables. For example, you try to eliminate any duplicate data (referred to as *data redundancy*). You would avoid a database design that requires the same information to be entered multiple times; for example, separate tables for client information and orders rather than maintaining only one table and duplicating client data in multiple order records.

Access allows you to define relationships between fields in various tables. Using the associations you establish you can show data from more than one table on the screen or in a report.

Access provides two different views for tables. The design view, shown in Figure 1-2, is used when you are defining the data elements to be

FIGURE 1-1   An Access table in datasheet view

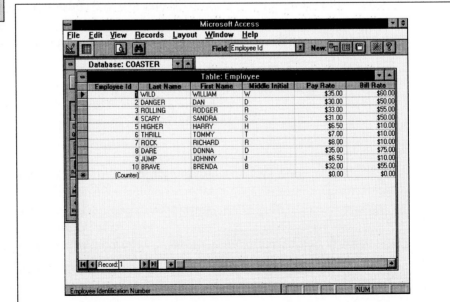

FIGURE
1-2

The design view of the table shown in Figure 1-1

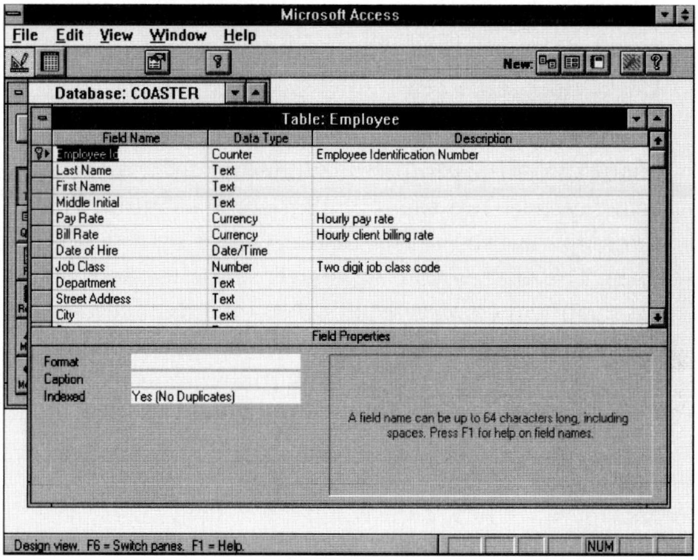

stored in the table. For each field in the table you define the field name and data type. You can also set field properties to change the field format and caption (used for the field on reports and forms), provide validation rules to check data validity, create index entries for the field, and provide a default value.

In the datasheet view you can enter data into fields or look at existing records in the table. Figures 1-1 and 1-2 show the same Employee table—Figure 1-1 presents the datasheet view of it and Figure 1-2 shows the design view.

Queries

Access supports three different kinds of queries: select, action, and parameter. Select queries choose records from a table and store them in a table called a *dynaset*. Action queries update values in a database table.

Parameter queries let you change the criteria for a query operation each time you use it.

Select Queries

Select queries are essentially questions that you want to ask Access about the entries in fields. When most database users think of queries, select queries are the type that come to mind. You can use your mouse to complete the entries in the Query-by-Example window that Access uses. The entries you make will define for Access the fields and records that you want in a special table—the dynaset—that contains the query results. You can use complicated combinations of criteria to define your needs and see only the records that you need. Figure 1-3 shows the data in the QBE grid that will select the records that you want. You can place entries in the Sort row to specify the order of records in the resulting query.

FIGURE 1-3 The QBE grid with query entries

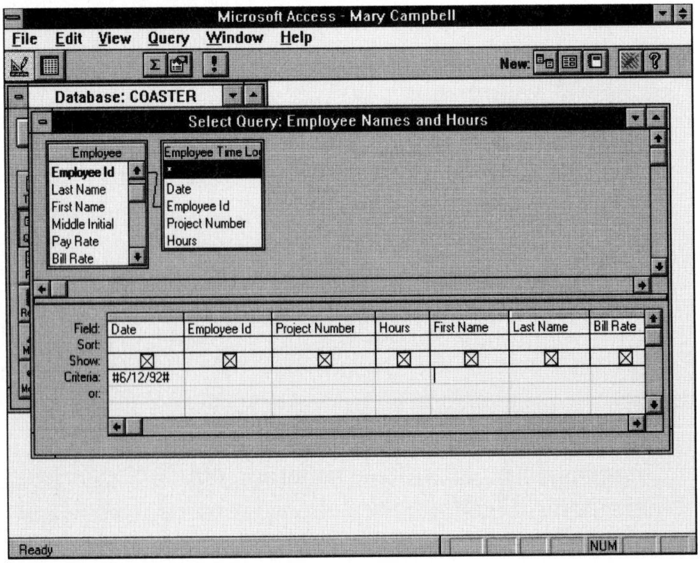

Action Queries

Action queries allow you to change an entire group of records in one step. For example, you can use action queries to remove records for former employees or increase the salary field for a specific job code by 10 percent. You must specify that you want an action query; Access notes your request with a special icon to ensure that records are not deleted or fields altered inadvertently.

Parameter Queries

Parameter queries allow you to change the criteria with each use of the query. Access will prompt you for criteria entries with the QBE grid. They are a useful tool that you can create for end users who want to fill in a dialog box rather than a QBE grid.

You can use Access query features for many different applications. Queries can calculate a total for records that match your specifications. You can even create a crosstab feature with select queries to summarize data according to your specifications. Access processes each record before computing totals.

If you have defined relationships between tables, Access recognizes these relationships and combines data from multiple tables in a query result. If the relationships are not defined you can still associate data in related tables by joining them.

Reports

Reports are the tool of choice when you want to print information from a number of records. You can see the detail as you can with a form on the screen but you can't look at many records at the same time. You can also look at summary information obtained after reading every record in the table. Reports can show the data from either a table or a query. Figure 1-4 shows a report created with Access.

For an easy approach to creating a report use the ReportWizards that come with Access. By responding to a series of questions you tell Access exactly what you want your report to look like. With the ReportWizards

FIGURE

1-4

An Access report

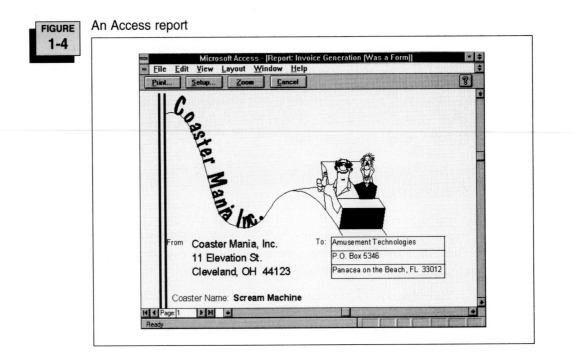

you can create a variety of different reports including mailing labels that might be needed for a customer file.

You do not have to use the ReportWizards to create a report entirely on your own. You can lay out exactly what you want. The report design screen shown in Figure 1-5 is divided into sections. The sections indicate whether the information prints at the beginning or end of a report, the top or bottom of each page, or for each new record processed. The controls that you add to each section control the data that prints at these locations in the report.

Since reports can be used to show a summary of all the records, you can present a summary view rather than the detail. You can add a graph to a report with Microsoft Graph. Graphs are frequently used to create a picture of the data in a few fields of a table or query.

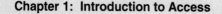

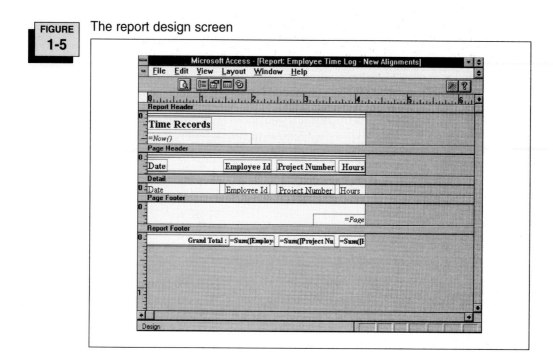

FIGURE 1-5   The report design screen

Forms

You can use forms to view the records in tables or to add new records. Unlike datasheets, which present many records on the screen at one time, forms have a narrower focus and present one record on the screen at a time (although they do allow you to use subforms to display related records from another table at the same time). You can use either queries or tables as the input for a form.

You can create forms with FormWizards and have Access help you with the creation process. A few quick choices enable you to create a form with little work. Your best bet may be to create a form with FormWizards and then customize it to meet your needs.

Controls are placed on a form to display fields or text. You can select these controls and move them to a new location or resize them to give your form the look you want. You can move separately the controls for fields and the text that describes that field. You also can add other text to the form. You can change the appearance of text on a form by changing the font or adding boldface or italic to it. You also can choose to show text as raised or sunken or to use a specific color. Lines and rectangles also can be added to a form to enhance its appearance. Figure 1-6 shows a form developed to present data in an appealing manner.

Like fields, the controls on a form have properties. You can change them to make a form function differently. Attached labels, sections of a form, and the form itself all offer different properties that you can change. You can choose options that let you display field values in a list or change the width of a column.

You can create filters to use with forms. Just like filters for water that trap objects and do not let them flow through to the other side, filters with forms stop records from being available when they do not match the criteria established for the filter.

Forms allow you to show data from multiple tables. You can build a query first to select the data that will appear on a form or use subforms

FIGURE
1-6

An Access form

to handle the multiple tables you want to work with. A subform displays the records associated with a particular field on a form. Subforms provide the best solution when you have a field in a record in one table related to many records in another table. They allow you to show the data from one record at the top of the form with the data from related records shown below it.

Macros, which allow you to record a set of actions, can be assigned to the events that occur on forms. *Events* happen at particular points in time in the use of a form. Moving from one record to the next is an example of an event that can have a macro associated with it. The macro will carry out the specified steps when the event occurs. Other events that are recognized are opening a form, changing the current record, changing data on a form, inserting a record, deleting a record, selecting a control, closing a form, pressing a command button, or double-clicking a control.

Modules

Modules are programs or sets of instructions designed to perform a specific task or series of tasks. Modules for Microsoft Access are written in Access BASIC code. Modules are slightly more complex than macros and should be avoided until you have mastered the basic package features.

Modules consist of a number of procedures written in Access BASIC, which is the programming language provided with the package. These procedures can be one of two types: function procedures that return a value that can be used within an expression and subprocedures that cannot be used in expressions.

Module code can be viewed and edited in a module window that looks like this:

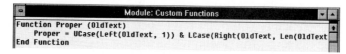

```
Module: Custom Functions
Function Proper (OldText)
    Proper = UCase(Left(OldText, 1)) & LCase(Right(OldText, Len(OldText
End Function
```

The module window provides a text editor that works similarly to your notepad or word processor, making it easy to enter and edit text.

Macros

Macros arc a series of steps or keystrokes that you record; you play back this "recording" when needed by pressing just one or two keys. Macros are an ideal solution for repetitive tasks. You specify the exact steps they should perform and they can do so whenever you need these steps again without making a mistake. Macros are like having an unpaid assistant, who's committed to perfection, ready to do your bidding.

Access macros are easy to work with since Access provides a menu-selectable list of all the actions that you can use in a macro. Once you select an action, you use *arguments* to control the specific effect of the action. Arguments differ for each of the actions since each action requires different information before it can perform a task. In Figure 1-7 the macro instructions are entered in a macro window. For many argument entries, Access provides its best guess at which entry you will want—you only need to change it if you want something different.

You can add a command button control to a form that will execute a macro when you select the button. You can even add a button to a form that will open a second form. Macros allow other sophisticated options such as custom menus and pop-up forms for data collection.

You can execute macros from the database window or other locations. Figure 1-8 shows a number of macros in the database window. You can highlight a macro and then select Run to execute it.

Requirements for Using Access

There are specific hardware requirements that must be met to use Access effectively. Although you might be able to start the program if you are missing one of these you will not be pleased with the performance of the package. You must have specific operating system software to install the package and adequate hardware to use it.

Microsoft Access is installed from within Windows; therefore, you must install the required operating system software first. Microsoft Access requires DOS 3.1 or later as well as Windows 3.0 or later.

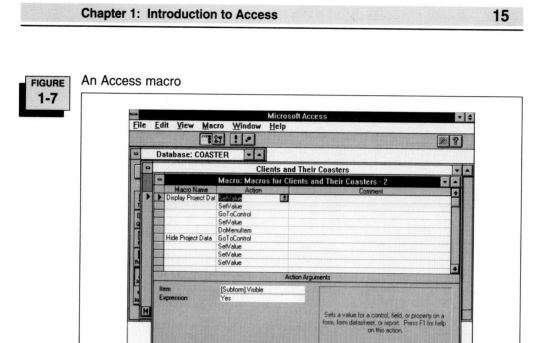

FIGURE 1-7 An Access macro

FIGURE 1-8 A window with many macros listed

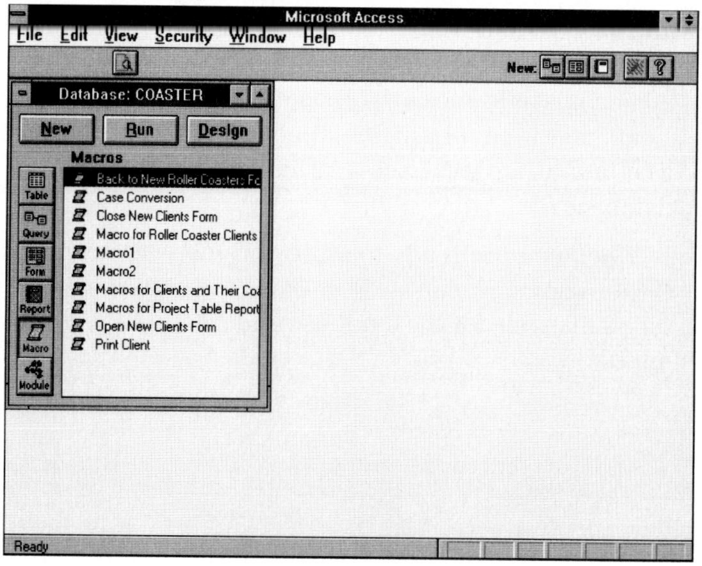

Hardware requirements include 11MB of free space on your hard disk and at least 2MB of RAM although performance will be much better if you have at least 4MB of RAM. You must have a computer with a 80386 or 80486 processor and a Microsoft-compatible mouse. A VGA monitor is recommended, although an EGA display can be used.

Acquiring the Basic Skills

Access uses the same techniques for navigating through Access objects, menus, and screens that other Windows applications do. If you have used Microsoft Word or Microsoft Excel you are already familiar with these techniques. If you focused solely on DOS applications such as dBASE IV you will need to learn to use Windows techniques and terminology before you are comfortable with Access. This section introduces you to some of the important windows in the package and discusses how to select various objects that you see on your screen.

The Access Window

When you first start Access, the Access window shown in Figure 1-9 appears. No database is open and there are only two menu options. You will use this window to open a database or to perform other tasks that are not possible once a database is open. These tasks include compacting a database to save hard disk space and encrypting the database to ensure that unauthorized users cannot decipher anything useful from the database file.

When you are ready to start working with an existing database or to create a new one, choose New Database from the File menu. You will then type a filename for the database and select OK. The database window will appear.

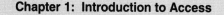

FIGURE
1-9

The first window you see upon starting Access

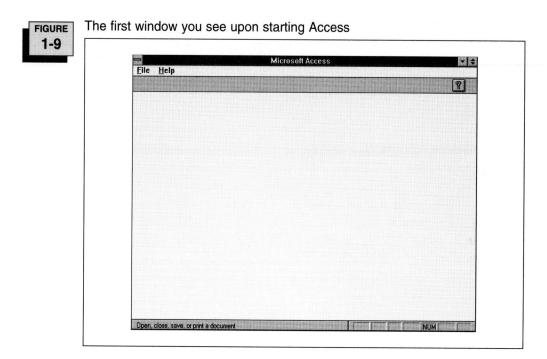

The Database Window

Once you have opened a database a window like the one in Figure 1-10 appears. This window allows you to access any object in the database with a quick selection of one of the object buttons. Initially the table button is selected and any tables in the database are listed.

If you want to look at a list of all the objects of another type, click the icon for any object and a complete list of all the named objects appears. This means that you can click the Macro button for a list of all the macros in the current database, or you can click the Query button to see if any queries have been created in the current database. The buttons that appear near the top of the window allow you to create a new object or perform another task.

FIGURE
1-10

The Database window

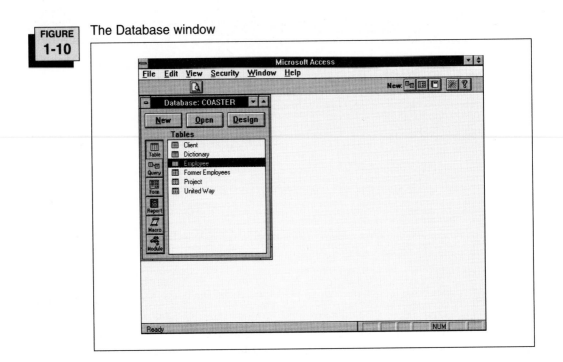

The menu that appears when the Database window is active is much more comprehensive than the initial Access menu although some of the Access menu options are not listed. Missing menu options are primarily due to the fact that some tasks such as encryption and compaction cannot be done while a database is open. The basic menu options remain the same even though you change the type of object that provides the entries in the current list of object names.

Using Menus

Menus offer choices within Access. You use them to select many different tasks as you work with the package.

As mentioned earlier, there are only two choices in the menu bar when you first start Access. After opening a database, the menu bar offers six different drop-down menu options.

You can pull down a menu in several ways. You can click the name of the menu in the menu bar. If you click File, a menu that looks like this will appear:

Another option is to press the ALT key in combination with the underlined letter from the menu name. Once the menu is displayed you can type the underlined letter to select an option or click the choice in the drop-down menu that you want. Menu options that appear dimmed or in a different color are not available for your selection at the current time. They may only be appropriate with a different object or after another action. Menu options that are followed by an ellipses (...) display a dialog box when you select them. Menu options followed by a triangle display another menu to give you more options.

Using the Toolbar

The toolbar appears beneath the menu bar. The icons it contains will vary depending on the object that you are working with. You can click the desired icon to make your selection.

When you are working with a table there are toolbar options for choosing a datasheet or a design view. When working with macros there are icons in the toolbar for single step mode and displaying conditions and macro names.

All of the toolbar choices have comparable menu selections. You can use either approach to accomplish the task but since the toolbar only requires a click it can be the quickest way to accomplish a task.

Completing Dialog Boxes

An ellipses after a menu option indicates that a dialog box will appear when you select the menu option. Unlike menus, there is no single simple way to interface with dialog boxes. Different techniques are used for informing Access of what you want depending on the type of reasons being elicited. Access does employ the standard techniques used for all Windows applications so you will know what to do if you have already used another Windows application.

If Windows is a new environment for you, you will need to learn how option buttons, drop-down list boxes, text boxes, check boxes, and command buttons work. The following illustration shows some of the possible components for a dialog box. You will notice names within the dialog boxes near most components. You can use the underlined letter to make that section of the dialog box active or simply click the mouse on the option you want.

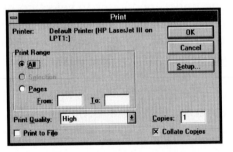

Text boxes offer the most flexibility for your entry. You can type whatever text you want into the box within the limitations for the entry you are making. If you are attempting to look for a record that contains a specific entry you will use a text box to specify what you are looking for. When you use the File Run Macro command a text box will be used to specify the macro name.

Check boxes offer choices. You can choose more than one check box option by clicking it. An x appears when the option is selected. Clicking it again removes the selection, and the x disappears. Check boxes are often grouped together. Unlike option buttons, discussed next, you can choose more than one.

Option buttons offer choices for a command but they are mutually exclusive. Selecting one unselects any other option button in the group that may be currently selected. You can select an option by pressing ALT and its underlined letter or simply clicking the button with your mouse.

A drop-down list box looks a lot like a text box with an entry already in it. It has an arrow to the right of the box that you can click to drop down a list of options. You can also activate the box with the ALT key and underlined letter and then use ALT and the DOWN ARROW key to display the list of options. A selection can be chosen by highlighting it and pressing ENTER or by clicking it with the mouse.

Command buttons finalize the actions in the dialog box. If you press ENTER with a command button highlighted, the box is closed when your request is completed. Most dialog boxes have command buttons representing OK and Cancel. OK executes the requested command with the current dialog box settings. Cancel cancels the request and ignores the dialog box entries.

Quick Reference

To Open a New Database   From the Access window choose New Database from the File menu. Type a name (one to eight characters in length) and then select OK.

To Make a Selection from the Menu   Click the menu name and then click the desired menu option (or press ALT plus the underlined menu letter) and then type the letter of the desired selection.

To Move to a Different Area of a Dialog Box   Click the desired location or press ALT plus the underlined letter.

CHAPTER

Designing an Access Database

An Access *database* is a collection of tabular information *and* the tools that you create to access the information. This terminology may differ from other databases in which each type of information is stored as a file and the entire collection of files is called a database; in those databases, information for creating reports and defining screens is kept in other types of files.

The tools included in an Access database are reports and forms. These integral components of the Access database unlock its power and usefulness, as you'll see throughout this book. Also, Access makes it easy to back up all of your important information since your data, reports, forms, queries, and indexes are all part of one database file.

All of the data within an Access database is stored in *tables*—rectangular arrangements of data that have a row and column orientation. An Access database can be as simple as a table containing the names and addresses of your clients or, if you are storing personal data, perhaps a table containing information about your CD collection. On the other hand, an Access database can be comprehensive tables of employees, suppliers, inventory, and billing information in addition to the table of clients. The Access database contains all the forms and reports that you designed to utilize the data tables just mentioned.

Microsoft refers to Access as a *relational database* because it allows you to define relationships between tables. For example, you can combine information from an employee file and a payroll file to put employee names and addresses on checks without recording them in both the employee and payroll files.

 Note This book adheres to Microsoft's terminology, calling Access a relational database to be consistent with Microsoft's documentation. However, many database experts feel that other requirements—which Access lacks—must be met before a database system may be called relational.

Whether you want to create an Access database that consists of a single table or utilize its ability to handle data relationships, you start the process by analyzing your needs and designing the database to meet those needs. You will find that an iterative approach to analysis and design will best serve your long-term goals. After making your best first attempt, take another look at both your analysis and design to see if you have forgotten any important data or if you can improve the organization and relationships that you initially define. Time invested in these vital tasks can save you significant time later since you will build a database that provides good performance and meets both short-term and long-term needs.

If you are an old hand at database design, you have already developed your own techniques for defining information needs and creating a workable database design. Your techniques will work with Microsoft Access just as they have for any other relational database package. Your database design may be complete, in which case you'll be eager to start setting up your own database rather than reading about the analysis phase of database creation. Skip to "Setting Up a Microsoft Access Database" later in this chapter, where you can apply your own design to creating a new Microsoft Access database.

Performing the Required Analysis

The objective of your analysis is to create a database design that will meet your short-term and long-term needs. To do this you must define what data is needed, and then look at options for organizing it into tables. The best way for you to do this is to examine current work flows and information sources. Look at the information that flows into various departments in the business as orders or invoices are processed, and then look at the information outflows as data is sent to accounting or shipping departments.

One of the initial steps in the design process is to define the *fields* or important pieces of information. A field can be a phone number, city, ZIP code, or part number. While designing your database, you will need to define each of the fields of information that you currently use. You will also need to list fields that you would like to use in the future to ensure that your design meets your needs for tomorrow as well as today. Figure 2-1 shows fields of information currently in use as well as new fields being compiled into a list.

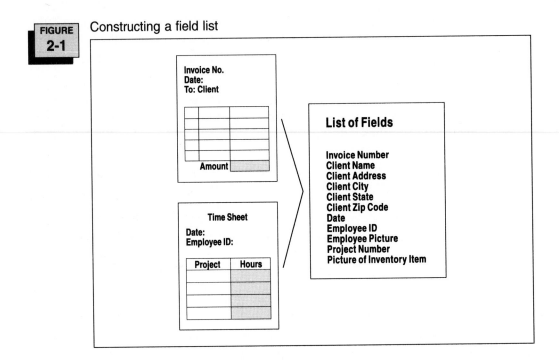

FIGURE 2-1   Constructing a field list

Defining Current Needs

Look at existing reports, computer applications, and all forms that you currently use. Approach one application area at a time if you are working with several. For example, explore all the information on employees before you address the projects that they might be assigned to or the clients they are assisting. As you address each new area, relevant data for other areas might come to light and can be added to the list for that area. You will do a more thorough job if you focus on one area at a time. Sometimes you will look at reports that actually bring together information from several different sources. Try to identify the basic categories of information and examine each in detail.

Jot down each field that you identify on a sheet of paper or, better yet, enter each field on a new line in a word processing document. This is the beginning of your *data dictionary* or list of relevant fields for your new database application. Later you can add information such as length, data types, definition, and database tables to your data dictionary as shown in Figure 2-2.

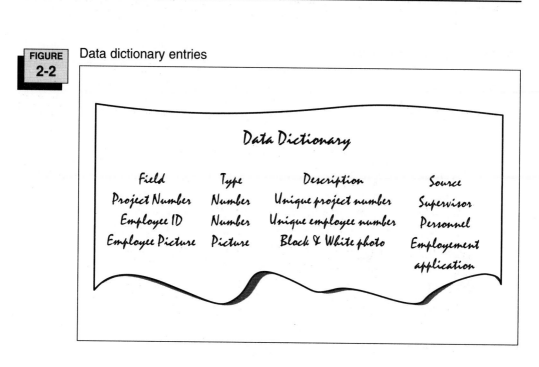

FIGURE 2-2   Data dictionary entries

Jot down or enter every field you come up with, even if you are not certain that you want all of them. This is not the time to eliminate information but rather a chance to make an exhaustive list of every field you might possibly want to include. Before creating the database tables you can purge fields that you do not need.

Defining Future Needs

After listing all the known fields of information that you currently use, focus on what you wish you had available. For example, the current employee report may show the employee's name, social security number, and salary. You might wish you had the employee's supervisor and phone extension on the report. Add these two elements to your field list. If you are aware of planned changes that might necessitate additional fields of data later, add them to your list. Maybe your company intends to add an employee health plan and will eventually need a field that indicates whether the employee subscribes to the plan. Although the plan is not yet in effect, this future need should be covered by the addition of a new field now.

Maybe payroll is currently handled by an outside service bureau. If you want to continue with the service bureau arrangement, fields for exemptions and filing status will not be needed in the employee table. If you think your company will ever consider bringing payroll processing in house, you will most likely need a social security number field and fields for benefit withholding such as medical insurance.

Ask people who use the information to list currently unavailable fields that would enable them to make better business decisions. If possible, look at systems implemented by others in your industry group to see what types of information they capture that you currently ignore. Industry trade groups are often good sources for this type of information as well as a free exchange of information with others in different parts of the country, enabling you to meet individuals perhaps more willing to share information than nearby competitors.

Allowing Adequate Time for Analysis

If your database has a single focus such as employee information, making the list might only take a few minutes. If you are creating a more comprehensive database that includes employees, suppliers, clients, orders, and accounts receivable information your task is much greater and will take much longer to complete. Focus on one area of the company at a time for the best results.

Since you might not be an expert in each of these areas, interview users who are experts to ensure that the comprehensive company database that you create will meet their needs.

 Tip Have several users from each area look over the list of elements that you have created to ensure that you have not omitted vital fields that are only needed occasionally.

Since a rushed design is often discarded for a new one at a later time, reports and forms must often be redone. To save yourself time, money, and frustration, do not rush through the design phase no matter how much you need the database application. If your time is limited or you are facing a deadline, your best strategy is to focus on one area and give it adequate time. You can add the other information later when you have sufficient time to explore your options more thoroughly.

Looking at a Fictional Example

One of the advantages of a product such as Access is that you can customize the database to meet your exact needs. This is important since even two companies in the same business are unlikely to design the same database. This also means that no example in this book will match your needs exactly. However, you can learn a lot about how to construct your ideal system by looking at existing system designs and deciding which features you want to incorporate into your own design and which features don't work for you.

The examples in this book use a fictitious company, Coaster Mania, which constructs amusement park roller coasters. This type of company was chosen because its records show different types of data and a variety of tables. Although your company probably does not construct roller coasters, it likely requires employee and client data just like Coaster Mania's. Also, you probably need to send invoices or bills for products or services just like Coaster Mania does.

Other aspects of Coaster Mania's needs may be quite different. You probably are not concerned with the cost of a coaster car or its angle of ascent. Even so, the opportunity for an in-depth look at Coaster Mania's design dilemmas and the decisions made here will help you design a database to fit your needs. Although some of the fields of information vary greatly from yours, the opportunity to look at the formatting and validating for Coaster Mania will help you define your own data tables.

During the analysis for Coaster Mania, employees, coaster projects, clients, and invoicing were examined. Coaster Mania has many other information areas not currently addressed as Figure 2-3 shows.

Every area is studied separately to create the most thorough field list possible. Each of the following sections describe the considerations in listing the Coaster Mania fields. You may have some of the same types of information in your database.

Other business areas, such as payroll and inventory, were not included in this analysis. Although some companies attempt to perform a complete conversion to automation for all areas at one time through the creation of a very comprehensive database, this is often the wrong approach. It's often best to get some of the application areas up and

FIGURE 2-3
Coaster Mania's many types of information

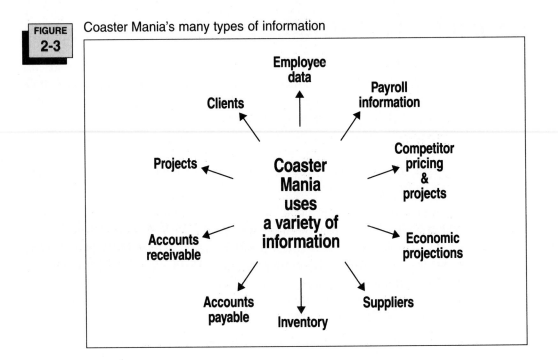

running, while you plan the addition of other information tables to the database for a later time.

Client Information

Although Coaster Mania has only a small number of active clients at one time, they include prospective clients in their client list. If the firm's management visits a current construction site they will often visit nearby amusement parks to check on the completed projects and to explore the potential for new coaster projects.

Currently Coaster Mania stores basic information on the various parks on index cards like the one shown in Figure 2-4. The initial fields taken from their list of existing clients might include any of these fields:

Client ID
Client Name
Contact

Park Location
Mailing Address
City
State
ZIP Code
Phone
Park Desc
YTD Invoices
YTD Payments
Total Invoices
Total Payments

In talking to the marketing people you find that they would like to include general information about each amusement park as well as a list of the park's current roller coasters. These fields are added as a result of those discussions:

Park Description
Park Coasters

FIGURE
2-4

Index card containing client information

CLIENT ID: 91   CLIENT NAME: Muskegon Park

CONTACT: ~~Judy Lyle~~ ~~Jim Smith~~ Susan Carter

PARK LOCATION: Muskegon Lakefront

MAILING ADDRESS: P.O. Box 3418

CITY: Muskegon   STATE: MI   ZIP CODE: 49081

PHONE: (616) ~~234-4444~~ ~~584-7211~~ 872-9999

PARK DESCRIPTION: Small family run amusement park
                   with 2 roller coasters and 14 other rides

Employees

Currently, Coaster Mania does not have an electronic file containing employee information. All of the available information on employees is maintained in personnel, and the file there is maintained by the employee's supervisor. Since it is unlikely that personnel will be dismantled, you don't need to add this information to your database list. Because payroll is handled by an outside service bureau, there is no need to add payroll fields to the list.

Although there has been some discussion of creating a Skills database to help select the best employee for a project, the company feels that there won't be sufficient knowledge of the information that must be maintained to make a Skills database workable until they have an opportunity to study the data stored by other companies. Management would like to include each employee's picture in the database. Thus far, this is the list of fields for the employee database:

Employee ID
Name
Pay Rate
Bill Rate
Date of Hire
Job Class
Department
Street Address
City
State
ZIP Code
Picture
Home Phone
Extension

After examining the initial list it is decided to split the Name field into three components: first name, last name, and middle initial.

Coaster Projects

The roller coaster projects that Coaster Mania maintains include information on proposed coasters, active construction sites, and completed coasters. These files are not currently stored in one central place. A proposed project file is kept by the member of the management team that is handling the proposal and current project folders are kept by the project manager. Completed project files can be in one of many locations and often are located only after a lengthy search. A database containing the information would offer the advantage of being instantly accessible to everyone. The company is especially eager to be able to share sketches or pictures of the coaster with everyone, and is looking for a database solution that will allow the use of these pictures in addition to other data.

The total number of coasters is less than 100, including those being planned, those under construction, and those completed. Although some fields are only pertinent to active projects, management wants to be able to enter queries that would include active, completed, and inactive sites—so all 100 will be stored in one table. Since there is no single correct design for a database, it is possible to develop another equally feasible solution that would not have all three types of projects in the same file. The fields of information relating to coaster projects are as follows:

Coaster ID
Coaster Name
Client ID Number
Completed
Operational
Est Cost
Actual Cost
Track
Height
Drop
Angle
Time
Speed
Capacity
Vehicles
Picture
Features

Separate fields for the park and the location were considered but since the Company ID field provides this information, management preferred to retrieve it from there when needed rather than duplicate it in the coaster records.

Time Reporting

Employees might work on several different projects at any one time. This is especially true for projects in the design phase when employees might put the finishing touches on several different blueprints or models in a given week.

Employees log their hours on weekly time sheets, which give total hours spent on each project that week. Figure 2-5 shows one of these time sheets. Although management considered having the employees account for time by activity, they decided that this would not give them any better information and so abandoned the idea.

This is the data from the time logs:

Date
Employee ID
Project
Hours
Comments

FIGURE 2-5 Weekly employee time sheet

Time Sheet

Employee name:
Employee ID:
Week ending: 7/24/92

Project	Hours	Comments
3	8.2	Meet with engineers
1	24	Complete project sketches
19	8.5	Site selection
Total	40.7	

Currently these sheets are processed monthly. Invoices are prepared manually to bill clients for hours on a cost plus basis. Time sheets are sorted by project, and the preparer then groups them by client. To automate this task, Client ID should be retained with this information (although it is not necessary for the employee to enter it since the time sheets can be processed against the project file to look up the Client ID and add it to the record). Including the Client ID will facilitate the preparation of invoices later.

Invoicing and Accounts Receivable

Coaster Mania charges clients a fixed up-front fee to cover the cost of all equipment, materials, and overhead. This payment is handled somewhat like a deposit on the project and is not part of the normal monthly time charges billing. Labor costs are billed monthly on a cost plus basis.

As shown in Figure 2-5, employees submit weekly time sheets showing the hours spent on each project. The individual who processes the time sheets verifies the project number and adds the Client ID to the record by looking up the Project ID. Later, costs are totaled by project and invoices are prepared.

An open invoice file contains invoices that have not yet been paid. When payments are processed, closed invoices are removed from this file, although these invoices would likely be stored in a history file for some time (for at least three to seven years to meet IRS tax record audit mandates). These closed invoice records aren't included in this database simply to keep the examples simple.

In addition to the employee time logs, these fields of information are needed to complete the invoicing and billing cycles:

Bill Rate
Invoice Number
Invoice Date
Invoice Amount
Payment Amount
Payment Date
Project ID
Hours
Employee ID

Some of this information is stored in fields in other tables. Year-to-date and total invoice and payment amounts are also needed but are grouped with the company information. Several different database tables probably will be used for this information in order to eliminate duplication between tables and to build the best relationships between tables.

Completing Design Activities

With the list of all the potential data elements completed, you still need to make a few decisions before setting things up in Microsoft Access. You must decide how to group your information into tables to organize information that seems to logically belong together. You need to decide which data type to assign to each element.

As you progress with your database definition you will also need to set properties and define relationships between the various tables. This chapter looks at the various data types that you can select. The discussion of relationships and setting properties has been reserved for Chapter 3. These two topics allow you to customize your database design and provide for more efficient operation of your database system.

Let's first consider your remaining decisions and then look at how you make your decisions known to Access.

Deciding How to Group Tables

After your analysis, usually you have a long list of data fields. There may seem to be some logical groupings in this list if you have explored one area at a time. Cut and paste from your list if need be; examine each of the areas that you explored and decide which information about an entity should comprise a table. You may have to move some fields to make this grouping possible. The Coaster Mania company will have an employee table, a project table, an employee time log table, an invoices table, and a client table.

Although we have eliminated some duplication by not storing time billing information with employee data and requiring multiple records for each employee, during the design phase this initial structure might still result in duplicate information in a number of records. Normally, creating a separate table will solve this problem. Check each of the tables that you initially propose to see if the design is likely to cause duplication. Eliminating duplication is easy at this point but much more difficult once you begin entering data.

Let's assume for a minute that Coaster Mania is handling purchases with this database. A table created for orders might have the same supplier information in many records. If it is necessary to process order information you might want two tables, one for orders and one for suppliers. This way you can put a supplier ID in each order record and only need to record each supplier once in the supplier table. Chapter 3 provides additional information about relationships between tables to eliminate duplicate data.

Refining Your Analysis

After you finish the initial table design, go back over what you have done. This second pass may bring to light important data that you overlooked. Ask yourself these key questions:

- ☐ Are there any missing fields?

- ☐ Are there fields in the database that can be calculated?

- ☐ Can any fields be eliminated?

- ☐ Should database fields be broken into several additional fields?

Adding and Eliminating Elements

Now that you have an organized list it may be easier to see what you left out or what you can discard. Show your list to business associates that work with the data. They may have some ideas for additional fields, such as for year end or quarterly processing. They may also be aware of fields that you can calculate versus those that must be stored in the database. These same users may be able to tell you that certain fields are no longer needed. If you look at old personnel systems you may find information on religious preference or disabilities; neither of these fields can be retained under the current law.

Splitting Fields

You might also decide that a field would be better broken into several different fields in order to allow each piece of information to be accessed separately. An example would be the contact name in the client database. If you want to be able to access first name, last name, and title separately you will want to split the contact field into three fields.

Sometimes dividing a field makes sense for almost every database. For instance, the second line of an address contains city, state, and ZIP code. For these often-used entities, it is always better to use three fields since at one time or another you are likely to want to query the database by state or ZIP code. Figure 2-6 shows a report created by state and mailing labels for a bulk rate discount created in ZIP code sequence.

FIGURE 2-6   Multiple fields make it easy to use the data in different ways

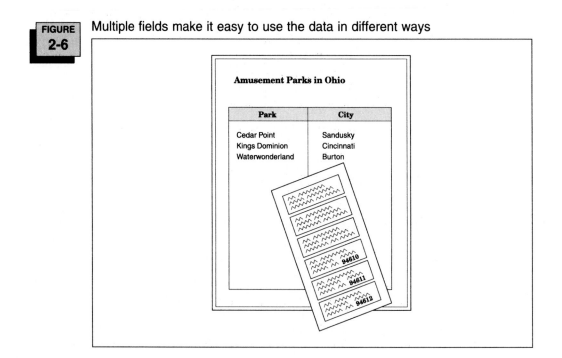

Dividing other fields can be more subjective. For example, a real estate management firm might need to be able to access street names separately from street numbers because they have more than one tenant on the same street. In this case, the database is designed with the street number and street name as two separate fields.

Deciding What Type of Data a Field Will Contain

Before you can create the first table in a new database you must decide what type of data you want to allow in each field. Do you want to allow the field to contain alphanumeric characters or just numbers? Will the field contain a date or time? If the field contains text is it a short entry or a number of paragraphs? Can you represent the field contents by a Yes/No answer or logical on or off state? Does the field contain an integer or a monetary amount? Should the field be incremented with the next sequential number in its record to provide a count of new records? If you think about these questions you will be prepared to make the correct selection of a Microsoft Access data type for each field.

Setting Up a Microsoft Access Database

As mentioned in the beginning of this chapter, a Microsoft Access database is a file that contains all of the tables you create for your information. It also contains forms, reports, and queries that you develop to use with your information. A Microsoft database can be as large as 128MB.

Because a database is a file, you must provide it with a unique filename, up to eight characters in length. Since Access allows only one open database at a time you will want to close any open database before creating a new one, although Access will do it for you if you forget.

Any database that you create will begin from the Access window shown in Figure 2-7. Follow these steps to create a database:

1. Choose <u>N</u>ew Database from the <u>F</u>ile menu.

2. Type a one- to eight-character filename in the File <u>N</u>ame box.

 Note The filename should only contain the characters A–Z, 0–9, and the underscore (_). Although DOS will allow other characters they do not add meaning to your name and should be avoided.

3. Choose OK to have Access create the file on your disk with an .MDB extension.

When the database window shown in Figure 2-8 appears you can add objects such as tables, forms, and reports to it. Your only real limitation is database size and disk space since you can have at most 32,768 tables.

Defining a New Table

A table is only one type of object that you can add to a Microsoft Access database. A table contains data about a specific topic or area. You can

FIGURE 2-7 Access window

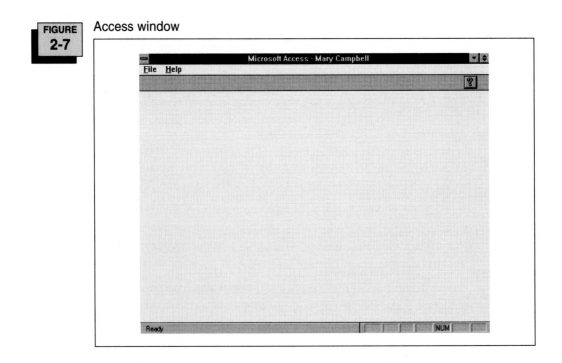

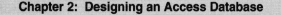

FIGURE
2-8

Database window

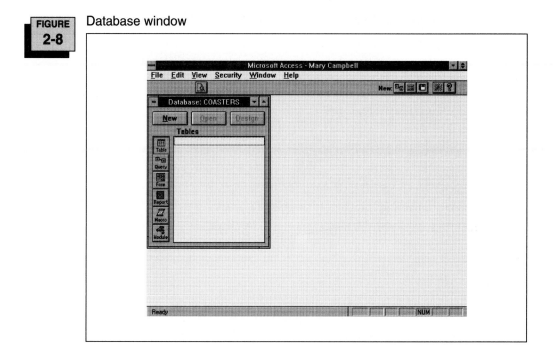

have as many as 255 fields in one table and as many as 32,768 tables in one database although you are limited to 254 open tables at one time.

A table is arranged in rows and columns much like a spreadsheet. Each column represents a field or individual piece of information and each row is a record or set of fields.

A table must be defined before you can enter data in it. You will define each field you plan to store in the table. At a minimum you must supply a field name and a data type for each field in the table.

To create a new Access table, follow these steps:

1. Click the Table button on the left side of the database window or choose Tables from the View menu.

2. Choose the New button at the top of the database window.

FIGURE
2-9
Design view for a Table window

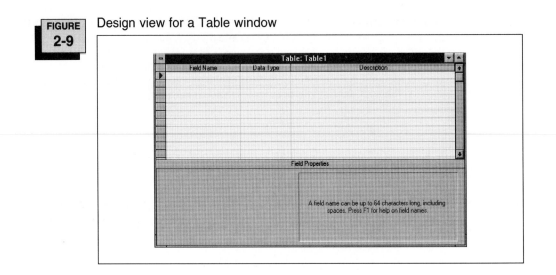

Access assigns the next sequential number to create Table*n*, where *n* is the next sequential number. The Table window appears in design view as shown in Figure 2-9 to allow you to define the fields you want to store in the table. Use the toolbar at the top of this window to access many commands quickly.

Naming a Field

Each field within a table must have a unique name. Try to make this name as descriptive as possible. You can use as many as 64 characters including letters, numbers, and spaces within this limit. If you are using a long name you will find that the Field Name column will not display a full 64 characters. You can continue typing and have your entry scroll off the screen or press SHIFT-F2 to display a Zoom box where you can see the entire entry with the field name, as shown here:

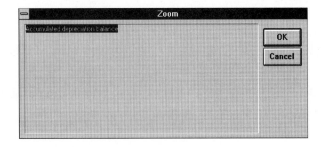

You will be able to define a shorter name later in Field Properties as a caption for use on reports and forms if you are concerned with a lengthy field name requiring too much space in these other objects.

After typing a field name for the first field in the form click the Data Type entry or press TAB to move to the next column.

Choosing the Correct Microsoft Access Data Type

Microsoft Access provides eight different data types to allow you to make this definition. You can use this drop-down list box to make your selection:

```
Text
Memo
Number
Date/Time
Currency
Counter
Yes/No
OLE Object
```

You must choose one of these data types for each field or Microsoft Access will use the default data type of Text, which allows as many as 255 alphanumeric characters in a field.

The eight data types offer variety. A Text field allows any alphanumeric character and a Yes/No field records only two different states for a field. A Memo data type is like a long text field that may contain paragraphs of information with a limit of 32,000 characters in a Memo field. A Number data type can contain an integer or decimal fraction. A Counter data type is automatically incremented by Access as you add each new record to a table. A Currency data type is designed to contain a monetary value. A Date/Time data type can contain only a valid date or time. An OLE Object is the most unique data type and can contain graphics, scanned pictures, binary data, or objects with a size limit of 128MB. OLE Object allows you to add such things as product sketches, employee pictures, and graphs to a database that would not otherwise be possible.

Your selection of a data type affects the amount of storage Access sets aside for your entries. Picking a data type that allows much more space than needed can be inefficient. An extreme example of a poor choice would be storing a Yes/No value in a Memo field rather than the much more efficient Yes/No data type.

The operations that you plan to perform with the data as you create reports and forms is another important factor. If you need to use a numeric entry to calculate a discount amount you must choose a Number or Currency field. Currency and Number fields are the only two options for calculations. If you store a number in a Text or Memo field data type you will not be able to use your data in a calculation.

Access allows you to sequence data in tables and reports by the values in a particular field. If you choose a Memo or OLE Object data type, you will not be able to use the field for sequencing your entries.

Although you can change data types before entering your data, look at Table 2-1 to see the size of each data type, what it contains, and any other limiting factors associated with the use of a particular data type. In Chapter 3, you will learn how to refine your selection with Property settings and how to specify a field size.

TABLE 2-1   Data Types

Data Type	Size	Contains	Limitations
Counter	4 bytes	An integer that is incremented by Access for each new record	Only one Counter in each table
Currency	8 bytes	A number representing a sum of money	
Date/Time	8 bytes	A date or time entry	
Memo	32,000 bytes max	Text in the form of phrases, sentences, or paragraphs	Cannot be used to index a table
Number	1 to 8 bytes	Numeric values	
OLE Object	128 megabytes max	Graphs, pictures, binary objects	Cannot be used to index a table
Text	255 bytes max	Alphanumeric characters	
Yes/No	1 bit	Boolean entries	

Adding a Field Description

Although the description for a field is optional you will want to use it unless the field name is fully descriptive. You are limited to 64 characters in your description entry.

For example, the Last Name field in the Employee table does not require further definition. The Angle field in the Projects table would require a definition to clarify which angle was being referred to. If you press ENTER or TAB, Access will move down to the next record.

Changing and Reorganizing Your Entries

You can make changes to a field name, data type, or description at any time. To change a field name or description press F2 to change from having the entire field selected to an insertion point. Once the insertion point appears in the entry, you can use the arrow keys to move the insertion point to a different location.

You can delete a field by clicking the field selector to the left of the field name to highlight the entire row, and then pressing the DEL key.

To insert a field press the INS key. A blank row is added above the current field name.

To move a field to a different location in the table layout, you must select it first. Click the field selector to the left of the field name. Next, click the selector again and drag this highlighted field to a new location. You can click another location on the window or press the RIGHT ARROW key to unselect the record.

Creating a Primary Key

A *primary key* uniquely identifies each database record. Although a primary key normally consists of a single field you can use more than one if you do not have a single field with unique entries.

You can also use a multiple key field if a single field does not contain unique entries. Although Access allows as many as 32 fields to be combined, you will want to keep the entries shorter than this in most cases for efficiency. If you have a table of class offerings for a college, for example, you might want to use each faculty member's last name in combination with the day of the week and time of the course as a key to the table. None of these fields would be unique by themselves as faculty members typically teach several courses and multiple courses are offered on the same day and time. Together they must be unique as you would not want a faculty member to teach two different courses at the same time. Access even helps you ensure that faculty members are not double-scheduled as it rejects all attempts to create a duplicate primary key entry.

To create a primary key, click the selector to the left of the field name. If you need to select multiple fields to create a key with unique entries, hold down CTRL as you click each field. Click the Primary Key button or choose Set Primary Key from the Edit menu.

Access indexes a table by the primary key and displays the records in this order on a form or datasheet.

Access enforces the unique entries within an index when you enter new records into the table. Access will reject an entry for a new record if it has the same primary key as an existing record.

If you save a table before designating a primary key, Access displays this dialog box:

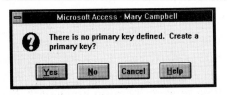

If you choose Yes and have a field with a data type of Counter, Access will use this field for a primary key. Access will add an ID field with a data type of Counter and automatically increment the value in the field for each new record. If you select No, the table is saved but no primary key is selected. If you choose Cancel, the save request is suspended and you can choose your own primary key.

Saving Your Work

Once you start entering data, saving is no problem since Microsoft Access saves a database record as soon as you move the *focus* to a new record. You can tell if the focus is on a record by the pointer to the left of the record in the table. You can also tell where the focus is by where the insertion point is located.

The design is not saved for you automatically. You must choose Save As from the File menu to save the current design settings. If the database design has been saved before, you only need to select OK to save it. If you choose Save from the File menu and have not saved the design before, the Save As window will appear anyway and prompt you for a table name.

Subsequent save requests can be made by choosing Save from the File menu unless you want to save the table under a new name. You must choose Save As to specify a new name.

If you have a table open and choose Close from the File menu, Access will close your table. If there are object changes that have not been saved, a dialog box displays the message "Save changes to Table *X*?" where *X* is the name of the table that has unsaved changes. You can decide whether or not to save and choose Yes, No, or Cancel. When the table is closed the database window displays again unless there are other open tables.

If you choose Close Database from the File menu in the database window, the database is closed and the Access menu appears again.

Accessing Data in Existing Databases and Tables

You must open a database before you can use any of its tables. To open an existing database choose Open Database from the File menu. Once the new database is open you can select the desired table and then select Ok. If you choose Exit from the File menu, Access will close the database for you. If you are wondering why there is no Save option in the File menu, it is because Access saves database changes to records automatically. Your only real concern should be saving changes to objects such as tables in which you work for long periods of time. You can save every five minutes, save every hour, or in any increments in between; how often you save depends on how much work you can stand to redo in the event your machine crashes unexpectedly.

Keeping a Copy of the Table Design

Microsoft Access does not provide a command for printing the table structure. There are two different approaches that you might take to keep a hard copy record of each table design. One method requires the use of a screen capture program such as Collage to capture the design view from the screen. The drawback to this method is that it may not show all the fields at one time and you might need a number of screens to see everything.

Another method involves more work but it does not require another package and can give you a more complete perspective, including settings for field properties. To use this approach create another table as a data dictionary. The fields in this table will be database table, field name, type, table, size, format, decimal places, caption, default width, and so on. Each data element in your database system would have an entry in this dictionary database. You could index by database and field name to group all the elements for a table in the same location. Your design for this table might look something like Figure 2-10.

You can create reports like the one in Figure 2-11 that show the fields in your tables.

FIGURE 2-10   Data dictionary

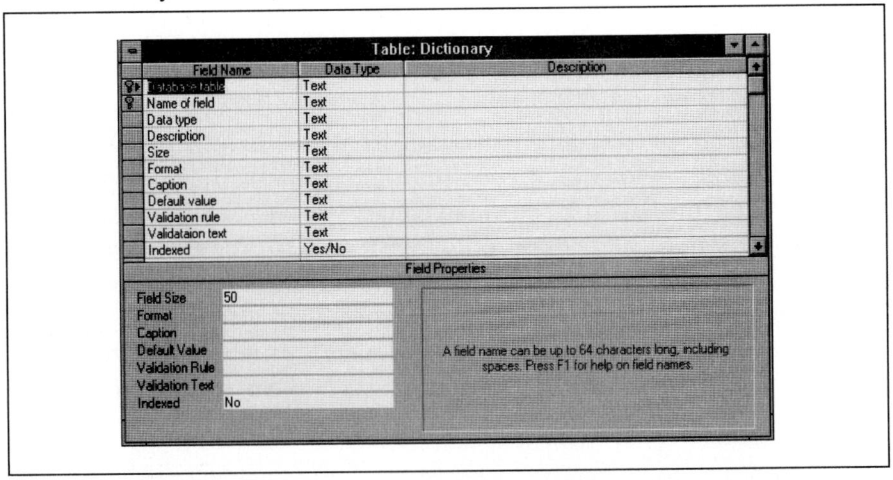

Field Name	Data Type	Description
Database table	Text	
Name of field	Text	
Data type	Text	
Description	Text	
Size	Text	
Format	Text	
Caption	Text	
Default value	Text	
Validation rule	Text	
Validataion text	Text	
Indexed	Yes/No	

Field Properties

Field Size	50
Format	
Caption	
Default Value	
Validation Rule	
Validation Text	
Indexed	No

A field name can be up to 64 characters long, including spaces. Press F1 for help on field names.

FIGURE
2-11

Report showing fields in different tables

Dictionary of Fields Used in Coaster Database

Table	Name of field	Data type	Description
Client			
	City	Text	
	Client Id	Number	Unique client identification number
	Client Name	Text	Name of the amusement park
	Contact	Text	Contact individual
	Mailing Address	Text	P.O. Box or other mailing address
	Park Desc	Memo	Park description and information on other par
	Park Location	Text	Location of park rather than mailing address
	Phone	Number	
	State	Text	
	Total Invoices	Currency	
	Total Payments	Currency	
	YTD Invoices	Currency	
	YTD Payments	Currency	
	Zip Code	Text	
Employee			
	Bill Rate	Currency	Hourly client billing rate
	City	Text	
	Date of Hire	Date/Time	
	Department	Text	
	Employee Id	Counter	Employee Identification Number
	Extension	Number	
	First Name	Text	
	Home Phone	Text	
	Job Class	Number	Two digit job class code
	Last Name	Text	
	Middle Initial	Text	
	Pay Rate	Currency	Hourly pay rate
	Picture	OLE Object	
	State	Text	
	Street Address	Text	
	Zip Code	Text	
Employee Time Log			
	Date	Date	First day of the week
	Employee Id	Number	Matches up with Employee Id in the Employee
	Hours	Number	Number of hours spent on project
	Project Number	Number	Matches up with Coaster Id in the Project tabl
Invoice Register			
	Invoice Amount	Currency	
	Invoice Date	Date/Time	

Creating the Database Tables for Coaster Mania

Creating the tables for your Access database is quite easy once you have created a solid design. The actual creation process represents only a small fraction of the time needed since it represents the time required to enter the data resulting from your analysis.

The first step is to create the COASTERS database. Next you create each table separately. You then establish field names and data types. Where needed, add descriptions to clarify the field contents. Chapter 3 discusses properties for these tables.

Table 2-2 shows the field names, data types, and descriptions used to establish the Project table. The data type choice for Coaster Id requires

TABLE 2-2

Projects Table

Field Name	Data Type	Description
Coaster Id	Counter	Unique coaster identification number
Coaster Name	Text	Name of coaster ride
Client Id	Number	Number from client table
Completed	Yes/No	Completed project
Operational	Date/Time	Projected or actual operational date
Est Cost	Currency	Projected out-of-pocket cost for labor and material
Act Cost	Currency	Actual labor and material costs
Track	Number	Length of ride track
Height	Number	Maximum height
Drop	Number	Maximum drop
Angle	Number	Greatest angle of descent
Time	Number	Length of ride in minutes
Speed	Number	Greatest speed in mph
Capacity	Number	Maximum number of riders in 1 hour
Vehicles	Number	Total number of vehicles
Picture	OLE Object	Picture of model or operational ride
Features	Memo	Unique features of the ride

an explanation. A Counter data type is automatically incremented for each new entry so this field handles numbering all of your new and old projects.

The Coaster Id field was set to be the primary key field before saving the table.

The decisions made for the Client table are recorded in Table 2-3. The Client Id field is a counter field for the same reason that Coaster Id was established as a counter field. The Phone field was set up as a number although text would have been another possibility. It depends on whether you want to be able to list telephone numbers using letters (such as FO7-8999 or LIM-OS4U) or want to always use numbers (367-8999 or 546-6748).

The primary key is Client Id.

The Employee table fields are shown in Table 2-4. Employee Id was set up as a Counter data type primarily to show you how to use functions

TABLE 2-3   Client Table

Field Name	Data Type	Description
Client Id	Counter	Unique client identification number
Client Name	Text	Name of the amusement park
Contact	Text	Contact individual
Park Location	Text	Location of park rather than mailing address
Mailing Address	Text	P.O. Box or other mailing address
City	Text	
State	Text	
Zip Code	Text	
Phone	Number	
Park Desc	Memo	Park description and information on other park coasters and planned projects
YTD Invoices	Currency	
YTD Payments	Currency	
Total Invoices	Currency	
Total Payments	Currency	

to link it with data in another table in a later chapter. Although you would normally use the same data type for all phone number fields, the Home Phone field is a Text data type to allow you to see the different ways to handle formatting for this field depending on its data type. Employee Id is the primary key.

The Employee Time Log table contains records for each project an employee worked on during the week. The definition of the table contains the elements shown in Table 2-5. The primary key consists of three fields to create unique entries: Date, Employee ID, and Project ID.

The tables for invoices and payments require only a few fields. For Coaster Mania, they are combined into a single table. Their primary key is the Invoice Number field. Table 2-6 contains the fields for Invoice Register.

TABLE 2-4   Employee Table

Field Name	Data Type	Description
Employee Id	Counter	Employee Identification Number
Last Name	Text	
First Name	Text	
Middle Initial	Text	
Pay Rate	Currency	Hourly pay rate
Bill Rate	Currency	Hourly client billing rate
Date of Hire	Date/Time	
Job Class	Number	Two-digit job class code
Department	Text	
Street Address	Text	
City	Text	
State	Text	
Zip Code	Text	
Picture	OLE Object	
Home Phone	Text	
Extension	Number	

Employee Time Log Table

Field Name	Data Type	Description
Date	Date/Time	First day of the week
Employee Id	Number	Matches up with Employee Id in the Employee table
Project Number	Number	Matches up with Coaster Id in the Project table
Hours	Number	Number of hours spent on project

Invoice Register Table

Field Name	Data Type	Description
Invoice Number	Number	
Invoice Date	Date/Time	
Invoice Amount	Currency	
Client ID	Number	
Payment Amount	Currency	
Payment Date	Date/Time	
Project Id		Matches up with Coaster Id in the Project table

Quick Reference

To Create a New Database   From the Access window choose New Database from the File menu. Type a filename in the File Name box (between one and eight characters long) and click OK.

To Create a New Table   Click the Table button, and then click New.

To Save the Table Design   Choose Save As from the File menu and type a name between 1 and 64 characters and spaces in length. You can also choose Save the first time you save but the Save As dialog box will be displayed anyway. With subsequent save requests choose Save unless you want to save the table with a new name.

To Close a Table   Choose Close from the File menu. You will be prompted to save the table if you have not already saved it.

To Close a Database   Choose Close database from the File menu.

To Create a Primary Key for a Table   Click the selector to the left of the field name you want to use and then click the Primary Key button or choose Set Primary Key from the Edit menu. If you want a multiple field primary key, press the CTRL key while selecting fields.

To Delete a Row of a Table Definition   Click the field selector to the left of the field name, and press the DEL key.

To Add a Row of Table Definition   Click the field selector to the left of the field below where you want to add the new field, and then press INS.

CHAPTER

Defining Properties and Relationships

Although you can skip to Chapter 4 and begin entering data as soon as you have the fields and data types defined for your initial table, first consider the relationships between tables in your database and customizing properties. This means examining the relationships between all of your tables, which might require creating yet another table or revising the design to eliminate redundancy and create usable relationships between tables. You will also want to define properties for the various table fields. Changing properties later can result in data loss and may allow errors to be entered into tables that can be prevented if validity check properties are used. The properties that you set will also affect the forms and reports that you create as these objects inherit the current property settings of a field at the time you design the report or form.

Defining Relationships

Access lets you link information from multiple tables on its reports, queries, and forms. This ability to link information from multiple tables is referred to as a *relationship.* In order to establish relationships between tables you first define a unique field or combination of fields for each table that can be used as the primary key to identify a specific record.

Planning for a Primary Key

Just as you use a social security number, serial number, or vehicle identification number to uniquely identify something, Access can use a key to bring together information from multiple tables. Access can locate records much faster when it has a primary key field for a table since it builds an index of primary key values and the record number in the table that corresponds. This makes it faster to locate a record than searching through the records themselves. Assigning a primary key is the essential first step if you plan to link the data from the table to data in a different table.

Entries in a primary key field must be unique. Nicknames, last names, and company names will not work since there can be duplicates in these fields (even if current data does not contain a duplicate, future entries may be duplicates). Be certain that future entries in a primary key field are not duplicates of current entries.

If you do not have one field that is unique you can use a combination of fields together as a primary key. For instance, you might have a database of parcels of land located in various states. Each piece of land has a plat number recorded in the county in which it is located. Although you will not have duplicate plat numbers within one county, as you cross county and state borders there could be duplicate plat numbers. If you use a combination of the county, state, and plat number as the primary key there will not be any duplicates.

Figure 3-1 shows how several fields in a Properties table are designated as a primary key. You learned in Chapter 2 that you can select more than one field by holding down the CTRL key while clicking to the left of each field you want to include in the primary key.

Warning　　Do not include unnecessary fields in the primary key as long keys adversely affect database performance.

If you do not have a unique field or if a unique combination would result in too lengthy a key, use a Counter field that simply assigns the next sequential number to each record in the database. The advantage

FIGURE 3-1　　Selecting several fields as a primary key

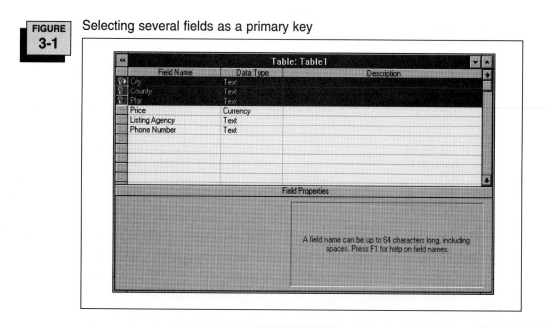

of using a Counter field is that its entries will be short until you have many records, and having a short primary key makes Access operate more efficiently.

Tip   Boost performance by choosing a primary key that works along the lines of how you normally search the table for answers to specific questions. Do you search by product ID, a combination of first name, last name, and location, or employer ID? Whatever the answer, consider using that field or combination of fields as your primary key.

Understanding Possible Relationships Between Tables

To establish a relationship between tables, place the primary key from the first table into the second table. (Once in the second table, this key is referred to as a *foreign key.*) Access can find the record in the first table and use this key to locate one or more records from the second table. Figure 3-2 shows how the Client Id from the Client table is added to the Project table to provide a connection to the client data. In most cases, the data types for both fields are the same (in this case, both Number). The only exception to this rule is since Client Id is a Counter field, in which case a Number data type is used in the Project table.

Consider the relationship between the records in each table to achieve the best database design. The most important component of the relationship is how many records in the associated table match entries in the first table. For instance, if you look up the Supplier ID in the Inventory table are there likely to be many records or a single record?

Associated tables may have one of three possible relationships: a one-to-one relationship, a one-to-many, or a many-to-many relationship. In most cases a one-to-many relationship provides the best design. A one-to-one relationship may be an appropriate solution in limited instances, especially if the data in one table is needed only temporarily. A many-to-many relationship should normally be restructured with the addition of a third table in order to achieve a one-to-many relationship. The following sections explore each of these types of relationships.

Diagram the relationship between your tables by drawing a line between related fields. You can even write "One" and "Many" at the end

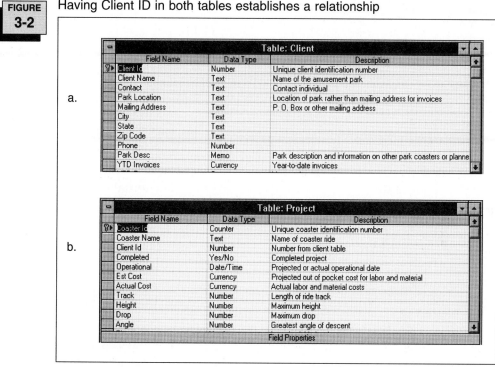

FIGURE 3-2 Having Client ID in both tables establishes a relationship

a.

Table: Client

Field Name	Data Type	Description
Client Id	Number	Unique client identification number
Client Name	Text	Name of the amusement park
Contact	Text	Contact individual
Park Location	Text	Location of park rather than mailing address for invoices
Mailing Address	Text	P. O. Box or other mailing address
City	Text	
State	Text	
Zip Code	Text	
Phone	Number	
Park Desc	Memo	Park description and information on other park coasters or planne
YTD Invoices	Currency	Year-to-date invoices

b.

Table: Project

Field Name	Data Type	Description
Coaster Id	Counter	Unique coaster identification number
Coaster Name	Text	Name of coaster ride
Client Id	Number	Number from client table
Completed	Yes/No	Completed project
Operational	Date/Time	Projected or actual operational date
Est Cost	Currency	Projected out of pocket cost for labor and material
Actual Cost	Currency	Actual labor and material costs
Track	Number	Length of ride track
Height	Number	Maximum height
Drop	Number	Maximum drop
Angle	Number	Greatest angle of descent

Field Properties

points to remind you of the type of relationship the tables have. Figure 3-3 shows an example of a diagram.

A One-to-Many Relationship

In a one-to-many relationship, a record in table 1 may have many matching records in table 2 but each record in table 2 will match no more than one record in table 1. It is important that you examine the relationship between tables from both tables.

Although the one-to-one relationship (explained next) is also an acceptable relationship between some tables, a one-to-many relationship yields the best design in most cases. The tables established for Coaster Mania, shown in Figure 3-4, have a one-to-many relationship between the tables that have a relationship. One record in the Client table can have many records in the Project table yet there is only one client for each project. One record in the Employee table can have many records in the Employee Time Log table yet there is only one employee record for each

FIGURE 3-3
Diagraming a relationship between tables

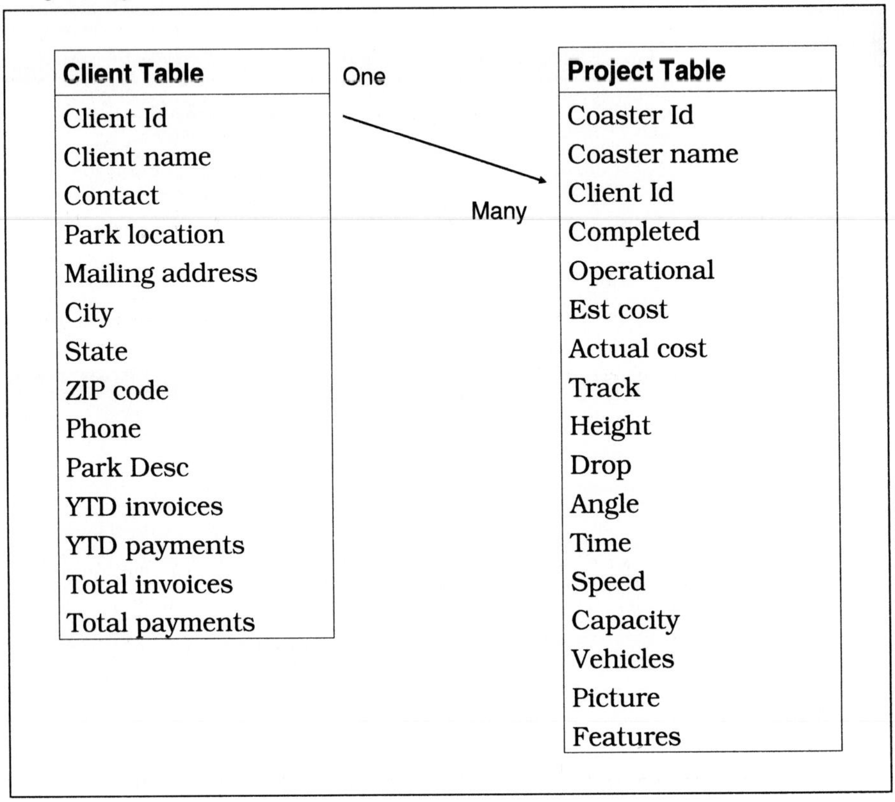

Client Table	One	Project Table
Client Id		Coaster Id
Client name		Coaster name
Contact		Client Id
Park location	Many	Completed
Mailing address		Operational
City		Est cost
State		Actual cost
ZIP code		Track
Phone		Height
Park Desc		Drop
YTD invoices		Angle
YTD payments		Time
Total invoices		Speed
Total payments		Capacity
		Vehicles
		Picture
		Features

time record. One client record can have many invoices yet there is only one client for each invoice.

Figure 3-5 shows how one client record might have several related project records. Even though most clients have only one project at a time, there are cases in which one client has more than one active project.

A One-to-One Relationship

If two tables have a one-to-one relationship, for each record in one of the tables there will be no more than one record in the other table. If comparing the Employee table and the Payroll table (which would contain the information necassary to process the payroll), for example, each employee would have no more than one record in the Payroll table and each record in the Payroll table would match with no more than one of the current employees.

FIGURE
3-4

Coasters relationships

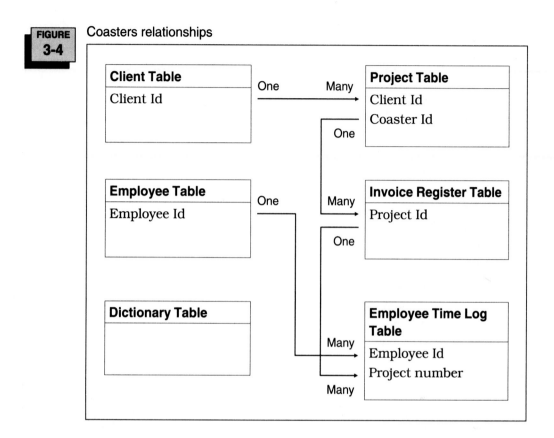

Whenever you have a one-to-one relationship between the records in two tables, you can probably combine the fields into one table. No relationships are needed because all of the data can be placed in one location.

FIGURE
3-5

Client record and related project records

Two projects for the same client

Table: Projec

Coaster Id	Coaster Name	Client Id	Completed	Operational	Est Cost
1	Scream Machine	3	No	10/4/93	$7,800,000.00
2	Blue Arrow	2	No	8/20/92	$4,000,000.00
3	Astro Transport	3	Yes	5/21/92	$7,500,000.00
4	Red Dragon	1	No	4/15/93	$4,500,000.00
5	Taurus	4	No	6/1/94	$4,500,000.00
6	Corker	5	No	7/4/93	$2,500,000.00
7	Wild One	6	No	9/15/92	$3,900,000.00
8	White Lightnin	7	Yes	2/15/91	$2,800,000.00
9	The Runaway	2	Yes	3/28/90	$3,215,000.00
(Counter)		0	No		$0.00

Creating one combined table is the best approach unless the data is only needed for a short time—such as during the United Way campaign. Figure 3-6 shows one table for employee data and another table for the United Way. You also probably wouldn't combine two one-to-one tables when only a few of the table entries actually contain data. A separate database table would be the best idea in these situations.

Examine the relationships between the database tables you have established. See if you have any one-to-one relationships between tables in which it makes more sense to combine the two tables.

A Many-to-Many Relationship

In a many-to-many relationship you have many entries from table 1 that potentially match entries within table 2 and many entries in table 2 that match entries in table 1. This type of relationship—in which many records in both tables match a record in the other table—is not acceptable.

FIGURE 3-6

A one-to-one relationship

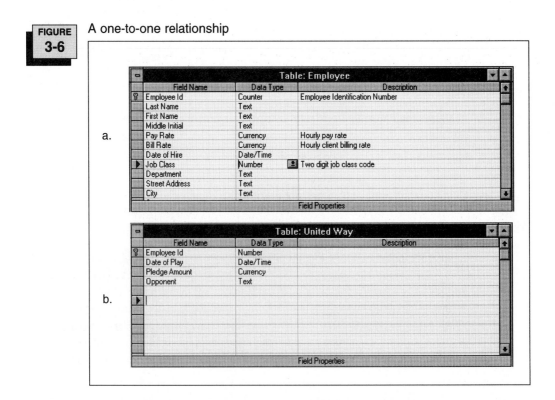

The data in two tables like this cannot be related directly as Access cannot handle this combination. The data from the two sources can be brought together through the use of a third table.

The potential for a many-to-many relationship exists for the Coaster Mania database. If billing information was entered directly into the Employee table you would need multiple records for each employee since there would be a record for each time period. Each record could reference multiple projects. If an employee ID was entered in the Project table to identify the project leader there would be many employee records when this ID was looked up in the Employee table. With one employee record containing references to several projects and one project record referencing many employee records, the many-to-many relationship would be built into the database design. Since this is not acceptable, a different approach was used.

If you attempted to relate Coaster Mania's Employee and Project tables, a many-to-many relationship would exist. There are many different employees that work on a single project. Also a given employee may work on many different projects. For this reason, no direct link should be established between these tables. The Employee Time Log table contains a link to both the Employee table and the Project table. The invoices can be created with both the employee's name and project name on the invoice. Using a third table eliminates many-to-many relationships. The individual links within this third table represent one-to-many links to the other tables.

Defining Default Relationships

You can wait until you create a form, report, or table to define the relationship between multiple tables used in these objects. There are several advantages to defining this relationship when you create the tables.

One advantage is that Access will check the referential integrity when you add or delete records. *Referential integrity* is the set of rules controlling the valid relationships between tables to ensure that your data continues to relate in the way you originally defined the relationships. Part of maintaining referential integrity means making sure that records are added to the primary table before they are added to a related table. This means adding a record to the Employee table before using the

Employee ID to record billing data. It also means preventing the deletion of an employee record when there are billing records that reference the employee ID that you are about to delete.

Another advantage to setting default relationships is that Access can use them to perform tasks for you. Access uses the default relationships that you define to create joins in queries as well as subforms and subreports that show related records.

You can have Access enforce referential integrity for you or take on the responsibility yourself. When Access enforces the referential integrity of a primary table, it prevents you from making changes to records in a primary table where the changes would cause a mismatch of records in a related table. When Access does not enforce referential integrity, it is your responsibility to make the records from a related table match the records in a primary table.

Defining a relationship between two tables is easy once you have diagrammed the relationship between your tables. In a one-to-many relationship, the table with one is the *primary table* and the table with many is the *related table*. In a one-to-one relationship, the main table, if there is one, is the primary table. For instance, if you have an Employee table and a table with employee table tennis scores from the company's tournament, the Employee table would be the primary table.

From the database window, define the tables you want to relate by following these steps:

1. Choose Relationships from the Edit menu. The Relationships dialog box appears, as shown here:

2. Select the primary table from the Primary Table drop-down list box. You are telling Access that you want to relate the primary key from this table to another table. Access displays the primary key beneath the list box.

3. Select the related table from the Related Table drop-down list box.

4. Select the One button if this is a one-to-one relationship.

5. Select Suggest if the related fields have the same names in both tables or select the fields in the Select Matching Fields drop-down list box that correspond to each field in the primary key.

6. To stop the referential integrity check, select the Enforce Referential Integrity check box to clear it.

7. Select the Add button.

8. Repeat steps 2 through 7 for all related tables, and then select the Close button.

An Example of Defining a Relationship

Use the procedure that you just learned with the Client and Project table. The Client table is the primary table in which the primary key is Client Id. This field name is used again in the Project table, which allows you to choose Suggest in the Relationships dialog box.

If you wish, continue defining default relationships as the Employee Time Log, Invoice Register, and Employee tables all have default relationships that can be defined. These relationships are easy to identify because the related tables all use the same fields as the primary keys in the Employee and Project tables.

Defining Table Properties

Table properties allow you to set the size for data entered in a field, change default values, and establish criteria for valid entries. You can also establish indexes for tables in addition to the primary key to make it quicker to access data needed for queries, forms, and reports.

Consider each of the property settings that you can make. Take special note of the different options available—these depend on the data type selected for the field. Although some of the Coasters fields are mentioned in the property changes that can be made, feel free to customize the settings for these tables. Appendix C lists the fields and properties for the tables used in this book.

You need to be in the design view of a table to make any of the property setting changes. If you have already closed the table, reopen it as a datasheet and then switch to the design view by clicking the Design button. You can also open the design view directly by clicking the Design button or by clicking a table with the right mouse button.

Activating the Field Properties

When the design view is visible, activate the field properties for any field with the F6 key. The exact steps that you need to perform are listed here:

1. In the top part of the design window, highlight the field that you want to change.

2. Press F6 to activate the Properties area.
   You can change any of the property settings for the field using the property setting controls in the bottom part of the design window.

3. When ready to work with another field, press F6 again to move to the fields at the top of window.

Changing the Field Size

The default size established for each field in a table depends on the data type that you select for the field. You can change the default sizes for text and number fields if your data requires a different size. The default size for a Text field is 50 and the default size for a Number field is Double, which allows the entry of any number from -1.797 times 10^{308} to 1.797 times 10^{308}.

Options for Text Fields

If entering a Text field for a part number that cannot exceed 12 characters, you can change the field size to 12 to ensure that no user accidentally enters a part number with more than 12 characters. On the other hand, if you want to enter an account description and want to allow for more than the 50-character default, increase the field size to 75 or even 100 characters. In either case, as mentioned earlier, all you need to do is highlight the field name on the design screen, press F6 to move to the properties, change the field size to a new number, and then press F6 again.

Options for Number Fields

If working with a field with a Number data type, you can alter the Field Size property but you need to know a little more about the option. Table 3-1 shows each of the options that you can select. There is not any option larger than the default size of Double since Access wants to ensure that you have a size that will hold any number when it sets the default. You can make your database more efficient by reducing the size of fields that do not require Double.

One of the changes you might consider making to the Project table is to change the Field Size setting to a Byte. None of the coaster projects will ever have more than the maximum of 255, which this setting allows.

Field Size Property Options for Number Fields

Field Size	Max Decimal Places	Storage Range	Storage Bytes
Byte	0	0 – 255	1
Double	15	$-1.797 \text{ times } 10^{308}$ to $1.797 \text{ times } 10^{308}$	8
Integer	0	$-32,768$ to $32,767$	2
Long Integer	0	$-2,147,483,648$ to $2,147,483,647$	4
Single	7	$-3.4 \text{ times } 10^{38}$ to $3.4 \text{ times } 10^{38}$	4

You might consider changing the Field Size setting for Capacity in this same table to Integer since the capacity of this field type extends to 32,767, which would be adequate for any coaster ride. Long Integer would be a suitable choice for the invoice and payment number fields in the tables with the same names because this field type will allow a number of 2,147,483,647. Single and Double Field Size settings are appropriate when the number entries are even larger. You must choose one of these two settings when you want to store nonmonetary values that have decimal fractions as they are the only two Field Size settings that support decimals.

If you create the sample application in this book you would not notice improved performance even if you changed all the fields to their smallest possible settings. There are too few records in the tables in these applications to notice the impact of an efficient choice of Field Size settings. In a table that has tens or hundreds of thousands of records you will notice performance differences between a system with optimized settings and one without them.

Setting the Format

You can change the default Format settings for fields with Number, Currency, Date/Time, and Yes/No data types. Access provides a number of predefined Format settings for each data type or lets you create custom formats for Number, Date/Time, and Text fields.

To change the Format setting for a field from the default general setting, highlight the field, press F6, and then use the drop-down list box and select the desired format with the mouse or by highlighting it and pressing ENTER. If you prefer a custom format, type your specification in the Format property box. Once you save the table design again this format appears in the table datasheet, forms, reports, and query dynasets.

Format changes can make a significant difference in appearance. You can display a field like the phone number from the Client or Employee table as 7998769876 or as (799)876-9876. Formatting makes the number much more readable.

Table 3-2 shows what the default general format provides for each of the data types with the Windows Control Panel International Country setting as the United States. You can change the Country setting to

TABLE 3-2 Appearance of the General Format with the United States Country Setting in the Windows Control Panel

Data Type	Entry	Appearance with the General Format
Text	Abc	Abc
Number	2378.6	2378.6
Currency	2378.6	$2,378.60
Date/Time	1/22/94	1/22/94
Yes/No	Yes	Yes

change the way that data with the general format appears. You can also change to a format other than the general format.

Selecting a Format for Number and Currency Data Types

Access provides six different formats for fields with a Number or Currency data type. In addition to General Number you can choose from Currency, Fixed, Standard, Percent, and Scientific. All of these formats work with the Decimal Places property discussed later to allow you to adjust the number of decimal places displayed. If you do not change the default Decimal Places property from its default setting of Auto, two places will display for all formats except Fixed, which displays zero decimal places unless you specify another number. Table 3-3 shows the effect of each of the Format selections that are predefined for your use.

Warning You will not get the same calculation results if you set a Number field to a Currency format as when the data types in the calculation are Currency. Choose the Currency data type whenever you want to work with numbers having from one to four decimal places; otherwise, you will not have the rounding you expect in calculations since Number field calculations use floating-point arithmetic usually reserved for scientific calculations.

Tip Although you can display an entry with a Number data type with a Format setting of Currency you should set the data type to Currency instead to ensure proper results in calculations.

Format Options for Number and Currency Data Types

Format	Effect	Entry	Displays As
Currency	Adds monetary symbol for the country Adds thousands separator Displays two decimal places	45667.8	$45,667.80
Fixed	Rounds to the nearest whole number unless you specify Decimal Places	45667.8	45668
Percent	Multiplies number by 100 Adds a percent symbol (%) Displays two decimal places	.456	45.60%
Scientific	Displays number as a power of 10	4566.7	4.57E+03
Standard	Adds thousands separator and displays two decimal places	45667.8	45,667.80

Note   Different country code settings in the Windows Control Panel will cause Access to use a different monetary symbol, a different thousands separator, and a different decimal separator.

In the Project table in the Coasters database you can improve the display of Capacity with a format of Standard. You can try other options if you like since a format change affects the display of your data, not the entries stored in the table.

Selecting a Date/Time Format

The default format for dates with the Control Panel International settings as United States looks like this:

7/15/92

Time entries display like this:

3:15:00 PM

This default setting is called General Date even though it applies to both date and time entries. If you change the International setting of Windows, this same format option will look very different, as the most common date and time representations for the selected countries are used.

Each of the other time and date settings correspond to either a date or a time entry. Like the first option, these settings will look different when International option in the Control Panel is changed. The other standard choices and their effect on the date and time entries that you have already seen are given here:

Long Date	Wednesday, July 15, 1992
Medium Date	15-Jul-92
Short Date	7/15/92
Long Time	3:15:00 PM
Medium Time	3:15 PM
Short Time	15:15

In the Coasters database, Invoice Date, Payment Date, and Date of Hire from the Invoice, Register, and Employee tables can all use any of the default formats. For at least Invoice Date and Payment Date, choose the same format.

Selecting a Yes/No Format

The default format for a field with a Yes/No data type is to display a Yes or No in the field. If you delete the format setting, a –1 appears for No and a 0 appears for Yes values. You can also change the format to True/False or On/Off with the first display option in each of these settings corresponding to a Yes entry.

In the Coasters Project table Yes or No is probably the best format choice for the field Completed in the Project table. True/False is often the best selection for fields in a database that contains survey responses. If you were to record a series of switch settings for a machine's Control Panel or printer switch in different database fields, the On/Off setting might be a more appropriate format choice than other options.

Creating a Custom Format

After looking at the standard formats you might wonder why custom formats are even needed. Later, as you begin to create reports and screens for other users, you are likely to find that users request changes to the appearance of their data to conform with the way it looked in the system prior to Access or to conform with handwritten documents. You will find that the custom format provides a significant number of new options, each of which are suitable in specific situations.

You can add fixed text to entries with custom formats. You can provide different formats for fields that are empty or fields that contain a negative number. You will build your custom format with an entry in the Format property using symbols valid for the data type. All custom formats cause data to be right-aligned unless an exclamation point (!) is used to left-align the entries.

The Number, Text, and Date/Time data types each have their own symbols used in creating formats. Most symbols are valid with only one data type although there are six symbols that can be used with any data type: ! for left alignment, [color] to specify a color for the data, \ to display the next character as a literal, * to fill the field with the next character, a space to insert a space, and quotation marks to enclose literal text. These universal symbols are discussed in more detail in the section on entering custom number formats, later in this chapter. Other than these six options you cannot mix symbols for multiple data types in one format.

Defining a Custom Format for a Number Field When you construct a custom format for a field with a Number data type you can have four different parts to your entry. The first part of the format will be used if the field contains a positive number and the second part if the field is negative. The third part of the format is used if the entry contains a zero and the fourth part is used only if the field is empty or null. Semicolons are used to separate the different parts of the format when you use multiple parts.

The symbols that you can use and their effect on the data are as follows:

Symbol	Effect
"*xxx*"	Displays the characters between the quotation marks exactly as they are entered
\	Displays the character after the backslash as a literal "N/A" and \N\/\A are equivalent entries
0	Displays a digit or a zero if no digit is provided
#	Displays a digit or a blank if no digit is provided
.	Marks the decimal location
%	Multiplies the entry by 100 and displays a percent symbol after it
, Inserts a thousands separator	
E– e–	Displays the number using scientific format with a – for negative exponents
E+ e+	Displays the number using scientific format with a – for negative exponents and a + sign for positive exponents
–	Displays the – as a literal
+	Displays the + as a literal
$	Displays the $ as a literal
( )	Displays the ( ) as a literal
[color]	Displays the number in the color specified. Useful for showing negative numbers as red. Colors supported are black, blue, cyan, green, magenta, red, yellow, and white
*	Fills the field with the character that follows

You could use the following formats for some of the Coasters database fields:

Client->Client Id   000000

Client->Phone   (000)000-0000

Client->Total Invoices	$##,###,###.##[Blue];-$##,###,###.##[Red]
Client->Total Payments	$##,###,###.##[Green];-$##,###,###.##[Red]
Employee->Job Class	00;"Temporary Employee";"Management", "Management"
Project->Angle	##" Degrees"
Project->Capacity	#,###" rph"

The format for the Client ID will display zeros when a smaller number is entered if you want to always display a six-digit client ID. The Phone number format adds parentheses and a dash to make the number more readable. The following shows the effect of changing some of the default formats for fields in the Project table:

Table: Project					
Height	**Drop**	**Angle**	**Time**	**Speed**	**Capacity**
168 ft	160 ft.	54 degrees	3 min	70 mph	1,800 rph
205 ft	182 ft.	60 degrees	2 min	73 mph	2,300 rph
68 ft	30 ft.	58 degrees	2 min	50 mph	1,900 rph
78 ft	60 ft.	48 degrees	2 min	42 mph	2,000 rph
135 ft	119 ft.	56 degrees	3 min	65 mph	3,500 rph
100 ft	85 ft.	54 degrees	2 min	50 mph	1,800 rph
100 ft	87 ft.	52 degrees	2 min	50 mph	1,000 rph
68 ft	60 ft.	48 degrees	3 min	50 mph	2,500 rph
120 ft	100 ft.	53 degrees	2 min	46 mph	1,350 rph
ft	ft.	degrees	min	mph	rph

The Total Invoices and Total Payments fields display in different colors depending on whether the values are positive or negative. The Job Class displays in different ways depending on the number entered. Constants are added after Capacity and Degrees.

Tip Try to use consistent changes for all fields that contain similar information. For example, to provide a consistent appearance all phone numbers should have the same format whether they are in the Employee table or the Client table. This is true for other properties such as validation rules although there are instances in the Coasters database where this has not been followed so as to expose you to the maximum number of options.

Defining a Custom Format for a Text Field There are two types of symbols that you can use for format characters for text fields. One type affects only a single character and the other type affects all the characters in the string. A *string* is considered to be all the characters entered in a text field.

The format options offered are to use a space or a null when a character is not supplied in a position, to change the display from uppercase or lowercase, and to change the alignment of characters in the field.

Format expression can consist of one or two sections. When only one section is defined it applies to all strings. If a second section is defined it applies to null strings or empty strings.

The following lists the characters that you can use and the effect of each:

<	Displays all characters in the field as lowercase
>	Displays all characters in the string as uppercase
!	Uses the characters in the field to fill from left to right rather than right to left
@	Displays a character if one is entered; otherwise use a space for a placeholder
&	Displays a character if one is entered; otherwise leave the position empty

You can enter symbols and text within a string by entering it in the format string; for example, use @@@-@@-@@@@ to provide dashes for social security number entries.

You can combine the symbols that affect the entire string with ones that affect only a single position as in !&&&&& where alignment is from left to right due to the exclamation point (!). The placeholder directions for characters that are not supplied are given by the ampersands (&).

The following lists string formats that you can use for the Coasters database and gives the effect of each:

Employee->First Name	>
Employee->Last Name	>;"***Missing Information***"
Employee->Home Phone	(@@@)@@@-@@@@

The first format displays the First Name in all capital letters although it does not change the storage of the data from the way that it was entered. The second format displays the Last Name in all capital letters if a name is supplied and displays ***Missing Information*** if the field is left blank. If the Phone Number is a Text data type, this format will display the parentheses for the area code and the hyphen separator.

Defining a Custom Format for a Date/Time Field   Date and time serial numbers are stored in database tables as numbers, which means you can use the Number format options for them although you will probably want to use a more traditional date or time display. Since a date and time display each have multiple components with a month, day, and year, or hour, minute, and second, the options are somewhat overwhelming. Keep in mind that the more abbreviated displays are represented with a minimum of symbol entries. This list shows each symbol and its effect:

c	Displays both the date and time using *ddddd ttttt* if the number has both an integer and a decimal portion
a/p	Uses a 12-hour clock and displays a lowercase *a* with hours before noon and a lowercase *p* with the noon hour and later
A/P	Uses a 12-hour clock and displays an uppercase *A* with hours before noon and an uppercase *P* with the noon hour and later
am/pm	Uses a 12-hour clock and displays *am* with hours before noon and *pm* with the noon hour and later
AM/PM	Uses a 12-hour clock and displays *AM* with hours before noon and *PM* with the noon hour and later
AMPM	Uses a 12-hour clock and uses the WIN.INI file's 1159 string with hours before noon and the WIN.INI file's 2359 string with hours after noon
h	Displays an hour between 0 and 23 with no leading zero
hh	Displays an hour between 0 and 23 with a leading zero if the hour is one digit
n	Displays a minute number between 0 and 59 without a leading zero
nn	Displays a minute number between 0 and 59 with a leading zero if the minute number is one digit
s	Displays a second number between 0 and 59 without a leading zero

ss	Displays a second number between 0 and 59 with a leading zero if the second number is one digit
ttttt	Uses the default time format h:mm:ss with the time separator defined in the Control Panel International setting
d	Displays the day number without a leading zero
dd	Displays the day number with a leading zero if the day number is one digit
ddd	Displays a three-character abbreviation for the day of the week (Sun–Sat)
dddd	Displays the full word for the day of the week (Sunday–Saturday)
ddddd	Displays the date using the Short Date setting in the Control Panel International setting. The default format is m/d/yy
dddddd	Displays the date using the Long Date option in the Control Panel International section. The default format is ddddd mmmm, yyyy
m	Displays a month number without a leading zero
mm	Displays a month number with a leading zero for a one-digit month number
mmm	Displays a three-character abbreviation for the month (Jan–Dec)
mmmm	Displays the full month name (January – December)
q	Displays the quarter of the year (1–4)
w	Displays the day of the week as a number (1 for Sunday)
ww	Displays the week of the year as a number (1–53)
y	Displays the day of the year as a number (1–366)
yy	Displays the year as a two-digit number (00–99)
yyyy	Displays the year as a four-digit number (100–9999)

The date field in the Employee table could be customized to present the date in another format. As you construct an entry with the special symbols and finalize it, Access checks for a match with predefined formats and displays the name of the predefined format instead of the symbols if there is a match. For example, if you type **c** and press ENTER,

General Date displays. If you are only interested in showing the month and year the employee was hired you could enter a format of **mm/yy** to display 01/91.

Establishing Decimal Places for Currency and Number Fields

You can set the decimal places to Auto or a specific number of decimal places. Choosing the default of Auto causes Access to display zero decimal places for a Fixed Format field and two decimal places for other formats.

You can set decimal places for a Number or Currency field regardless of the format you have chosen. If you choose decimal places greater than zero for a field with a Byte, Integer, or Long Integer Field Size, they will always display as zeros since no decimal places are stored with the entries. If you were to type a number such as **5.5** in an Integer field set with two Decimal Places, it would display as 6.00. Consider this when making your selections for these fields as the numbers you display could appear to contain decimal accuracy that does not exist.

 Warning Choose carefully between Number and Currency data types. Setting the accuracy in Decimal Places will not solve accuracy with monetary calculations if you accidentally choose the Number data type.

In the Coasters database you might want to set the decimal places for some of the fields in the Project table. Try one, two, or three decimal places for the Speed measurement. The Time field should probably have one or two decimal places. Track could have one or two decimal places. Vehicles should definitely be set as zero decimal places since it is not possible to have a partial vehicle.

Using a Different Field Name on Reports and Forms

When you create a columnar report, the amount of space that a field uses depends on its contents and the heading used at the top of the column. Since the width of a printed page is a limiting factor to the amount of data that you can show on a columnar report, you don't want a field three or four characters long consuming 30 or 40 positions of the report width due to a long field name. Likewise, a form that displays a field will use the width of the field name plus its contents. Although the space on a form does not seem to be a limiting factor as often as it is with a columnar report, sometimes you may want to show three or more fields on the same line of the form—yet lengthy field names would prevent this combination. The solution in both cases is to provide a Caption property for fields that have a small field size yet have a long name.

You might decide that Job Class should be shortened in reports and forms since the data itself only requires two digits. Shorten the entry to Class by typing **Class** in the Caption Property. The new caption will be used in all reports and forms created from that point.

 Tip   In addition to using the Caption to shorten a field name you can also change the caption when you are designing a report or form for a specialized need. For example, you might have a field named Uncollectible Accounts that you will include when you create several reports labeling this field as Bad Debts. You can add Bad Debts as a Caption, create the reports, and then delete the caption so that other new reports will use the field name.

Establishing a Default Value

Default values are used to provide a value for a field when records are added to a table with a datasheet or form. Any field with a Number data type is automatically assigned a default value of 0. Fields with a Yes/No data type have a default value of No. If you make no changes to these fields they will retain the default setting for all fields of these types. You can delete the default to have a null entry in each new record or you can enter another value.

In the Coasters Employee table you might want to use OH as the State code for new employees if most employees reside in Ohio. You would highlight State in the Design view, press F6, and type **OH** in the Default Value property. If you wanted to make the default Pay Rate $6.00 an hour, move to Pay Rate, press F6, move the Default value, and type **6**.

Each new employee record would have a Pay Rate of $6.00 unless you changed the record at entry time.

You can also use expressions to establish default values. (Chapter 12 fully covers the use of expressions.) Use the Date function to supply the current date for the Date of Hire field in the employee table if employee records are typically entered on their date of hire. The entry would look like Figure 3-7. This same expression could be used for the Date field in the Invoice and Register table.

Performing Validity Checking

Validity checking screens your entries rather than supplying an entry for you. Even if you leave the Validation Rule property blank on all of your fields, some validity checking is still performed to see that your entry is valid for the data type that you have selected. Although Access will

FIGURE 3-7

Default value for date

Field Name	Data Type	Description
Employee Id	Counter	Employee Identification Number
Last Name	Text	
First Name	Text	
Middle Initial	Text	
Pay Rate	Currency	Hourly pay rate
Bill Rate	Currency	Hourly client billing rate
Date of Hire	Date/Time	
Job Class	Number	Two digit job class code
Department	Text	
Street Address	Text	
City	Text	

Table: Employee

Field Properties

Format	Medium Date
Caption	
Default Value	=Date()
Validation Rule	
Validation Text	
Indexed	No

A field name can be up to 64 characters long, including spaces. Press F1 for help on field names.

Default Value property for the Date of Hire field

accept any entry for a Text or Memo data type, it will ensure that Number and Currency fields do not contain text. It also ensures that Date/Time and Yes/No fields have acceptable entries. Likewise, OLE Object fields cannot contain a number or text.

Validation rules are entered as expressions. These expressions can include constants and functions as well as references to other fields.

Validation rules can be as long as 255 characters although in most cases you will be able to express the checking you want to perform more succinctly. Your validation rules will apply to all new forms that are created. Existing forms must have their controls modified to perform the same check that you just defined. Even if you alter the controls for an existing form, existing data will not be rechecked to see if it conforms to the validation rule. Data that does not meet the rule that you establish will be rejected.

Validation text can be as long as 255 characters. If you are going to reject users' entries, ease their frustration by using the Validation Text property to explain exactly what is wrong with an entry. For example, if the expected entry for Pay Rate in the Employee table lies between $4.25 and $35.00, your Validation Text entry might be "Pay Rate must be between $4.25 and $35.00. Please enter a valid Pay Rate." Another possible entry for the same example could be "Pay Rate must be between minimum wage and $35.00."

Validating Number and Currency Fields

It is easy for data entry operators to transpose a number when entering digits. You can sometimes trap an occasional error by using validation rules with numeric fields. You might have an upper or lower limit for the value entered in a field, you might find any number except zero an acceptable entry, or you might only allow one of four numeric codes. You can even reference the value in another field within the table if you enclose the field name in square brackets. Any of these conditions can be checked by adding an appropriate rule and accompanying text.

The following are examples of some rules and text that might be appropriate for fields in the Coasters database:

Rule	Text
Project->Vehicles	
Validation Rule >0	
Validation Text	Each coaster ride must have at least one vehicle
Employee->Job Class	
Validation Rule	10 Or 20 Or 30
Validation Text	10, 20, and 30 are the only valid job class codes
or	
Validation Rule	>=10 And <=70
Validation Text	Job Code must be between 10 and 70
Employee->Bill Rate	
Validation Rule	>=[Pay Rate]*1.15
Validation Text	Billing Rate must be at least 15% higher than the Pay Rate

Validating Text Fields

Text fields must sometimes follow a set pattern such as when valid part numbers always begin with AT and are followed by a dash and four characters. The Validation Rule property would be "Like AT—????" and an appropriate message would be placed in the Validation Text property. You can ensure that the entries match the defined pattern. You can also check for a set of codes such as valid states where your company delivers or has retail stores at the time of entry.

In the Coasters database you might set this Validation Rule property for the State field in the Employee table:

"OH" Or "PA" Or "MI"

The Validation Text property would read "Employee state code must be OH, PA, or MI."

Validating Date Fields

Access automatically validates a date entry to ensure that it is a valid date. It will not allow a user to enter a date such as 2/31/93 since February never has 31 days. There are other validations that you can perform on date and time fields to ensure that they meet your needs. You may only want dates within the current calendar year entered in fields or you may want to ensure that the date entered is before or after the current date.

For the Coasters database you might consider these validation settings:

Employee->Date of Hire

Validation Rule	>="1/1/93#
Validation Text	Date must be later than 1/1/93

Invoice->Invoice Date

Validation Rule	>=#1/1/92#
Validation Text	Date must be later than 1/1/92

Creating Indexes for a Table

You can create indexes for tables beyond the primary key that you learned about in Chapter 2. Additional indexes are useful when you need to search frequently for specific values in a field. Indexes can also speed up a request to display records in a sorted sequence if you already have an index in the desired order.

You can create indexes that require unique entries for a field or allow duplicates. If you have only a few values for a field that occurs many times, an index may not be efficient since the same index entry will point to many different database records.

You can create an index for one field or use multiple fields when building the index entries.

Indexing with One Field

Create an index for any individual field with the Indexed property. Options for this property are No, Yes (Duplicates OK), and Yes (No Duplicates). Changing a setting from Yes to No deletes an existing index on the field. Figure 3-8 shows the property setting for Indexed in the Employee table Job Class changed to Yes (Duplicates OK). The index that is created can have duplicate entries since a number of employees have the same job class.

Indexing Multiple Fields

Although you could create a multiple field primary key from the design window, you must use the menu to create a multiple field index. You can create as many as five of these multiple field indexes.

Indexed property changed

	Table: Employee		
Field Name	**Data Type**	**Description**	
Employee Id	Counter	Employee Identification Number	
Last Name	Text		
First Name	Text		
Middle Initial	Text		
Pay Rate	Currency	Hourly pay rate	
Bill Rate	Currency	Hourly client billing rate	
Date of Hire	Date/Time		
Job Class	Number	Two digit job class code	
Department	Text		
Street Address	Text		
City	Text		

Field Properties

Field Size	Integer
Format	General Number
Decimal Places	Auto
Caption	
Default Value	0
Validation Rule	[Job Class]>9 And [Job Class]<5
Validation Text	Job Class must be between 10 a
Indexed	Yes (Duplicates OK)

The data type determines the kind of values that users can store in the field. Press F1 for help on data types.

Indexed property

To create a multiple field index from the table design view, follow these steps:

1. Click the Properties button or choose Table Properties in the View menu.

2. Click the next unused index.

3. Type the fields to be used in the index separated by semicolons.
   The fields should be listed in order of priority with later fields in the list serving only as tiebreakers when there are duplicate entries in earlier fields.

4. Choose Save from the File menu to save these changes.

The following shows multiple field indexes for the Employee table on Last Name, First Name, and Middle Initial as well as Department and Job Class.

Table Properties	
Description	
Primary Key	Employee Id
Index1	Last Name; First Name; Middle Initial
Index2	Department; Job Class
Index3	
Index4	
Index5	

Changing Table Definition and Property Defaults

In Chapter 4 you will begin entering data into tables. Although you can change anything that you want before data is entered, you can encounter some potential problems after data in entered. This does not mean that you cannot change your tables; it does mean that you should be fully aware of the consequences of certain types of changes.

The changes that you need to be concerned with are new and deleted fields, a change to an incompatible data type, and a change to a Field

Size property. Access will display a warning when you save the table design if data will be lost in the conversion process. Watch closely for these messages and take appropriate action to avoid losing data.

 Tip Create a backup of your database before making significant changes. If you do lose data, you can always use the copy.

Adding and Deleting Fields

You can add a new field to a table at any time. You can enter new values for this field at any time by using the Datasheet view but if you want to add the data with an existing form, you will need to modify the form design first. Likewise, seeing this new data on reports requires a modification to the existing report design.

If you delete a field from a table you will lose all the data stored in this field. Deleting the field from the table will not remove this object from forms, reports, and queries, which you will need to revise.

In addition to deleting fields you sometimes need to rename them. Although you will not lose data in a rename operation, the data will not be available on existing forms and reports until you revise them to include the field's new name.

Changing Data Types

Before changing data types think about whether the new data type is more or less restrictive than the original. For example, changing a Number data type to a Text data type is no problem since the new field type will accept anything that might be in the field. Changing a Text data type to a Number might not work as well; if the entries in the Text data type are not numbers, they will be changed to null values. Your original data will be lost and indexes for the data will no longer exist.

When you convert from other data types to Text all of the formatting characters such as currency symbols and thousands separators are lost. When you convert from Text to another format these characters are recognized and handled correctly.

If you change a field's data type from Text to Memo, none of the data will be lost but any index created with the field will no longer exist since Memo fields cannot be indexed. If you change a field's data type from Memo to Text, the integrity of your data will depend on the length of the Memo field entries. A maximum of 255 characters can be converted although the Field Size default setting is 50 and may need to be changed.

Changing Properties

If you change the Default Value or Validation Rule properties, the existing data will not be altered. These new properties will only apply to new entries. Format, Caption, and Decimal Places property changes do not have potentially damaging effects either. It is the Field Size for Number fields that you need to be concerned about.

If you change the Field Size property to a smaller size you can lose data from the field if the numbers need to be larger to represent your data. For instance if 124578.8976 is stored in a field as Double and you change it to Byte or Integer, you can lose data. If the only difference is that the new Field Size property does not support decimal places, the number will be rounded and the decimal accuracy will be lost forever.

Quick Reference

To Set Default Relations Between Tables   Open the database for which you want to establish relationships, and choose Relationships from the Edit menu. Select the main table you want to relate from the Primary Table drop-down list box. Select the table that contains related data from the Related Table drop-down list box. Select One to relate two tables by their primary keys or select the field containing related data in the Select Matching Fields drop-down list box. Choose Add.

To Define an Index for One Field   From table design view, press F6. Change the Indexed property to Yes (Duplicates OK) or Yes (No Duplicates).

To Define a Multiple Field Index   From table design view click the Properties button. Add the names of the fields in one of the Index properties using semicolons (;) as separators.

To Change Field Properties   From the table design view, press F6 to move to the properties section and make the desired changes. Press F6 and move to the next field you want to change.

CHAPTER

Entering and Editing Data

With the design of your database complete, you are ready to enter data into one or more tables. You can enter data directly in the datasheet view or create a more sophisticated form to handle data entry. This chapter shows how to enter data in the datasheet; Chapter 8 shows how to use forms for data entry. This chapter teaches you to recognize the special indicators for the status of records, cut and paste data on a datasheet, and make customizing changes to the layout of a datasheet. You also will learn how to print entries made in the datasheet and create another table by copying an existing table.

Adding Records

You must have an open table in order to add records. From the Microsoft Access window, choose Open Database from the File menu and select the database that you want from the File Name list box. From the database window select any existing table and then choose Open. You also can double-click the name of the table in the database window to open the table immediately. Another shortcut is to choose one of the databases listed at the bottom of the File menu (there can be as many as four). Selecting which database you want to open from the bottom of the File menu gives the same results as opening the database with the Open Database command in the File menu.

You use the blank record at the bottom of the datasheet to enter new records into a table. A new table will display nothing other than this blank record until you have entered data. Access uses an asterisk to mark this blank record when it is not the current record. When it is the current record, the regular current record indicator (which looks like an arrowhead) points to it. Figure 4-1 shows some data in the Client table with an asterisk marking the blank record and the current record indicator pointing to the record before it. Press CTRL-END to move to the last field in the last record, and then press HOME to move to the first field in this record quickly. You can also choose Go To from the Records menu and choose New.

As you enter data in new records, Access applies all the knowledge it has about your table definition to check that the entries you make match the data type and properties you set for each field.

FIGURE
4-1
An asterisk marks the blank record

Client Name	Park Desc	Mailing Address	City	State	Zip Cod
Family Fun Land	Large amusement park that H	P.O. Box 345	Houghton	MI	49312
Teen Land	Turn of the century amuseme	P.O. Box 786	Ashtabula	OH	44321
Happy Park	Small family park	1211 Lake St	Muskegon	MI	49231

Microsoft Access - Mary Campbell - [Table: Client]
File Edit View Records Layout Window Help
Field: Mailing Address   New:
Record: 3
P. O. Box or other mailing address   NUM

Entering the Data

To enter data into a blank record when another record is active, click the first field in the record to make it the current record. An insertion point marks your place in this field. Unless you have changed the default setting for Editing Allowed in the Records menu you will be able to begin making entries immediately. If Access rejects your attempt, choose Editing Allowed from the Records menu to allow the table records to be added or edited.

You normally start entries with the leftmost field and move to the right, completing each field. There are two exceptions to this pattern: you skip a counter field since Access supplies the next sequential number automatically and you skip fields where data is unavailable.

As you type values for each field, press TAB to move to the next field. Access scrolls data from the left side of the screen as you move to the right. Later in this chapter, you will learn how to freeze the display to keep critical identifying data at the left visible as you type in fields to the right.

Table 4-1 shows some of the messages that Access might display if you enter data that does not match the definition you have supplied for a field. Access checks both the data type and the Validation Rule property that you establish for the field.

Errors that present a dialog box require that the box be removed by selecting OK before the error can be corrected. The exception is when you attempt to type an entry in a counter field. Although no dialog box appears, the message is shown at the bottom of the table window. Press TAB to move to the next field and the message will disappear.

You can press ESC to Undo the change in the record that caused the problem or edit the entry to correct it. The following shows the message that appears in the dialog box when you attempt to enter text into a field with a Number data type:

Microsoft Access - Mary Campbell
The value you entered isn't appropriate for this field.
OK   Help

Sample of Data Entry Messages

TABLE 4-1

Error Message	Reason for Error
The value that you entered isn't appropriate for this field	Data type does not match.
Can't have Null value in index	Index field was left blank and it is not a Counter data type.
Can't have duplicate key; index changes were unsuccessful	You attempted to use an index entry that already existed when the Indexed property was set to No duplicates.
To make a profit the billing rate must be at least 10% more than the pay rate	Customized Validation Text that matches a custom Validation Rule. Since the entry does not fulfill the rule, the text is displayed.

Entering Client Records

Try the data entry process for one of your tables. Appendix C lists the records entered in each table in the COASTERS database. For now, try a few records in the Client table. All you need to do is open the Client table and begin entering the data shown here:

Record 1

Field	Entry
Client ID	None needed - Counter data type
Client Name	Family Fun Land
Contact	Jeff Jackson
Park Location	Isle Royale
Mailing Address	P.O. Box 345
City	Houghton
State	MI
Zip Code	49312
Phone	6162239999
Park Desc	Large amusement park that has been popular for over 50 years. Only access to the park is by ferry. Three adult's and two children's coasters are already operational.
YTD Invoices	2500000.00
YTD Payments	2300000.00
Total Invoices	2500000.00
Total Payments	2300000.00

Record 2

Field	Entry
Client ID	None needed - Counter data type
Client Name	Teen Land
Contact	Mary Morris
Park Location	Ashtabula Park
Mailing Address	P.O. Box 786
City	Ashtabula

Record 2

State	OH
Zip Code	44321
Phone	2169999090
Park Desc	Turn of the century amusement park with many family riders and some superb coasters
YTD Invoices	3900000.00
YTD Payments	1900000.00
Total Invoices	7100900.00
Total Payments	5100900.00

As you finish the entry of the last field in the second record you can choose Save Record from the File menu or simply move to another record.

Skipping Fields

Most of the time you will move across the row in the table placing an entry in each field and using the TAB key to move to the next field. You can also use SHIFT-TAB to move left and complete an entry. Move to the first field in the record by pressing HOME; move to the last field by pressing END. To move to a specific field use the Field list box on the toolbar, as shown here, to select from a list of field names:

Field: Client Id

When you select the Field list box for the Employee table, you see the list displayed here:

Either click the field that you want or highlight it and press ENTER.

Adding an OLE Object to a Record

Access supports OLE objects for field entries in your tables as long as the type is OLE object. This allows you to use graphs, worksheet objects, drawings, and scanned pictures or art within a table record. Any objects created with applications that support object linking and embedding can be included.

Existing objects must be created by an application that supports OLE or be in a binary format. The Microsoft Paintbrush and Microsoft Graph applications provided with Access are two options for creating OLE objects. You might also have a picture or drawing scanned by a service bureau and stored in a format such as .BMP or .PCX. After selecting the field that will contain this object, follow these steps:

1. Choose Insert Object from the Edit menu to display the dialog box shown here:

2. Select the File button.

3. Select the name of the file that you want to use.

You will be able to see the selected object on your screen.

If you need to create the object, you must start the application that will create it. This application must support OLE. You proceed in the same manner as when adding an existing object by choosing Insert Object from the Edit menu but you select the application that you want from the Insert Object dialog box. Next you need to create a document that comes as close as possible to the actual size you want your form or report to be. Choose Exit or Return from the File menu to continue with your entries in the Access table.

Tip You might want to create all of your OLE Objects in a separate session rather than trying to create them while doing your data entry. In most applications, it is more efficient to work in the drawing or graph program to create all the pictures or graphs that you need, and then complete data entry.

Using Undo to Remove a Change

Access allows you to undo editing changes as well as your last action. Because the extent of the editing changes can affect one field or many and the last action may differ, Access displays different Undo options in the Edit menu depending on what is possible at a given time.

Access allows you to undo one editing change to a field or to undo all the changes you make to a record. You must request that Access undo your changes *before* you start editing another record or switch to a different window. If you change the current field and want to undo the change, choose Undo Current Field from the Edit menu. If you have made other changes to this record and want to eliminate them, choose Undo Current Record from the Edit menu.

You can also undo the last action taken in a datasheet. Perhaps you deleted records, typed some data, or saved a record and want to eliminate the change. If you edit the ZIP code in a client record and then realize that you have changed the wrong record, choose Undo Typing from the Edit menu.

 Tip Press CTRL-Z to quickly undo your last action.

Editing

Although Access saves changes to a record as soon as you move to another record, you can always make further changes if you wish to. When you start making changes to a record, the Pencil icon appears, indicating that you are modifying the record. Choose Save Record from the File menu to save your changes or simply move to another record.

Moving to the Record You Want to Change

To move to the record that you want to change, either click the record or use the UP ARROW and DOWN ARROW keys to move to it. Here are some other key combinations that can help you get where you are going quickly:

CTRL-PAGE DOWN	Move to the right one screen
CTRL-PAGE UP	Move to the left one screen
CTRL-HOME	Move to the first field in the first record
CTRL-END	Move to the last field in the last record

In many situations you will not know the record number; however, when you know it you can choose Go To from the Records menu. You can choose First, Last, Next, Previous, or New. Choosing New moves you to a blank record.

Moving to the Field You Want to Change

When you want to edit a record, you may only want to change one field. Moving across the record one field at a time with the TAB, LEFT ARROW, or RIGHT ARROW keys may be too slow. Use the END key to move to the last field, and then use SHIFT-TAB to move one field to the left or HOME to move to the first field. A more precise approach is to select the field by clicking it or using the Field list box in the toolbar to move to a field that is not visible. You learned to use this technique earlier when adding data in the Adding Records section earlier in this chapter.

Access Record Indicators

The current record is the record that you are working on. Access provides indicators that appear to the far left of the current record and indicate its status. Access refers to the current record as the record that has the focus and marks it with this symbol:

As you make changes to this record, Access marks the current record with this symbol:

If a record has this Pencil icon you know it still has the focus but is being edited.

These editing changes are not saved until you change the focus to another record or choose Save Record from the File menu.

Not saving the record allows you to change your mind and eliminate all of your changes by choosing Undo Current Record from the Edit menu; however, this only works if you haven't yet moved to another record.

When a record is locked by another user, you will not be able to make changes to it. Locking is designed to prevent two overlapping sets of changes, which could result in the loss of one of the user's changes. This symbol marks a record that is locked:

Selecting Data

You need to master the techniques for selecting data in fields and records to work effectively with the data in your datasheet. You will use these techniques to edit data in existing records. You will also use these techniques when you copy, move, and delete data in fields or records. You can use either the keyboard or the mouse for most options.

Using the keyboard can be convenient in some situations as it is quicker to press F2 to select an entire field than to maneuver the mouse pointer to the correct location before clicking; however, in other situations using F2 requires extra steps. When selecting part of a field using the keyboard, move the insertion point to the location where you want to start. When using the keyboard to select an entire record, first move to the record that you want to select.

Both keyboard and mouse alternatives are provided where possible to allow you to choose the approach that seems easiest for each activity. Both options highlight the selected data. You can choose from the selection options in the table that follows:

Option	Action	Device
Select part of a field	Click the location where you want to start the selection and drag across	Mouse
	Move the insertion point to the desired start location, press SHIFT-LEFT ARROW or SHIFT-RIGHT ARROW to complete your selection	Keyboard
Select the entire field	Click the left edge of the field (the mouse pointer will appear as an arrow rather than an I-beam)	Mouse
	Press F2	Keyboard
Extend the selection within a field	Press SHIFT and click the new ending position	Mouse
	Press SHIFT-LEFT ARROW or SHIFT-RIGHT ARROW	Keyboard
Cancel the selection for a field	Click another location	Mouse
	Press F2	Keyboard
Select a record	Click the record selector to the left of the record	Mouse
	Move to the desired record and press SHIFT-SPACEBAR	Keyboard
Select multiple records	Click the selector of the first record and drag to the selector of the last record	Mouse
	Press SHIFT-SPACEBAR and then SHIFT-UP ARROW or SHIFT-SPACEBAR and then SHIFT-DOWN ARROW	Keyboard
Select all records	Click the selector in the upper-left area of the datasheet	Mouse

Editing Options

With editing options you can either replace the entire contents of a field or make a subtle change. You can move or copy data between fields.

To replace the entire contents of the field, select the field using the techniques described in the previous section and begin typing your new entry. The previous entry is replaced by what you type.

To eliminate an entry in a field, select the field and then choose De̲lete from the E̲dit menu. To delete part of a field, select the portion of the field that you want to eliminate before taking this action.

You can insert missing letters, digits, or words in a field by moving the insertion point to the desired location and typing the new data. The data is inserted at the insertion point. The distinction between inserting and replacing is that the entire field is not selected (and overwritten) when you insert.

When you move or copy data from a field, you can use that data to fill an empty field, replace the contents of a field, or add it to the current field entry. Regardless of which approach you choose, these steps will work for you:

1. Select the data to be moved or copied as shown in Figure 4-2.

2. Choose C̲opy or Cu̲t from the E̲dit menu depending on whether you want to copy or move the data.

3. Select the destination field or place the insertion point where you want to add the data.

Figure 4-3 shows the destination field with the field selected.

4. Choose P̲aste from the E̲dit menu, and the data that you cut will replace the data in the field that you're pasting.

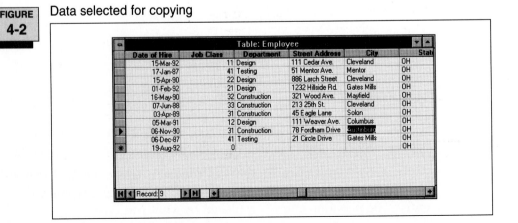

FIGURE 4-2

Data selected for copying

Date of Hire	Job Class	Department	Street Address	City	State
15-Mar-92	11	Design	111 Cedar Ave.	Cleveland	OH
17-Jan-87	41	Testing	51 Mentor Ave.	Mentor	OH
15-Apr-90	22	Design	886 Larch Street	Cleveland	OH
01-Feb-92	21	Design	1232 Hillside Rd.	Gates Mills	OH
16-May-90	32	Construction	321 Wood Ave.	Mayfield	OH
07-Jun-88	33	Construction	213 25th St.	Cleveland	OH
03-Apr-89	31	Construction	45 Eagle Lane	Solon	OH
05-Mar-91	12	Design	111 Weaver Ave.	Columbus	OH
06-Nov-90	31	Construction	78 Fordham Drive	Contributo	OH
06-Dec-87	41	Testing	21 Circle Drive	Gates Mills	OH
19-Aug-92	0				OH

Table: Employee

Record: 9

FIGURE
4-3

The destination field selected

Date of Hire	Job Class	Department	Street Address	City	Stat
15-Mar-92	11	Design	111 Cedar Ave.	Cleveland	OH
17-Jan-87	41	Testing	51 Mentor Ave.	Mentor	OH
15-Apr-90	22	Design	886 Larch Street	Cleveland	OH
01-Feb-92	21	Design	1232 Hillside Rd.	Gates Mills	OH
16-May-90	32	Construction	321 Wood Ave.	Mayfield	OH
07-Jun-88	33	Construction	213 25th St.	Cleveland	OH
03-Apr-89	31	Construction	45 Eagle Lane	Solon	OH
05-Mar-91	12	Design	111 Weaver Ave.	Columbus	OH
06-Nov-90	31	Construction	78 Fordham Drive	Austinburg	OH
06-Dec-87	41	Testing	21 Circle Drive	Gates Mills	OH
19-Aug-92	0				OH

Record: 1

Moving or Copying Records

You can move or copy records from one Access table to another. This is useful if, for example, you keep prospects and client information in separate tables. You could move a record from the Prospects table to the Client table as soon as you had an active project for an individual or company. You also might want to move records between tables for the Coaster Mania's employee table. If you choose to maintain only current employees in this table, you could move a record for a terminated employee to a table containing information on former employees, as shown here:

Employee Id	Last Name	First Name	Middle Initial	Pay Rate	Bil
1	WILD	WILLIAM	W	$35.00	
2	DANGER	DAN	D	$30.00	
3	ROLLING	RODGER	R	$33.00	
4	SCARY	SANDRA	S	$31.00	

Record: 3

Table: Former Employees

Employee Id	Last Name	First Name	Middle Initial	Pay Rate	Bil R
(Counter)				$0.00	

Record: 1

To move or copy a record into another table, the fields must have the same data types even though the field names may be different. The fields must be in the same order on the datasheet since the fields are kept in the order of the destination file. The fields in the destination datasheet must have a sufficient length to receive the data. If the data is to be placed in the *primary key* or a key that is indexed that allows no duplicates, the value in the source field cannot already exist in the destination table. Also, you cannot paste a record into a table if one or more field entries violates a Validation Rule property. Records that cannot be pasted for these reasons are written to a special table called Paste Errors for your review. You can change the source data as needed and attempt to move the records to the destination table again.

To move or copy a record to another datasheet, follow these steps:

1. Select the records to be copied.

2. Choose Cut or Copy from the Edit menu.

3. Open the table that you want to move or copy the records to.

4. Rearrange the fields to match the order of the source records if necessary.

5. Select the records to be replaced and then choose Paste from the Edit menu or append the records at the end of the table by choosing Paste Append from the Edit menu.

Deleting Records

Removing records is easy. If you make a mistake and delete the wrong records you can undo your mistake as long as you take the correcting action immediately.

To delete one or more records, select them by clicking the record selector. To select multiple records select the first record selector and drag to the last record. Choose Delete from the Edit menu or press the DEL key. The dialog box that appears indicates the number of records about to be deleted when the records are saved and lets you determine whether or not to proceed.

Customizing the Datasheet Layout

You can use the view of the datasheet that appears when you open a table or make some significant changes to its appearance. You may find that changing the display speeds up your work or makes the data that you need to work with more accessible or attractive. While the datasheet view is ideal for looking at the contents of many records at the same time, limiting the data that is displayed can make it easier to spot any changes that you have to make. You can use each layout technique singly or combine them to achieve the best possible display. To make your changes a permanent part of the datasheet layout, choose Save Layout from the File menu. If you want the changes to be temporary, just close the table without choosing Save Layout from the File menu.

Freezing the Display

Often identifying fields appear at the left side of the datasheet. As you move to the right, these fields scroll off the display, which can make it difficult to tell which record you are entering or editing. You can freeze fields at the left of the display. These fields will remain in view as you scroll to the right so that you easily can see the identifying data such as employee ID or last name.

To freeze fields on the display, select the field selectors at the top of the column and then choose Freeze Columns from the Layout menu. Select multiple columns by pressing the SHIFT key as you click the field selector at the top of the columns. Figure 4-4 shows the Client Name and

FIGURE 4-4

Frozen columns

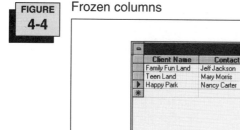

Contact frozen at the left of the window while other fields from the right side of the display are viewed.

To unfreeze the columns when you no longer need to lock them in place, choose Unfreeze All Columns from the Layout menu. The columns that were frozen now appear at the left of the datasheet. To put them back in another location, move them using the instructions in the next section or close the table without saving the layout.

Reordering the Column Display

Initially the column order for a datasheet corresponds to the order of the fields in the table. If you need to enter only a few fields or check the values in several fields, your task would be much easier if the fields appeared in adjacent columns on the datasheet. Also, you may have frozen columns and found when you unfroze them that they reside on the far left of your datasheet even if they were originally in a different location.

To move a column to a new location, select the field selector for the column. Select multiple adjacent columns if you wish. Next, click the field selector again and drag the column to the new location. After freezing the Client Name and Contact from the Client table and unfreezing the display, these fields now appear to the left of the Client Id in the Client table. You can select these columns as shown in Figure 4-5. Next drag the field selector to the right of the Client Id and release it.

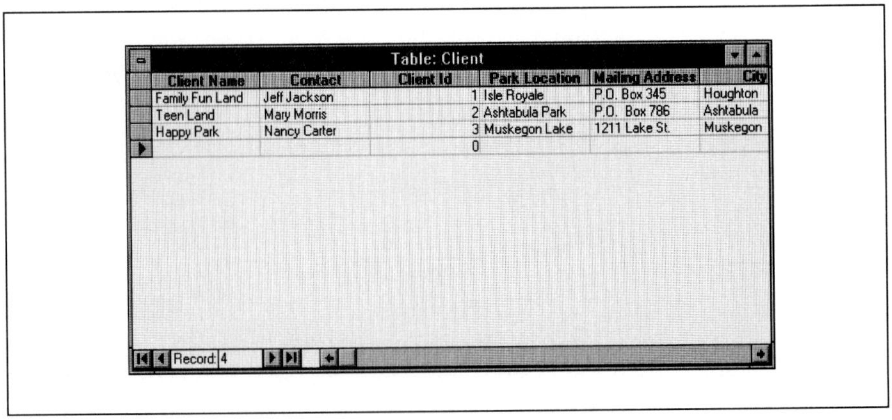

FIGURE 4-5

Two columns need to be moved to the right of Client Id

	Client Name	Contact	Client Id	Park Location	Mailing Address	City
	Family Fun Land	Jeff Jackson	1	Isle Royale	P.O. Box 345	Houghton
	Teen Land	Mary Morris	2	Ashtabula Park	P.O. Box 786	Ashtabula
	Happy Park	Nancy Carter	3	Muskegon Lake	1211 Lake St.	Muskegon
			0			

Table: Client

Record: 4

Hiding Columns

If your datasheet has more than a few fields it is probably not possible to show all the fields on the screen or on one sheet of paper when printed. If you do not need to work with the information in all the columns you will find that hiding unneeded columns can make it easier to work with the data that you need. Hidden columns not only do not appear onscreen, they also don't print when you use the Print command in the File menu to print the contents of the datasheet.

To hide one or more columns, select the columns and choose Hide Columns from the Layout menu. To select multiple columns, hold down the SHIFT key as you click the columns.

For example, if you are working with the Client datasheet and do not need to see Mailing Address, City, State, and Zip Code, select these fields and then choose Hide Columns from the Layout menu. Although the columns are not permanently deleted there is no evidence of their existence onscreen or on paper when printed.

Tip Since you cannot hide nonadjacent columns without multiple selections, you might find it easier to use the Show Columns command from the Layout menu when hiding a large number of columns. Choose fields from the list of field names and click the Hide button for each field that you want hidden.

To redisplay columns that you have hidden, choose Show Columns from the Layout menu. The Show Columns box appears. Choose the column that you want to display again and then choose the Show button. Continue selecting until all the columns you need have been selected. Select a column and choose Hide if there are columns that you want to eliminate. When you are finished making changes, choose Close to remove the Show Columns box from the screen. Figure 4-6 shows how the Client table appears with many of its columns hidden.

Changing the Column Width

Access establishes the column width based on the Field Size property established for each field. You may not need all the space allowed to

Hidden columns

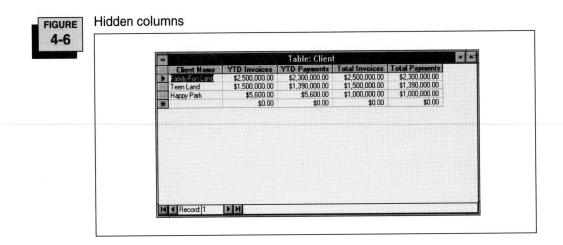

display a meaningful amount of data and may choose to shrink the column width. This will allow you to show more columns from the datasheet on the screen. It will not limit the length of the entries that you can place in a field the way that changing the Field Size property will.

Since the default width for a Text field is 50, users often reduce the column width of a Text data type field. Since Currency fields for small unit prices and other numeric data do not always fill the space allocated, determine whether you can reduce these fields as well. Even Counter fields are often too large if you have a datasheet with a limited number of records. With a Text data type you may want to actually reduce the Field Size property so as not to have to change the field display each time you use it. With other field types, you have chosen the data type and property setting with other reasons in mind and may not be able to make any modifications.

Tip If you need to narrow the columns to see the fields that you want and cannot see the full contents of some fields, increase the row height to double or triple the standard height to allow multiple lines of data to display for a field. Although you will see fewer records, you may find this optimizes viewing the screen for some situations.

To change the width of a column, simply position the mouse pointer at the right side of the field selector for the column and drag it right or left to achieve the desired size. Figure 4-7 shows the Park Description field widened to show more text onscreen.

Changing the Font or Row Height

You can change the font for a datasheet to any available screen font option. Although this does not guarantee that the appearance of the printed datasheet will match the screen display, Access will select the closest possible match when printing your data depending on what printer options you have available. You can have Access automatically adjust the row height to match a new font height or you can customize the row height to display multiple rows of data for a field.

Changing the Font

When you change the font for a table you can change the character design and character set with your selection of a font. You can change

FIGURE 4-7   Column width changed

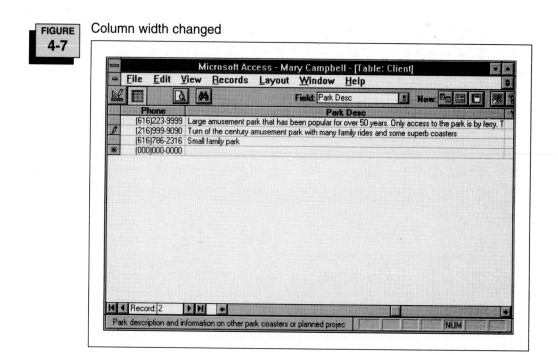

the style, size, and special effects as well. All of these changes are made by choosing Font from the Layout menu to display the dialog box shown here:

Font Style options include boldface and italics. The characters and selected font stay the same; only the new style option is added for all the table entries.

A change in the point size affects the height of each character. Point size is measured in 1/72-inch increments if you are using decimal measurements and 1/28-cm increments if you are using metric. This means that a point size of 8 is approximately 1/9 of an inch or 2/7 of a centimeter in height. When you change the point size, the row height is automatically adjusted as long as you have not changed the Standard Height check box for Row Height. If you change the point size from the default of 8 to 18, Row Height is automatically adjusted from 10.5 to 22.5.

Tip When you change a font you can see what it will look like immediately by looking at the Sample text box in the Font dialog box.

Figure 4-8 shows one of the Coaster tables displayed in a serif font with a larger point size. The height of the rows is adjusted automatically.

Changing the Row Height

Access automatically resizes the height of the rows in a table when you change the font as long as you do not remove the check from the check box for the Standard Height setting. The row heights shown are

FIGURE 4-8

A serif font selected for display in a point size larger than the default

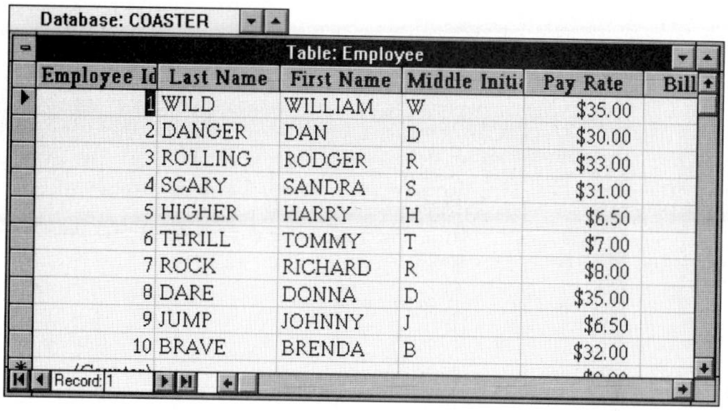

| Database: COASTER | | | | | |

| Table: Employee | | | | | |
Employee Id	Last Name	First Name	Middle Initi	Pay Rate	Bill
1	WILD	WILLIAM	W	$35.00	
2	DANGER	DAN	D	$30.00	
3	ROLLING	RODGER	R	$33.00	
4	SCARY	SANDRA	S	$31.00	
5	HIGHER	HARRY	H	$6.50	
6	THRILL	TOMMY	T	$7.00	
7	ROCK	RICHARD	R	$8.00	
8	DARE	DONNA	D	$35.00	
9	JUMP	JOHNNY	J	$6.50	
10	BRAVE	BRENDA	B	$32.00	

Record: 1

specified in point sizes (just as the fonts are) with a larger row height size automatically selected as the standard height to make the datasheet entries readable.

You can also change the row height without changing the font and leave text the same point size. This will display more than one line of the text in a row. If you want to display more than one line of text within a row when entries are longer than the column width will display, choose a row height that is larger than the standard row height. For example, when a point size of 8 is chosen, the standard row height is set at 10.5; if you change the point size to 33, you can see more of lengthy entries in three lines as shown in Figure 4-9.

Printing a Table

Although the reports that you will learn about later in Chapter 9 give you more sophisticated options, you can print your data directly from the datasheet. Hidden columns will not appear, which allows you to limit the amount of data displayed in the printout. Other customizing options such as font and height changes also affect the printout. You can retain the gridlines or remove them by choosing Gridlines in the Layout menu.

Preview the appearance of the printout by choosing Print Preview from the File menu. If you need to select another printer, change the configu-

Multiple rows of long fields display due to a larger row height setting

ration of the current printer, or print to a file, choose Printer Setup from the File menu. If you want to print selected records, choose them and then select Print from the File menu. You can select from All, Selection, or Pages to control the amount of data that will print.

Copying a Table

You might want to make a copy of an existing table and then modify the copy. The copied table can contain all the data or only the table structure in order to create a history or archive file for data. You can also use the Copy option to add records from one table to the end of another table.

Follow these steps to copy a table:

1. Open the database containing the table that you want to copy.

2. From the Database window, select the table that you want to copy and then choose Copy from the Edit menu.

3. Choose <u>P</u>aste from the <u>E</u>dit menu to copy the table to the current database and supply a new name.

You must open the destination database first if the new table is not needed in the current database.

4. Complete the Paste Table As dialog box by selecting the type of paste operation and supplying a new filename.

5. Select OK.

Quick Reference

To Move to Another Field Use TAB or SHIFT-TAB to move to the next or previous field. Click the name of the field you want in the Field list box.

To Move to Another Record Click the navigation buttons at the lower-left corner of the datasheet to move to the first, last, next, or previous records. Use the UP ARROW or DOWN ARROW keys or choose <u>G</u>o To from the <u>R</u>ecords menu and choose the option that meets your need.

To Undo a Change Choose <u>U</u>ndo Typing, U<u>n</u>do Current Field, or U<u>n</u>do Current Record from the <u>E</u>dit menu.

To Delete a Record Select the record and then select D<u>e</u>lete from the <u>E</u>dit menu or press DEL.

To Copy a Field or Record Select the data to be copied and choose <u>C</u>opy from the <u>E</u>dit menu. If you want to replace data, select the destination or move the insertion point and then choose <u>P</u>aste or Paste Appen<u>d</u> from the <u>E</u>dit menu. You use Paste Append when you want to add records that you are copying to the end of the table.

To Move a Field or Record Select the data to be moved and choose Cu<u>t</u> from the <u>E</u>dit menu. If you want to replace data, select the destination or move the insertion point and then choose <u>P</u>aste or Paste Appen<u>d</u> from the <u>E</u>dit menu. Use Paste Append when you want to add records that you are moving to the end of the table.

To Freeze the Display Select the field selector for the columns to be frozen and then choose Freeze Columns from the Layout menu. To unfreeze columns choose Unfreeze All Columns from the Layout menu.

To Move a Column Click the field selector for the column to be moved. Click the field selector a second time and drag the column to its new location.

To Hide a Column Click the field selector for the column that you want to hide. Choose Hide Columns from the Layout menu.

To Show a Hidden Column Choose Show Columns from the Layout menu and then select the column you want to display and select Show. Choose Close after selecting all the columns to be displayed.

To Change the Column Width Drag the field selector for the column to the right or left.

To Change the Font Choose Font from the Layout menu and then select Font, Font Style, Size, or Underline. Select OK when you are finished making changes.

To Change the Row Height With the pointer between two record selectors, drag up or down to change the row height or choose Row Height from the Layout menu and specify the row height in points.

To Print a Table Select Print from the File menu and select OK.

To Copy a Table From the Database window, select the table to be copied. Choose Copy from the Edit menu. Open another database, or place the copy in the current database by choosing Paste from the Edit menu immediately. You can choose to copy the structure and data, the structure only, or just the records. Specify a name for the table and select OK.

CHAPTER

Importing and Exporting Data

*I*f you use a personal computer regularly, you may already be acquainted with other programs. You may have data from these programs that you would like to use with Access. Also, you may want to use some of your new Access data in these other formats.

You can use data from Access in other database applications or import data into Access. Access supports access to dBASE, Paradox, Btrieve, and SQL. You can create an Access database from data stored in a spreadsheet or word processing programs, or use your Access data in the other programs.

Because Access is a Windows application, you can easily share data with other Windows applications. You can copy one or more Access objects to the Clipboard and then paste them into another application. This allows you to transfer data from Access to products such as Word for Windows or Excel for Windows and allows you to transfer data from one Access database to another.

If you have data in these other formats, take the time to explore using the data with Access now since you can build a database table with minimal work this way. If you are new to database management, skip this chapter and focus on other Access topics in the chapters that follow this one. You can return to importing and exporting when it applies to your work.

Accessing Data in Other Database Applications

The investment you have made in building a base of information is not lost if you decide to begin using Access for your database tasks. Using Access with your existing data requires a minimum of work. Access is so flexible that it allows you to continue to maintain the data in the original file format while creating Access forms and reports. You simply attach the data in the other database file or table to one of your Access databases. When you *attach* data, it behaves as if it is part of the Access database although it is not. You can edit data in both Access and the other application and view it as if it is an Access table although an Access table is not created. Attaching is the perfect solution when you need to continue to use the other program with the data.

When you no longer need to use your existing data with the program that created it, you can import the data into Access. *Importing* converts the data from its original format into an Access table. Access supports attaching and importing with dBASE, Paradox, Btrieve, and SQL. If you want to add data from an existing application to an Access table, you can append the data to an Access table as long as its format matches the existing table entries.

The difference between importing and attaching data is where the data is stored when you use it in Access. When you import data, you are taking a copy of the data and placing it in a table in an Access database, as you can see in Figure 5-1. When you use data in an attached table in Access, you are using the data that is stored in a file in another application's format. The data is *not* in your Access database although you use your Access database to look at and use the data.

FIGURE 5-1   Difference between importing and attaching files

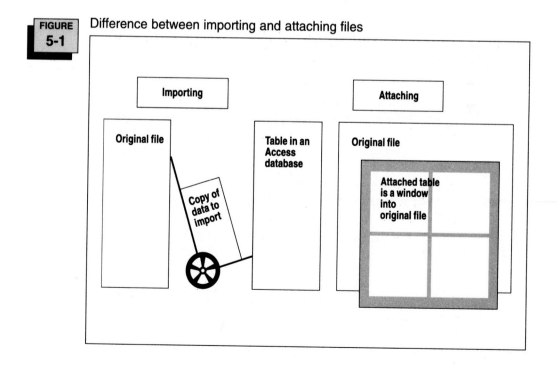

General Guidelines for Importing and Attaching

When you want to use data stored in another application's format, you must decide whether to import or attach the data. The decision hinges on this question: Do you want to use the data in the other application again? When the answer is yes (you are importing data from dBASE that you will continually fine-tune in dBASE, for example), attach the data to an Access database table. When the answer is no (you are upgrading to Access from your old software, for instance), import the data.

Either attach the data from the other format or import the data. Don't do both because then you'll have more than one copy of the data. With more than one copy, you can't always be sure which copy is the most recent.

Tip Make the original table your only copy, and attach it to the tables that require the information whenever necessary; this way you'll know that the original table always contains the most up-to-date information. When you change the data in the original tables or in one of the attached tables, the data is updated both in the original table and in all databases that use the data as an attached table.

The steps for importing a file are summarized in the next section, "Importing Data into a Table." The steps for attaching a table into an Access database are summarized in the section after that, "Attaching a Table." Sections throughout this chapter will refer you to these two sections whenever you need to import into a table or attach a table in Access. When you either attach or import data into a table, you are creating a new table that has the same name as the file that contains the imported or attached data.

Tip If you run into a problem importing or attaching, check to see that SHARE is loaded. SHARE is a DOS program that allows multiple applications to use a file. You may want to include this command in your AUTOEXEC.BAT file by having a line containing C:\DOS\SHARE assuming DOS is installed in C:\DOS\. If you do not want to include SHARE in your AUTOEXEC.BAT file, you will want to enter **SHARE** at the DOS prompt before starting Windows.

Importing Data into a Table

To import the data in a file into a table in the current database, follow these steps:

1. Switch to the Database window by pressing F11 or clicking it.

2. Choose Import from the File menu.

3. Select the format of the data you want to import from the Data Source list box in the Import dialog box, the directory from the Directories list box, and the drive from the Drives drop down list box, and then select OK.

4. Select the filename of the file you want to import and select the Import button.

Access imports the file you have selected. When Access is finished, it displays a message that it successfully imported the file.

5. Select the OK button.

6. Repeat steps 4 and 5 for each file of the selected file type you want to import.

7. Select the Close button.

If the Database window is displaying the database's tables, you can see the newly imported tables in the list of tables. If you are prompted for a password when the file you select is password-protected, you must enter the same password you would enter in Paradox, Btrieve, or an SQL database when you use the data in that application.

Attaching a Table

To attach data stored in another file as a table in the current database, follow these steps:

1. Switch to the Database window by pressing F11 or clicking it.

2. Choose Attach Table from the File menu.

3. Select the format of the data you want to import from the Data Source list box in the Import dialog box and select OK.

4. Select the filename of the file you want to attach and select OK. You can also change the drive and directory just as you can with Import.

Access attaches the file you have selected. Once the attachment process is finished, Access displays a message saying that attachment of the file is complete.

5. Select the OK button to return to the Attach Tables dialog box.

6. Repeat steps 4 and 5 for each file you want to attach.

7. Select the Close button after attaching all the files you want of the type you selected in step 3.

Differences Between Attaching and Importing

The tables that you import differ in several ways from tables that you attach. These differences include the icon, what happens to the table's data when you delete a table from the database, and whether the data you are adding to a database can be added as a new table or appended. The following sections cover these differences.

The Icon   Imported tables and attached tables use different icons in the Database window. Imported tables use the same icon as the tables you create in Access. Attached tables use the same icon with an arrow to indicate that it is attached, as shown here:

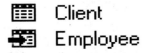

Deleting a Table   When you delete an imported table, the table's contents are removed just as they are when you delete a table that you have created in Access. When you delete an attached table, you are breaking the link from the current database to the database that contains the table. The data continues to be available in the original database as well as in all other databases that use the table as an attached table.

Adding Data When you import data into a table, the data can be placed in a new table or the data can be added to an existing table. For example, when you import several files containing different parts of your customer list into an Access table, you'll want all the files to be imported into the same table. Appending the data into the table means the data you are importing must have the same field definitions and order as the table to which you are appending the data. When you attach a table, the table is separate from the other tables in the database and cannot be combined with any of them.

 Tip You can rename the tables you import and attach. Most of the tables you import and attach use the same eight-character limitation imposed by DOS for filenames. You can rename the imported and attached tables to provide better descriptions of the table's contents. Rename the new tables with the Rename command in the File menu.

Working with Attached Tables

When you use an attached table in an Access database, you will notice that it differs in several ways from a table stored in the database. Attached tables in Access are not as fast as the tables stored in Access files because the data from the attached table must be constantly read from the original file. Also, while you can change the data in the table, you are more limited in the changes you can make to the table's design.

Table Design One difference is how the table behaves when you display the table's design. First, when you switch to a table's design, Access displays a message reminding you that the table is attached and not all table properties can be modified. After you select OK, you will notice that you cannot change the field names or data type. You also cannot rearrange or add fields in the table or delete any fields. However, you can change the Format, Decimal Places, Caption, Default Value, Validation Rule, and Validation Text properties.

Increasing Speed You can make attached tables work faster just by changing how you use them. With dBASE attached database files, you can improve performance by including an index file when you attach the database file (you'll see how to do this later in this chapter). The difference in speed between other operations on an attached table may not be noticed when you are using an attached table that is not shared. But if you are using an attached SQL table or a file stored on a network, you will want to use these suggestions to speed your work on attached tables. The more you move between the records in the table, the more Access must reread data from the disk. By only moving to the records you need, you make the attached table perform faster.

Also, if you only need to work with a select group of records from the attached table, create a query that selects only the records you want. When you create queries that use attached tables, avoid functions, especially aggregate functions such as DSUM. If you want to add records to the attached table, add them faster by creating a form that has the Default Editing property set to Data Entry (you will learn how in Chapter 10). When finished using the data in the attached tables, close the table window.

Tip   If you need to bring in data that is not already in one of the acceptable formats, you probably can convert the data by saving the data in the original application in one of the acceptable formats. For example, import data stored in a Quattro Pro format (which is not an acceptable format) by saving the file in Quattro Pro with a .WK1 extension to save the file in a Lotus (WK1) format, which is supported.

Sharing Data Between Access Databases

The tables and other objects you create for an Access database can be used by more than one database. You can import tables and other objects from an Access database. You can also attach a table from one Access database into another. You will import tables from other Access databases when you want to transfer a table to a different database. You will import other objects into an Access database when you want to create a separate copy of the object for the current database.

For example, you can import a form or report that you have created with another database to use as a model for a form or report you want to use in the current database. It's best to attach a table from another database when you want to both keep the table in the original database and also use it in the current database. You'll see yet another option for sharing data between databases later in this chapter in the "Exporting Access Data" section. When exporting a table or other object from one Access database to a second one, the results are the same as when you import the object from the first database into the second one.

Importing Objects from Another Access Database

When you import an object, you are placing a copy of it in your current database just as if you had originally created it in the current database. Most of this chapter focuses on importing tables but when you import from another Access database, you can import other database objects as well. For example, you can create a report in one Access database and import it into another Access database to use with one of the tables in the second database.

To import an object from an Access database into the current database, follow the same steps you use to import data files although steps 4 and 5 will differ slightly. First, after you select Microsoft Access from the Data Source list box in the Import dialog box, select the database name containing the object you want to import and select OK. Next, select the type of object you want to import from the Object Type drop-down list box. You have the same Tables, Queries, Forms, Reports, Macros, and Modules choices for the different objects listed in the Database window. Notice that when you select Tables from the Object Type drop-down list box, you can select the Structure Only or the Structure and Data radio button. These radio buttons select whether you are importing only the table's structure or importing both the data and the table's structure. Finally, select the object you want to import from the Objects in the Database list box, and the Import button.

Attaching Tables from Another Access Database

Rather than importing a table from another Access database when you need to use it in the current one, you can attach it. Attaching a table lets you share the data in the table between more than one database application. For example, you can have an employee table that you share between the personnel database and the payroll database. To attach a table from another Access database as a table in the current database, follow the steps described for attaching a table, although instead of selecting the filename you want to attach, first select the database containing the table to attach and then select which table from the database you want to attach.

Pasting Objects from Another Access Database

You can also use the Clipboard to transfer tables between databases. When you copy tables with the Clipboard, you can put the copied data in a new table or in one of the existing ones. You can also use the Clipboard to copy the data from a table to another table in the database.

To copy a table with the Clipboard, switch to the Database window. When you have highlighted the table you want to copy, choose Copy from the Edit menu. Next, switch to the database where you want to place the copied table. Choose Paste from the Edit menu. Access prompts for a name for the table. Type a table name and select OK. You can select the Structure Only or the Structure and Data radio button to choose whether to copy the structure of the table or the structure and the data of the table. Another option is to select the Append Data to Existing Table radio button and type an existing table name in the Table Name text box to have the data in the Clipboard added to the end of the selected table.

Note While this example only focuses on copying a table, you also can copy the other types of Access objects you will learn about later such as forms, reports, and queries.

You can copy the Clipboard's contents into the same database from which you cut; this means that you can have two similar reports in the same database by creating the first report, copying it to the same database, and then editing it and saving it under a different name.

Tip If you want to append data to an existing table but are unsure if the format of the existing table and the data you want to import are the same, import the data as a new table. You can then check to see that the tables are similarly organized. If they are, copy the new table and paste it to the existing one.

Using dBASE Data with Access

dBASE III and IV are popular database programs. If you have your data stored in dBASE III or IV files, you can import or attach these files. You use the same steps to attach and import data from dBASE III as you do to attach and import data from dBASE IV.

In dBASE, the tables of data are stored in database files. When you use dBASE data in Access, the dBASE Character fields are set to Text, the Numeric and Float fields are set to Number with a double width, the Logical fields are set to Yes/No, the Date fields are set to Date/Time, and the Memo fields remain memo fields. In an attached table, the table continues to have the original field types that it had in dBASE since the different field types only affect how they are treated in Access.

Importing Tables from dBASE Data

When you no longer need to keep dBASE data in its original file and you want to use the data in an Access database, import it to the current database. Once you import a dBASE data file, you can use the data in Access just as if you had originally created the table in Access. To import a dBASE III or IV database into the current database, follow the same steps that you use to import other data files. Figure 5-2 shows the dBASE data in dBASE and then the same data imported into an Access table.

Attaching Tables from dBASE Data

When you need to keep dBASE data in its original file, attach it to the current database. Once you attach a dBASE data file, you can use the data in dBASE as well as in the current Access database. To attach a dBASE database as a table in the current database, follow the steps described earlier in this chapter in the "Attaching a Table" section.

The only special feature in attaching a dBASE table is that you can select the indexes the attached table uses. After you select the dBASE file you want to attach, you can select the index files this dBASE data will use in Access. The index files organize the data in the dBASE file and improve how Access performs with the dBASE data.

FIGURE
5-2

dBASE data imported into Access

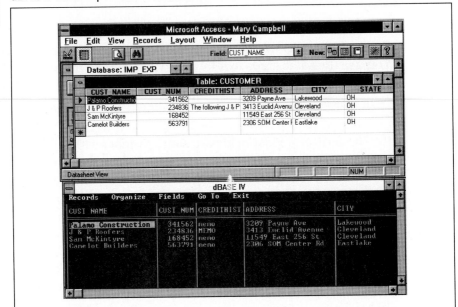

Access can use the .NDX files that provide one order for the records or the .MDX files that provide multiple orders for the records in the file. You can select the index files the same way you select the dBASE file. You can repeat selecting indexes. When you select all of the indexes you want, choose the Select button. A prompt tells you that Access has attached the selected dBASE database. Assuming you have selected index files when you attached a database, Access creates an index information file in the same location as the dBASE data and marks index files with an .INF extension. Be sure to keep the indexes you have selected current since Access cannot open the attached table if the index files are out of sync with the information in the table.

 Tip Some products that work with dBASE data are not designed to work as part of attached dBASE files. For example, Access does not support Clipper .NTX files. This is not an issue if you use dBASE solely to access dBASE data. When you work with dBASE data in an application that is not dBASE, you may want to try attaching a test table to see how attaching the table works both with Access and the non-dBASE application.

Using Paradox Data in Access

Paradox is another popular database management program. You can use your Paradox 3.0 and 3.5 tables in Access. Like other database management files, you can either import or attach these files. In Access, the Paradox Alphanumeric fields are set to Text, the Number fields are set to Number, the Logical fields are set to Yes/No, the Date fields are set to Date/Time, and the Memo fields remain Memo fields. In an attached table, the table continues to have the original field types in Paradox since the different field types affect only how they are treated in Access.

Importing Paradox Data

When you want to use Access in place of Paradox for your data management needs, import your Paradox tables into Access databases. Once you import your Paradox data, you can use the tables in Access just as if you had originally created the table in Access. To import a Paradox table into the current database, follow the same steps that you use to import other data files.

Attaching Tables from Paradox

If you plan to continue using data in Paradox, you can still use the same data in Access by attaching the table to a database. Once you attach a Paradox table, you can use the data in Paradox as well as Access. To attach a Paradox table as a table in the current database, follow the steps described earlier in this chapter for attaching a table.

If the Paradox table has an index file with a .PX extension, Access uses this file to keep track of the table's primary key. You want to keep this index file with the Paradox data file since you cannot open the attached table if Access cannot find the file. If the Paradox table does not have a primary key, you cannot update the Paradox information in Access.

Using Btrieve Data in Access

Importing and attaching Btrieve tables is done differently than importing and attaching data from packages such as dBASE and Paradox.

Btrieve has an Xtrieve dictionary file that contains information about the database that contains the Btrieve tables. You use the Xtrieve dictionary file to select the files you want to import or attach.

In Access, the Btrieve String, Lstring, and Zstring fields become Text fields, the Integer, Float, and Bfloat fields become Number fields, the Money fields become Currency fields, the Logical fields become Yes/No fields, the Date and Time fields are set to Date/Time, the Note fields become Memo fields, and the Lvar fields become OLE Object fields. In an attached table, the table continues to have the original field types in Btrieve since the different field types affect only how they will be treated in Access.

Importing Btrieve Data

When you want to use Access in place of Btrieve for database tables, import your Btrieve tables into an Access database. Once the data is in Access, the field is just as if you entered it in Access originally. To import a Btrieve table into the current database, follow the same steps you use to import other data files except instead of selecting the file of data to import, you select the Xtrieve dictionary and then the table listed in the Xtrieve dictionary file.

Attaching Tables from Btrieve

When you plan to continue using Btrieve tables with Btrieve, you can share the data in the table between Btrieve and Access by attaching the table to the current database. After attaching a Btrieve table, you can use the data both in Btrieve and in Access. To attach a Btrieve table into the current database, follow the same steps you use to attach other data files except instead of selecting the file of data to attach, select the Xtrieve dictionary and then the table listed in the Xtrieve dictionary file.

Using SQL Tables with Access

You can import and attach SQL tables with Access but you must use the Microsoft Open Database Connectivity (ODBC) drivers to do so. Access includes the ODBC drivers for Microsoft SQL server versions 1.1

and later. If you need an ODBC driver for another SQL database server, contact Microsoft. Your SQL database server must support ODBC to import and attach tables in Access, and you must use the Setup program provided with Access to add the ODBC drivers to Access. Once ODBC is set up, you have the same import and attach capabilities for SQL tables that you have with the other supported databases.

An Overview of ODBC

To utilize the ODBC SQL server drivers, you must have the system configuration that you need to run Microsoft Access with the following additional requirements:

❑   A computer with an Industry Standard Architecture (ISA) or Micro Channel Architecture (MCA). An IBM/PC-AT or IBM PS/2 qualifies. An 80386 or 80486 are recommended for satisfactory performance.

❑   OS/2 version 1.2 or higher on the server and MS-DOS version 3.3 or higher for the workstation.

❑   An installed and running DBMS application software that supports ODBC.

❑   A network connection installed to connect to a remote data source if you are attempting to use SQL tables that are not on your PC. This network software must support fully named pipes. Novell and Microsoft are examples of vendors whose software supports this.

❑   A gateway server installed if your request will need to pass through a gateway before being processed.

❑   Available space on your hard disk for the ODBC drivers.

The ODBC driver that is copied to your hard disk will establish a link to a specific DBMS software product, remote operating system, and a network unless you are running both the DBMS product and Access on your PC. This combination of three components is referred to as a *data source*. Each data source that you plan to use must be set up separately as each requires a separate section in the ODBC.INI file in order to make the connection.

To install the required ODBC drivers, start Windows and then choose Run from the File menu in the Program Manager and enter **A:SETUP** in the text box to run the setup program. Be sure to put the ODBC disk that accompanies Access in drive A. Follow the directions in the dialog box to select the check boxes for the options that you want to install. Selecting the ODBC Administration Utility as one of the options will make it easier for you to add new data sources later.

Importing SQL Database Tables

Importing an SQL table copies the SQL data into Access. For example, you may want to use Access when you no longer need to keep the SQL tables on the network or SQL server. When you import an SQL table, instead of selecting the filename of the data to import, select the SQL data source. Next, log in to the SQL server by entering the user name and password in the two text boxes of the dialog box Access presents. Once the connection is made, you can select which SQL table you want to import and then select the Import button. If you encounter any problems, check to be sure you can use the SQL table from the SQL server.

Attaching SQL Database Tables

Attaching an SQL table lets you use Access rather than the SQL server to manage the data in the SQL table. You can use Access instead of the SQL server while other SQL users use a different interface. When you attach an SQL table, instead of selecting the filename of the data to attach, select the SQL data source. Next, log in to the SQL server by entering the user name and password in the two text boxes in the dialog box Access presents. Once the connection is made, select which SQL table you want to attach and then select the Attach button. If you encounter any problems, check to be sure that you can use the SQL table from the SQL server.

Importing Text

Access can also import text files. Text files are files that contain the data you would see in a table with just the extra characters separating them. Text files usually do not include the unprintable characters other types of files contain that tell your computer the instructions in a program you are running or how you want data in a data file formatted. In a text file, each record is on a separate line. Each of the fields within a line is either separated with specific characters or starts in a specific column. Figure 5-3 shows two text files in different Notepad accessory windows.

The DELIMIT.TXT file has the fields separated by colons with the text enclosed in quotes. This is a *delimited text file*. The FIXWIDTH.TXT file has the fields separated by spaces so each of the fields starts in a specific column. This is a *fixed width text file*. You have a lot of freedom in formatting text files you import because you set up how the data is imported. When you import a text file, each column or section of delimited data should contain the same type of information. For example, if you had the following two lines, you would not want to import them because they do not follow a pattern.

```
Joe Smith,Vice President,ABC Company
23192 Main Road,Akron,OH
```

FIGURE 5-3

Fixed width and delimited text files

```
┌──────────────────────────────────────────────────────────┐
│                  Notepad - FIXWIDTH.TXT                    │
│ File  Edit  Search   Help                                  │
│ STR Rentals       5 231-4567 Dallas    10   75             │
│ XCU Company       3 341-4545 Chicago   5    60             │
│ Tower College     5 431-9092 New York  15   85             │
│ Lower Rentals     3 498-2123 Dallas    20   60             │
│ Nelson Products   4 213-9845 Albany    3    60             │
│ Tower College     5 431-9092 New York  30   85             │
│ Lower Rentals     3 498-2123 Dallas    2    60             │
│ Nelson Products   4 213-9845 Albany    14   60             │
│ XCU Company       3 341-4545 Chicago   15   60             │
│ Tower College     5 431-9092 New York  22   85             │
└──────────────────────────────────────────────────────────┘

┌──────────────────────────────────────────────────────────┐
│                   Notepad - DELIMIT.TXT                    │
│ File  Edit  Search   Help                                  │
│ "Expense Code":"Division":"Region":"Branch":"Amount":"Sort-Key" │
│ "RT-1000":1:1:300:$998.00:"11300RT-1000"                   │
│ "RF-1265":1:2:200:$6,785.00:"12200RF-1265"                 │
│ "ST-8978":1:2:200:$1,050.00:"12200ST-8978"                 │
│ "RX-1254":2:1:110:$1,200.00:"21110RX-1254"                 │
│ "ST-8978":2:1:110:$2,341.00:"21110ST-8978"                 │
│ "ST-1100":2:2:500:$7,500.00:"22500ST-1100"                 │
│ "RX-1254":3:1:100:$1,208.90:"31100RX-1254"                 │
│ "ST-1100":3:1:110:$560.00:"31110ST-1100"                   │
│ "RF-1265":3:2:610:$2,341.00:"32610RF-1265"                 │
│                                                            │
└──────────────────────────────────────────────────────────┘
```

When you import a text file, you set up a pattern for each line in the file to be broken into different fields. The first step of importing a text file is to create this pattern and then use the pattern setup to import the file.

 Tip   To create a text file you can import into Access, enter the data in your word processor and save the file in an ASCII text format. The exact steps to do this depend on your word processor.

Importing a Fixed Width Text File

When you import a fixed width text file, you must tell Access the pattern of how to break each line into fields in a separate step before importing the text file. To set up the pattern for a fixed width text file, choose Imp/Exp Setup from the File menu. The first step is to type a name for the specification in the Specification Name drop-down list box. Later, when you want to modify a specification, select an existing name using the drop-down list box. If you do not supply a name, you are prompted for one after you select OK. When you finish entering the setup for how to import a text file, select OK and your setup is ready to use to import a text file.

In the File Type drop-down list box, select Windows (ANSI) or DOS or OS/2 (PC-8) to tell Access whether the text file you are importing was created with Windows or with a DOS or OS/2 application. Under Dates, Times, and Numbers, you may want to select the order of the information in a date, how the parts of dates and times are separated, whether dates have a leading 0 for single digit months and days, and whether years use four or two digits.

The important part of setting up the import specification for a fixed width text file is telling Access the names for the fields, the field types, the column each field starts at, and the width of each field. The Field Name, Data Type, and Width columns are just like the same columns for a table's design. The Start column counts the number of columns from the left where the field starts. Figure 5-4 shows the FIXWIDTH.TXT file and the Import/Export Setup dialog box setup to import this text.

 Tip   To see how the data is arranged in a text file to set up the import, open the text file using the Notepad accessory. The Notepad lets you see how the text file is organized.

FIGURE 5-4 Setup completed for a fixed width text file

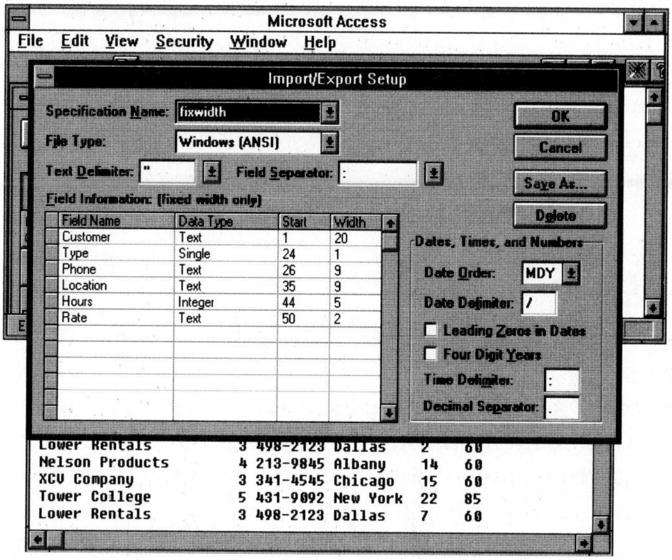

When the setup is complete, you are ready to import the text file. Choose Import from the File menu and then choose Text (Fixed Width) from the Import dialog box. Select the name of the file to import (for example, FIXWIDTH.TXT is the filename in Figure 5-4).

Next, select whether you are creating a new table or appending the data to an existing one, and choose the import specification you will use. Select the Create New Table radio button if you want the text file imported as a new table or the Append to Existing Table radio button if you want the text file added to an existing table. If you select the Append to Existing Table radio button, select one of the existing table names from the adjoining drop-down list box. In the Specification Name drop-down list box, select a specification name that contains the pattern you want to use. When the specification name is selected, select OK to import the file. When you see the message about Access importing the data, select OK and Close.

The next step ensures that the data is imported correctly. Open the table you have just created and check that the data is correctly imported.

Since you might miscount the columns, you can easily have the data off by a column and incorrectly imported. For example, the FIXWIDTH.TXT file when imported looks like Figure 5-5.

Tip Since you can easily enter the wrong starting column for importing a fixed width text file, import the data to a new table. Later, when you are sure you have correctly imported the text file, you can copy it to an existing table.

Importing a Delimited Text File

The text file pattern you use when you import a delimited text file tells Access how the different fields in each line are separated. To set up this pattern for a delimited file, choose Import from the File menu, Text (Delimited) from the Import dialog box and the file you want to import. At this point, you can select between the Create New Table radio button to import the delimited text file into a new table or the Append to Existing Table radio button to import the delimited text file to an existing table. If

FIGURE 5-5

Fixed width text file imported into Access

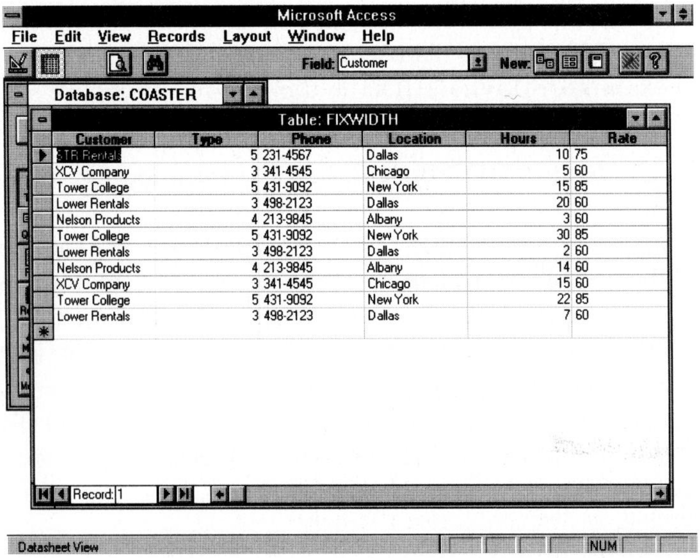

you select the Append to Existing Table radio button, select one of the existing table names from the adjoining drop-down list box.

Another selection just for delimited files is the First Row Contains Field Names check box. Select this check box if the first row of the delimited files has text you want to use as the field names in the table. If you want to change how the delimited file is imported, select the Options button. You only need to make changes if you want to use settings different from the defaults.

When you import a delimited file, you must tell Access which characters separate the fields and whether any special characters enclose text data. These characters are selected in the Text Delimiter and Field Separator drop-down list boxes. For example, to import the DELIMIT.TXT file in Figure 5-3, leave the default values of " and : for the text delimiter and field separator characters.

In the File Type drop-down list box, select Windows (ANSI) or DOS or OS/2 (PC-8) to tell Access whether the text file you are importing was created with Windows or with a DOS or OS/2 application. Under Dates, Times, and Numbers, select the order of the information in a date, how the parts of dates and times are separated, whether dates have a leading zero for single-digit months and days, and whether years use four or two digits. If you want to keep the specification for later use, either name it by typing a name in the Specification Name drop-down list box or select an existing name.

When specifications are set to your satisfaction and you are ready to import the file, select OK. When you see the message about Access importing the data, select OK and Close. Look at the table you have just created to check that the data is imported correctly.

You can also set up a pattern for a delimited file using Imp/Exp Setup from the File menu. When you do this, you must provide a specification name but can ignore the Field Information section.

Importing Spreadsheet Data

Besides using data management packages to store your data, you can import data from spreadsheets into an Access table. For instance, you may have used Excel or Lotus 1-2-3 as a data management package and you want to use this data in Access now. As an example, you may want to import the spreadsheet data shown in Figure 5-6. You have several possibilities for importing spreadsheet data into an Access table. Importing spreadsheet data has several more options so you will want to follow these steps:

1. Switch to the Database window by pressing F11 or clicking it.

2. Choose Import from the File menu.

3. Select Excel, Lotus (WKS), Lotus (WK1), or Lotus (WK3) as the format of the data you want to import from the Data Source list box in the Import dialog box and select OK.

4. Select the name of the spreadsheet you want to import and then select OK.

Access displays an Import Spreadsheet Options dialog box that contains selections that apply solely to importing spreadsheets.

FIGURE 5-6

Spreadsheet to import into Access

A1: [W10] "Date

	A.	B	C	D	E	F	G
1	Date	Days	Location	Meals	Lodging	Airfare	Misc.
2	02–Jul–93	12	Dallas	$350.04	$2,067.25	$350.46	$211.40
3	02–Jul–93	2	Akron	$58.34	$123.29	$474.34	$14.02
4	03–Jul–93	3	Chicago	$87.51	$526.36	$490.22	$51.87
5	06–Jul–93	12	Denver	$350.04	$2,130.42	$462.29	$161.12
6	07–Jul–93	5	Phoenix	$145.85	$551.08	$353.75	$44.57
7	08–Jul–93	4	Atlanta	$116.68	$280.65	$361.29	$53.46
8	10–Jul–93	6	New York	$175.02	$787.16	$439.04	$70.65
9	12–Jul–93	3	Portland	$87.	$257.18	$420.02	$43.89
10	12–Jul–93	5	Cleveland	$145.85	$818.31	$456.53	$56.86
11	14–Jul–93	8	Seattle	$233.36	$1,361.24	$499.69	$110.93
12	15–Jul–93	1	Atlanta	$29.17	$129.04	$391.61	$13.60
13	17–Jul–93	6	New York	$175.02	$441.86	$433.51	$13.31
14	19–Jul–93	3	Washington D.C.	$87.51	$356.61	$463.60	$9.54
15	19–Jul–93	7	San Diego	$204.19	$696.79	$433.53	$57.28
16	23–Jul–93	6	Houston	$175.02	$659.89	$402.64	$63.77
17	23–Jul–93	7	Miami	$204.19	$656.68	$420.70	$134.31
18	24–Jul–93	4	Los Angeles	$116.68	$535.76	$352.65	$18.70
19	26–Jul–93	2	Charlotte	$58.34	$336.57	$338.55	$23.91
20	28–Jul–93	4	New York	$175.24	$876.58	$475.04	$47.63

14-Jul-92 01:15 PM

   5. Select the First Row Contains Field Names check box if the spreadsheet range you are importing has labels in the first row that you want to use as the field names in the table.

Figure 5-6 is a good example for which you would select the check box. In this spreadsheet, the entries in A1..G1 contain labels you want to use as field names. By selecting the check box, Access uses the labels in A1..G1 as the field names for the table and imports data records starting in row 2.

   6. Select the Create New Table radio button if you want the spreadsheet data imported as a new table or the Append to Existing Table radio button if you want the spreadsheet data added to an existing table. If you select the Append to Existing Table radio button, select one of the existing table names from the adjoining drop-down list box.

   7. Type the range name or range address that contains the data you want to import in the Spreadsheet Range text box.

The spreadsheet range tells Access the data you want to import. When you do not make an entry in the text box, Access imports the entire spreadsheet. As an example, for the data in Figure 5-6, you can import only A1..G65, which is the range containing the database data. If the spreadsheet contains other information, you do not want to import the entire spreadsheet but only the range A1..G65.

   8. Select the OK button.

When Access finishes importing the spreadsheet, it displays a message that indicates whether Access found any errors while importing the spreadsheet. If the first row in the spreadsheet contains entries that do not make valid field names when you have selected the First Row Contains Field Names check box, you cannot import the data as is. You must either modify the spreadsheet data so the first row contains valid field names or select the First Row Contains Field Names check box again to clear it.

   9. Select the OK button again.

   10. Repeat steps 4 through 9 for each spreadsheet you want to import.

11. Select the Close button.

Tip   Name the range in the spreadsheet you want to import. You can remember the range name much easier than the range address of the cells you want to import.

Import Problems

When you import spreadsheets and text files, if Access encounters data that it cannot properly import, Access creates a table that lists the problems. This table is called Import Errors followed by your name. When you import data and you get a message that Access found errors, immediately check to see what the errors are before importing more data. For each error Access finds, it creates a record in this table that lists the row number, field, and error description, as shown in Figure 5-7. The following is a list of some of the reasons you may have errors.

Import problems table

	Error	Field	Row
	Type Conversion Failure	7	3
	Type Conversion Failure	7	4
▶	Type Conversion Failure	7	5
	Type Conversion Failure	7	6
	Type Conversion Failure	7	7
*			

Table: Import Errors - Mary Campbell

Record: 3

- Access tried putting data into a field that is inappropriate for the field's type. For example, if you import a spreadsheet that contains a column of values except for where the label "N/A indicates missing data, each occurrence of "N/A in the column is reported as an error.

- Access made a bad guess about the contents of a field. When you import to a new table versus appending to an existing one, Access looks at the first row of data (or second if the first row is used for field names) to decide the best field type. While Access makes the best possible guess, sometimes it picks the wrong type.

- Access found a row in the original file that contains more fields than it has set up in the new table or in the table to which you are appending the data. For example, if you have entries in A1..G16 and A17..I20 of a spreadsheet you import to a new table, Access creates a table that has seven columns for the entries in columns A through G of the spreadsheet. For rows 17 through 20, Access will find errors since the new table does not have room for the entries in columns H and I.

- Access found an entry that is wider than the field's size. If you are appending your customer address database into a table that has two spaces reserved for the field for the state, Access finds errors with the state names for which you used a longer abbreviation or spelled out.

- Access tried importing the contents of a field that matches another record's entry for that field when the field has an index property set to Yes (No Duplicates).

To see the errors, open the Import Errors table just as you would open other tables in the database.

Exporting Access Data

Besides using data from another application with Access, you can put your Access data into a format other applications can use. This process is called *exporting* and creates a separate file that contains the data you have stored in one of your tables. Your data continues to be in your Access table. The steps for exporting a table are summarized in the next section.

Exporting a Table

To export the data in a table to a file in a format other applications can use, follow these steps:

1. Switch to the Database window by pressing F11 or clicking it.

2. Choose Export from the File menu.

3. Select the format of the data you want to export from the Data Source list box in the Export dialog box and select OK.

4. Select the table you want to export and select OK.

5. Select the name of the file where you want the data exported and select OK.

6. Select any information Access needs to export the table. The exact information you are prompted for depends on the format you select in step 3. The Access, delimited text, fixed width text, Btrieve, and SQL formats prompt for additional information.

Exporting to Another Access Database

Earlier you learned about importing a table or other database object from another database into the current one. You can obtain the same results by exporting the table from the current database into the other database. You import when the current database is the database where you need a copy of the table or other object, and you export when you are in the database that contains the object or data you want copied to another database.

When you want to export a table or other database object to another database, follow the steps for exporting a table. In the fourth step, you can select another object besides a table by selecting an object type from the Object Type drop-down list box and then selecting which object of that type you want to export. When Access prompts for the name of the file, select one of the existing databases.

After selecting the name of the database to which you want the object exported, you have an additional prompt for the name of the object in the database you have just chosen. Use the default of the same name that the object uses in the current database or type a new one. After exporting the table or other object, the table or other object is both in the current database and in the database you have selected while exporting the file.

Exporting a table or other object is different from attaching a file. After you export a table, for example, any changes you make to the table in the current database are not updated in the database to which you exported the table.

Putting Access Data in a Fixed Width Text File

Earlier you learned about fixed width text files that Access, like other applications, can use to accept data. You can also create fixed width text files from your Access tables. Before you export a table to a fixed width text file, you must set up the pattern you want the exported data to follow. For example, each field should start at a different column. This is just like the pattern you established for importing fixed width text files earlier. You can even use the same setup specification you used for importing a fixed width text file if you already have one that is appropriate. Once you have the setup specification, you can export the file. To export a table to a fixed width text file, follow the steps for exporting a table. After you select the name for the file you are creating, select the setup specification name in the Specification Name drop-down box.

Putting Access Data in a Delimited Text File

Besides exporting a table to create a fixed width text file, you can also export a table to create a delimited file. For example, you may want to use the Employee table from the COASTER database as the data for a mail merge document in your word processor. When you want to export a table to a delimited text file, follow the steps for exporting a table. After selecting the filename for the delimited text file you are creating, select export options. Select the First Row Contains Field Names check box when you want the first row of the delimited file to contain the field names from the table. To change the characters used to separate the fields and enclose text as well as change the options used by dates, times, and numbers, select the Options button. Selecting the Options button expands the dialog box to include the same delimited setup settings you see when importing a delimited file.

Putting an Access Table in a Spreadsheet

While you can use Access for all of your data management needs, you may want to use your Access data in a spreadsheet package such as Excel or Lotus 1-2-3. For example, you may want to perform regression analysis on data in a table. When you want to export a table to a spreadsheet format, follow the steps for exporting a table. The only difference between exporting to an Excel or Lotus file is the format you select in the Export dialog box. When Access finishes exporting the table, you can retrieve the file you have just created in your favorite spreadsheet program. As an example, if you export the Employee data from the COASTER database to a Lotus WK1 spreadsheet, your data in Lotus 1-2-3 Release 2.4 will look like Figure 5-8.

Exporting dBASE or Paradox Data

You can put your Access data into both dBASE and Paradox formats. Once you have the dBASE or Paradox files, you can use them in these applications to take advantage of reports or other product features you have already designed. To export a table to a dBASE or Paradox format, follow the steps for exporting a table. The only difference between exporting to a dBASE III, dBASE IV, or Paradox file is the format you select in the Export dialog box. When Access finishes exporting the table, open the file you have just created in dBASE or Paradox.

FIGURE 5-8 Employee data exported to Lotus 1-2-3

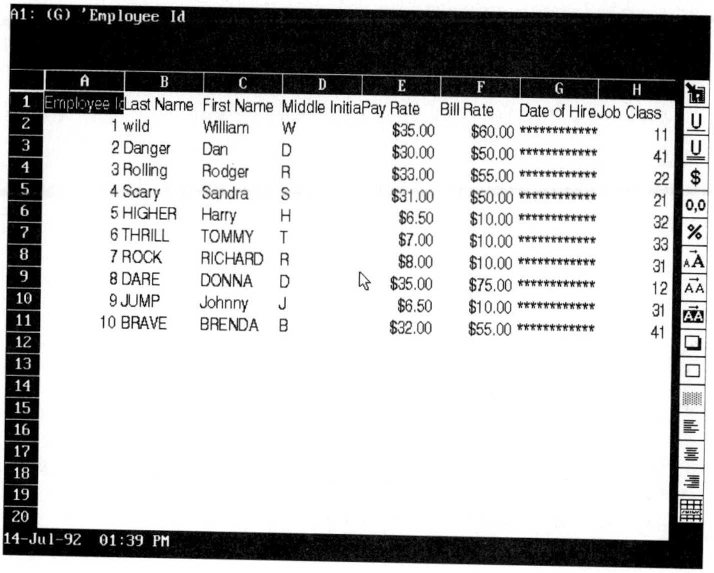

A1: (G) 'Employee Id

	A	B	C	D	E	F	G	H
1	Employee Id	Last Name	First Name	Middle Initia	Pay Rate	Bill Rate	Date of Hire	Job Class
2	1	wild	William	W	$35.00	$60.00	*************	11
3	2	Danger	Dan	D	$30.00	$50.00	*************	41
4	3	Rolling	Rodger	R	$33.00	$55.00	*************	22
5	4	Scary	Sandra	S	$31.00	$50.00	*************	21
6	5	HIGHER	Harry	H	$6.50	$10.00	*************	32
7	6	THRILL	TOMMY	T	$7.00	$10.00	*************	33
8	7	ROCK	RICHARD	R	$8.00	$10.00	*************	31
9	8	DARE	DONNA	D	$35.00	$75.00	*************	12
10	9	JUMP	Johnny	J	$6.50	$10.00	*************	31
11	10	BRAVE	BRENDA	B	$32.00	$55.00	*************	41
12								
13								
14								
15								
16								
17								
18								
19								
20								

14-Jul-92 01:39 PM

Putting Access Data in a Btrieve Table

You export your Access tables to Btrieve tables using the Xtrieve dictionary file just as you do when importing. Use the Xtrieve dictionary file to select the tables you want to export. To export a table to a Btrieve format, follow the steps for exporting a table. Instead of entering the name of the file to contain the Btrieve table, select the name of the Xtrieve dictionary file. This file is usually called FILE.DDF. Once the dictionary file is chosen, you are prompted for the name of the table in Btrieve; enter the table name and select OK.

Putting Access Data in an SQL Table

Exporting to an SQL table lets you copy an Access table onto your SQL server. You may want to do this when you need to share the database's data with other users. By exporting an Access table to an SQL table, you can subsequently attach the SQL table to the current database and continue using Access for the interface between you and your data. When you export an SQL table, instead of typing the name for the file to which you want the data exported, first enter a name for the table in the SQL database. After selecting OK, select the SQL data source to which you want the table exported. After selecting OK again, log in to the SQL server by entering the user name and password in the two text boxes of the dialog box Access presents. Once the connection is made, Access exports the table and places it on the SQL server.

Using the Clipboard to Share Data Between Applications

Besides transferring data between Access and other applications by importing, attaching, and exporting data, you can also transfer information between applications using the Clipboard. The Clipboard is Windows' temporary area where it can store information from any application designed to use it. The Clipboard can store entire tables or other objects you create in Access. You can put Access information on the Clipboard and then paste that Clipboard information in another application's file or you can take information stored in another application, copy it to the Clipboard, and paste it into Access. You can also use the Clipboard to transfer data from one database to another.

When copying data from a table in Access, select the records or the table you want to copy. To select several records, drag the mouse over the record numbers of the records you want to copy. Select the entire table by either choosing Select All Records from the Edit menu or by clicking the upper-left corner of the table's datasheet view. When you select the entire table this way, you are selecting the table's data rather than the entire table. Once you have selected the records or table you want, copy the data to the Clipboard to copy the information to another table or another application. You can also select entire tables or other Access objects by selecting them in the Database window.

Transferring Access Objects Between Databases

Besides importing and exporting tables and other objects, you can also transfer information from one database to another with the Clipboard. To transfer Access tables or other objects, select the object you wish to copy from the Database window. To put the selected object on the Clipboard, choose Copy from the Edit menu. You can also choose Cut from the Edit menu to put the selected object on the Clipboard while removing the object from the current database. Next, switch to the database to which you want the object copied and choose Paste from the Edit menu. You can even paste the selected object to the same database—for example, if creating two similar reports by using one as the basis for the other.

Transferring Access Data to Another Application

When you need your Access data in other applications that allow the Windows Clipboard, you might find it easier to copy the data to those applications using the Clipboard rather than exporting the table's data to a file then importing it to the application. For example, you may want to put your Employee table in the COASTER database into Word for Windows. To do this, you select the records or the table's contents you want to copy. Next, choose Copy from the Edit menu to put the table or record's contents on the Clipboard. At this point, switch to the application where you want the copy of the Clipboard data and choose Paste from that application's Edit menu. Figure 5-9 shows the Employee table from the COASTER database in a Word for Windows document.

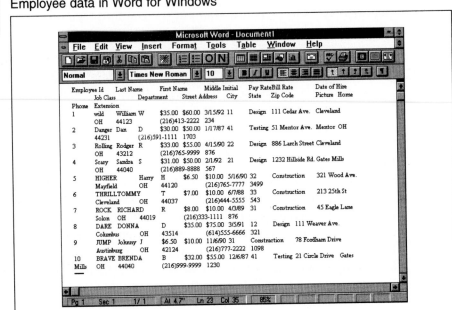

FIGURE 5-9

Employee data in Word for Windows

Transferring Data from Other Applications to Access

You also can copy data between applications when you want to take data from another application and use it in Access. For example, you may want to add data from a table in Word for Windows into a new table in Access. To do this, select the data in the other application that you want to copy. Choose Copy from that application's Edit menu to put the data on the Clipboard. Switch to Access and move to where you want the data inserted. Choose Paste from the Edit menu. You can use the Clipboard to transfer large blocks of text—for example, if you want to copy to a record's Memo data type field.

Quick Reference

To Import a File   Choose Import from the File menu from the Database window. Select the application that created the data you want to import and select OK. Choose the file you wish to import and select the Import button. Select the OK button and then the Close button.

To Attach a File   Choose Attach Table from the File menu from the Database window. Select the application that uses the file for data you want to attach and choose OK. Choose which file you want to attach and select OK. Select the OK button and the Close button.

To Export a File   Choose Export from the File menu from the Database window. Select the application for the data you want to export and select OK. Select the table you want to export and choose OK. Select the name of the file to which you want the data exported and select OK.

PART

II

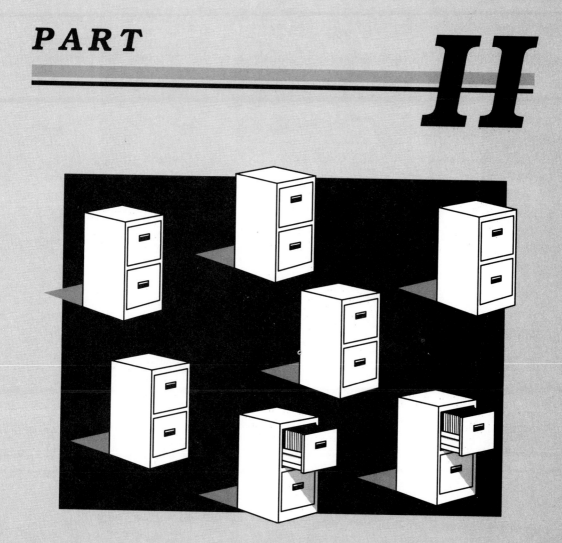

Queries

CHAPTER

Designing Queries to Select Data

A query lets you zero in on the information from your database that interests you at the current moment. The result of a query is a set of records that matches your specifications. These records are presented in a datasheet that makes it seem as though you're looking directly at a table containing only the information you need.

Queries are separate database objects so they are always available. You do not have to reenter the description of the data every time you want to look at the same subset of the table's data. Also, a query always uses the most up-to-date data you have stored in your tables. Changing a table's data also changes the data a query shows when the query uses that table.

Queries offer many features that select the data presented. In a query, you add, remove, and rearrange the fields presented.

You enter *criteria* that select the records from the table. Other options for queries let you sort the data, hide fields, and calculate values. When you finish the query's design, you can view the records that match the criteria you select. This data is the query's *dynaset.*

A dynaset is a temporary presentation of data in a table format. The data is real but the presentation is not. As you edit data that appears in a dynaset, you are changing the data in the table that the query uses to create that dynaset. You can print the dynaset as well as save the query's design for later use.

The most common query is a *select query.* Access also has other types of queries. These types of queries summarize groups of records, delete specific records, add records to another table, and create new tables containing specific records. You will learn about these additional types of queries in Chapter 7. You can use these select queries as the basis of the data you present in forms and reports. You will learn how to create forms and reports starting in Chapter 8.

Creating a Query

You can create a query while displaying tables or queries in the database window. Creating a query opens a query design screen just like creating a table opens a design screen. Part of creating a query is selecting the table you want the query to use. A query can use more than one table; you will learn in Chapter 7 how to combine tables in one query. For now, as you learn the basics of creating a query, you will use a single table. The table you select is the source of the data you want to present in the query.

Follow these steps to create a query:

1. Add the table you want the query to use.
2. Add the fields from the table you want to use in the query.
3. Add any criteria that selects the records to appear in the dynaset.
4. Add any sorting selections you want to organize your data in the dynaset.
5. Display the selected data.

Initially you can skip step 3. As you create queries with more and more query features, the basics of selecting the table, the fields, and displaying the dynaset remain the same. Several features such as saving queries, printing queries, and organizing the output of the dynaset are so easy you'll want to quickly put these skills to use. Finally, you will learn about the wide assortment of criteria entries you can make to select which records appear in the dynaset.

Starting the Query Design

A quick method of creating a query is to select the table you want the query to use when the database window is displaying tables. Next, from the toolbar, select the New Query button, which looks like this:

This button tells Access that you want to create a new query using the highlighted table as the basis for the query. Access opens a query design window with the table you will use already selected. Assuming the Client table is highlighted when you click this button, your screen looks like Figure 6-1. Another way you can open a query design window using the

FIGURE
6-1

A sample query design screen

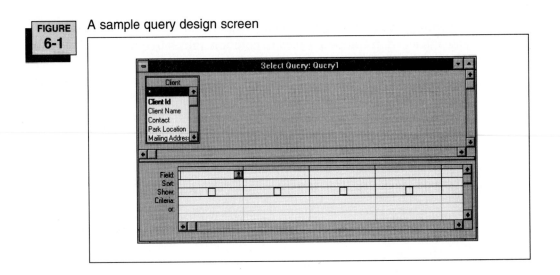

highlighted table for the query is to choose New from the File menu and then choose Query.

You can also create a new query by displaying queries in the database window. First, switch to the database window and choose Queries from the View menu or click the Queries button. Next, choose the New button at the top of the database window. You can also choose New from the File menu and then choose Query. Since you do not have a table selected for the query to use, you need to tell Access which table you want to use. Your Access window now looks like this:

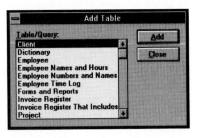

Select the table from the list in the Add Table window. After selecting the table, double-click it or select Add to add it to the query design. Once the table is added, select Close to close the dialog box. With the table added, the query design looks like Figure 6-1. Now that you have a query design, look more closely at the various sections of this window.

 Tip You can create a query that uses the data from another query. Simply select the query name when you create the new query. You can use a query as a basis for another query when you want to make further changes to a query without changing the original query design.

Looking at a Query Design Window

As shown in Figure 6-1, a query design window contains several parts that you want to be familiar with as you create queries. First, the title bar shows Select Query followed by the name of the query. The default name for a query is Query followed by the next unused number. When you learn how to create different types of queries in Chapter 7, you will see Select Query replaced with other text to describe the type of query the design represents.

The smaller window in the top half of the query design screen is a field list window. This window has the table name in the title bar and contains all of the fields from the table in its list. The table's primary index appears in bold. The list of fields also includes an asterisk (*), which represents all of the fields in the table.

Notice that the bar below the horizontal scroll bar divides the top half from the bottom. You can change the proportion of the window that displays the top and the bottom information by dragging this bar up or down. You can switch between the two sides by clicking the side you want to work on or by pressing F6.

Finally, the bottom half of the query design window contains the QBE grid. QBE stands for query by example, since you select records you want to see in the query by providing examples. This grid contains the field names a query uses, whether they appear in the query's datasheet, how they are sorted, and the criteria that selects which record appears. This grid contains separate columns for each of the fields the query uses. Just like you did in a datasheet, you can make the columns wider or narrower by dragging the right side of the column at the top of the column right or left. The rows of the grid contain the data the field uses in the query.

Most of your entries go into this area. The first entries you make into this area are the fields the query uses.

Adding Fields to a Query

Once in the query design window, the first step is to select the fields the query uses from the field list window. You can add fields one at a time or you can add all of them simultaneously. The order in which you add fields sets the order the fields appear in the dynaset. The only exceptions are fields that are used for sorting since they are rearranged on the grid where you define the query. The fields you add include all the fields you want to see in the query as well as the fields that select the data you see in the query.

When adding fields to a query design, add them to the top row of the QBE grid. You can add these field names in one of two ways. One way is to select the field name from the field list window for the table and then drag it to one of the empty cells in the top row of the QBE grid. As you drag the field from the field list to the QBE grid, the pointer changes shape to indicate that you are copying the field and adding the field to the QBE grid. When you release the mouse in the QBE grid, the field name is added to the top of the selected column and the check box below the field name is selected. Figure 6-2 shows a query design after several fields are selected.

The other method for adding a field to a query design is to click or move to the cell in the Field row of the QBE grid where you want to add the field. You can see the down arrow that is part of all drop-down list boxes. Select one of the listed fields or type the field name. Like dragging a field name to the QBE grid, the check box below the field name becomes selected.

You can also add the table name, a period, and an asterisk, as in Client.*, which adds all of the table's fields to the grid. Even though the asterisk column only uses one column, when you display the datasheet for this query, all of the fields are shown. One advantage of using the asterisk rather than adding all of the fields separately, is if the table changes its fields, the asterisk in the query design adopts the new fields.

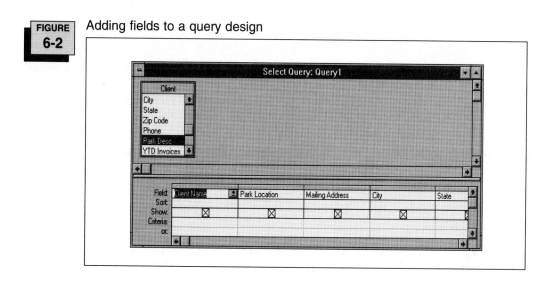

FIGURE 6-2 Adding fields to a query design

Otherwise, when you add a new field to a table, you must add the field to queries that you want the new field to appear as part of. You cannot use the asterisk as a field name for sorting or selecting the records that will appear in the query. When you want to use the asterisk and use sorting and criteria, you must have more than one copy of the field in the QBE grid.

You can also add all of the fields by using the field list window. If you double-click the table name in the field list window, all of the fields become highlighted except for the *. With all of these fields selected, drag any one of them to the QBE grid. You have just added all of the fields from the table to the QBE grid just as if you had added them individually.

Tip If creating a query that you will use in a form or report, include all of the fields that you plan to use in the field or report.

Deleting, Inserting, and Moving Fields in a QBE Grid

As you add fields to the QBE grid, you can rearrange them as you change your mind about how you want the information displayed. You can add, delete, and rearrange the fields.

Before you make any of these changes, decide whether you want to change one or more columns in the QBE grid. If you only want to change one column, point above the field name in the column so the pointer becomes a black downward-pointing arrow. Click this column to select it. When a column in the QBE grid is selected, the column becomes black. If you want to change more than one adjoining column, drag the mouse right or left to cover the columns you want to select. Once the column or columns are selected, you can insert, delete, and move the columns. When you delete, insert, or move the columns, you are moving the field and all of the settings the field has in the query. To rearrange non-adjoining columns, adjust each column separately.

To delete the selected columns, press DEL or select Delete from the Edit menu. You can also use the Delete Column command in the Edit menu to get the same results. The remaining columns of the query are shifted to the left. To insert as many columns as the ones you have selected, press INS or select Insert Column from the Edit menu.

To move the selected columns to the left or right, click on the bar above one of the selected columns and hold the mouse down. You will notice that the selected column has a white line on the left side of it. This line indicates where Access will place the selected columns when you release the mouse. You can drag the mouse right or left; when the line is to the left of the field where you want the selected columns added, release the mouse.

Viewing a Query

When finished adding fields to the QBE grid, you can start viewing the query's results. The query's results, or the dynaset, contain the data that you have selected to appear in the query design screen. Display the dynaset by clicking the Datasheet View button in the toolbar. You can also select Datasheet in the View menu. Figure 6-3 shows the dynaset for the query design in Figure 6-2.

The datasheet that displays the dynaset looks just like the datasheet you use to display a table. The only visible difference is the title bar, which

FIGURE
6-3
A datasheet showing the dynaset created by the query

Client Name	Park Location	Mailing Address	City	State	Zip Code
Family Fun Land	Isle Royale	P.O. Box 345	Houghton	MI	49312
Teen Land	Ashtabula Park	P.O. Box 786	Ashtabula	OH	44321
Amusement Techn	Panacea on the Be	P.O. Box 5346	Panacea on the Be	FL	33012
Arden Entertainmer	Indianapolis	100 Federal Avenu	Indianapolis	IN	67821
Family Amusements	Stanton	P.O. Box 123548	Stanton	PA	78378
Playland Consortiur	Wheeling	P.O. Box 5839	Wheeling	WV	45678
Island Waterplay In	Raleigh	1 Waterplay Lane	Raleigh	NC	12378
Entertainment Plus	Jersey City	P.O. Box 4892368	Jersey City	NJ	08767

Record: 1

says Select Query followed by the query name. Because the query selects which fields appear, which records appear, and the order of the fields and records, the fields and records appearing may differ from what you see in the query's underlying table. If the query design contains two copies of a field, the second copy of the field in the datasheet will use Field and the next unused number. You will learn how to change the name of the fields later in the chapter.

While looking at the datasheet for the dynaset, you can edit the data just as you would edit the data in a datasheet for a table. The dynaset creates a pathway from the query's datasheet to the table the query uses to create the dynaset. When you edit an entry in the dynaset's datasheet, you are changing the data in the table that the data originally came from. Also, any table properties that affect data entry in the table's datasheet still affect data entry in the query's datasheet. The commands you learned about in previous chapters to change the appearance of a datasheet— hiding columns, fonts, row heights, column widths, and grid lines—also apply to a dynaset's datasheet.

If the query shows the data you want, you are ready to save and print the dynaset. If not, switch back to the query's design by clicking the Design View button in the toolbar or choosing Query Design in the View menu. Once back at the query's design, modify the design and continue switching between the design and datasheet view until you have created the query you want.

Saving a Query

When you have a query you want to keep for future use, save it. Saving a query means saving the settings of the query—not the dynaset. This means each time you use the query, Access reapplies the same query settings to the current table data. Saving just the query's design means every time you use the query, you are using the most current version of the data in the table the query uses.

Saving a query is just like saving other objects in a database. You can save a query with the Save or the Save Query command (depending on which view you are in) in the File menu.

When saving the query for the first time, you must supply the query name. In the Query Name text box, type the name that you want for the query and select OK. You can have up to 64 characters in the name (the rule for naming all Access objects). You cannot name a query with the same name as a table or another query in the database. When you select a table or query as a source of data for another object in Access, Access does not distinguish between tables and queries. You are also prompted to save the query when you close its window. When you save a query after the first time, the query is saved using the same name.

If you want to change the name of the query you are saving, choose Save As or Save Query As (depending on the view you are in) in the File menu and type a new name for the query before you select OK. For example, you may have one query that you want to use as the basis for another. In this case, save the original query with a new name and modify the new query to fit your changing needs.

Once you have saved the query, you can return to it at a later point. To open a query that is no longer displayed, select the query in the list of queries from the database window. You can double-click the query name or select the Open button to open the query and show the datasheet containing the query's dynaset. You also can use the right mouse button to double-click the query's name or select the Design button to open the query and show the query's design.

Renaming a Query

Just as with other objects in the database, you can rename queries. You may decide that an existing query could be more aptly named. To give it a new name, select the query from the database window and choose Rename from the File menu. In the Query Name text box, type the new name for the query and select OK. Before you rename a query, close any window the query design or its dynaset datasheet appears in.

Printing a Query

Later, starting with Chapter 8, you will learn about creating forms and reports that give you more sophisticated options but you will also want to print your data directly from the datasheet. Printing a query's datasheet is just like printing a table's datasheet. Figure 6-4 shows a printed query using the query design shown in Figure 6-3. You can also preview the appearance of the printed datasheet before you print it by choosing Print Preview in the File menu.

FIGURE 6-4

A printed datasheet of the query

Client Name	Park Location	Mailing Address	City	State	Zip Code
Family Fun Land	Isle Royale	P.O. Box 345	Houghton	MI	49312
Teen Land	Ashtabula Park	P.O. Box 786	Ashtabula	OH	44321
Amusement Techn	Panacea on the Be	P.O. Box 5346	Panacea on the Be	FL	33012
Arden Entertainme	Indianapolis	100 Federal Aven	Indianapolis	IN	67821
Family Amusemen	Stanton	P.O. Box 123548	Stanton	PA	78378
Playland Consortiu	Wheeling	P.O. Box 5839	Wheeling	WV	45678
Island Waterplay I	Raleigh	1 Waterplay Lane	Raleigh	NC	12378
Entertainment Plus	Jersey City	P.O. Box 489236	Jersey City	NJ	08767

Tip   If your query has more fields than can fit across the page, you may want to hide some columns in the datasheet. Hidden columns are not printed so you can limit the data printed to just the information that you need to see for a particular use. Hide columns by selecting them and choosing Hide Columns from the Layout menu.

Printing Options

When you print a query's datasheet, you have several choices for how to print the data. These options are available through either the Print dialog box displayed by the Print command in the File menu or the Print Setup dialog box displayed by the Print Setup command in the File menu. All of these printing options apply when printing either tables or queries. When you learn about forms and reports starting in Chapter 8, you can use the same printing options to change how the forms and reports are printed.

In the Print dialog box, the printing options let you select which data is printed and the quality. The three option buttons under Print Range set the data Access will print. All prints the entire query datasheet. Selection, which is only available when you have selected some of the records or fields in the query, prints only the highlighted data as if only this data appeared in the datasheet. Pages prints only the range of pages you enter in the From and To text boxes after Access decides the data that would appear on each page if you printed all of the query datasheet.

From the Print Quality drop-down box, select between High, Medium, and Low. The higher the print quality, the longer it takes to print and the better the output looks. With some printers, such as Hewlett-Packard LaserJets, changing the print quality has no effect.

Finally, set the number of copies to print by entering a number in the Copies text box and pressing OK. This number is reset to the default of 1 every time you print. The Print to File and the Collate Copies check boxes are described in Chapter 9.

In the Print Setup dialog box, shown next, you can set the printer, orientation, page size, and margins.

The printer is selected by leaving the Default Printer option button selected or by selecting the Specific Printer option button and selecting one of the printers installed through the Windows' Control Panel program from the adjacent drop-down list box.

You can select whether the data is printed on the page normally or rotated to print sideways by selecting the Portrait or Landscape option buttons. With the Size drop-down list box, select one of the listed paper sizes that you know your printer supports. After Source, select one of the paper feeding choices your printer has available. You may want to select the Data Only check box when you do not want to print the query datasheet with the borders and grid lines. In the Margins text boxes, type the new margins you want the printed copy to use. Use inches or centimeters as the current setting shows or type **in** or **cm** after the new margin to indicate which measurement system you want to use.

Finally, select the Options command button to display the Windows settings for the selected printer. You see the same settings when you select Configure then Setup in Windows 3.0 or select Setup then Options in Windows 3.1 from the Printers dialog box in the Control Panel. The changes you make from the Options dialog box affect all Windows applications. The More button is not available since this button is used to provide options applicable only to forms and reports.

Additional Query Design Features

Your queries can use other features that change how the data appears in the dynaset. These features include renaming fields in a query, sorting the dynaset's data, and hiding fields.

Renaming Fields in a Query

By default a query uses the same field names in its dynaset as the table the data comes from. You can change the name for a field in a dynaset to another acceptable field name. For example, you might want to rename fields in a query when the table the query uses has abbreviations in the field names. Later, when you learn about calculated fields in a query, you can rename these fields so you have better descriptive names than the default. Also, if you have multiple copies of a field, especially when one of the copies is hidden, you may want to rename both copies.

To rename a field, move the insertion point to the beginning of the field name you want to rename in the QBE grid of the query's design. Type the name you want to use for the field, followed by a colon. When the column previously contained a field name, leave the field name after the colon as in Estimated Cost:Est Cost. The field name after the colon tells Access the source of the data in that field. When you view the dynaset in a datasheet view, the column uses the new field name—Estimated Column, as shown here.

Coaster Id	Coaster Name	Completed	Client Id	Actual Cost	Estimated Cost
1	Scream Machine	No	3	$4,000,000.00	$7,800,000.00
2	Blue Arrow	No	2	$3,900,000.00	$4,000,000.00
3	Astro Transport	Yes	3	$7,800,000.00	$7,500,000.00
4	Red Dragon	No	1	$2,500,000.00	$4,500,000.00
5	Taurus	No	4	$198,000.00	$4,500,000.00
6	Corker	No	5	$1,500,000.00	$2,500,000.00
7	Wild One	No	6	$3,200,000.00	$3,900,000.00
8	White Lightnin	Yes	7	$3,100,000.00	$2,800,000.00
9	The Runaway	Yes	2	$3,200,900.00	$3,215,000.00
(Counter)		No	0	$0.00	$0.00

Record: 1

If the new field name includes a colon as part of the name, enclose the field name in brackets as in [Cost: Estimated]:Est Cost. When the field name for the column replaces the field name Access gives to a calculated field, remove the previous field name. Like naming fields in a table, each field name in a dynaset must be unique.

Sorting the Dynaset

You can use the query to rearrange your data as you combine sorting with other features in a query. Sorting the data in a query organizes the records presented according to the values of one or more fields. You can use any field type except Memo and OLE Object for sorting. Sorting does not change the order of the records in the table that the data in the dynaset comes from. Sorting a dynaset only changes the order in which records are presented in the dynaset's datasheet view.

Sorting records in a query is done from the query design view. First, in the QBE grid, move to the column of the first field you want to use for sorting. This is the field in which all records are sorted according to their values. Then, in the Sort row, the second line in that column, select between Ascending, Descending, and (not sorted). Ascending sorts the records using the values for that field in increasing order. Descending sorts the records using the values for that field in decreasing order. The third choice, (not sorted), gives the same results as deleting the Ascending or Descending—that is, it halts the use of that field for organizing the dynaset's records. As soon as you select Ascending or Descending, the records in the dynaset are sorted.

If the field you select for the first field has the same value for two or more records, you may want to use another field's value to order those records having the same value for the first field. To organize the dynaset's records using a second field as a tiebreaker for only the records with the same value as the first field, click the Sort row of the field you want to use as the second field to organize the dynaset's records, and select Ascending or Descending from the drop-down list box. To tell Access that you want to use this field as the second field to sort the records, the field must be to the right of the field you want to use as the first field.

Access sorts the dynaset's records by the fields that have Ascending or Descending in the Sort row of the QBE grid. Access starts with the field in the left side of the grid and continues to the right. When two or more records have the same values for the first and second fields, you can use a third field to order the records by selecting Ascending or

Descending in the Sort row of the QBE grid and placing the field to the right of the fields you are using for the first and second fields. You can repeat this for as many as ten fields.

Figure 6-5 shows a dynaset using two fields to organize its records. The first field is Project ID so all of the records are placed according to their project number order. The records that have the same Project ID field values are sorted by the Invoice Date field, which is the second field that sorts the records. The query design for this dynaset is shown in Figure 6-6. You can see by the order of the fields that the query's records are sorted by Project ID and Invoice Date. For each field used for sorting, the Sort row contains Ascending or Descending.

When you save a query that uses sorting, the fields used for sorting are shifted in the QBE grid so they are on the left side of the grid. If you want the fields used for sorting to appear in different locations than the beginning of the dynaset, place two copies of the field in the query's design and hide the copy used for sorting (you'll see how later). Also, you may need more than two copies of a field when one of the columns in the QBE grid contains the table name followed by an asterisk as in Client.*, and you want to use one of the table's fields to sort the records.

Tip Create indexes for the fields in a table that a query uses for sorting. Having indexes for the fields a query uses to sort makes using the query faster.

FIGURE
6-5

The sorted dynaset

Project Id	Invoice Date	Invoice Number	Invoice Amount
1	6/30/91	1057	$500,000.00
1	10/31/91	1062	$1,200,000.00
1	3/31/92	1078	$1,700,000.00
1	5/31/92	1092	$600,000.00
2	2/29/92	1073	$400,000.00
2	5/31/92	1094	$1,500,000.00
2	7/31/92	2011	$2,000,000.00
3	12/31/90	1021	$250,000.00
3	7/30/91	1058	$2,750,000.00
3	10/31/91	1063	$3,000,000.00
3	6/30/92	2005	$1,800,000.00
4	1/31/92	1068	$400,000.00
4	1/31/92	1071	$300,000.00
4	2/29/92	1072	$200,000.00
4	2/29/92	1074	$1,600,000.00
5	5/31/92	1093	$198,000.00
6	1/31/92	1070	$350,000.00
6	4/30/92	1085	$1,150,000.00

Select Query: Sorting Invoices

Record: 1

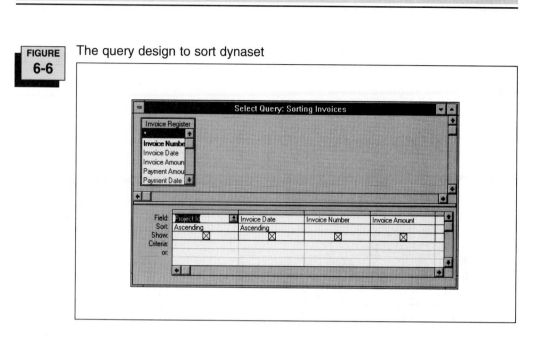

FIGURE
6-6
The query design to sort dynaset

Hiding Fields in a Query

A query can contain more fields than you actually see in the dynaset's datasheet. A query can have hidden fields for a variety of purposes. You can use hidden fields when you have multiple copies of a field in a query. You also use hidden fields when the QBE grid contains an entire table added with an asterisk and you want to use some of the table's fields for sorting and adding criteria.

Note Do not hide fields that you want to include when you use the query in a form or report.

Hiding fields in a query is easy—just clear the Show check box under the field in the QBE grid. For example, in the query design shown in Figure 6-7, the first three fields in the query's dynaset are First Name, Last Name, and Date of Hire, which have checked boxes.

You hide fields when you want multiple copies of a field from a table. For example, to use the Last Name field to sort the records for the query in Figure 6-7, you can have two copies of the field—one copy to contain Ascending or Descending in the Sort row to organize the data and another

FIGURE
6-7

Selecting which fields to display on the datasheet

copy with the field shown in the datasheet. In the first copy the field is hidden, while in the second copy it is not. When you include an asterisk in the QBE grid as well as adding a field separately to sort or select the data, the field may appear in the table twice.

When you close and save a query, Access rearranges the fields in the QBE grid so the hidden fields are shifted to the right. At the same time, sorting fields are shifted to the left. When a field is both hidden and used to sort, the field is placed on the left side.

Creating Criteria to Select Records

While sorting records, rearranging field order, and hiding fields are useful features of a query, a select query's real power comes from selecting which records out of all the records in a table you want to work with. To select the records from a table, you enter criteria, against which Access compares each record to see if it fits your requirements. For each record, Access looks at the data in the record and the criteria to see if they match. When a record matches the criteria, the record appears in the query's dynaset. When a record does not match the criteria, the record does not appear in the dynaset. You will learn how and where to enter criteria first. Then you will learn about the different types of criteria. Once you have criteria entered, you can switch to the datasheet to see the criteria applied to the dynaset's data.

Entering Criteria

Criteria is entered in a query's design in the criteria rows in the QBE grid. The criteria rows start with the row labeled Criteria and continue downward as many rows as necessary. You can have one line of criteria or multiple lines. Each line can have one or more criteria that must be met. Where you place the criteria tells Access how the criteria is used. For this section, all of the criteria are exact matches that look for specific entries in a field (for example, State equaling OH). Later you will learn about different types of criteria you can create.

To input exact match criteria, enter the text, number, or date you want to find in a particular field. The column in which you enter this text, number, or date is the column for the field that you want to contain the text, number, or date.

To enter the simplest of criteria, enter a single criteria under a single field. As an example, say you want to find the records for Design department employees using employee information. The QBE grid for this query looks like this:

Field:	First Name	Last Name	Department	Job Class	
Sort:					
Show:	☒	☒	☒	☒	
Criteria:			Design		
or:					

To enter this criteria, move the insertion point to the first criteria row under the Department field and type **Design**. When you move to another cell in the QBE grid, Access adds quotes around the text. When you display this query's datasheet, Access checks each record to see whether the value for the Department field equals Design. If it does, the record is part of the dynaset; if it does not, the record is ignored by the query. The query's datasheet looks like this:

Another type of criteria is when you want to find records that have two or more values for the same field. For example, you might want to know which employees are working on projects 2 and 7. To find this out using a query based on the Employee Time Log table, type **2** in the first criteria row underneath Project Number and **7** in the row below it as shown here:

When Access evaluates this criteria, it checks each record to see whether the Project Number field equals 2. If it does, the record is included in the dynaset. If the record's Project Number field does not equal 2, Access then checks whether this field equals 7. If it does, the record is included in the dynaset. If the record's Project Number field does not equal 7, the record is omitted from the dynaset. Figure 6-8 shows the dynaset's datasheet that includes only records containing 2 or 7 in the Project Number field.

When you use multiple criteria lines in a QBE grid, the criteria does not have to be for the same field. For example, you may have criteria that looks like this:

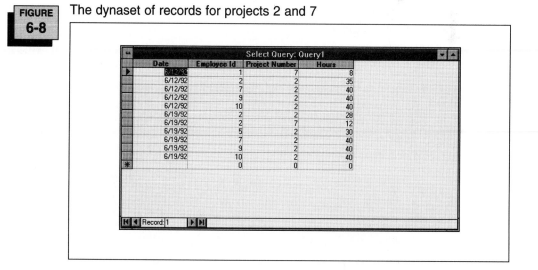

For the date, you can type **6/12/92** and let Access add the # signs to enclose the date. This criteria matches records from the Employee Time Log table that have a value of 2 for the Project Number field or have a value of 6/12/92 for the Date field. A record must meet just one of these conditions to be included in the dynaset.

Think of different lines of criteria in the QBE grid as similar to tracks in a race course that include hurdles as diagramed in Figure 6-9. Each

FIGURE 6-8

The dynaset of records for projects 2 and 7

FIGURE
6-9

Diagram of how the different rows of criteria work

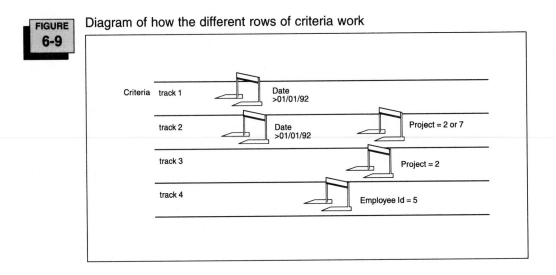

record must run the length of the track to get to the finish line (be included in the dynaset). Each track has separate hurdles that may be at different locations than the hurdles in other records. When a record cannot pass one of the hurdles in the track, it tries the next track. When a record cannot make it through any of the tracks, it is not included in the dynaset. Access does not care which track the record uses to get through the hurdles.

Another way to enter criteria is to have more than one piece of criteria in the same row. For example, you can select records from the Employee Time Log table whose Date field equals 6/12/92 and Project Number field equals 2. When you create criteria like this, each part of the criteria a record must match is entered in separate columns on the same row as shown here:

Field:	Date	Employee Id	Project Number	Hours		
Sort:						
Show:	☒	☒	☒	☒		
Criteria:	#6/12/92#		2			
or:						

For a record to match this criteria, the Date field must equal 6/12/92 *and* the Project Number field must equal 2. Records equaling 6/12/92 for the Date field but not equaling 2 for the Project Number field are not included. Only records matching both criteria make it to the dynaset.

You can also combine both multiple lines and multiple pieces of criteria on the same lines. For example, you may want records from the Employee Time Log table for project 2 for the week of 6/12/92 and records for the employee with the employee identification number of 5 for the week of 6/19/92. A criteria that selects these records looks like this:

For a record to match this criteria, a record must either have a Project Number of 2 and a Date of 6/12/92 or have an Employee ID of 5 and a Date of 6/19/92. Records must meet both of the conditions of either row to be included in the dynaset.

Types of Criteria

Besides the exact matches you saw in the examples just given, you can create additional types of criteria. These other types of criteria let you test for more than just whether a specific field matches a specific value. Some of the types of criteria you can use for queries include using patterns of text, comparisons, and arithmetic. Several of the types of criteria you can create take advantage of *operators*. These operators tell Access to perform some operation such as math or a comparison.

All of the criteria you enter is converted to Access's syntax. For example, you noticed earlier how Access adds quotes around text and # symbols around dates. As you enter criteria, you may notice other small changes that Access makes, such as adding spaces to make the criteria more readable. When Access changes the criteria you enter, it is creating statements that it uses to select the records. Access prefaces each cell in the criteria section of the QBE grid with the field name and an equal sign as in State="OH". You will not see the field names or equal sign added but Access provides this for itself behind the scenes.

Using Wildcard Characters in Criteria

Sometimes you will want criteria that match a pattern of characters. For example, you may want a list of all the roller coaster names that start with a W. You might want a list of all clients that include Entertainment in their name. When an entry must match a certain pattern, you can use *wildcard characters* to create a pattern. When a field's value matches the pattern, that record matches that part of the criteria. To enter this type of criteria, enter the pattern the matching entry must follow.

When you move to another cell in the QBE grid, you will see the pattern enclosed in quotes and the term "Like" preceding the pattern. Like is an operator that tells Access you want to match a pattern with a field's value. If you use a range in the pattern (described later in this chapter), you must enter the Like and the quotes yourself.

The pattern can contain four entries. The first type of entry a pattern contains is the specific characters that you want to appear in the matching entries. A pattern can contain one or more question marks, the second type of entry, when you want Access to fill in for the question marks any possible character that result in matches with your data. An example of using question marks in a pattern is C??st??, for which Access finds the matches Coaster, Caustic, Crested, and Crystal.

A pattern can contain an asterisk when you want the field's entries to contain zero or more characters in that location. An example of an asterisk in a pattern is *the*, for which Access finds the matches other, theory, and lithe.

The fourth entry you can use in a pattern is a *range*, which allows one of a set of characters in the range's location. A range contains the available characters in brackets as in [ABCDE] or [A-E]. The hyphen indicates that all the characters between the characters on either side of the hyphen are included in the range.

Access distinguishes between uppercase and lowercase characters in the brackets, so [A-E] is not the same as [a-e]. The characters in ranges must be in ascending order so you can use [A-E] but not [E-A]. You can also use the brackets to exclude characters by putting an exclamation point after the opening bracket as in [!A-E] to not match an A, B, C, D, or E. An example of a range is [123][ABC]* which matches 1A, 3B, and 2 Coaster.

To return to our example of finding every coaster that starts with a W—to do so, using wildcard characters, just enter **W*** under the Coaster Name field in the Criteria row of a query. When you display the dynaset, the datasheet includes the records for Wild One and White Lightnin, whose names match the pattern.

The In operator is an alternative to the Like operator. The In operator also determines whether a value matches a pattern. An In operator tests whether a value is part of a group. You can use this in place of multiple logical operators. For example, you can use the In operator for criteria that matches records from the Employee table that have Design or Testing in the Department field. To use the In operator for these two departments, enter **In** ("**Design**","**Testing**"). Usually, you will type the different entries you want for a field into separate lines rather than using this operator.

Comparison Criteria

Instead of looking for specific entries with criteria, you may want to use criteria to match records that are more or less than another value. You can use comparison operators to create criteria that match records based on their relative value to one another.

The comparison operators you can include in criteria are the less than, equal to, greater than, and a combination of these. These are the comparison operators:

<	less than
<=	less than or equal to
>	greater than
>=	greater than or equal to
=	equal to
<>	does not equal

When the part of the criteria containing the comparison operator is true, the record matches that part of the query's criteria. Otherwise, the record does not match that criteria row. When you compare text, relative values are decided by the character's position in the alphabet. When you compare numbers, relative values are determined by which number is larger or smaller. When you compare dates, relative values depend on which date occurred before or after the other.

For example, you can use comparison operators to select invoices for 1992 by finding invoices with dates of 1/1/92 or later. The completed dynaset looks like Figure 6-10. To create this criteria, type **>=1/1/92** under Invoice Date as shown here after moving to another cell in the QBE grid:

Field:	Invoice Number	Invoice Date	Invoice Amount	Payment Amount	Payme
Sort:					
Show:	☒	☒	☒	☒	
Criteria:		>=#1/1/92#			
or:					

If you need to test whether an entry falls inside or outside of a range, you can combine the comparison and the logical operators (as described later) or you can use the Between ... And operator. A record matches a criteria containing this operator when the field's value is within the range

FIGURE 6-10

A dynaset created using a comparison operator in the criteria

			Select Query: Query1			
Invoice Number	Invoice Date	Invoice Amount	Payment Amoun	Payment Date	Project Id
1074	2/29/92	$200,000.00	$0.00		
1078	3/31/92	$1,700,000.00	$1,700,000.00	5/3/92	
1092	5/31/92	$600,000.00	$300,000.00	7/15/92	
2005	6/30/92	$1,800,000.00	$0.00		
1071	1/31/92	$300,000.00	$300,000.00	2/20/92	
1074	2/29/92	$1,600,000.00	$1,600,000.00	4/5/92	
1068	1/31/92	$400,000.00	$400,000.00	2/13/92	
1093	5/31/92	$198,000.00	$0.00		
1070	1/31/92	$350,000.00	$350,000.00	4/4/92	
1085	4/30/92	$1,150,000.00	$1,150,000.00	7/18/92	
2006	6/30/92	$1,800,000.00	$1,800,000.00	7/29/92	
1073	2/29/92	$400,000.00	$400,000.00	6/1/92	
1094	5/31/92	$1,500,000.00	$1,500,000.00	7/17/92	
2011	7/31/92	$2,000,000.00	$0.00		
0		$0.00	$0.00		

Record: 1

set by the entry before and after the And. As an example, you can have criteria of Between 1000000 And 2000000 under the Invoice Amount field in a query based on the Invoice Register table. To create the same criteria with a comparison operator, the criteria is > 1000000 And < 2000000.

Using Field Names as Parts of Criteria

Sometimes you need criteria that compares the value of one field with the value of another. For example, when looking at the Invoice Register table, you might want to show records in which invoices have not been fully paid. In this case, compare the Invoice Amount and the Payment Amount fields. You can do this using comparison operators but you need to include one of the field names in the QBE grid when you enter the criteria. To make sure Access understands where each field name begins and ends when you enter criteria, enclose field names with brackets as in [Invoice Amount]. Access knows to use the field value for the current record in the criteria. For the example of finding records for unpaid invoices, you can type a criterion of **<[Invoice Amount]** below the Payment Amount field or **>[Payment Amount]** below the Invoice Amount field. Either criterion provides the same results, which look like this:

Invoice Number	Invoice Date	Invoice Amount	Payment Amoun	Payment Date	Project Id
1079	2/29/92	$200,000.00	$0.00		4
1092	5/31/92	$600,000.00	$300,000.00	7/15/92	1
2005	6/30/92	$1,800,000.00	$0.00		3
1093	5/31/92	$198,000.00	$0.00		5
1056	6/30/91	$500,000.00	$0.00		8
2011	7/31/92	$2,000,000.00	$0.00		2
0		$0.00	$0.00		0

Select Query: Query1 — Record: 1

Arithmetic Operators in Criteria

Criteria can use arithmetic operators for mathematical calculations. Usually these operators are combined with other operators. Here are the arithmetic operators:

+   addition

–   subtraction

*   multiplication

\ and /   division (\ when both numbers are integers and / for other cases)

^   exponentiation

mod   calculating the modulus

Exponentiation raises a number to another power as in 3 to the fourth power (3*3*3*3, which you write as 3^4). The modulus is the remainder from when you divide two numbers so when you divide 11 by 5, the result is 2 with a remainder, or modulus, of 1.

An example of an arithmetic operator in a criterion is the query using the Client table in Figure 6-11. This figure shows two copies of the same query so you can look at the query design and the results at the same time. The criterion is [Total Invoices]–[Total Payments]>1000000. The query only lists the client records when the difference between total invoices and total payments is more than one million. When you later look at this query, you will find that Access has created a hidden calculated field that subtracts the total invoices from the total payments

FIGURE
6-11

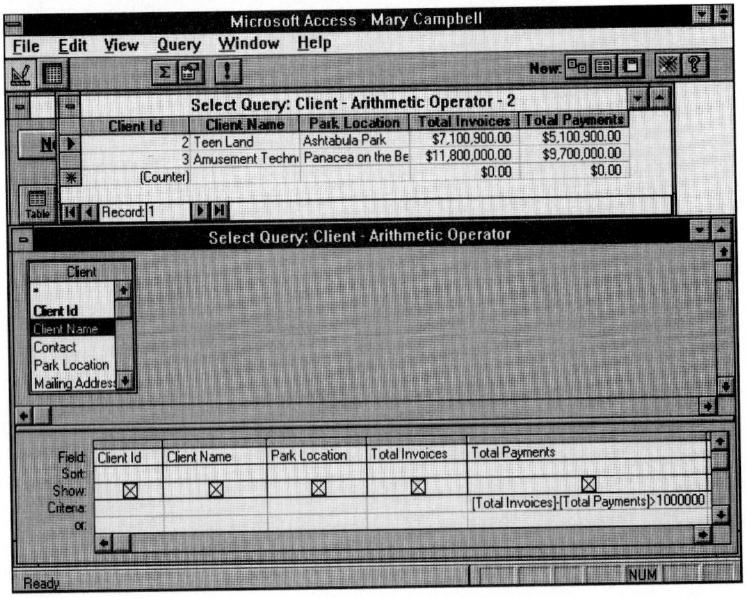

A datasheet and design of a query using an arithmetic operator

and uses the calculated field for the query. You will learn about calculated fields later in this chapter.

Operator Precedence

When you have several operators in the same part of a criterion, Access makes decisions about the order in which it evaluates them. Access has a *precedence order* that selects which operators are evaluated before others. This means that if you have both a comparison and an arithmetic operator in the same piece of criterion, Access performs the arithmetic before the comparison. You can always include parentheses to tell Access to evaluate one part of a criterion piece before the other. When you have several sets of parentheses, Access works from the inside out.

Access evaluates operators in this order:

( )	parentheses
^	for exponentiation
–	to indicate negative numbers
* and /	for multiplication and division
\	for integer division
mod	for the modulus
+ and –	for addition and subtraction
&	for concatenation (described later)

comparison and the Like operators and logical operators

Access starts evaluating operators at the top of the table. All operators at the same level are evaluated from left to right.

Testing for Empty Field Values

You can create criteria that match records that have no value for a field. Using Is Null as a criterion finds fields with empty or null values. For example, to check your Client table for any empty values, use Is Null as a criterion for the different fields on separate lines; only records that have one or more empty fields will be listed. You can also combine Is Null with Not so records only match that part of the criteria when the field contains any value.

Logical Operators

You also will want to compare two true and false values you have from other calculations. For example, you can have a criterion that determines whether an invoice is more than 100,000 and less than 1,000,000. With this example, you may want records to match the criterion when both conditions are true and not to match the criterion when either or both of the conditions are false. To make this type of evaluation, you use the *logical operators*.

Most of the logical operators compare two true or false results such as the ones created by comparison operators. Only the Not uses a single condition. These include logical operators:

And	Both conditions are true
Eqv	Both conditions are either true or false
Or	One or both conditions are true
Xor	Only one condition is true
Not	Reverses the result of the condition

You will use the Not operator most frequently in criteria. Use the Not operator to flip the result of an operator by putting the Not logical operator at the beginning of a criterion so that criteria that would otherwise match the record no longer do and criteria that do not match the record now match the criteria. For example, changing a criterion from Is Null to Not Is Null means that criterion now matches records with an entry for that field instead of matching records that do not have entries for that field.

Using Functions in Criteria

You can use functions to provide ready-made formulas and return information that is not readily available. While Access includes functions that are used in forms, reports, macros, and programming, you can use some of the functions in your criteria.

Functions have the format of the function name followed by its arguments surrounded in parentheses. The function's arguments are the information you must supply for the function. The arguments a function uses depends on the function since each function may need different information. Function arguments are often field names, or literals such as a number, date, or a string. Appendix B lists all of the available functions with the arguments they use and the results the functions provide.

An example of using a function in a query is when you want to compare a field's date to the current date. For example, you can compare the current date of 12/2/92 to the dates in the Invoice Date field to see if they are 180 days overdue by creating a criterion that looks like this:

Field:	Invoice Number	Invoice Date	Invoice Amount	Payment Amount	Payme
Sort:					
Show:	☒	☒	☒	☒	
Criteria:		>Date()-180			
or:					

In this query, the Date function returns the current date. This function does not return arguments. The criterion subtracts 180 days from the current date and compares this value to the value of the Invoice Date field. Records with an invoice date that come later than 180 days ago match this criterion.

Calculated Fields in a Query

When designing your database in Chapter 2, you learned that you do not want to include fields in a table that contain values that can be calculated. Instead, you can create a query that contains calculated fields that are updated every time you use the query and do not occupy data storage space. For example, if you want to calculate the difference between invoices paid and invoice sent, you can create a calculated field in the query that computes this amount for you. This is the calculated field Access created for you when you entered the example of criteria shown for arithmetic operators earlier in this chapter.

To create a calculated field in a query, move to the Field row in the QBE grid where you want to add the calculated field (you may need to insert a column first). Next, type the formula you want calculated for each field. The formula often uses names of other fields that you can enter by enclosing the field names in brackets. When you move to another cell, the formula changes to include Expr followed by the next unused number and a colon as in Expr1:[Total Invoices]–[Total Payments]. As mentioned earlier, you can replace the Expr# field name with another name.

When you display the datasheet for the dynaset containing the calculated field, the calculated field looks just like the others. The difference is that you cannot change the entry. When you try making a new entry, the status line changes to "Control bound to read only column field name".

You can use a calculated field in a query much the same way you do with the other fields, for example hiding it or using it to organize data. Figure 6-12 shows two copies of the same query created for the Invoice Register table that has the calculated field renamed to Total Still Due and uses this field to sort the data in descending order. Only the records with amounts still due are displayed because the criterion entered in the criteria row below this calculated field is >0.

Joining Characters in a Calculated Field

One operator you did not see for criteria but that you might use in a calculated field is the concatenation operator, the ampersand (&). The

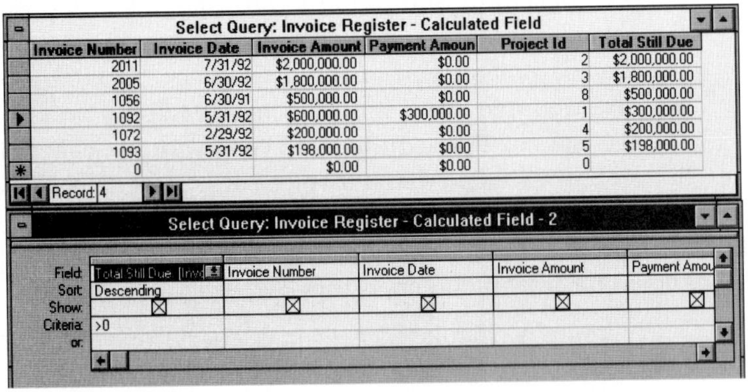

FIGURE 6-12   A datasheet and design of a query with a calculated field

ampersand joins two entries as if they are one. For example, you can create a calculated field that combines the city, state, and ZIP code. A calculated field that performs this function is [City] & ", " & [State] & " " & [Zip Code]. The concatenation operator is placed between the two entries you want to combine. The following shows a query's datasheet that uses the calculated field created with Second Line: [City] & ", " & [State] & " " & [Zip Code] entered in the Field row:

First Name	Middle Initial	Last Name	Street Address	Second Line
WILLIAM	W	WILD	111 Cedar Ave.	Cleveland, OH 44123
DAN	D	DANGER	51 Mentor Ave.	Mentor, OH 44231
RODGER	R	ROLLING	886 Larch Street	Cleveland, OH 43212
SANDRA	S	SCARY	1232 Hillside Rd.	Gates Mills, OH 44040
HARRY	H	HIGHER	321 Wood Ave.	Mayfield, OH 44120
TOMMY	T	THRILL	213 25th St.	Cleveland, OH 44037
RICHARD	R	ROCK	45 Eagle Lane	Solon, OH 44019
DONNA	D	DARE	111 Weaver Ave.	Columbus, OH 43514
JOHNNY	J	JUMP	78 Fordham Drive	Austinburg, OH 42124
BRENDA	B	BRAVE	21 Circle Drive	Gates Mills, OH 44040

Select Query: Employee - Combined Address — Record: 1

Quick Reference

To Create a New Query   Click the <u>N</u>ew button at the top of the Database window while displaying queries, click the New <u>Q</u>uery button on the toolbar while looking at a table or query, or choose Ne<u>w</u> from the <u>F</u>ile menu and then <u>Q</u>uery. If a table or query is not selected when you create the query, select a table or query from the Add Table dialog box and then select <u>A</u>dd and <u>C</u>lose.

To Add a Field to the Query   Drag the field name from the field list window to one of the spots in the QBE grid or select the field name from the drop-down list box available in the Field row of the QBE grid.

To Display a Query   Click the Datasheet View button in the toolbar or choose Data<u>s</u>heet from the <u>V</u>iew menu. You can return to the design by clicking the Design View button in the toolbar or by choosing Query <u>D</u>esign from the <u>V</u>iew menu.

To Print a Query Choose <u>P</u>rint from the <u>F</u>ile menu and select OK. You have all the same printing options available for printing tables.

To Rename a Field in a Query Type the name you want to appear on the datasheet and a colon before the field name you are renaming in the Field row of the QBE grid. To rename a calculated field, replace the existing field name in front of the colon with a different field name.

To Sort Dynaset Records Select between Ascending and Descending in the Sort row of the QBE grid below the field you want to use to sort. The fields for sorting must be in the order you want them sorted.

To Hide Fields in a Query Clear the check box below the field you want to hide in the Show row of the QBE grid.

To Add Criteria Move to one of the criteria rows below the field you want to use as the basis for deciding whether a record is included in the dynaset. Type the criteria you want tested for each record.

To Add a Calculated Field to a Query Move to an empty cell in the Field row where you want the calculated field and type the name for the field, a colon, and the calculation whose values you want to appear as the calculated field. If you omit the field name and colon, Access supplies the default field name. Other field names you include in the calculation must be enclosed in brackets ([]).

CHAPTER

Creating Sophisticated Queries for Selections, Actions, and Parameters

You can do much more with queries than just select data as you did in Chapter 6. Queries can be dynamic and change how they select the records every time you use them with parameter queries. Queries also can combine data from multiple tables to let you join the data stored in several locations and treat it as a unit. Queries can summarize the data in the records that a query selects so you can choose whether to see the individual records or the overall data. Access has a special crosstab query that creates a compact summary of data selected by a query. Finally, you can create action queries that perform actions on the data in the query's underlying tables. These actions include deleting records, adding records, creating a table, and updating values.

Parameter Queries

The queries created in Chapter 6 always use the same entries in the criteria. Here you will see how to create *parameter queries* that let you change the criteria added to a QBE grid every time you use a query. In a parameter query, you are prompted for data. The query uses the data you enter just as if you entered that data into different parts of the query's QBE grid.

To create a parameter query, first create the query as if you do not intend it to be a parameter query. You may want to enter sample criteria where you will eventually have criteria that changes every time you use the query. Using criteria in these locations lets you test that the parameters for the query criteria are in the correct place. For example, your QBE grid at this point may look like this:

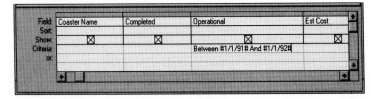

Next, replace the temporary criteria you have added to the QBE grid with the prompts you want to see when you run the query. Enter the prompts enclosed in brackets as in **[Enter the first date:]**. These prompts ask for entries and replace the entries you supply with the prompts in the QBE grid. For example, if you type **[Enter the first date:]** in a cell in the QBE grid, when you run the query, you will see the prompt Enter the first date:. Your entry in response to this prompt replaces the [Enter the first date:] in the QBE grid. Each time you run the query, you can enter a different response to the prompt, and Access substitutes the different responses in the QBE grid. Using the same query, when you replace some of the criteria with prompts, the beginning of the query might look like this:

Notice how the prompts in the brackets are placed anywhere you will otherwise have a value. For example, the criteria entered under the Operational is Between [Enter the first date:] And [Enter the second date:].

After you have entered the queries, you need to tell Access the type of data that is allowable for each of the prompts. Selecting the data types of the query's parameters makes sure you make acceptable entries when you run the query. To set the data type of the parameters in a query, choose Parameters in the Query menu. The dialog box looks like this:

In the left half of the dialog box, type the parameter prompts without the brackets. Your entries must exactly match the prompts entered in the QBE grid including whether letters are in uppercase or lowercase. In the right half of the dialog box, select one of the data types available from the drop-down list box. The choices are Yes/No, Byte, Integer, Long Integer, Currency, Single, Double, Date/Time, Binary, Text, Memo, OLE Object, and Value.

You can see that number data types are selected by their field size. After filling in the parameters and data types, select OK. Make sure that the entries in the Parameters dialog box exactly match the text in the QBE grid. If you forget part of the entry, even something as small as a colon at the end, you will see the prompts appear twice—once for the prompt stored in the QBE grid and then again as the prompt stored in the Parameters dialog box. The completed dialog box for the example query contains Enter the first date: and Enter the second date: in the first column and Date/Time for both prompts in the second column.

Now that you have the parameter query created, you are ready to use it. When you click the Datasheet View button in the toolbar or choose Datasheet in the View menu, Access prompts for the parameters you want to see. The prompts are displayed in the order in which they are added to the Parameters dialog box. The first prompt for the sample query looks like this:

You can enter any valid date in response to this prompt. The date will be entered in the query design in place of the [Enter the first date:] prompt. After you select OK, Access displays another prompt for the second date. When you select OK the second time, Access displays the dynaset created by the query design using the other criteria in the QBE grid as well as the dates you have provided as part of the criteria under the Operational field. Every time you display the dynaset for this query, Access displays the two prompts and then displays the appropriate data.

If you enter data that is not a valid date to either of the two prompts, Access displays a message that the value you have entered is inappropriate for the field. Access checks that the data is valid because you used the Parameters command in the Query menu. If you do not use this command, Access lets you make any entry in response to the prompts; in this case that will result in the display of an empty dynaset since none of the records will fall within the range of an invalid date.

 Tip You can select the prompt in the QBE grid and copy it to the Clipboard. Once the prompt is in the Clipboard, paste it into the Parameters dialog box. Copying the prompt ensures that the prompt in the parameters exactly matches the prompt in the QBE grid.

Using Multiple Tables in a Query

One of the advantages of using a query instead of just tables is that you can include more than one table in a query. With more than one table in a query, you can show how the data in one table relates to the data in another. You can also use queries as the data source in another query. The steps for using tables or queries are the same since the lists from which you select the tables to use as a basis for a query also include all of the queries.

When you use multiple tables in a query, you either use the tables to create a one-to-one relationship or a one-to-many relationship. In a one-to-one relationship, one record from one table combines with one record from the second table to create a single record in the query. In a one-to-many relationship, one record from one table combines with several records from the second table to create as many records in the query as there are records from the second table.

When creating queries that use multiple tables, you may find it easier to display the table names in the QBE grid. To display the table names, choose Table Names from the View menu. This adds a Table row to the QBE grid as shown in Figure 7-1. You can remove this row by selecting the command again since the Table row only appears when the Table Names command in the View menu has a check mark by it.

The table name never appears as part of the query's datasheet. When a table is selected in the Table row, the Field row's drop-down list box only contains the field names from that table. When you use multiple tables in a query, you must add the additional tables to the query and join the tables to show how the records between the tables are related. You use these multiple tables in a query design just as you use a single table although Access has a few special options that change which of the records from the joined tables are displayed.

Adding Tables

To use additional tables in a query, you need to add to the query design the tables you want to use. You can add these tables in one of two ways. When you first create a query and Access is displaying the Add Table dialog box, you can repeatedly select tables and then double-click them or click the Add button. You can add all the tables you want to use in the query at this point.

The other way to add tables to the query is by choosing Add Table from the Query menu. This opens the same Add Table dialog box you see when you first create a query. Just as when adding tables in other situations, you select a table or query from the list and double-click it or click the Add button.

In either case, when you add tables to a query, you are adding field list windows to the query design window. If you have created relationships between tables, you will see a line between the field list windows connecting the fields that contain common data, as shown in Figure 7-1.

A special shortcut you can use to add tables to a query design is available by not maximizing windows. From the query design window, switch to the database window. Next, select the table or query you want to add to the query design you are working on. Drag the pointer from the table or query name to the query design. As you drag the table or query name, notice that the pointer changes to the shape of a table or query icon. When you release the mouse while pointing to the top half of the query design, Access adds that table or query as a field list window in the query design.

FIGURE 7-1

A query design showing the Table row in the QBE grid

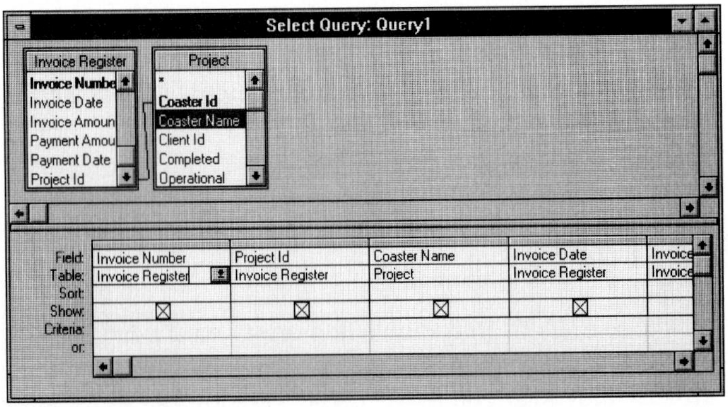

Deleting Tables

If you accidentally add too many tables or queries to the query design, you can remove them. You may also need to remove tables and queries from a query design as you change the information you want in the query. Remove tables by clicking the field list window of the table you want to remove and choosing Remove Table from the Query menu. You also can select the field list window you want to remove and press DEL.

Joining Tables

When a query has more than one table or query, you need to tell Access how the data from one table or query relates to the data in the other table or query. For example, how do the records in the Client table connect with the records in the Project table? Fortunately, Access makes this easy if you already have defined relationships. When you add tables that already are related, Access joins the tables for you.

Joined tables contain lines that connect the field from one table with a field in another table that contains the same value. Figure 7-2 shows an example of this type of line connecting the Employee and Employee Time Log tables. If one of the sources of data for a query is another query, or you do not have relationships between the tables defined, you must join the tables or queries yourself.

FIGURE 7-2

A query design combining Employee and Employee Time Log tables

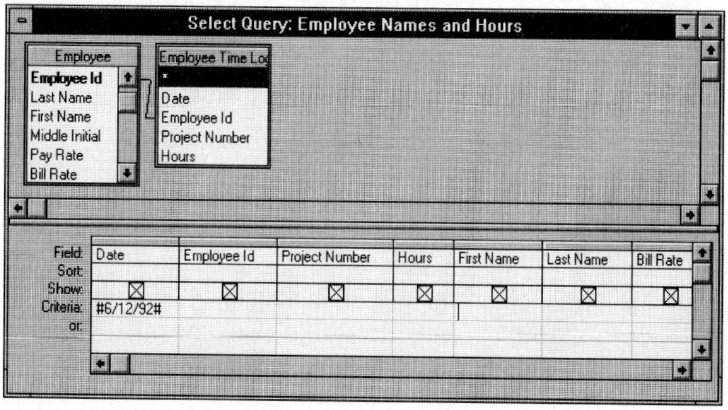

To join tables and queries, first check that the fields from each table or query you will use to join the tables or queries appear in the field list window. Then, select the field from one of the field list windows that you want to connect with a field in another table. Next, drag the field from the field list window to the field you want to link it with in the field list window of the other table or query. For example, in Figure 7-2, you would drag Employee ID from the Employee table's field list window to the Employee ID field in the Employee Time Log table's field list window.

 Warning   Do not join tables using a Single field size Number field from one table and a Double field size Number field from the other.

If you do not join tables, Access joins every record in one table or query with every record in the other. For example, if you include the Project and Client tables in a query and the tables are not joined, the query will have 72 records since every one of the nine records in the Project table will match up with every one of the eight records in the Client table. When you do not join tables on larger queries, the dynaset will be huge and slow.

If you need to delete joins—for example, when you drag one field on top of the wrong field in another table or query—click the join line. When the join line is selected it appears heavier. To delete the selected join, press DEL. Adding and deleting joins only affects the query—not the database. If you create a join between tables in a query, only the query uses that join; every time you want a join between the tables you must re-create it.

Using Multiple Tables in a Query

When using several tables and queries in a query, designing the query is just like designing one that uses a single table or query. Add fields by dragging the field names from the different field list windows or by selecting the field names in the drop-down list box in the Field row of the QBE grid.

You can intermingle the fields from each of the tables and queries. The drop-down list box in the Field row contains all of the fields from all of the tables and queries in the order that the tables or queries are given in the field list windows. If you display the table or query names in the QBE grid with the Table Names command in the View menu, the drop-down list box in the Fields row only contains the fields of the table selected in the Table row. Figure 7-2 shows part of a query design that includes fields from both tables.

The only special difference between entering criteria and calculated fields when a query contains one table or query or contains several is how you tell Access which table contains the field used by both tables. For example, if you have a query that uses the tables in Figure 7-2 and you want to use the Employee Id field in criteria, you need to tell Access which table it should use since Employee Id is in both of them. Tell Access which table to use by putting the table name in brackets before a period. For example, to include Employee Id from the Employee table, enter **[Employee].[Employee Id]**. Here is an example of a query design with a field name that uses this method of indicating the table:

Field:	First Name	Last Name	Project Number	Date	H
Sort:					
Show:	☒	☒	☒	☒	
Criteria:			<[Employee].[Employee Id]		
or:					

In this query design, only the records that have an employee Id number lower than the project number will match the query. You only need to include the table with the field name when the field name is used by more than one table. This also applies to queries used in another query.

Changing the Join

Access has three ways it can create records for the query based on the join established between the tables. The default is for the query to only include records from both tables that share a common field. This means in a query that combines the Client and Project tables, the query only uses data from the Client table that is joined to a record in the Project table and only uses data from the Project table that is joined to a record in the Client table.

The second way is to include records from one of the tables whether or not a record matches a record in the other table. This means that the query can include all the Client records whether or not the records match records in the Project table.

The third way is that the query can include all the Project records whether or not the records match records in the Client table. To make this change, double-click the line joining the two tables. Access displays a dialog box like the one shown here:

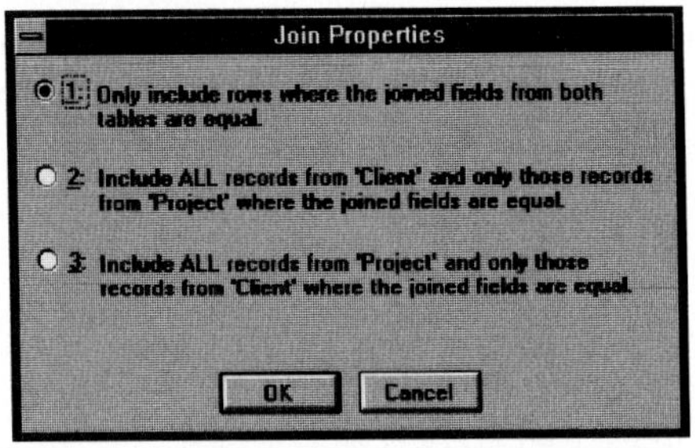

The top option button, the default, only includes records from both tables when the records have a field with the same value. The second option button includes all records from the first table even when the records do not have a field with the same value. The last option button includes all records from the second table even when the records do not have a field with the same value. For the Client and Project table example, if you select the middle option button, the query's results will include the record for the eight Client records although no roller coasters are being built for the eighth potential customer yet.

Editing a Query

With all of the choices you have in a query, you may be surprised when you try editing data and find you cannot. While the data in some fields in a query can be edited, the data in other fields cannot. Also, in some types of queries, none of the fields can have their data changed. The limitations on whether you can edit the data in a query are created by the query's design rather than the data itself. When a query is based on a table, you can edit the data in the dynaset's datasheet. The only fields you cannot edit are calculated fields.

When a query uses multiple tables that have a one-to-one relationship, you can edit all of the fields except the field that creates the link to the other table. For example, if you have a table containing other roller coaster information that has a one-to-one relationship with the Project table and is linked by the Coaster ID field in both tables, you can edit any of the data in the query except for the Coaster ID fields.

When a query uses multiple tables that have a one-to-many relationship, you can edit all of the fields from the table that contains the multiple records except for the field that creates the link to the other table. For example, if you have a query that includes the Project and Invoice Register tables, you can edit any fields from the Invoice Register table except for the Project ID field.

The only exception to this is when the query does not display any fields from the many side of the relationship. With this exception, you can edit the fields from the one side of the relationship. An example of this is when you use fields from the Invoice Register table to select which records from the Project table appear in the query's dynaset, and none of the fields from the Invoice Register table appears in the dynaset. In this example, you can edit all of the fields, including the field that links the two tables. In Chapters 8 and 13, you will learn to create forms that contain more than one table. Using a main/subform form that you will learn about in those chapters, you can edit the data from both tables.

 Note You will learn about some advanced query features later in this chapter; when a query contains these features—which include only displaying unique values, including a Total row in the query design, and crosstab queries—none of the data in the query can be edited.

When a query is based on another query, the limitations created by the current query are added to the previous query. If the data from a previous query can be edited, you may still be able to edit the data when you use the query in another query. Any restrictions the previous query places on editing the data in the dynaset also apply to the current query.

Changing a Query Through Query Properties

A query has several properties that you can change to change the data presented. These properties include only including unique records and selecting which fields appear in a field list window when you use a query as the basis for another object. These changes are made by displaying the query's properties. You can display these properties by choosing Query Properties from the View menu or, from the toolbar, clicking the Properties button, which looks like this:

You can add and remove query properties from the Query Properties dialog box. The query properties you select only apply to the current query and not to any other tables or queries in the database. The Query Properties dialog box looks like this:

The Run With Owner's Permission option is set whether permissions for underlying tables applies to the query using the table. This is used with multiuser applications such as networks when you go through the process of assigning ownership to the parts of a database. You will learn how to do this in Chapter 19. Later, when you create other types of queries, the dialog box will include additional properties. These additional properties are described with the types of queries that use the properties.

Displaying Unique Records

When displaying a subset of the fields available in a query, you may have several records that look identical. For example, if you are displaying the Bill Rate and Department fields from the Employee table, you will see four records that contain 10 for the Bill Rate field and Construction for the Department field since all of the employees in the Construction department have the same values for these two fields. Rather than displaying every record, you may want to show only unique combinations.

You can display only unique combinations by selecting the Unique Values Only check box in the Query Properties check box. When this check box is selected, only the unique records of those selected by the query's criteria appear. When the check box is cleared, all records that match the criteria appear. Uniqueness is determined according to the fields that you include in the QBE grid. For example, you can create a query that shows the unique combinations of the Bill Rate and Department fields for the Employee table records that looks like this:

Bill Rate	Department
$10.00	Construction
$50.00	Design
$50.00	Testing
$55.00	Design
$55.00	Testing
$60.00	Design
$75.00	Design

Select Query: Query1

Record: 1

The dynaset only shows the unique combinations of the Bill Rate and Department fields in the table. Also, notice that you do not have an extra line at the bottom of the data. The data in the datasheet is read-only so you cannot edit the data or add new records. If you want to limit which records are included, simply include criteria in the QBE grid. You also can clear the Show check box for fields that you add to the QBE grid for the criteria so their field values are not considered when determining which records are unique.

 Tip You can use uniqueness to create queries that list the unique values of a field. Chapter 10 shows you how to use a query like this for a form to provide the selections that appear in the list box.

Displaying All Query Fields

When you use a query as the basis for another object, the query only contains the fields that appear as part of the QBE grid in the query's design. At this point, you will use queries only to create other queries but later you will learn about forms and reports that can use queries as the source of the data they present.

When you add a query as a field list window in another query's design, the field list window only includes the fields that appear in the query's QBE grid. However, you also can display not only all of the fields that appear in the query's QBE grid but also all of the fields from the tables or queries that the query uses as the source of its data. Show all of these fields by clearing the Restrict Available Fields check box in the Query Properties dialog box. When this check box is selected, only the fields in the QBE grid appear.

For example, if you use the query with the design shown in Figure 7-3, if the Restrict Available Fields check box is selected for this query, when you use this query as the basis for another query, the field list window only includes the Coaster Name, Features, Client Name, and Park Desc fields. If the Restrict Available Fields check box is cleared for this query, when you use this query as the basis for another query, the query's field list window includes the 17 fields from the Project table and the 14 fields from the Client table. As this example indicates, changing this property for a query affects the objects that subsequently use the query. Changing this property does not change the fields included in the field list windows of the current query.

FIGURE 7-3

A query design using only some of the available fields

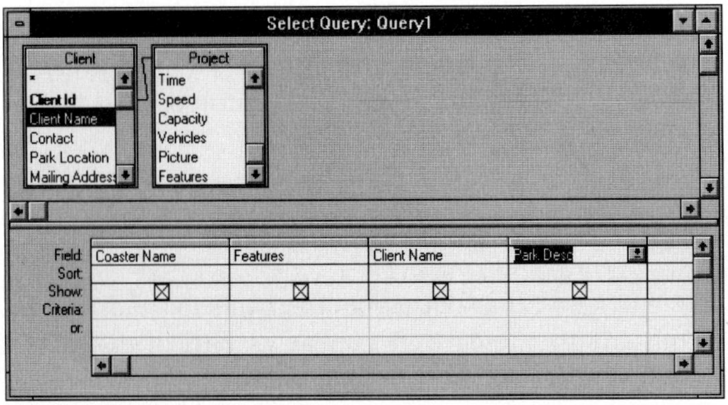

Adding Summary Calculations to a Query

Often with queries, you may be less interested in the individual records and more concerned with the total or another statistical computation involving all of the records selected by a query. For example, you may want the total of all the invoices by project for the records in the invoice register.

To create a query that summarizes its records, you first create a *select query* that selects the records you want to summarize. Creating a select query lets you check that the query selects only the records you want to summarize. Once the query chooses just the appropriate records, you remove the fields that will not be included in the summary statistics. The fields that remain in the query design are the fields you want to use for criteria, fields you want to summarize, and fields you want to use for grouping the records. When only these fields remain, add the summary calculations to the query's design.

Figure 7-4 shows a query design that has had these steps applied. Originally, the query design included all of the fields in the Invoice Register table. Then the criteria >=1/1/92 was added. The query's datasheet was displayed and you can see that only the invoices for 1992 are displayed. Next, the Invoice Number and Payment Date fields are removed from the QBE grid. The remaining fields are the ones you will use for the summary statistics. The Invoice Amount and Payment

FIGURE 7-4

A select query before adding summarizing statistics

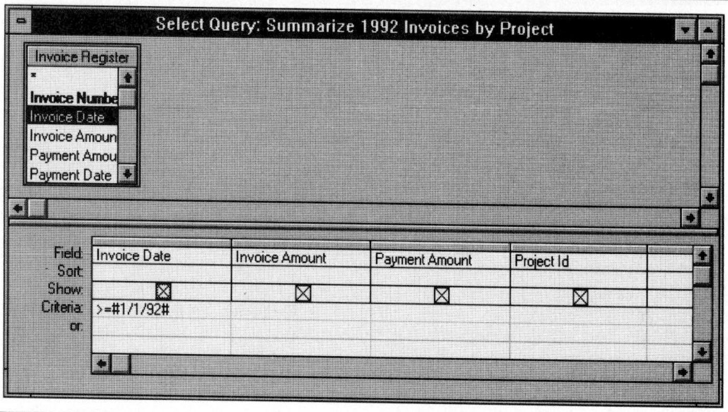

Amount fields will be totaled, the Invoice Date will be used for criteria, and the Project ID field will be used to group the records that are summed according to their project number.

Adding Summary Statistics to a Query Design

After adding the criteria to the design to select only the records you want, add the summary statistics to the query design by adding a Total row to the QBE grid. To add this row, choose Totals from the View menu or, from the toolbar, click the Totals button, which looks like this:

This command adds a Total row as shown here:

Field:	Invoice Date	Invoice Amount	Payment Amount	Project Id
Total:	Group By	Group By	Group By	Group By
Sort:				
Show:	☒	☒	☒	☒
Criteria:	>=#1/1/92#			
or:				

The Group By entries in this row can be replaced with other choices that summarize fields and select fields. Once the Total row is added, you can change the Group By for different fields to other choices. When the query design contains criteria like the >=#1/1/92# below Invoice Date, the Total row needs to change to tell Access to use this field's criteria but not to summarize this field. Do this by changing the Group By to Where. Since you do not want this field to summarize the data, clear the Show check box. The criteria is still part of the query but you will not see it when you look at the datasheet. You should also change the Group By for fields that you want to summarize. For these fields, change the Group By to one of these choices for the following summary statistics:

Operator	Effect
Sum	Adds the values of that field
Avg	Averages the values of that field
Min	Returns the smallest value of the values in that field

Max	Returns the largest value of the values in that field
Count	Counts the number of records for that field
StDev	Calculates the standard deviation of the values in that field
Var	Calculates the variance of the values in that field
First	Returns the first value of the values in that field
Last	Returns the last value of the values in that field
Expression	Calculates a formula's value that is entered like a calculated field in the Field row

For the query design in Figure 7-4, you replace the Group By with Sum for the Invoice Amount and Payment Amount fields.

The fields in which you want to leave Group By in the Total row are the fields you want to use to divide the data into groups that are summarized by the other fields. For the query design in Figure 7-5, which has the Total row completed, the Project ID field retains the Group By in the Total row. When you display this query's dynaset, the records that match the query are divided into groups according to the Project ID field values.

Once you have made any changes you want with the Total row in the QBE grid, you are ready to display the query's dynaset. Switch to the datasheet view just as you have for other queries. Figure 7-6 shows the

FIGURE
7-5

A query design incorporating summarizing statistics

dynaset that the query design in Figure 7-5 creates. For all of the records that match the criteria set by the columns that have Where in the Total row, Access divides these records into groups according to the field values of the columns that have Group By in the Total row. For all of the records in each group, Access calculates the summary statistic for the columns in the query design that have a summary statistic in its Total row. For the dynaset shown in Figure 7-6, this means that the invoice records with dates on or after 1/1/92 are divided into groups according to project numbers. For each group of recent invoices for a project, Access totals the Invoice Amount and the Payment Amount fields. Also, notice that this datasheet does not have a row at the bottom to add new data. The dynaset data cannot be changed.

Warning Do not use an asterisk (*) in the Field row of the QBE grid for a query that will use a Total row.

Tip: Make sure the Total row is still visible when you save the query so all of the settings made in the Total row are saved as part of the query design.

Using More than One Field for Grouping Records

In the query design and datasheet shown in Figures 7-5 and 7-6, the query groups the records only according to the values of one field. You also can use more than one field's values to group the records. For

FIGURE 7-6 A query datasheet that includes the summarizing statistics (the dynaset for the query design in Figure 7-5)

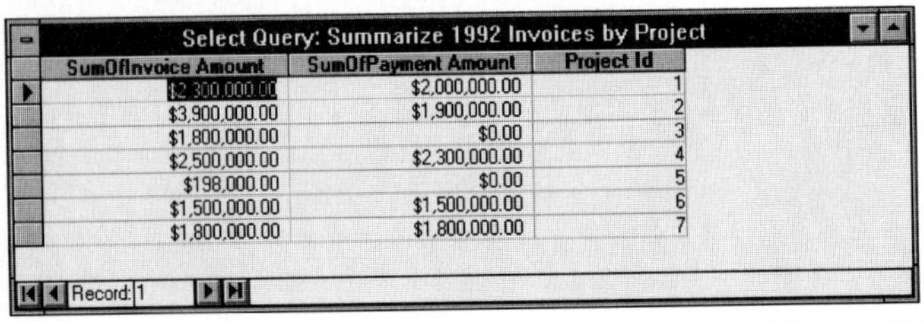

SumOfInvoice Amount	SumOfPayment Amount	Project Id
$2,300,000.00	$2,000,000.00	1
$3,900,000.00	$1,900,000.00	2
$1,800,000.00	$0.00	3
$2,500,000.00	$2,300,000.00	4
$198,000.00	$0.00	5
$1,500,000.00	$1,500,000.00	6
$1,800,000.00	$1,800,000.00	7

Select Query: Summarize 1992 Invoices by Project

Record: 1

example, suppose, instead of just looking at the total invoices and paid amounts for the current year, you wanted to see the total invoices and paid amounts for each of the projects for each year. Calculate the year by creating a calculated field using the Year function that returns the year from a date. This calculated field can be entered as **Invoice Year:Year([Invoice Date])** in the Field row of the query design. Now you can remove the Invoice Date from the query design with its criteria. This field also uses Group By in the Total row of the query design shown here:

Field:	Project Id	Invoice Year: Year([Invoice Date])	Invoice Amount	Payment Amount
Total:	Group By	Group By	Sum	Sum
Sort:				
Show:	☒	☒	☒	☒
Criteria:				
or:				

When you display this query's dynaset, Access divides the records according to the values of two fields. For each unique combination of field values of the two fields, Access calculates the summary statistics for the records that have that combination. The result of the query design you just saw is shown in Figure 7-7. In this query, all of the table's records are divided into groups since the query does not include criteria to exclude records. Each group includes the records for a project for a particular year. Several of the projects have several rows in Figure 7-7 so that each year of the project's billing is totaled.

FIGURE 7-7 Grouping by two fields with summarizing statistics

Project Id	Invoice Year	SumOfInvoice Amount	SumOfPayment Amount
1	1991	$1,700,000.00	$1,700,000.00
1	1992	$2,300,000.00	$2,000,000.00
2	1992	$3,900,000.00	$1,900,000.00
3	1990	$250,000.00	$250,000.00
3	1991	$5,750,000.00	$5,750,000.00
3	1992	$1,800,000.00	$0.00
4	1992	$2,500,000.00	$2,300,000.00
5	1992	$198,000.00	$0.00
6	1992	$1,500,000.00	$1,500,000.00
7	1991	$1,400,000.00	$1,400,000.00
7	1992	$1,800,000.00	$1,800,000.00
8	1990	$2,600,000.00	$2,600,000.00
8	1991	$500,000.00	$0.00
9	1989	$3,000,000.00	$3,000,000.00
9	1990	$200,900.00	$200,900.00

Select Query: Summarize Invoices by Project and by Year

Record: 1

When you group by fields, Access divides the records according to the unique combination of field values for the fields that contain Group By in the Total row. When you group by only one field, the groups are divided solely by that field's values. When you group by two groups, the groups are divided by the unique combination of values in the two fields. If you group by more than two fields, the records are grouped by as many unique combinations of field entries among the fields that have Group By in the Total row.

Tip You can summarize calculated fields as well as the fields that come from the table or query the current query uses.

Other Types of Criteria in a Summary Select Query

Besides the criteria you add to a column when you change the Group By in the Total row to Where, you can add criteria in other locations. You also may want to add criteria in two other locations: to columns that contain Group By in the Total row and to columns that contain summary statistics in the Total row.

If you add criteria to a field that has Group By in the Total row, only the groups of records that match the criteria are displayed. For example, if you put 2 and 7 in two rows below the Project ID field in the query design shown in Figure 7-5, the query only includes the groups of records for projects 2 and 7 so you only have two lines in the query datasheet. The criteria in a Group By column selects which of the groups that the query otherwise creates are included in the dynaset.

You also can put the criteria in the columns that summarize the values. These are all of the columns that do not use Group By or Where in the Total row. In these cases, the criteria is applied to the results the dynaset would otherwise show. As an example, suppose you entered **>500000** in the Criteria row below Invoice Amount in the query design shown in Figure 7-5. When you display the dynaset, the datasheet looks like this:

SumOfInvoice Amount	SumOfPayment Amount	Project Id
$2,300,000.00	$2,000,000.00	1
$3,900,000.00	$1,900,000.00	2
$1,800,000.00	$0.00	3
$2,500,000.00	$2,300,000.00	4
$1,500,000.00	$1,500,000.00	6
$1,800,000.00	$1,800,000.00	7

Select Query: Summarize 1992 Invoices by Project
Record: 1

Notice how all of the numbers are the same as the ones you saw in Figure 7-6. The only difference is that the row for project 5 is missing. When you look at the dynaset in Figure 7-6, you can see that the total Invoice Amount is less than 500,000. Since you have added this criteria, the dynaset excludes the records whose summary statistics do not match the criteria.

Tip If you want to use summary statistics on the output of a query that shows unique records, create a query that shows the unique records. Then, use the query you have just created as the basis for the query to which you add the summary statistics.

Crosstab Queries

Another method of summarizing your data in a query is through a *crosstab query*. Crosstab queries create tables out of your data where a set of entries is in the left column, another set of entries appears as column headings, and the table is filled in with values. For example, suppose you want to show how many hours each of the employees worked on each project. Create a query like the one shown in Figure 7-8 that uses the Total row in the QBE grid to group records by their combination of project number and employee number. This query may not supply the layout you want To create a table that has the project numbers across

FIGURE
7-8
Using summary statistics to group records by two fields

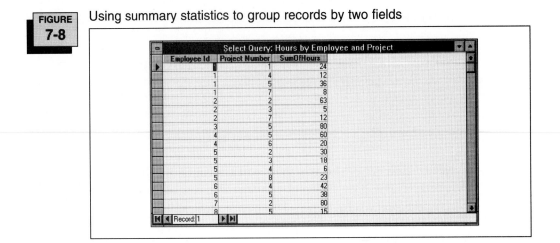

the top and the hours each employee works on the project filling in the columns, create a crosstab query.

A crosstab query is like the summary statistic select queries you saw before. The difference is that the field values of one of the fields you used to group records are shown across the top of the datasheet as if they are field names. The different summary statistics are shown at the intersection of the column of the field value of one of the grouping fields and the row of the field values of the other grouping fields. A crosstab query only calculates a summary statistic on one field at a time. Figure 7-9 shows the same data in Figure 7-8 presented as a crosstab query.

FIGURE
7-9
A crosstab query showing the same information as shown in Figure 7-8

To create a crosstab query, first create a select query that selects the records you want to summarize. Creating this select query first lets you check that the query only includes the records you want to summarize. Once the query chooses only the appropriate records, remove the fields that you don't want included in the crosstab query. The only fields you want to remain in the query design are the fields that contain criteria, fields you want to summarize, and fields that you want to border the top and left side of the results.

Once you remove the extra fields, you can change this select query into a crosstab query. If you are using all the records from the Employee Time Log table as the basis for a crosstab query, your query will contain the Employee ID, Project Number, and Hours fields.

Once you select the fields to appear in the crosstab query, change the select query to a crosstab query by choosing Crosstab from the Query menu. The Show row you saw in Figure 7-5 is replaced by the Crosstab row as you can see here:

If the QBE grid did not previously include the Total row, it is added to the QBE grid. Once the Crosstab row is added, you can make entries in this row to tell Access how you want the data to appear in the crosstab query. You have three entries that you can put in this location: Row Heading, Column Heading, and Value, as well as leaving the entry blank.

If the QBE grid includes criteria to select the records used by the crosstab query but you do not want the field used in the crosstab query, leave the entry empty. You can later change the entry in the Crosstab row to (not shown) if you want to hide a field.

On the top of the crosstab query's datasheet are the field entries that you use to divide the crosstab entries into columns. For the crosstab query datasheet shown in Figure 7-9, this field is the Project Number field. You can have only one field whose entries appear as column headings across the top of the query. To tell Access which field's entries you want to use, select Column Heading in the Crosstab row.

On the left of the crosstab query's datasheet are the field entries that divide the datasheet into rows. You can select more than one field to appear on the left side of the crosstab query datasheet. To select these fields, select Row Heading in the Crosstab row. Access creates the rows by presenting the unique combinations of field value entries just as if the fields you use as row headings are in their own query with the Unique Values Only check box for the query properties selected. To create the crosstab query shown in Figure 7-9, the Employee ID field has its Crosstab row changed to Row Heading.

The remaining field you will want to change the Crosstab row for is the field that you want to summarize. For this field, change the Crosstab row to Value and then select from the Total row one of the choices that summarizes data. These choices are Sum, Avg, Min, Max, Count, StDev, Var, First, Last, and Expression. At this point, with the crosstab query designed, your QBE grid may look something like this:

Field:	Employee Id		Project Number	Hours		
Total:	Group By		Group By	Sum		
Crosstab:	Row Heading		Column Heading	Value		
Sort:						
Criteria:						
or:						

To view the crosstab query, switch to the datasheet view just as you do for other query types. The design just shown creates the crosstab query shown in Figure 7-9.

Adding Fixed Column Headings for Crosstab Queries

Besides letting Access create the field headings for the fields in a crosstab query, you can set these field headings yourself. You may want to do this when you want the field headings to appear in a different order. You will also want to use fixed column headings when you use the crosstab query as the basis for a report (Chapter 13 shows an example of this).

To set the fixed column headings that appear in a report, choose Query Properties from the View menu or click the Properties button. The last property is now Fixed Column Headings. You can add the fixed column headings by selecting the Fixed Column Headings check box and then entering the entries you want in the text box below. When entered, the column headings are separated by a semicolon or by pressing CTRL-ENTER, which puts the column headings on separate lines.

Creating Action Queries

Besides using queries to present data, you can also use queries to perform actions. Using action queries, you can put the contents of a query's datasheet into another table, delete records, add data to another table, or change many records in a table at once. Action queries are permanent database objects so every time you want to perform an action you have the query ready to perform the action for you.

Action queries look different than select and crosstab queries in the database windows. You can see the different icons shown here:

Action Queries
Select and Crosstab Queries

 Tip Make backup copies of your database when you first start working with action queries. You can make a tremendous amount of changes to your database through action queries. If you make the wrong changes, removing the effects of the changes may take a long time.

Setting Up an Action Query

The first step in using action queries is creating a select query that selects only the records on which you want the action performed. For example, if you want an action query to delete a group of records, you first create a select query that selects only the records that you want to delete so you do not accidentally delete records you want to keep.

Once the query chooses the appropriate records, change the query type by choosing the type of query you want the action query to become from the Query menu. After changing the query type, you may need to make further changes depending on the action the query performs. These further changes are described next, along with the different actions queries can perform.

When the action query design is completed, run the query by choosing Run from the Query menu or, from the toolbar, clicking the Run button, which looks like this:

You will see some confirmation to which you must respond before Access completes the action. After the query design window closes, the next time you want to run the query, select the query and double-click it, press ENTER, or select Open. You may need to respond to a confirmation that running the action query will modify a table's data. When you run an action query, you cannot undo the effects of it. This is why it is so important that you create the select query first before you convert the query into an action query. When you first run an action query, check that you get the results you expect to be sure you have designed the query correctly.

Tip   You can make parameter action queries by changing parts of the criteria as just described for select parameter queries. Parameter action queries prompt for the data to use in the query just like parameter select queries. The parameter action queries use the data you enter to select which data you are affecting.

Creating an Action Query to Create a New Table

When you create a query that contains the data that you want to save to a separate table, you can create a *make table action query* that takes the data a query selects and puts it in a separate and new table. You might use this type of an action query when you want a table to contain a subset of information that changes every time you run the action query. For example, suppose you want to create a table from the Employee Time Log table that only includes records for the week of 6/12/92. You might want to create a separate table when you plan to export the data to another application.

You also can use a make table action query when you want to create a table of the records you plan to delete from a table with a delete action query. The table you create with a make table action query will contain all of the data the select query would otherwise contain, even if the data comes from multiple tables.

To make a query a make table action query, choose Make Table from the Query menu. From the Query Properties dialog box that displays this command, type the name for the new table in the Table Name text box or select an existing table name using the drop-down list box, as shown here:

This table by default is placed in the current database but you can select the Another Database option button and type the filename of the other database in the File Name text box. The Unique Values Only and Run With Owner's Permission check boxes are for the same query properties as described earlier for select queries. When the table name, and possibly the database name is entered, select OK. The table is not created, however, until you run the query.

Once you have selected the new table you are creating, you are ready to run the action query. Choose Run from the Query menu or click the Run button in the toolbar. Access displays a message telling how many records it will place in the new table. Select OK to create the new table. The new table you have created has the same data type and data size as the table that originally contained the data but the table does not adopt any of the other table or field properties.

When you run this action query a second time, Access will prompt you for whether it can delete the previous table before continuing with the action query. Select Yes to delete the previous table and continue the action query or No to cancel the action query and preserve the existing table.

Creating an Action Query to Delete Records

When you want to systematically remove records from a query, you can create a query that performs this action for you. A *delete action query* quickly removes entire records that you select from one or more tables. After you have created the select query to ensure you are selecting the correct records, add * (an asterisk) to the Field row of the QBE grid for the table from which you want to delete the fields.

To make a query a delete action query, choose Delete from the Query menu. The Sort and Show rows in the QBE grid are replaced with a Delete row. This Delete row contains Where for all the fields except the one with the * (asterisk). The Where tells Access that these columns contain criteria to select which records are deleted. The From in the Delete row for the column containing the * tells Access that this is the table from which to remove records. With this preliminary step completed, you are ready to run the action query.

Choose Run from the Query menu or click the Run button in the toolbar. Access displays a message telling you how many records it will delete. Select OK to remove the selected records.

When the query contains multiple tables, you may be able to delete records from one or both tables. If the tables have a one-to-one relationship, you can delete the matching record from both tables. Make sure you include the * (asterisk) in the Field row of the QBE grid for each table. If the tables have a one-to-many relationship, you can first use the delete action query to delete the records from the table with the many records by including the * for the table name. After you check that the correct data is selected, run the action query to delete the records. Then, replace the * for the table of the many side of the relationship and run the action query again.

 Tip   Before you run a delete action query the first time, count the records in the select query that you use as the basis for selecting records to delete. Then when you run the delete action query, the number of records Access tells you it will delete should match the number of records displayed by the select query.

Creating an Action Query to Append Data to a Table

When you have data in one query that you want to add to another table, you can use an *append action query* to transfer the data between tables. You can use an append action query when you have data in an attached table that you want to add to a nonattached table. You also can use an append action query when you want to combine data from a separate database into a table in the current one. This may occur when someone else has entered the data at another machine.

The query you are taking data from must have certain features in common with the table you are appending the data to. First, if the appending table has a primary key, the query must contain a field with the same name and data type as well as entries that are unique. If the data you are appending includes duplicate information or is empty for the primary key field, Access will not paste the record to the table.

To make a query an append action query, choose Append from the Query menu. The Query Properties dialog box looks just like the one for the Make Table command except Make New Table is Append To. Type the name of the table to contain the appended data in the Table Name text box or select an existing table name using the drop-down list box. Access assumes this table is in the current database but you can select the Another Database option button and type the filename of the database containing the table in the File Name text box. The Unique Values Only and Run with Owner's Permission check boxes are for the same query properties as described earlier for select queries. When the table name, and possibly the database name are entered, select OK. The data is not appended, however, until you run the query.

After you convert the table to an append action query, the Show row in the QBE grid becomes an Append To row. The Append To row selects the fields in the table to which you will append the data. You can select from any one of the field names available through the drop-down list box or type the field name. If some of the fields have the same name, Access fills these cells with the field names for you.

All of the fields in the QBE grid must have an entry in the Append To row. If the QBE grid includes an asterisk (*) in the Field row, Access copies the contents from the query to the table for all of the fields in the query that have the same names as the fields in the table. If you include an asterisk (*) in the QBE grid, you don't include other fields from the same field list window since Access will try to copy the field's contents twice for each version of the field name. When one of the fields in the table you will append to is a Counter field, delete the field contents from the query's data so the Counter field's data is updated and renumbered in the table. You only leave this field's contents intact when you want the appended records to retain the same values for the Counter field in the table.

When the Append To row in the QBE grid is completed, you are ready to run the append action query. Choose R̲un from the Q̲uery menu or click the Run button in the toolbar. Access displays a message telling you how many rows it will append to the table. Select OK to add the rows. If the table has data that it cannot append to the table, the record is added to the Paste Errors table, creating it if it does not exist. This is the same table Access creates and adds data to every time you unsuccessfully paste data from the Clipboard to a table. After appending the data, if the table you are appending to is open, press SHIFT-F9 to reapply the query.

 Tip If the field order in the query's QBE grid exactly matches the fields in the table, copying the records from the query's datasheet and pasting them into the table is faster.

Creating an Action Query to Alter Data to a Table

If you have a group of records that you need to make the same change to, creating a query to select the records and then manually making the change to each record can be time-consuming. A shortcut is to create an *update action query* that selects the records and then updates the records for you. All of the records selected by an update action query have selected field values altered. This type of an action query lets you globally change all of the records in a group. You can also use an update query to delete the field values of specific fields.

After you create a select query that correctly selects only the records you want to update, convert the query into an update action query by choosing Update from the Query menu. After you use this command, the Sort and Show rows in the QBE grid become an Update To row. This row is where you enter the formula of the new value you want the field to equal. These formulas are just like the criteria and calculated field formulas you have entered previously. Some of the possible entries (and the change each would perform) are listed here:

Entry	Result
"Safety"	Changes the values of the field to the text Safety
#12/31/92#	Changes the values of the field to the date 12/31/92
7	Changes the values of the field to 7
[Actual Cost]*[1.05]	Changes the values of the field to five percent more than the current value of Actual Cost

You only need to include entries in the Update To row for the fields whose values you want to change. With the Update To row complete for the fields you want to change, you are ready to update the field values. When you want the data in the field updated, you must run the query. Choose Run from the Query menu or click the Run button in the toolbar. Access displays a message telling you how many records it will update in the table. Select OK to make the changes.

 Tip To double-check that the formula is correct, create a calculated field that calculates what the new values for the field will be. If the query's datasheet contains the correct values for the calculated field, copy the formula from the calculated field to the Update To row in the QBE grid for the original field.

Tip To confirm each replacement as it is made, view the data in the table or in a query and then use the Replace command in the Edit menu to selectively make field value replacements.

Quick Reference

To Create a Parameter Query   Create a select query that selects a sample of the data you want. Replace the entries you want to change each time with the text you want to appear as a prompt enclosed in brackets. Choose Parameters in the Query menu. In the Parameter column, enter the prompt and in the Data Type column, select one of the available data types. Select OK after entering the prompts and data types for each parameter value. The parameter prompts will appear every time you display the query's datasheet.

To Add Tables to a Query   Choose Add Table from the Query menu. Select a table or query from the Add Table dialog box and then select Add. Repeat until you add all the tables you want to the query and then select Close. You can also drag a table or query name from the database window onto the query design.

To Remove Tables from a Query   Select the field list window from the table or query you want to remove. Press DEL or choose Remove Table from the Query menu.

To Join Tables in a Query   Drag the field from one field list window to the field in the other field list window you want to use to join the records in the tables. Access automatically joins tables for which you have already defined a relationship.

To Display Unique Records in a Query   Create the select query to select the records you want and set the QBE grid to only display the fields you are interested in. Choose Query Properties from the View menu or click the Properties button in the toolbar, select the Unique Values Only check box, and select OK.

To Add Summary Statistics to a Query   Choose Totals from the View menu to add the Total row to the QBE grid in the query design. For columns that contain criteria to select which records you want to summarize, change the Group By in the Total row to Where. For the columns in the QBE grid you want to summarize, change the Group By to Sum, Avg, Min, Max, Count, StDev, Var, First, Last, or

Expression. Display the datasheet just as you normally do. The query displays the summary statistics for the records grouped according to the unique field value combinations of the columns that contain Group By in the Total row.

To Create a Crosstab Query Choose Crosstab from the Query menu to change the select query to a crosstab query. In the Crosstab row, change the column's entry to Column Heading for the field whose values you want to appear as the column headings in the crosstab query. Change the column's entry in the Crosstab row to Row Heading for the fields whose combinations of unique values you want to divide the crosstab query into rows. Change the column's entries in the Crosstab row to Value for the field that you want summarized and change the entry in the Total row to Sum, Avg, Min, Max, Count, StDev, Var, First, Last, or Expression for the summary statistic you want calculated for the different combinations of row heading and column heading values. You can display the crosstab query by switching to the datasheet view as you normally do.

To Create a Make Table Action Query After creating a select query that correctly chooses the records you want placed in another table, change the select query to a make table action query by choosing Make Table from the Query menu. In the Query Properties dialog box, type the name for the new table in the Table Name text box or select an existing table name using the drop-down list box. If the table is to be added to another database, select the Another Database option button and type the filename of the other database in the File Name text box. Select OK. Run the query by choosing Run from the Query menu or clicking the Run button in the toolbar. Select OK to confirm that Access is copying the number of rows copied to the new table.

To Create a Delete Action Query After creating a select query that correctly chooses the records you want deleted, change the select query to a delete action query by choosing Delete from the Query menu. The Delete row contains Where to indicate columns containing criteria to select the records to delete and From to indicate which tables contain the records to delete. Run the query by choosing Run from the Query menu or clicking the Run button in the toolbar. Select OK to confirm deleting the number of rows displayed.

To Create an Append Action Query   After creating a select query that correctly chooses the data you want added to another table, change the select query to an append action query by choosing Append from the Query menu. In the Query Properties dialog box, type the name of the table to append the data to in the Table Name text box or select an existing table name using the drop-down list box. If the table is in another database, select the Another Database option button and type the filename of the other database in the File Name text box. Select OK. In the Append To row, select the field names from the table you have selected in the Query Properties dialog box where you want the query's data appended. Run the query by choosing Run from the Query menu or clicking the Run button in the toolbar. Select OK to confirm that Access is adding the number of rows copied to the table.

To Create an Update Action Query   After creating a select query that correctly chooses the records in which you want to change the data, change the select query to an update action query by choosing Update from the Query menu. In the Update To row, enter formulas that calculate the value you want the current field values replaced with. Run the query by choosing Run from the Query menu or clicking the Run button in the toolbar. Select OK to confirm the number of records updated by the query.

PART III

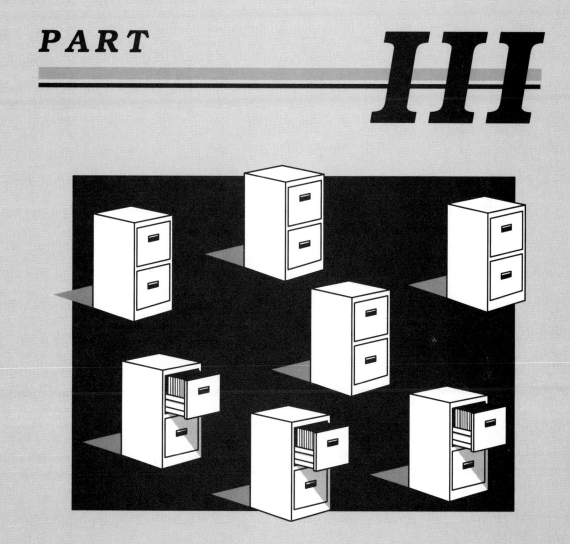

Forms and Reports

CHAPTER

Creating a Basic Form

A form is a definition of the data that you want to work with and an arrangement of how and where you want the information to appear on your screen. You can design a form by yourself or get help from Microsoft Access FormWizards.

Forms let you present and input information in a format that is easier to use than a table or datasheet. You use forms to present or input one record at a time. You can easily switch between a form and a datasheet to change between looking at one record and looking at a table.

Forms are usually used to display the information on the screen but you can also print the form when you want a hard copy of a record's information.

Tip When you want to create a customized output of a table or query, create a report rather than printing a form. You will learn about reports in Chapter 9.

How products are marketed provides a good analogy for how fields can be used in forms. When advertising a product to one group of consumers, marketers might stress its health benefits. When advertising the same product to another group of consumers, perhaps low cost and quick preparation time would be emphasized instead. Different advertising campaigns focus on different features of the same product. Similarly, with a database table you might have several different form designs that you use with the same set of fields; which form you use for a given task depends on the task.

You will often have multiple forms and reports so that you can enter your information differently depending on your application. The forms you create with Access let you select which data from a table or dynaset you present and how this information is presented. For example, if updating a mailing list for a client, you only need to show the customer name and address on the form. If you are updating account balances for the same client, the best form design would show the client's name and other identifying information along with the account balances. Tailoring the form to the application makes the task of updating information easier. You don't need to show every field within a table on a form unless your application adds new records to the table and you need to be able to enter data in each field.

This chapter gives the basics of creating a form. Most of the forms discussed can be created with FormWizards, which you will learn how to use next. You will also see how to name, save, and print the forms you create. Since forms and reports share many aspects of design and creation, what you learn in this chapter will be applicable to creating reports in Chapter 9.

Creating a Form with FormWizards

Microsoft's answer to having an intelligent assistant help you with form creation is FormWizards, which offer the easiest and quickest method for creating a new form. FormWizards create a form out of a table or query by prompting you with questions. The form most appropriate for your needs appears, based on your answers to the questions.

Access has four types of forms that you can create with FormWizards. Figure 8-1 shows the four different Wizard types. The title bar in each of the four windows indicates the Access Wizard that created the form. If none of the FormWizards options meet your exact needs you can still save time by creating a form with FormWizards and then changing the design to better meet your needs.

To create a form with FormWizards, tell Access you want to create a form. Click the New button at the top of the Database window when displaying forms or choose Ne_w from the _File menu and then _Form. You can also create a form by clicking the New Form button on the toolbar as shown here:

The advantage of choosing Ne_w from the _File menu and then _Form or clicking the New Form button on the toolbar is that you can do this when you are not displaying forms in the Database window. Access displays the New Form dialog box shown in Figure 8-2. The Select a Table/Query drop-down list box tells Access the table or query from which you want to pull data for the form you are creating. When you create a form with a table or dynaset window displayed or selected in the Database window, the table name or query is already supplied.

Four types of FormWizards form types

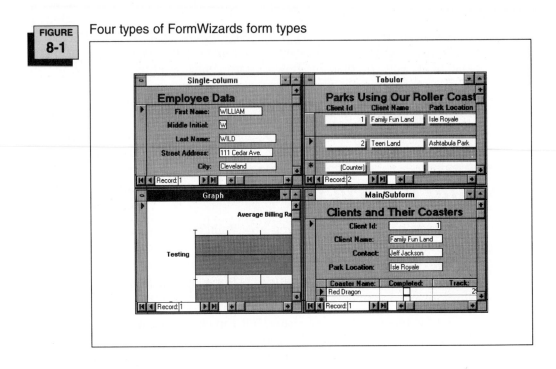

Dialog box from which you create forms

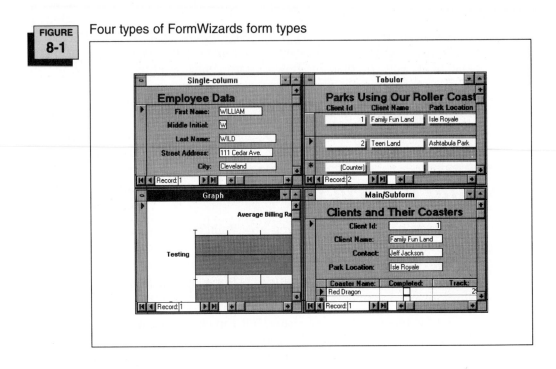

After selecting the table or query name whose data you want to use in the form, choose the FormWizards or Blank Form button to create the form. Selecting FormWizards creates the form using one of the four FormWizards options. Later you will learn about creating a form with the Blank Form button to create an empty form that you can fill as you want.

Once you select the FormWizards button, choose which FormWizard form you want to create. Access has four types—single-column, tabular, graph, and main/subform. These form types result in basic styles, which you can later embellish. When you select the FormWizard you want to use, it asks questions about the information that appears in the form. The questions vary depending on which FormWizard you select.

Single-Column and Tabular FormWizard Forms

Single-column and tabular FormWizard forms are created the same way. A *single-column form* puts all of the fields you select into a single column. A *tabular form* puts all of the fields you select into a row. A tabular form is similar to the table format of tables and queries but the form includes more space between each record. Both types of forms let you select a style for the boxes that contain the field's contents and a selected title.

From the first dialog box, shown here, you select the fields to appear in the form.

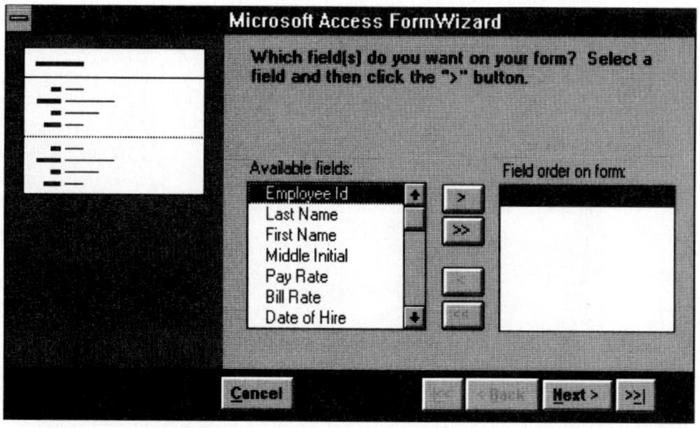

Add the fields to the form in the order you want them to appear. When you select the field in the Available fields list box and select the > button, the field is added to the form. Select the >> button to add all of the fields. You can also select a field in the Field order on Form list box and the < button to remove the field from the form. The << button removes all fields from the Field order on Form list box. The fields that are included in the form are indicated in the Available Fields list box with a > character. Once the fields you want the form to use appear in the order you want, select the Next button.

Now select the look for the form. A single-column or tabular FormWizard form has five predefined looks, each shown in Figure 8-3 and named with the descriptions in the five title bars. The look decides the style of the box for each of the fields in the form: where the fields' names appear relative to the fields, the lines added, and the background color. Select one of these styles and then select Next.

All Access needs to complete the form is the title, which appears at the top. Note that the title is separate from the form's name. You can type any text you feel is appropriate. If you do not type a title, the form will

FIGURE 8-3   Different styles for FormWizard forms

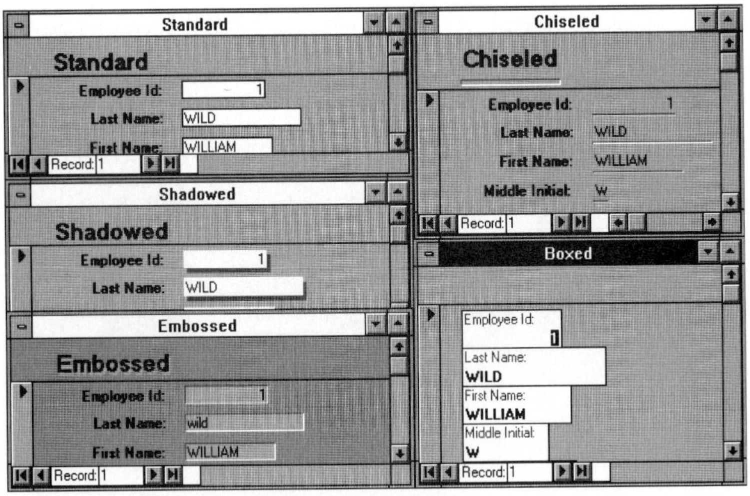

have an empty Form Header section, which is the part of the form design where a form's title appears.

Once you have a title, select Open to display the form. Figure 8-4 shows a single-column FormWizard form that includes all of the fields in the Employee table of the COASTER database in a different order. Figure 8-5 shows a tabular FormWizard form that includes some of the fields in the Clients table of the COASTER database. You can also select the Design button to display the form's design that you have created through the FormWizard.

Once you create the form and display the table using the form, save it by choosing Save in the File menu. Access also asks if you want to save a form when you try closing the window containing the form. When you save the form, type a name for the form following the same rules for naming tables. If you later want to save the form with a different name, save again by choosing Save As in the File menu.

Tip Use the title to add a heading to the form so the form's user knows the purpose of the form.

Single-column FormWizard form

Employee Data	

Employee Data

First Name:	WILLIAM
Middle Initial:	W
Last Name:	WILD
Street Address:	111 Cedar Ave.
City:	Cleveland
State:	OH
Zip Code:	44123
Home Phone:	(216)413-2222
Date of Hire:	15-Mar-92
Job Class:	11
Employee Id:	1
Office Ext.:	234
Photo:	

Record: 1

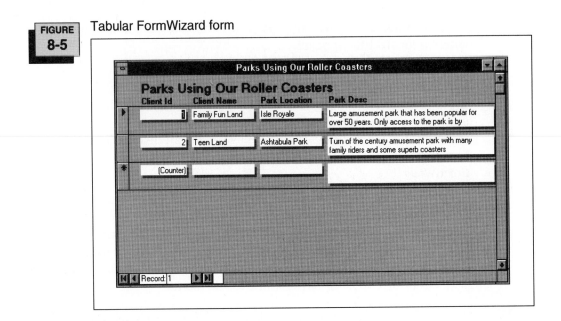

FIGURE 8-5　Tabular FormWizard form

The Graph FormWizard Form

A *graph form* creates a graph out of the data in a table or query. This FormWizard form type lets you choose from 11 graph types. Figure 8-6 shows an example of a graph FormWizard form. In this graph, the X axis is the axis along the left side of the graph since the graph is rotated. Entries on the X axis match the departments that the Department field has. Each of the bars represents the average of the values of the Bill Rate and Pay Rate fields for the three departments. The points along the graph can be averaged or totaled.

First choose the type of graph you want this form to create by selecting one of the 11 buttons representing the different graph types. Six of these are actually different graph types: area, horizontal, vertical, bar, line, pie, and a line graph variation similar to a high/low stock graph. The remaining five are three-dimensional versions of the first five graphs. Besides selecting the type of graph, you can select whether you are graphing the total or average of the values for each point along the X axis.

At this point, just as you did with the single-column and tabular forms, select the fields to appear in the form. The first field you select is usually

FIGURE 8-6

Graph FormWizard form

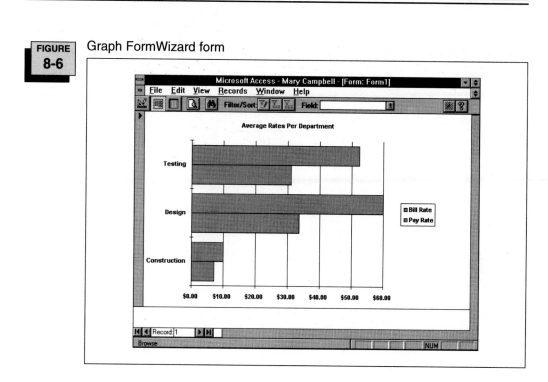

the field you want along the X axis. This can be a field that contains text, a value, or a date. Adding fields for this form type is just like adding fields for the single column or tabular FormWizard forms. Most of the fields you select to include in the form are the fields that contain numbers. You can only select one field that is not a number data type.

When you select Next, Access looks at the Data Type property of the fields you have selected. Access may need more information. If one of the fields has a text data type or they are all number data types, you can use one or more fields to label the X axis. The FormWizard prompts for the selected fields to use for labeling the points on the graph. Usually, you select the text field to have the points along the axis labeled with the entries in the text field. In this case, the other field names in the graph become the text for the legends as Figure 8-6 shows.

Select multiple fields when you want the field names to label the X axis and the contents of the remaining series to be used as the legend text. For example, in Figure 8-7, the two fields Pay Rate and Bill Rate label the X axis and the entries of the Department field are the legend

FIGURE
8-7

Another graph FormWizard form

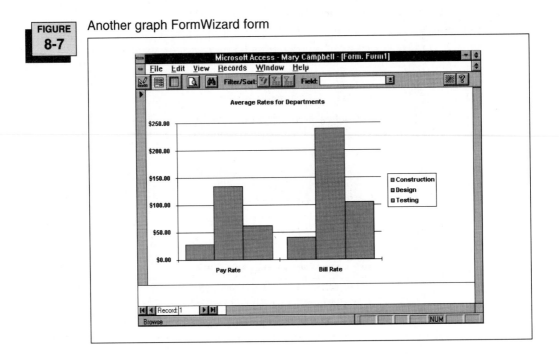

entries. When you have finished selecting fields in response to this prompt, select Next.

If one of the selected series is a Date/Time data type, Access assumes you want the dates or times to identify the different points along the X axis. You have two options for using dates: You can choose how the dates or times in the Date/Time data type field are grouped by selecting a term in the Group [field] By drop-down list box. (The drop-down list box lets you group dates or times by years, quarters, months, weeks, days, hours, or minutes.) You can also select whether to use all the dates and times or only use the dates and times within a range. The default is to use all of the dates and times but you can select the Use Data Between radio button and modify the dates and times to select the range of dates and times you want to use. The range of dates and times determines which records from the table or query the form uses for the graph. When finished selecting options for the Date/Time data field, select Next.

Finally, enter the title for the form in the Form Title text box. The title is the title that appears above the graph just like Average Rates Per

Departments appears above the graph in Figure 8-6. With any title completed, select Open to display the form, which may look similar to the one shown in Figure 8-6. In this graph, each of the bars represents the average pay and billing rate for the different departments.

You can also select the Design button to display the form's design that you have created through the FormWizard. This FormWizard form type creates a graph using the table's or query's data using Microsoft's Graph program, which is included with Access. The graph you create is an *embedded object*. Think of an embedded object as one that appears to be part of the current application but is really on-loan from the application that created it and is still controlled by the original application (the one it was created in). If you double-click the embedded graph either in the form or in the form's design window, you start the Microsoft Graph application. If you have used Microsoft's Word for Windows, you may already know how to use Microsoft Graph to build graphs to put into your word processing documents.

Once you create the form and display the table using the form, save the form by choosing Save in the File menu. Access also asks if you want to save a form when you try closing the window containing the form. When you save the form, type a name for the form following the same rules that you use when naming tables. To save the form later under a different name, choose Save As in the File menu.

The Main/Subform FormWizard Form

A *main/subform form* is a form that combines two tables or queries. One of these tables or queries is the main part of the form and the second table or query is the subform portion of the form although the two parts do not look any different on the completed form. Usually you have a link that connects the items from the main form to the subform.

When you create this type of FormWizard form, the table or query you select when you create the form is the table or query used for the main form. Once you select Main/Subform from the Microsoft Access Wizard dialog box, you must select the table or query you want the form to use as the subform. Select one of the listed tables and queries, and then select Next.

Now, Access needs to know which of the fields from the main table or query you want to use for the main form. Just as you selected fields for single-column and table forms, you select the fields you want the main form to use. After selecting the fields and Next, select the fields from the second table or query that will appear on the subform. You do not have to include the field that the two tables share. After following the same steps to add the fields you want the form to use, select Next.

The next step tells the FormWizard how the data in the main form and the subform are related. Usually, the two tables or queries each have a field with the same type of data. For example, if you are creating a form that combines your Client and Project tables, use the Client Id field to select which records from the Project table appear in the subform when a record with the matching value in the Client Id field appears in the main form.

If you have created a relationship between the main and the subform table or query, you do not have to tell the FormWizard how to relate the tables or queries because the FormWizard takes this information directly from the relationship you have created before. You only need to tell the FormWizard how to connect the tables or queries when you are creating a form with two tables or queries that are not related. To create this link, select the field from the main form's table or query in the first column that matches the values in the field you select from the subform's table or query you select in the second column. Select Next to continue.

The next step is to select the look for the form. You can choose from the same five predefined looks available for the single-column or tabular FormWizard forms, as shown in Figure 8-3. The look decides the style for both the main form and the subform. Once one of the styles is selected, you can select Next.

Finally, enter the title for the form in the Form Title text box. The title is the title that appears above the main form. After entering the title, select Open to open a main/subform FormWizard form. As the FormWizard creates the form, Access will prompt you about naming the subform. When prompted about saving the file, select OK, type a name for the file, and select OK again. Figure 8-8 shows this type of form created for the Client and Project tables. The table displays the selected information from the Client table at the top and shows the selected fields from the Project table below it. Since the two tables are related by their client identification numbers, the table only shows the projects that apply to the client shown on top. The buttons that move you from record to record

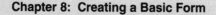 Main/subform FormWizard form

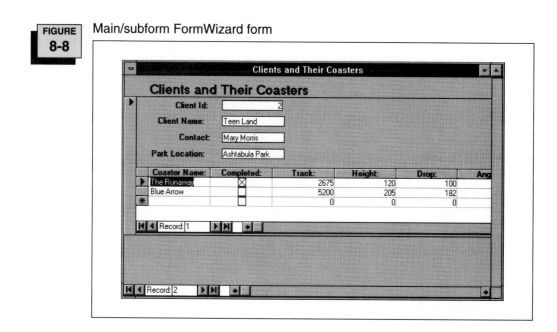

for the Client table are different than the ones that move you between records for the Project table.

Once you create the form and display the table using the form, save the form by choosing Save in the File menu. Access also prompts you to save a form when you try closing the window containing the form. When you save the form, type a name for the form following the same rules you use for naming tables. If you later want to save the form with a different name, choose Save As in the File menu.

Tip When you save a form that is a subform to another form, indicate that in the name of the subform. For example, if you name the main form Clients and Their Coasters, name the subform Subform of Clients and Their Coasters.

Using the Form

Whether you've created your form with or without FormWizard, select the Open button to begin using the form. Using the form is just like using the datasheet for the table or query, in that you use the buttons at the bottom of the window to move between records or to move to the first or last one. You can also enter a number after Record to move to that record. The graph forms you create with FormWizards behave differently as described previously in "The Graph FormWizard Form" section. When you use a main/subform FormWizard form, you can edit the data from either table or query that appears on the form.

Forms have the ability to pick up the features of the table from which the data in the form originates. For example, when you use the Employee data form created for the Employee table of the COASTER database, the entries in the Last Name, First Name, and Middle Initial fields appear in uppercase even if you type them in lowercase. This is due to the fact that the three fields have a Format property of >.

As you learned in Chapter 3, there are many variations for the data types and properties that you can use for your data. The current setting for each of these at the time that your form is created determines exactly how your data looks on the form. Once created, the form continues to have the properties it picked up from the table or query. Later, you can change the properties of the table or query without changing the properties of the form, although you must change the properties of the form yourself; Access does not make this change for you. Also, any Validation Rule entered in the table affects the data that a user can input with the form. The data must pass validation rules or the Validation Text will display.

When you add a field to a table or query, the new field is not added to the forms that otherwise include all the fields of the table or query.

Renaming a Form

You can rename forms just as you can any other objects in the database. If you use the default name for forms, rename them as you add more so the forms have better descriptive names. To rename a form, select the form from the Database window and choose Rename from the File menu. In the Form Name text box, type the new name you want for the form and select OK. Before you rename a form, close any window in which the form or its design appears.

Looking at the Form's Design

Even if you use FormWizards to create forms, usually you will change the form's design somewhat. Working with a form design lets you adjust the contents, size, and position of everything that appears in the form. You can adjust form design and add additional features that do not appear in a form created with FormWizards. You can also display an empty form design and add everything you want the form to contain one piece at a time. Each small piece of a form or report is called a *control*. Controls include a field's data, text, pictures, and calculations.

The steps for looking at a form design of an existing form differ from the steps you take to look at a new form. To look at an existing form design, select the form you want in the Database window and then select the Design button. From the window displaying the form, click the Design toolbar button or choose Form Design in the View menu. Figure 8-9 shows the form design for the Employee Data form created for the Employee table of the COASTER database using a single-column FormWizards form.

FIGURE 8-9   Employee Data form's design

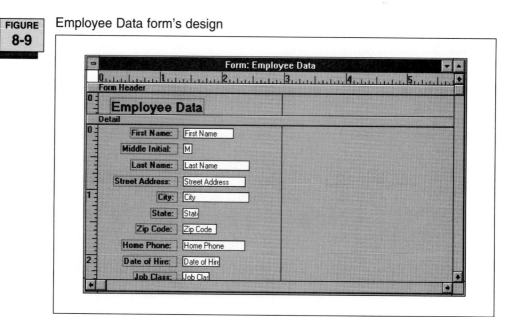

To look at the form design of a new form, you tell Access you want to create a form just as you did for a FormWizards form. Click the Form button in the Database window or choose Forms from the View menu, and then click the New button in the Database Window or choose New from the File menu and then Form. You can also create a form by clicking the New Form button on the toolbar. Next, select the table or query from the Select a Table/Query drop-down list box to use for the form. Finally, select the Blank Form button. Selecting the Blank Form button opens the form design screen with an empty form that you can fill as you want. Figure 8-10 shows an empty form design screen.

You can have several extra windows open while you design forms that make creating and modifying forms easier. One of these is the Toolbox window shown in Figure 8-10 that includes the arrow at the top of it. You can display this window by choosing Toolbox from the View menu. Later you will learn about other windows such as the Field List window, which lets you list the fields you can add to the form. Chapter 10 discusses the Palette window and the Properties window, which allow you to change the colors and different features of the form's controls.

FIGURE 8-10

Form design of a blank form

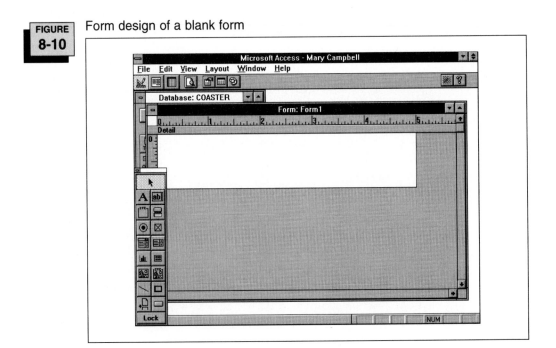

The rest of this chapter focuses on basic form design features. These include changing the size of the form, moving and sizing the controls you place on the form design, and adding fields to the form.

Whenever you choose to, save the form using the same commands you use to save when creating FormWizards forms. Choose Save in the File menu to save the form. Access also asks if you want to save a form when you try closing the window containing the form. When you save the form, you can type a name for the form following the same rules for naming tables. If you later want to save the form with a different name, save by choosing Save As in the File menu.

When you want to see the form you are designing, choose Form from the View menu. You can also click the Form button, which is the second button in the toolbar.

Moving and Sizing Controls

Most of the controls you place on a form can be moved and sized to improve the form's appearance. Before you move or size a form, you must select it. Since you usually want to move or size more than one control at a time, you'll learn here how to select groups of controls as well as any single control.

Selecting a single control is as simple as clicking it. As you select controls, the selected controls are marked with handles. These handles show which controls you have selected. When you click a control for a field, you are often selecting the label of the field name as well. For example, when you click the Last Name field, shown in Figure 8-9, you are selecting both the box containing the field and the adjoining text.

When you want to select more than one control, select the first control you want and then hold down the SHIFT key while you continue clicking the other controls you want to select. Another option for selecting a group of controls is to draw a box on the form design that selects every control included in the box. To draw this box, click an empty area of the form design near the controls you want to select and drag the mouse so the box you are drawing contains the controls you want to select. The box only appears while you are drawing it, so as soon as you release the mouse the box disappears as Access selects all of the controls that appeared in the box.

Tip   The style you select with FormWizards often adds extra controls that you may not initially consider when you want to move fields and field names. For example, the Shadowed style adds a grayed box slightly to the right and below the box containing the field. The Boxed style adds an extra box around the field name and field. When you move the field name and field, you will want to include these additional controls.

Once you have selected the controls you want to move, all you have to do is drag the controls to a new position. Move the pointer to one of the selected controls so the pointer looks like a flat hand. When you drag this hand from one position to another, all of the selected controls are moved with it.

You can also move a part of a control that includes more than one part, such as moving the field name (just the field name) from its position above the field it describes. To move just part of the selected control, move the pointer to the upper-left corner of the part of the control you wish to move so that the pointer looks like a hand holding up one finger. Drag the pointer to a new position and the part of the control is moved to that new location. If you have multiple controls selected, just the part of the control you are pointing to moves.

You can size selected controls just as easily. First, move the pointer so the pointer looks like a double-headed arrow. Drag the pointer to where you want the new corner of the control to be. Since the opposite corner remains in place, the selected control is resized to fit the rectangle set by the two corners. If you have multiple controls selected, resizing one of them only affects the size of the control you are pointing to. Changing the size of a control containing text does not change the size of the text but only the size of the area that may contain text.

Figure 8-11 shows a single-column form for the Employee Data table created with the FormWizard after moving and sizing some of the fields. In this form, the fields have been dragged to new positions and some of the boxes have been enlarged. This form also has been renamed to Modified Employee Data using the Save As command in the File menu.

Changing the Form's Area

A form has a default size but its size is only a starting point for the amount of space the form occupies. You can change the size of the form

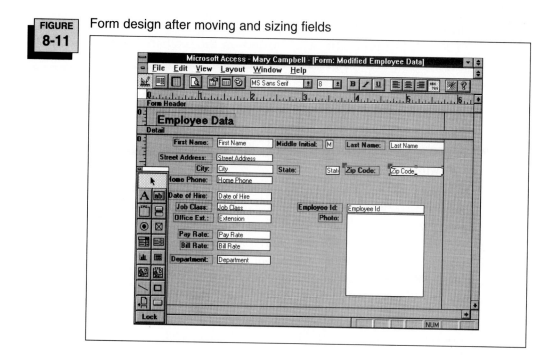

FIGURE 8-11

Form design after moving and sizing fields

when you need to put more or less information on the form. A form initially occupies a small part of the window so you may want to enlarge the form as you put more information on it. You can resize a form by moving to the form's boundary. Notice that the pointer changes to a double-headed arrow. When you drag the mouse to a new location, the edge of the boundary moves with the mouse but the opposite boundary remains stationary—so the form expands.

Adding Fields to a Form

When you create a form from scratch, you add fields from the table or query. You can add any fields from the selected table or query. You also need to add fields as part of a form's design when you modify existing forms after adding fields to the table or query that the form uses.

To add a field, get the list of fields from the table or query that you can add to the form. This Field List window is added by clicking the Field List button in the toolbar or by choosing Field List in the View menu. The Field List button is the sixth button on the toolbar. When you add the Ficld List window to the desktop, it looks like Figure 8-12. The primary key field appears in boldface. From this window, select the field or fields you want to add to the form. You can select one field by clicking it or pressing the arrow keys. You can select more than one field from the list simultaneously by holding down CTRL while you click the additional fields. A quick method of selecting all the fields is to double-click the Field List window title bar.

When you have selected the fields you want to add to the form, drag one of the selected fields from the Field List window to where you want the fields to start. The field names are added to the left of the fields. You can repeat the field selection and addition to the form as many times as you want so you are not adding all the fields you want the form to use at once. When the fields are added to the form, you have the same sizing and moving capabilities you learned about earlier.

When finished adding fields, clear this Field List window. Do this by double-clicking its control box, pressing ALT-F4 when the window is active (with the default colors the title bar is blue), choosing Field List in the

FIGURE 8-12

Form design that includes form and page headers and footers

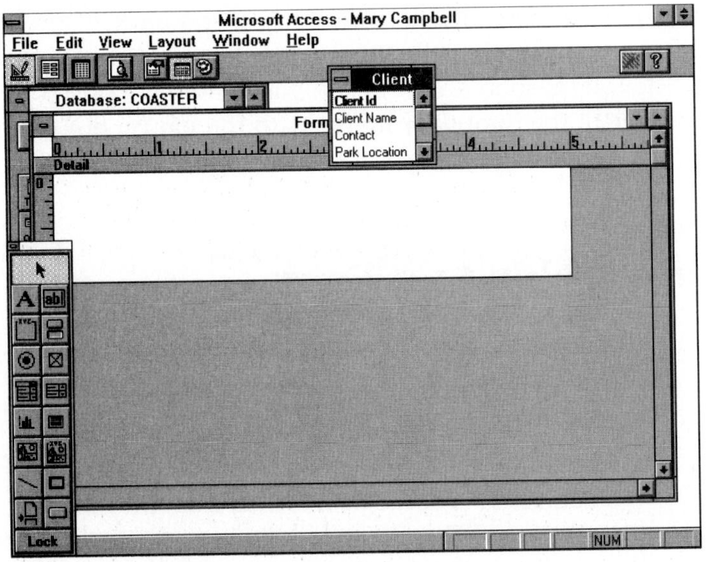

View menu, or clicking the Field List button in the toolbar again. When you add a field using the Field List window, the field appears as a text box of a default size. For some field types, you can create other types of controls that are better suited to making entries in the form. For example, Chapter 11 discusses other controls such as using check boxes for Yes/No fields, option buttons for fields that have few possible entries, and list boxes to choose from a more extensive list.

Deleting Fields from a Form

Besides adding fields that you need to include you may have some on the form that you want to remove. For example, if modifying a form created with FormWizards that includes all of the fields, you may want to remove some of them. You remove a field by pointing to the field and pressing DEL or choosing Delete from the Edit menu. Both the field name and the field are removed. You can also point to just the field name when you do this to delete the field name without deleting the field. This is helpful when you want to show a field without its field name or you want to create a separate label that identifies the field's contents.

Tools for Aiding Design

The form design window has several tools that make creating a form easier. One of these is the ruler that measures the distance from the top and left corner of the ruler. The other is a grid, which is an organized layout of dots. Use the ruler and grid to make placing or sizing the controls you add to the form easier. A third method of quickly sizing controls is using the menu to align controls relative to one another.

If you do not find the ruler helpful, remove it so you have more room for the form design. To remove the ruler, choose Ruler from the View menu. If you want to add the ruler back, choose Ruler from the View menu again. This command is a toggle switch that turns on and off the display of the ruler.

Another command that operates as a toggle is the grid. You may have noticed that when you move and size controls on the form, the control hops from one location to another as you slowly drag the control. The form has a grid pattern; every time you move or size a control, Access hops to the nearest grid point. You can see this grid by choosing Grid from the View menu. When you choose the command again, the grid disappears. Displaying the grid does not affect the form since the grid only appears when you are working on a form's design.

The controls hop to the nearest grid point because the Snap to Grid command in the Layout menu is chosen. If you turn off Snap to Grid (removing the check mark next to Snap to Grid), the controls are then placed exactly where you drag them. This command is also a toggle, so when you choose it again, the check mark is added again and the controls you subsequently move and size hop to the nearest grid point.

You can temporarily ignore the grid when you move or size a control by holding down the CTRL key while dragging the control you are moving or sizing. The grid setting only controls the position of controls at the time you move or size them so when you turn the Snap to Grid on, you will not change the size and position of controls you have sized and moved while the Snap to Grid was off.

Another grid feature that controls the size of controls is the Size to Grid command in the Layout menu. When you choose this command so the command has a check mark next to it, all four corners of every control hop to the nearest grid point. Usually Size to Grid does not have a check mark next to it. Both Size to Grid and Snap to Grid operate whether or not you are displaying the grid in the form design. You can continue using the default grid placement or you can change its size. Chapter 10 teaches how to change the grid's size.

Besides using the grid or the ruler to position controls, use Align in the Layout menu to position controls relative to each other. For example, if you have several fields you want left-aligned, you can tell Access to left-align those controls rather than placing them individually. To align the controls, select the controls you want aligned relative to one another. Next, select Align in the Layout menu and choose how you want the controls aligned. Left moves all of the controls to the left edge of the control furthest to the left. Right moves all of the controls to the right edge of the control furthest to the right. Top moves all of the controls up to the top edge of the highest control. To Grid moves all of the controls to start at the closest grid point.

Changing the Tab Order

When you use a table or query, every time you move from one field to another, you are moving to the fields in the order they appear as well as the order they are in the table or query. In a form, you might put the fields in a different order but you will still want to move through them in the order they appear. To change the order of fields you move to as you move through the form, you change the tab order. Initially, a form's tab order is the same order in which you add the fields to the form. To change a form's tab order, select Ta_b_ Order from the _E_dit menu. This opens the Tab Order dialog box. In this dialog box, the fields are shown in the order that you will move between the fields in the form.

If a field uses a form header or form footer, you can also set the tab orders for those sections of a form by first selecting the Form _H_eader or Form _F_ooter radio buttons. To rearrange the fields, point to the bar to the left of the first field you want to move and drag the mouse down to cover the fields you want to move. Next, click one of these selected fields and drag the fields up and down in the list to where you want the fields placed. As you drag the mouse this time, Access draws a line indicating where the selected fields will be in the tab order. Repeat moving fields in the tab order until the fields are in the order you want.

You can select the _A_uto Order button as a shortcut. When you select this button, Access reorders the fields in the form to match the order in which they appear on the form design. The new order after selecting the _A_uto Order button is left to right and top to bottom.

Changing the Text of a Field Name Label

Sometimes the labels that Access adds to a field name may be exactly what you want—but when they're not you can change the text that appears in this label. Once you have selected the field name label control, changing the text is easy since you just click at the point in the label where you want to add the insertion point just as you do when editing an entry in a table or query. You can modify the field name label just as if you are making an entry. Continue to edit the label and then press ENTER or click another part of the form design to finish the changes. Later in Chapter 10, when you learn how to add other types of label controls to a form, you can modify the text in these controls the same way.

Adding Form Headers and Footers

If you look at the form designs of the forms you created with FormWizards, you will notice that the title you have provided for your form appears in a section called Form Header. A form that has a Form Header section also has a Form Footer section. The Form Footer section appears at the bottom of every form. You can use these two sections to include a title or any other information you want. These two sections are added by choosing Form Hdr/Ftr in the Layout menu. As you learn to add controls and change properties of forms, keep in mind that you can also add controls and change properties of the controls in the Form Header and Form Footer sections.

Forms can also have a page header and page footer, which you will learn about in Chapter 9 when you create reports. These sections can have controls added as you have learned how to do in this chapter and in the subsequent ones. A Page Header section and Page Footer section only appear when you print the form. You will not see these sections when you look at the form in a window. These two sections can be added by choosing Page Hdr/Ftr in the Layout menu. Figure 8-13 shows a form design that includes Page Header and Footer and Form Header and Footer sections. This command is a toggle so selecting it again removes these sections from the form. When you print a form, even though the printed copy includes the Page Header and Page Footer sections, you will notice that it does not include the Form Header and Form Footer sections. The Form Header and Form Footer sections only appear when you look at a form in a window.

Printing a Form

Besides using the form to input new data and display data, use the forms you create to print the information in the table or query. Printing a form is just like printing databases, queries, and, as you will learn in

FIGURE
8-13

Field List added to a form design

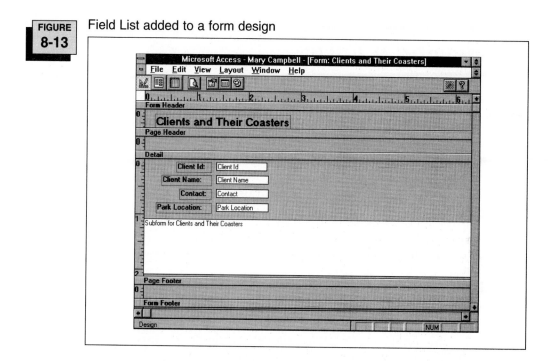

Chapter 9, printing reports. Printing a form has no new options over printing tables and queries.

To print a form, either select the form from the Database window or select a window displaying the form or the form's design. Next, choose Print from the File menu. From the Print dialog box, you have the same choices for the print range, print quality, printing to a file, number of copies, collating copies, and printer setup that you have for printing tables and queries. When you select OK to print the form, Access prints the form for all of the records in the table or query. The following shows a sample printout of one of these forms for the first example. In Chapter 10, you will learn how you can add a page break at the end of the detail band so the form skips between pages.

Previewing a Form

You can also preview how the printed copy will appear. Use the Print Preview command in the File menu to see a screen showing how the form will print before you print it. While previewing the printed form, you can change the setup. When you see that the format of the printout is what you want, select the Print button to print the form. Usually, if you see something you do not want in the form, you will change the form's design rather than the print settings you use to print the form.

Quick Reference

To Use FormWizards to Create a Form   Click the New button at the top of the Database window while displaying forms, click the New Form button on the toolbar while looking at a table or query, or choose New from the File menu and then Form. Select a table or query the form uses from the Select a Table/Query drop-down list box. Select the FormWizards button. Next select the type of FormWizard form you want to create. For each of the subsequent dialog boxes, select the information it requests such as the fields the form includes, its style, and its title. When you select the Open button from the final dialog box, the form opens.

To Create a Form Starting with an Empty Design   Click the New button at the top of the Database window while displaying forms, click the New Form button on the toolbar while looking at a table or query, or choose New from the File menu and then Form. Select a table or query the form uses from the Select a Table/Query drop-down list box. Select the Blank Form button. In the form design window, add the controls you want to appear in the form. You can use the toolbar, toolbox, and other features that make designing forms easier. When you want to see the data displayed with a form view, you can choose Form from the View menu or click the View menu.

To Rename a Form   Select the form that you want to rename from the Database window. Choose Rename from the File menu. Type the new name for the form and select OK.

To Display a Form's Design   Select the form in the Database window. Click the Design button in the top of the Database window. If you already have the form design displayed, click the Design button in the toolbar or choose Form Design from the View menu.

To Move a Control on a Form   Click the control in the form design you want to move. Point to the control so the mouse pointer looks like a hand. Drag the control to a new position. You can tell when the control has another control attached to it (such as a field and its field name), because the pointer looks like a hand holding up one finger. At this point you can move one without moving the other by simply dragging it to a new location.

To Size a Control on a Form   Click the control in the form design you want to resize. Point to one of the handles on the control so the pointer looks like a double-headed arrow. Drag the handle to a new location.

To Add a Field to a Form   With the Field List showing in the form design, select the fields you wish to add from the Field List window. Drag one of these fields to where you want the fields to appear on the form design.

To Delete a Control on a Form   Click the control in the form design you want to remove, and then press DEL or choose Delete from the Edit menu.

To Change the Text of a Field Name of a Control on a Form
Click the field name control in the form design. Click again where you want the insertion point added. Make the changes to the text and press ENTER or select another control to finish the editing.

To Print a Form   Display the form or form design, or select the form name in the Database window. Choose Print from the File menu and make changes to the Print dialog box if you wish. Select OK to print the form. You can also preview your form by clicking the Preview button in the toolbar or by choosing Print Preview from the File menu.

CHAPTER

Creating a Basic Report

A *reports a description of how you want the data in a table or query* presented. Unlike forms, reports are meant to be printed rather than displayed onscreen. You can design a report by yourself or ask Microsoft Access ReportWizards to help you.

Re ports let you present information in a format that is easier to understand than a table or query. Also, reports let you select the data you want to present. You can customize your reports to produce exactly the output you want.

Note If you want a customized presentation to display your records on the screen, create a form, not a report.

When you create reports in a database, you will have multiple reports to match the multiple information requests the database supplies. The reports you create with Access let you select which data from a table or query you present and how this information is presented. For example, for a mailing list of clients, you print just the customer name and address. If you are preparing billing information, the report will also include the items the clients have ordered or services rendered. A report does not need to show every field within a table.

This chapter gives you the basics of creating a report. Most of the reports you will learn about and see here are created with ReportWizards. You will also learn how to name, save, and print the reports you create. Since forms and reports share many design and creation features, you will perform the same steps in designing a report that you used to design a form in Chapter 8.

Creating a Report with ReportWizards

ReportWizards offer the easiest and quickest methods for creating a new report. ReportWizards create a report out of a table or query by prompting you with a few questions, and basing the report on the answers you give. Access has three types of reports that you can create with ReportWizards—single-column, groups/totals, and mailing label. You'll learn about all three in this chapter. Figure 9-1 provides a sample of the three ReportWizard types. If none of the ReportWizard options meet your exact needs you can still save time by creating a report with ReportWizards then changing the design to better meet your requirements.

To create a report with ReportWizards, tell Access you want to create a report. Click the New button at the top of the Database window when you are displaying reports or choose New from the File menu and then Report. You also can create a report by clicking the New Report button on the toolbar, as shown here:

The advantage of choosing New from the File menu and then Report or clicking the New Report button on the toolbar is that you can do this when you are not displaying reports in the Database window. When you

FIGURE
9-1

Three report types offered by Access ReportWizards

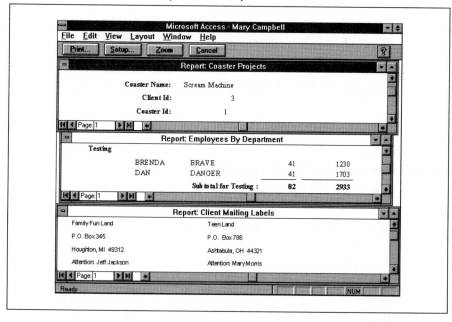

start to create a new report, Access displays the New Report dialog box shown here:

The Select A Table/Query drop-down list box tells Access which table or query you want to pull data from for the report you are creating. When you create a report with a table or query displayed in a window or selected in the Database window, the table name or query is already supplied. After selecting the table or query name, select the ReportWizards or Blank Report button to create the report. Selecting ReportWizards creates the report using one of the three ReportWizard types. Later in this chapter you'll see how to create a report with the Blank Report button to create an empty report that you can fill as you want.

Once you select the ReportWizards button, choose which ReportWizard report you want to create. As you saw in Figure 9-1, Access has three types—single-column, groups/totals, and mailing label. Each of these report types gives you a different basic style of report, which you can embellish as you like. When you select which ReportWizard you want to use, the ReportWizard asks questions. Your answers to those questions determine the information that appears in the report. Each ReportWizard asks a different set of questions.

Single-Column ReportWizard Reports

A *single-column report* puts all of the fields you select into a single-column with their field names to the left. This type of report lets you select a style for how the field names and the contents are displayed as well as the title that appears at the beginning of the report.

From the first dialog box, shown here, select the fields you want to appear in the report:

Add the fields to the report in the order you want them to appear. When you select the field in the Available Fields list box and select the > button, the field is added to the report. Since the field is added to the report's field order where the highlight appears in the Field Order on Report list box, you can insert a field into the report's order by highlighting the field where you want the next selected field placed in the Field Order on Report list box. Select the >> button to add all of the fields.

You also can select a field in the Field Order on Report list box and choose the < button to remove the field from the report. The << button removes all fields from the Field Order on Report list box. The fields that are included in the report are indicated in the Available Fields list box with a > character. Once the fields you want the report to use appear in the order you want, select the Next button.

Now decide how the records in the table or query will be sorted for the report. The records from the table or query can be arranged for this report using the values of zero to three fields. From the dialog box, select the fields that you want to sort the records by. The first field you select is the field that controls all of the table's or query's records. The second field you select controls only the order of records when a group of records has the same value for the first field. The third field you select only controls the order of the records of the group of records with the same value for both the first and second fields. You do not have to select any fields in cases in which you want the report to present the information in the order the data appears on the table or query. When the fields you want the records sorted by are selected, select the Next button.

Once you have chosen how you want to sort the records for the report, select the look for the report. A single-column ReportWizard report has three predefined looks—Executive style, Presentation style, and Ledger style—as shown in Figure 9-2. The look decides the appearance of the field names and the field contents in the report. Select one of the styles and choose Next.

All Access needs to complete the report is the title. The title appears at the beginning of the report and is separate from the report's name. Type any text you feel is appropriate. If you do not type a title, the Report Header section that is part of the report's design will only contain the current date.

Once you've entered a title, select Print Preview to display the report in the Print Preview window. Figure 9-3 shows a single-column ReportWizard report that includes all of the fields in the Project table (except for Picture and Features) in a different order than they appear in the table.

FIGURE 9-2

Different styles for ReportWizard reports

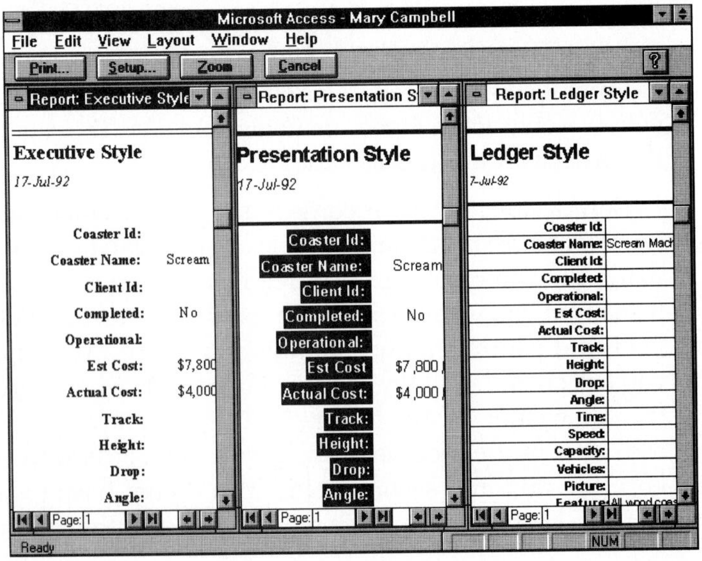

FIGURE 9-3 Single-column ReportWizard report

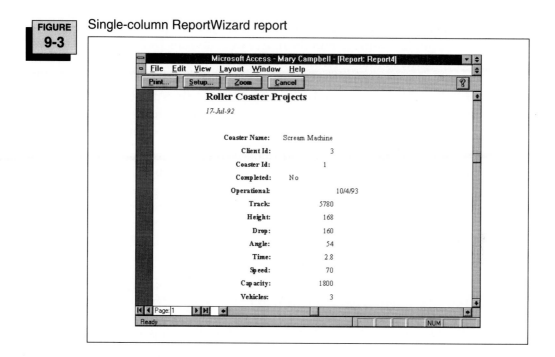

You can also select the Design button to display the report's design that you have created through the ReportWizard. If you do this, note how Access has added the date to the report. When you move to the bottom of the page or print out the report, notice how the bottom of every page contains the page number. The date and page numbers are added as expressions to the report's design. You will learn more about expressions in Chapter 12.

Tip Use the title to add a heading to the report so the report's user knows the purpose of the report.

Groups/Totals ReportWizard Reports

A *groups/totals report* puts the fields you select into a row and groups the records according to the value of a field in the table or query. You can group the records by as many as three different fields. Grouping fields lets you organize your data into manageable groups. As an example, suppose you want a report of all city mayors for the United States and you want to be able to find the mayor by searching by location. You group the records for each mayor first by state, then by county, and finally by city. When you want to find the mayor of a particular city, you can look first for the state, then for the county, and then for the city. You can select a style for how the field names and the contents are displayed as well as how the title appears at the beginning of the report.

Just like the single-column ReportWizard report, you now select the fields that will appear in the report. Add the fields to the report in the order you want them to appear. When you select the field in the Available Fields list box and select the > button, the field is added to the report. By changing where the highlight appears in the Field Order on Report list box, you can select where a field is added to the report's field order. Select the >> button to add all of the fields.

You can also select a field in the Field Order on Report list box and the < button to remove the field from the report. The << button removes all fields from the Field Order on Report list box. The fields that are included in the report are indicated in the Available Fields list box with a > character. Once the fields you want the report to use appear in the order you want, select the Next button.

Now select how the records in the table or query will be grouped for the report. The groups are divisions within a report that includes all records that have a value for a specific field. You can also have groups within groups. Within each primary group, the records can be further divided into smaller groups according to the value of a second field. You can take this one step further by dividing each secondary group into smaller groups according to the value of a third field. (Remember the example of the city mayors report.)

From the dialog box, select the fields in the order you want the groups created. The first field you select is the field that divides all of the records in the table or query. Within each primary group, the records are grouped again by the second field you select. If you also have a third field selected, the secondary groups you have under the first one is divided into smaller groups that are divided according to the values of the third field. You do not have to select any fields if you do not want the records divided into groups. When you want a report in a table format but you do not want group divisions, you will not select fields.

When the fields you want the records grouped by are selected, select the Next button. As an example, you can use groups to create the report shown in Figure 9-4. In this report, Date is selected as the field for the first group and Project Number is selected as the field for the second group. The individual records are grouped by the ones that have the same date and project ID.

Next, decide for the fields just selected how you will divide each field's values into groups. You have several choices depending on the field's data type. With character values, you can divide the data according to the entire entry in the field, the first character, the first two characters, the first three characters, the first four characters, or the first five characters.

For example, when you look at a dictionary, notice that all of the entries are grouped by the first letter. When you divide addresses by a state field, you will select Normal to use the full field so your North Dakota addresses are not intermingled with the ones from North Carolina. Numbers can be grouped by their unique values or into groups of tens, hundreds, and so

FIGURE 9-4   Report containing primary and secondary groups

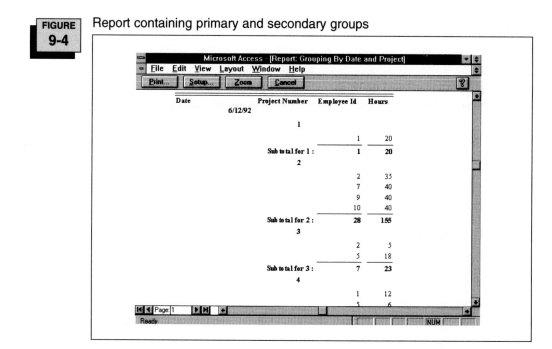

on. Dates can be grouped by years, quarters, months, and so on for days down to individual days. Time values can be grouped by hours or minutes.

The default for how to group the records is Normal, which means that whenever the value for that group field changes, the report starts another group. To choose how the values of a field are divided into groups, select the field name in the Available Fields list box. Select how you want the field values combined into groups from one of the listed choices in the Records Will Be Grouped By list box.

Next, select how the records in the table or query are sorted for the report. Access organizes the records to appear in the report first by the groups the report uses and then by any fields you select to further sort the records. The fields you select to sort by only sort the records within the smallest groups of the report. For the report shown in Figure 9-4, the records are first organized by date and then by project number for the groups the report creates; then, within the smaller groups, the records are listed in order of the Employee ID field.

From the dialog box, select the fields to sort the records by. Selecting fields for sorting is just like selecting fields to appear in the report. Only the fields not used to group the records in the report are listed. You can select multiple fields, and the records within each group are organized by the value of the fields in the order you select them. You do not have to use both sorting and grouping in a report since you only select the report features you want to include. When you have selected the fields you want to additionally sort, select the Next button.

Once you have chosen how you want to sort the records for the report, select the look for the report. Like a single-column ReportWizard report, a groups/totals report has three predefined looks—Executive style, Presentation style, and Ledger style—shown in Figure 9-2. The primary difference in appearance between a groups/totals report and a single-column report is that the field is below the field name in a groups/totals report and to the right of the field name in a single-column report. The look decides the style of the box for each of the fields in the report and also determines where the lines are added. Choose one of the styles and select Next.

Now add the report's title. The title appears at the beginning of the report, and it is separate from the report's name. Type any text you feel is appropriate. If you do not add a title, the report's Report Header section, which is the part of the report design where a report's title appears, will only contain a date.

At this point, select whether you want to squeeze the fields onto one page. When the Fit All Fields on One Page check box is selected, the fields in the report are truncated if Access needs room to fit all of the fields from one record onto a page. Usually this check box is cleared, which means when you use this ReportWizard report type on a table or query that includes many of the fields, some of the fields appear on separate pages.

Once you've entered the title, select Print Preview to display the report in the Print Preview window. Figure 9-5 shows a groups/totals ReportWizard report created using the Employee table. In this report, records are grouped according to department and sorted according to their job class. Each group is a separate section of the report. Also notice how the job class and extensions are totaled at the bottom of the report. The totals are calculated for each group in the report and then again at the end of the report. Like the single-column report type, this report has expressions for the date and page number added. (Expressions will be covered in Chapter 12.) This ReportWizard design totals all numeric fields. From the last dialog box of the ReportWizard, you can also select the Design button to display the report's design that you have created through the ReportWizard.

Mailing Label ReportWizard Reports

A *mailing label report* fits the fields you select into a rectangle that is designed to print labels. Unlike the other ReportWizard reports, this type of report does not include the field names. The mailing label report is specifically designed to print one of various sizes of labels. This report type also makes it easy to add text such as commas and spaces.

Once you select Mailing Label, you get a different dialog box for adding the fields than you did earlier for adding fields in the other two types of ReportWizards. This dialog box appears:

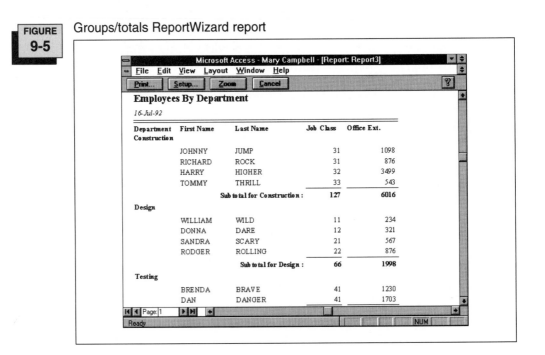

Besides selecting fields and then the → button to add them to the report, you can select which characters you want to add. The dialog box has buttons to add the characters most frequently used in a mailing label. When you click the colon, comma, hyphen, period, slash, or space buttons, these characters are directly added to the current line in the report design. You can also type text into the text box below the field

FIGURE
9-5

Groups/totals ReportWizard report

names and then click the Text → button to add the text you type to the report.

Unlike the other ReportWizard reports, the fields you add do not appear on different lines. The fields appear on the same line until you select the → button because as you add fields, as well as other characters to the report, you are selecting which line they appear in. Select the fields and text you want for each line. When finished with a line, select the → button to advance to the next line.

Another difference between this dialog box and the dialog box for adding fields for the other ReportWizard report types is when you click the < button, Access removes the last field, character, or group of text from the current row on the right side of the dialog box. You cannot insert and remove fields and characters from the middle of a row. When you are adding several fields and characters to a single row, you can shift the added fields and text left and right by clicking the left and right arrows. When you have the fields you want in the report layout on the right side, select the Next button.

Next, select how the records in the table or query are sorted for the report. This organizes the records into the order in which they are printed on the mailing labels. For example, you may want the printed mailing labels sorted by ZIP code. From the dialog box, select the fields to sort the records. The first field you select orders all of the table's or query's records. The second field you select orders records only when a group of records has the same value for the first field. The third field you select only controls the order of the records of the group of records with the same value for both the first and second fields. When you want the mailing labels printed in the order in which they appear on the table or query, you will not select any fields. When the fields you want the records sorted by are selected, select the Next button.

Now, select the size of the labels. The list box includes most available label sizes listed according to their Avery number. If you do not know the Avery label number, look at the Dimensions and Number Across columns to find the label size that matches your labels. Access will handle centering the data on the label. Select one of the label sizes from the list and select Next.

At this point, Access has created the label design for you. Select Print Preview to look at your mailing labels. Figure 9-6 shows the mailing label report created with the Client table. The comma, spaces, and the text

Mailing labels ReportWizard report

"Attention:" are added as part of the report's design. From the same dialog box from which you selected the Print Preview button, you can also select Design to look at the design of the report that Access has created for you.

Saving a ReportWizard Report

When you have finished using and printing the report, you will want to save it. Save the report by choosing Save in the File menu. Access also asks if you want to save a report when you try closing the window containing the report. When you save the report, type a name for the report following the same rules for naming tables. If you later want to save the report with a different name, save the report again by choosing Save As in the File menu. Any report title is separate from the name of the report.

Using the Report

Once you select the Print Preview button when you create a report with a ReportWizard or you display a report created without the ReportWizard, Access generates the report. Access substitutes the fields in the report with the data stored in the table or query.

To use a report you have created with the ReportWizard or to use one of the reports created from scratch, display the report names in the Database window. When you double-click a report name from the list or highlight the report name and press ENTER, the Print Preview window appears with a preview of how the report will appear when printed. Reports, unlike forms, do not show one record at a time. When you leave the report preview, you are returned either to the Database window or the report design screen.

A report picks up the table properties of the table or query the report uses. For example, when you use the Employees By Department report created for the Employee table of the COASTER database, the entries in the Last Name, First Name, and Middle Initial fields appear in uppercase even if you type them in the table in lowercase. This is because the three fields have a Format property of >. In Chapter 11, you will learn about other properties you can use with reports.

As you learned in Chapter 3, you have many variations for the data types and properties for your data. The settings in effect for the data types and properties at the time that your report is created determine exactly how your data looks on the report. Once created, the report keeps the properties it picked up from the table or query. Later, you can change the properties of the table or query without changing the properties of the report. If you want the properties of the report changed, you must do so yourself since Access does not make this change for you.

Printing a Report

The main use of a report is to print it so you have something in your hand that represents the data in your database. Printing a report is just like printing tables, queries, and forms. You have the same options when printing a report that you have when printing forms. Some of the printing options are used more frequently with reports than with forms.

To print a report, either select the Print Preview button when you are creating the report with the ReportWizard or select the report from the Database window. When looking at the report's design, display the report in the Print Preview window by clicking the Preview button in the toolbar or by choosing Print Preview from the File menu. When looking at the report in the Print Preview window, check that the report appears as you want so you do not waste time printing a report destined for the garbage. When the report preview looks satisfactory, select the Print button and OK. The Print dialog box gives you the same choices for the print range, print quality, printing to a file, number of copies, collating copies, and printer setup that you have for printing tables and queries. Later, when you are certain the report already contains what you want, print it by highlighting the report name in the Database window and choosing the Print command in the File menu.

Use the settings in the Print Preview window to change how the report is laid out on the paper. These changes are made by selecting the Setup button or choosing Print Setup from the File menu. You have used some of these options when printing your tables and queries but this dialog box also has other options that you will use most often with reports. Some of these options display when you select the More button to expand the dialog box so it appears as shown in Figure 9-7.

Printing Multiple Columns

The Coaster Projects report shown in Figure 9-1 was created to illustrate the single-column ReportWizard report type; notice that the report has a lot of empty space because the report information takes little space on the page. You can arrange the data of the report into several columns. Your telephone directory is an example of a report that uses multiple columns. If phone books used a single column to list names and numbers, nobody but weight lifters could move them. By using multiple columns, phone books are a more manageable size. Apply this same principle to your reports and display their information in several columns whenever appropriate.

To print your reports in multiple columns, display the setup for printing and select the More button. In the Items Across text box, select

FIGURE 9-7 Print Setup dialog box showing additional printing options

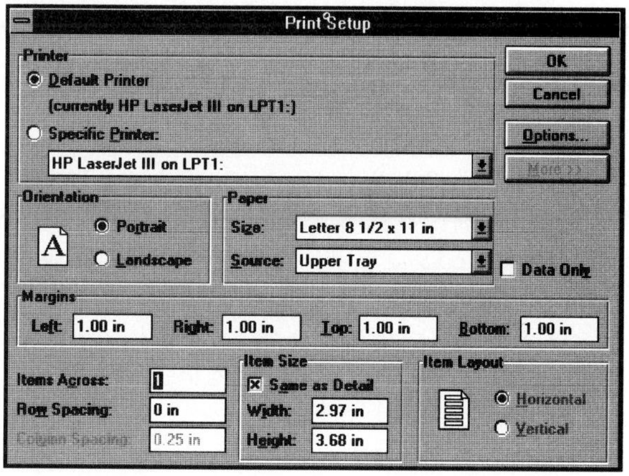

how many columns you want to display the report's information. For example, if you type **2** in this text box, after printing what would otherwise appear solely on the first page, the data that would appear on the second page is printed to the right of the first column of information as shown in Figure 9-8. You can use higher numbers when the columns in the report are narrow. Since the Coaster Projects report uses half of the page, you can fit only two columns on a page.

You can also control the amount of space that appears between the columns. Enter this distance in the Column Spacing text box in inches. When more than one record fits in a column, generally you will add space between the records. This distance between records in the same column is entered in the Row Spacing text box. When you select OK, the report uses the number of columns you select (assuming the columns can fit on the page). Figure 9-9 shows a previewed report where the Coaster Projects report is divided into two columns with 1 inch between columns and rows. While you cannot see the detail of the records, you can see the groups of data that make up each record.

Tip When printing multiple columns or printing a mailing label ReportWizard report, you can select whether the records are added to the report from top to bottom in the first column before going to the second

FIGURE
9-8

Two-column report

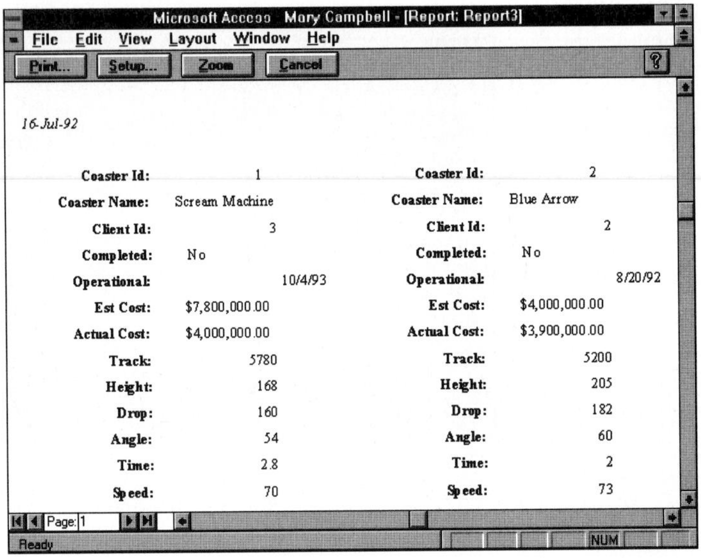

column or whether they are added left to right going across columns. If you select the More button in the Print Setup dialog box when the value in the Items Across text box is more than 1, you can select whether the records are added to the report from top to bottom or left to right by selecting the Horizontal or Vertical button under Item Layout.

Sample Preview Printing

When you have a report for a large table or query, you may not want to use the usual preview to check the report's appearance because it will take Access too long to generate the report. With large reports you have the option of using the sample preview. The sample preview quickly inserts data into the report while ignoring criteria and joins. This feature is useful if you want to check the overall look of the report rather than how specific pieces of data appear in the report.

To display the report using the sample preview instead of the regular preview, choose Sample Preview in the File menu. This displays a Preview

FIGURE 9-9

Preview showing row and column spacing between multiple columns

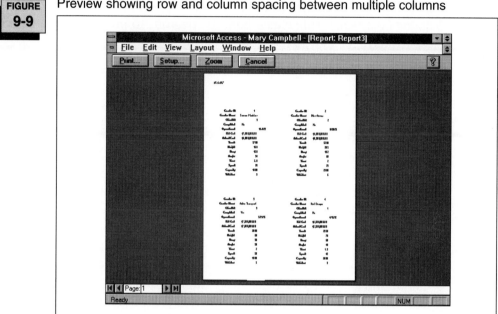

window just like the regular Print Preview window. The difference is that here you may see records that the report otherwise excludes since the sample preview ignores criteria and joins. If you print from the sample preview, the report will contain exactly the data that appears in the Preview window. When finished looking at the sample preview, click the Cancel button or choose Sample Preview in the File menu.

Collating Copies

You can also choose how many copies you want to print of your datasheet, form, or report. When you print multiple copies, Access can either print multiple copies of the first page, then the second, and so on for each page, or Access can print all pages in a report one by one and then print all the pages again for the next copy, and so on until Access has printed the number of copies you have selected. When you print large reports, the collating sequence can be important. Access prints multiple copies of lengthy datasheets, forms, and reports faster when it prints all the copies of the first page, then the second, and so on. Print your reports faster by not collating; clear the Collate Copies check box from the Print dialog box. Select this check box, the default, to print each copy of the report, form, or datasheet separately (but more slowly).

Printing to a File

Another printing feature that you will find more useful for a report is Access's ability to print the report to a file. When you print the report to a file, the file contains the information that Access and Windows will send to the printer. You print to a file for two reasons: to delay printing, if, for example, your computer is not currently connected to a printer or to bring the report into another application.

When you want to print to a file in order to bring the report into another application, change the printer to which you are printing to Generic/Text Only by selecting the Setup button or choosing Print Setup from the File menu, and selecting the Specific Printer radio button and Generic/Text Only from the drop-down list box. Then to print the report to a file, select the Print button or choose Print from the File menu. Select the Print to File check box. When you select OK, you are prompted for a filename. Type the name of the file and select OK. The file will contain exactly the same information that would have been sent to the printer. You do not have to worry about clearing the Print to File check box since Access clears it for you after you have printed to a file.

Printing Only the Data

When you print a report, the report includes all of the information included in the report design. When using a report to print the data for a preprinted form, you will not want to include information such as field names. Omit field names (and other information in a report that is not a field or expression) by selecting the Data Only check box. When you print the report, the field and expression values are the only information that prints. The default is for the Data Only check box to be cleared so all of the report's information is printed.

Renaming a Report

Just like the other objects in the database, you can rename reports. If you use the default name for reports, rename them as you add more so you can rely on descriptive names to know which one you want even when selecting from a long list of report names. To rename a report, select the report from the Database window and choose Rename from the File menu. In the Report Name text box, type the new name you want for the report and select OK. Before you rename a report, close any window the report or its design appears in.

Looking at the Report's Design

While you can continue using ReportWizards to create reports, usually you will want to change the report's design or create your own from scratch. Working with report design lets you adjust the contents, size, and position of everything that appears in the report. You can modify or add additional features that do not appear in the reports you create with the ReportWizard. You can also display an empty report design and put everything you want the report to contain on the report one piece at a time. As with forms, each small piece of a report is called a *control*. Controls include a field's data, text, pictures, and calculations. Many of the features relating to forms that you learned about in Chapter 8 also apply to reports.

The steps for looking at a report design of an existing report differ from those you use to look at a new report. To look at an existing report design, select the report you want in the Database window and then select the Design button. You can also display a report design by double-clicking the report name using the right mouse button. Figure 9-10 shows the report design for the Coaster Projects report created for the Project table using a single-column ReportWizard report.

To look at the report design of a new report, tell Access you want to create a report just like you did for a ReportWizard report. Click the

FIGURE
9-10

Report design of the single-column ReportWizard report

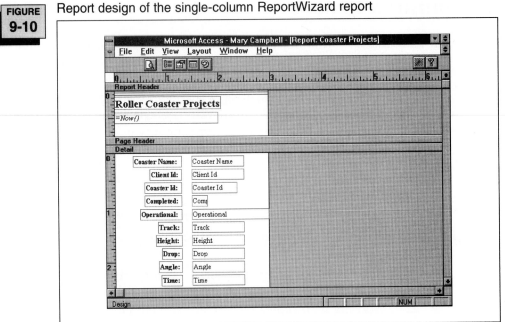

Report button in the Database window or choose Reports from the View menu and then click the New button in the Database window or choose New from the File menu and then Report. You can also create a report by clicking the New Report button on the toolbar. Next, select the table or query from the Select a Table/Query drop-down list box to use for the report. Finally, select the Blank Report button. Selecting the Blank Report button opens the report design screen with an empty report that you can then fill in as you want. Figure 9-11 shows an empty report design screen.

When you look at the report design of some of the reports you create with the ReportWizard, you will notice advanced features that you will learn about in later chapters. For example, the Employees By Department report in Figure 9-5 has a Department Header and Department Footer section. These sections start and end each group of records for the different departments in the report. You will learn about creating these sections and dividing a report's records into groups in Chapter 11. Also, when you look at the Clients Mailing List report created as an example of a mailing list ReportWizard report type, the boxes that contain the

FIGURE
9-11

Empty report design

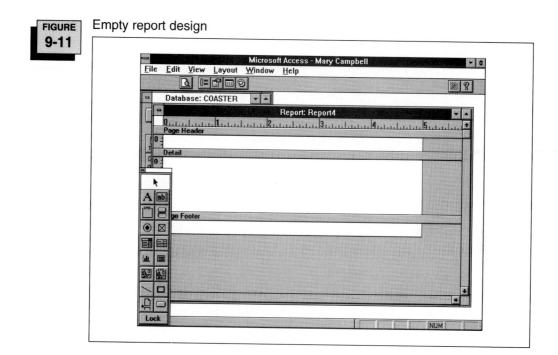

contents of each line in the mailing label do not contain the field names like the boxes that you see in Figure 9-10. Instead these boxes contain expressions. You will learn about expressions in Chapter 12.

Just like designing forms, when you design reports you can have extra windows open that make creating and modifying reports easier. One of these is the Toolbox window shown in Figure 9-11 that includes the arrow at the top of it. For now, remove this window by choosing Toolbox in the View menu. You will use this window in the next chapter to add controls to the report.

Later you will learn about other windows such as the Field List window to list the fields you can add to the report. In Chapter 10, you will learn about the Palette window and the Properties Sheet that you can use to change the colors and different features of the report's controls. When you display these three windows, they remain in the location you put them. You can move these windows around in the Access desktop so they are out of your way when you work on the report design. Also, displaying these windows also displays them for forms and for other database objects that use the windows. For example, if you display the Property for a table design, the Property Sheet is also open when you work on queries, forms, and reports.

The rest of this chapter describes basic report design features. These include moving and sizing the controls you place on the report design, changing the size of the report, and adding fields to the report. You use most of these features with reports exactly the same way you used them when designing forms in Chapter 8.

Save the report using the same commands you use to save ReportWizard reports. Choose Save in the File menu to save the report. Access asks if you want to save a report when you try closing the window containing the report. When you save the report for the first time, type a name for the report following the same rules for naming tables. If you later want to save the report with a different name, save the report again by choosing Save As in the File menu.

When you want to see the report you are designing, choose Print Preview or Sample Preview from the File menu, or click the Preview button. Print the report using the same printing commands and buttons that you use when you print datasheets and forms. When you select Cancel to leave the previewed report, you will be returned to the report design.

Moving and Sizing Controls

You can move and size most of the controls you place on a report to improve the appearance of the report. Before you move or size a control in a report, you must select it. Since you usually want to move or size more than one control at a time, you want to know how to select groups of controls as well as any single control.

Selecting a single control is as simple as clicking it. The selected controls are marked with handles to make selected controls easily seen. When you click a control for a field, you are often selecting the label of the field name as well. For example, when you click the Coaster Name field in Figure 9-10, you are selecting both the box containing the field and the adjoining text. This happens because the field and the field name are part of a *compound control*.

When you want to select more than one control, select the first control you want and then hold down the SHIFT key while you continue clicking the other controls you want to select. Another option for selecting a group of controls is to draw a box on the report design that selects every control included in the box. To draw this box, click an empty area of the report design near the controls you want to select and drag the mouse so the two corners of the box you are drawing form a box that surrounds the controls you want to select. The box only appears while you are drawing it; as soon as you release the mouse, the box disappears as Access selects all of the controls that appeared in the box.

When you want to move the selected group of controls, all you have to do is drag the controls to a new position. Move the pointer to the border of one of the selected controls so the pointer looks like a hand with the fingers extended. When you drag this hand from one position to another, all of the selected controls move to the new location.

You also can move a part of a compound control. For example, you can move a field without moving the field name that belongs to it. To move only part of the compound control, move the pointer to the upper-left corner of the part of the compound control that you wish to move so the pointer looks like a hand holding up one finger. Drag the pointer to a new location, and only the selected part of the compound control moves to the new location.

Note You cannot move parts of multiple controls simultaneously; if you have multiple controls selected when you move part of a compound control, only the part of the one compound control pointed to moves—the other compound controls remain the same.

You can size selected controls just as easily. To size the selected controls, move the pointer to one of the handles around the control so the pointer looks like a double-headed arrow. Drag the pointer to where you want the new corner of the control to be. Since the opposite corner remains in place, the selected control is resized to fit the rectangle set by the two corners. If you have multiple controls selected, resizing one of them only affects the size of the control you are pointing to. Changing the size of a control containing text does not change the size of the text but only the area that may contain text.

Figure 9-12 shows two copies of the same groups/totals report for the Employee table created with the ReportWizard that does not use any groups after moving and sizing some of the fields. The top window shows the preview of the report while the window on the bottom shows the report's design. In this report, fields have been dragged to new positions and some of the boxes have been enlarged or shrunk. (Also, some of the field names have been deleted as described next and the Detail section was expanded as described next.) Chapter 12 tells you how to create expressions so the city, state, and ZIP code are resized to fit the contents of those fields.

Changing the Report's Area A report design starts out at a standard size, which you can change as your needs change. You can alter the size of the report when you need more or less information on the report. A report initially occupies a small part of the window so you may want to enlarge the report as you add information to it.

You can resize a report by moving to the report's boundary. When you do, the pointer changes to a double-headed arrow with a thick line in the

FIGURE 9-12

Report design after moving and sizing fields

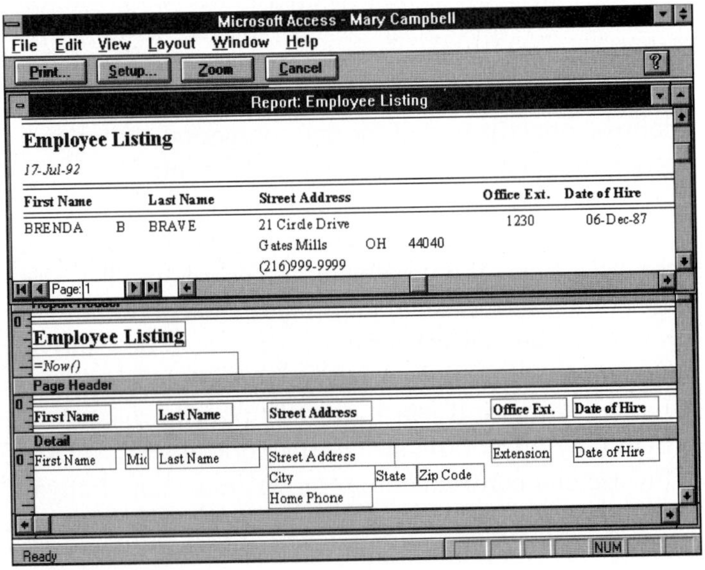

middle. When you drag the mouse to a new location, the report's size widens or contracts so the right edge of the report is where you release the mouse. Access will also enlarge the report's size for you when you move a control outside the report to accommodate the control's new position.

Adding Fields to a Report

When you create a report from scratch, you need to add the fields from the table or query. You also need to add fields when you modify a preexisting report design, for example, to add a field to accommodate data added to the table or query. You can add any fields of the selected table or query. For now, you will learn how to quickly add text boxes that are set to contain the contents of one of the table's or query's fields. Chapter 11 teaches how to add fields to a report in other formats such as check boxes. Chapter 12 shows how to create text boxes that contain expressions that let you add information to a report that is not directly available in one of the fields of the report's table or query.

To add a field, you need the list of fields from the table or query that you can add to the report. Obtain this Field List window by clicking the Field List button in the toolbar or by choosing Field List in the View menu. The Field List button is the fourth button on the toolbar. When you add the Field List window to the desktop, it looks like Figure 9-13. The primary key field appears in boldface.

From this window, select the field or fields you want to add to the report. Select one field by clicking it or pressing the arrow keys. Select more than one field simultaneously by holding down CTRL while you click the additional field names in the list. A quick method of selecting all the fields is to double-click the Field List window title bar. When you have selected the fields you want to add to the report, drag one of the selected fields from the Field List window to where you want the fields to start. The field names are added to the left of the fields. You can repeat the field selection and addition to the report as many times as you want so you are not adding all the fields you want the report to use at once.

Once the fields are added to the report, you have the same sizing and moving capabilities you learned about earlier.

Note   The Property Sheet appears whenever you double-click a control that is not currently selected. You can close the Property Sheet and have it still be available when you are ready to use it.

When finished adding fields, clear this Field List window by double-clicking its control box, pressing ALT-F4 when the window is active (with the default colors the title bar is blue), choosing Field List in the View menu, or clicking the Field List button in the toolbar again. When you add a field using the Field List window, the field appears as a text box of a default size. For some field types, you can create other types of controls that are better suited for the entries in the report. For example, in Chapter 11, you will learn about other controls such as using check boxes for Yes/No fields.

Deleting Fields from a Report

Besides adding fields that you need to include you may have some on the report that you want to remove. You can remove a field by clicking

FIGURE 9-13   Field List added to a report design

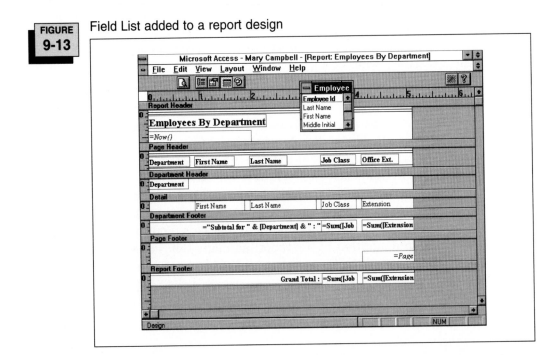

the field and pressing DEL or choosing Delete from the Edit menu. When you do this, both the field name and the field are removed. You can also click the field name when you press DEL or choose Delete from the Edit menu. This deletes just the field name without deleting the field. Do this when you want to show a field without its field name or you want to create a separate label that identifies the field's contents.

Tools for Aiding Design

The report design window has several tools that make creating a report easier. One of these is the ruler, which measures the distance from the top and left corner of the ruler. The other is a grid, which is an organized layout of dots. You can use the ruler and grid to simplify placing or sizing the controls you add to the report. A third method of quickly sizing controls is using the menu to align controls relative to one another.

If you do not find the ruler helpful, remove it to give your report design more room. To remove the ruler, choose Ruler from the View menu. If you want to add the ruler back, choose Ruler from the View menu again. The Ruler command is a toggle switch that turns on and off the display of the ruler.

Another command that operates as a toggle is the grid. You may have noticed that when you move and size controls on the report, the control hops from one location to another as you slowly drag the control. Every time you move or size a control, Access hops to the nearest grid point. Display the grid by choosing Grid from the View menu. When you choose the command again, the grid disappears. Displaying the grid does not affect the report since the grid only appears when you are working on a report's design and never actually prints.

The reason the controls hop to the nearest grid point is because the Snap to Grid command in the Layout menu is on. If you turn off this command by removing the check mark next to Snap to Grid, when you move and size controls they are placed exactly where you drag them. When you choose this command again, the check mark is added and the controls you subsequently move and size again hop to the nearest grid point. You can also temporarily ignore the grid when you move or size a control by holding down the CTRL key while you drag the control you are moving or sizing. The grid setting only controls the position of controls at the time you move or size them so when you turn the Snap to Grid on, you will not change the size and position of controls you have sized and moved while the Snap to Grid was off. Usually Snap to Grid is not turned on—that is, does not have a check mark next to it.

Another grid feature that controls the size of controls is the Size to Grid command in the Layout menu. When you choose this command, all four corners of every selected control hop to the nearest grid point, so the controls may enlarge or shrink depending on the locations of the closest grid points. Both Size to Grid and Snap to Grid operate whether or not you display the grid in the report design. You can continue using the default grid placement or you can change its size. Chapter 11 shows how you change the grid's size.

Besides using the grid or the ruler to position controls, you can use Align in the Layout menu to position controls relative to each other. For example, if you have several fields you want left-aligned, you can tell Access to left-align those controls rather than placing them individually. To align the controls, select the controls you want aligned relative to one another. Next, choose Align in the Layout menu. Choose how you want the controls aligned. Left moves all of the controls to the left edge of the control furthest to the left. Right moves all of the controls to the right edge of the control furthest to the right. Top moves all of the controls up to the top edge of the highest control. Bottom moves all of the controls down to the bottom edge of the lowest control. To Grid moves all of the controls to start at the closest grid point.

Aligning the controls does not necessarily align the contents of the fields you align. By default, Access left-aligns textual data and right-aligns numbers. In Chapter 14, you will learn about changing the alignment of the contents of the fields. Changing the alignment this way changes how the field's contents are aligned within the area you create for a field.

Changing the Text of a Field Name Label

The labels that Access adds to a field name may be exactly what you want on the report, but if they're not you can change the text that appears in this label. Once you have selected the field name label control, changing the text is easy since you just click where you want to add the insertion point in the label just as if you are editing an entry in a table or query. Modify the field name label as if you are making an entry. Continue to edit the label and then press ENTER or click another part of the report design to finish making changes. In Chapter 11, when you learn how to add other types of label controls to a report, you can modify the text in these controls the same way.

Report Headers and Footers

If you look at the report designs of the reports you created with ReportWizards, you will notice that the title you gave your report and the report's date both appear in a section called Report Header. A Report Header section appears at the beginning of the report design. A report that has a Report Header section also has a Report Footer section. The Report Footer section appears at the bottom of every report. When you create a groups/totals report using ReportWizards, this is the section that contains the totals of number-filled fields.

You can use these two sections to include a title or any other information you want. These two sections appear because Report Hdr/Ftr in the Layout menu has a check mark next to it. You can choose Report Hdr/Ftr in the Layout menu to remove this check mark and remove the two sections from the report design.

 Caution Remove these sections only if you do not want them at all since removing these sections permanently destroys the contents of the report design in these sections.

As you learn how to add controls and change properties of reports, keep in mind that you can also add controls and change properties of the controls in the Report Header and Report Footer sections.

Also, most report designs include a Page Header and Page Footer section. The Page Footer section is where Access has added the page number for you when you create a report with the ReportWizard. When you create a groups/totals ReportWizard report, the Page Header section is also the section where the field names are added as column heads. You can add controls to these sections just as you've added controls earlier. Usually your reports will have these sections; they appear whenever Page Hdr/Ftr in the Layout menu has a check mark next to it. If you select this command to remove the check mark, the contents of these two sections are permanently removed. This command is a toggle so selecting it again adds both sections again. Anything previously in those sections is no longer there.

Quick Reference

To Use ReportWizard to Create a Report   Click the New button at the top of the Database window while displaying reports, click the New Report button on the toolbar while looking at a table or query, or choose New from the File menu and then Report. Select a table or query that the report uses from the Select a Table/Query drop-down list box. Select the ReportWizards button. Next select the type of ReportWizard report you want to create. For each of the subsequent dialog boxes, give the information it prompts you for such as the fields the report includes, its style, and its title. When you select the Print Preview button from the final dialog box, the report is created.

To Create a Report Starting with an Empty Design   Click the New button at the top of the Database window while displaying reports, click the New Report button on the toolbar while looking at a table or query, or choose New from the File menu and then Report. Select a table or query the report uses from the Select a Table/Query drop-down list box. Select the Blank Report button. In the Report Design window, add the controls you want to appear in the report. You can use the tool bar, toolbox, and other features that make designing reports easier. When you want to see the data that is used in the report, choose Print Preview from the File menu or click the Preview button.

To Rename a Report   Select the report to rename from the Database window. Choose Rename from the File menu. Type the new name for the report and select OK.

To Display a Report's Design   Select the report in the Database window. Click the Design button in the top of the Database window.

To Move a Control on a Report Click the control in the report design you want to move. Point to the control so the mouse pointer looks like a hand. Drag the control to a new position. When the control is part of a compound control (such as a field and its field name), move one without moving the other by pointing to the control so the pointer looks like a hand holding up one finger before you drag the mouse to a new location.

To Size a Control on a Report Click the control in the report design you want to resize. Point to one of the handles on the control so the pointer looks like a double-headed arrow. Drag the handle to a new location.

To Add a Field to a Report With the Field List showing in the report design, select fields you wish to add from the Field List window. Drag one of these fields to where you want the fields to appear on the report design.

To Delete a Control on a Report Click the control in the report design that you want to remove. Press DEL or choose Delete from the Edit menu.

To Change the Text of a Field Name of a Control on a Report Click the field name control in the report design. Click again where you want the insertion point added. Make the changes to the text and press ENTER or select another control to finish the editing.

To Print a Report

Select the report name in the Database window. Double-click it, press ENTER, click the Preview button, or select Print Preview from the File menu to display the report in a Preview window. Choose Print from the File menu or the Print button. Make any changes to the Print dialog box. Select OK to print the report.

CHAPTER

Customizing Forms with Controls and Other Settings

*T*he forms that you create with Access FormWizards may sometimes meet your exact needs, but usually you will want to make some changes. To change a form, you add or remove controls that are part of its design. The techniques that you use to modify a form by adding controls also work when you want to build a form from a blank form to contain exactly the controls and features that you want.

You can also customize forms by organizing the records in each form in a different sequence. Changing the order of records is referred to as *sorting*. The same steps you use for sorting records can be used to create a filter. A *filter* selects records that meet criteria just like the queries you created earlier in Chapter 6.

A third way of customizing forms is by splitting a form into multiple pages. Using multiple pages in forms that have many controls lets you divide a large form into more manageable pieces.

Adding Controls to Forms

As you used FormWizards in Chapter 9, a control was added to the form for every field that you selected. You can add more of these text box controls if you have forgotten a field or two rather than start over again with a new FormWizards design. You can also add other types of controls to a form.

Access divides controls into three groups: bound controls refer to a field in a database table, unbound controls refer to other objects such as lines or text that you have added, and calculated controls require a computation. Bound controls are like the text boxes for the fields in the forms you created with FormWizards. Unbound controls are like the text that describes the fields you add to a form. Calculated controls are like the date and page number you have added to reports created with ReportWizards.

Types of Controls

The forms you create in Access can include the various controls you are accustomed to seeing as you work with Windows and Windows applications. You can add the same check boxes, option buttons, list boxes, and drop-down list boxes to your forms.

Regardless of the type of control that you add, you will use the toolbox shown in the lower-left corner of Figure 10-1. These different types of controls let you choose from various methods of using the form so you can select the one that best fits your data. These are the controls you can add to a form: labels, text boxes, option groups, toggle buttons, check boxes, combo boxes, list boxes, graphs, subforms, bound and unbound object frames, lines, rectangles, page breaks, and command buttons. The functions each provides are explained in the following sections.

Label   Adds text that does not change from record to record. Labels often identify other controls and can appear in other sections such as the Form Header, Form Footer, Page Header, and Page Footer sections. You add labels to a form when you add most other types of controls.

Text Box   Adds a box containing the value of a field that changes from record to record. This type of text box is a bound control. Text boxes can

FIGURE 10-1

Form design showing the toolbox

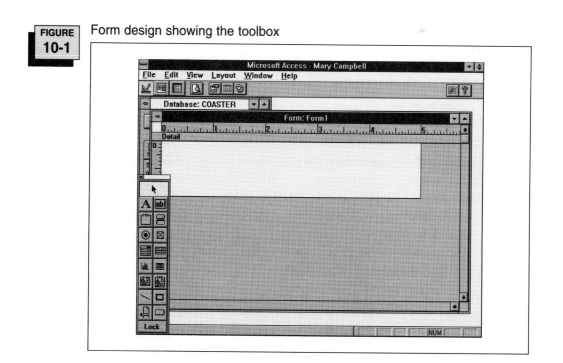

contain other types of entries such as the expressions you will learn about in Chapter 12. A text box that contains an expression is a calculated control.

Option Group   Adds a box that you can subsequently fill with option buttons, check boxes, or toggle buttons. When option buttons, check boxes, or toggle buttons are in an option group, you can select only one from the group.

Toggle Button   Adds a command button that looks recessed when selected and stands out when it is not. The first three buttons in the toolbar are toggle buttons that show whether you are looking at the form's design, form, or datasheet. When toggle buttons are in an option group, you can select only one from the group. When toggle buttons are not in an option group, each option button is separate from the others and functions as a check box.

Option Button   Adds an option button either to an option group or alone. When option buttons are in an option group, you can select only one from the group. When they are not in an option group, each option button is separate from the others and functions as a check box.

Check Box   Adds a box that is selected or cleared with an X. This control is used just like option buttons and toggle buttons. In a form design, check boxes, option buttons, and toggle buttons can be used interchangeably since they are treated the same way by Access. You decide which you want to use based strictly on the appearance of each.

Combo Box   Adds a text box with a down arrow after it. Like other drop-down list boxes, you can select a field's value using a combo box by selecting one of the items in the drop-down list box or typing an entry in the text box.

List Box   Adds a box containing a list of the available choices for a field. Using a list box lets you select the field's value by selecting one of the listed items.

Graph   Adds a graph created with the graph FormWizard. This graph is created with Microsoft's Graph program. When you select a location for the graph, the Graph FormWizard is started. You are prompted for information to put in the graph just as when you create a graph FormWizard form.

Subform   Adds a box that contains a subform or a form created from another table or query. More information about subforms is found in Chapter 13.

Bound and Unbound Object Frames   Adds a box that contains an object such as a picture or an OLE object. You will learn more about adding these types of objects to your forms in Chapter 15.

Line   Adds a line to a form. You will learn more about adding lines in Chapter 14.

Rectangle   Adds a rectangle to a form. You will learn about adding rectangles in Chapter 14.

Page Break   Adds a page break when you have several pages within the form design. A page break control is added on the left edge of the form design. This page break control lets you divide forms into multiple pages. Later you will learn how to set whether the form uses the page break on the screen, only when you print the form, or a combination of both. You can use page breaks in a form to divide up a large area of data that must be separated into smaller chunks.

Command Button   Adds a command button that performs macro instructions when you select them. The macros can be added to a command button to perform steps while working in the form.

   This chapter teaches you how to use most of these controls but not all of them. You will use the subform tool in Chapter 13 to combine multiple tables into a form. You will learn about the controls to add lines and boxes in Chapter 14. In Chapter 15, you will learn about adding pictures and graphs to your forms. In Chapter 16, you will learn about macros.

Adding a Control to a Form Design

In Chapter 9, you learned how to add a control that represents one of the fields from the table or query by dragging the field name from the field list window. Dragging fields from the field list window adds text boxes for the field and the adjoining labels that describe the field's contents. Besides using the field list window to add controls, you can use the Toolbox window. You can also combine the Toolbox window and the field list window to quickly create controls of different types that represent the different fields.

To add a control other than through the field list window, display the toolbox by choosing Toolbox from the View menu. Next, select the type of control you want to create from the toolbox. These controls are identified in Figure 10-2. Then click the part of the form design where you want the control you are adding to begin.

With some types of controls that can be resized, you can set the size of the control when you add the control to the form design, by dragging the mouse from where you want the control to start to where you want

FIGURE 10-2

Tools in the Form Design toolbox

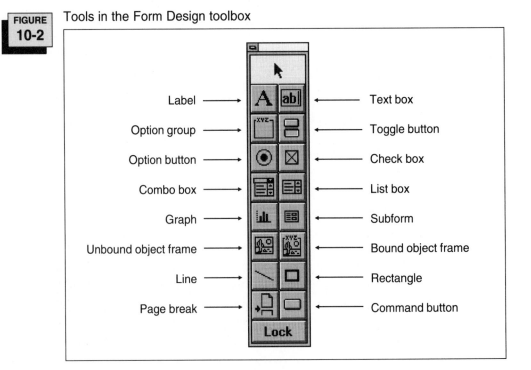

the opposite corner of the control. You may not want to set the size of label controls (including the labels that are part of other controls), since Access adjusts the control's size as you change the text that appears in the control. When you add these controls, Access puts an empty control in the location as shown in Figure 10-3. As soon as you add a label, immediately type the text you want to appear in the label.

When adding an option group, you are creating a group that you will subsequently add to other check box, option button, or toggle button controls. When you add these controls to the option group, the option group will reverse its colors to indicate that the area to which you are pointing is the correct place to add the control to the option group. When you add check boxes, option buttons, or toggle buttons to an option group, don't worry about whether the box will fit the controls you are adding. When you move one of the controls in an option group beyond the option group's boundary, the option group is resized to fit where you have moved its subsidiary controls. When you move an option group, you also move all of the check boxes, option buttons, and toggle buttons in that option group. The controls that you place in an option group are always part of an option group; the controls that are not originally placed in an option group are always separate from the option group.

FIGURE 10-3

New controls added to a form design

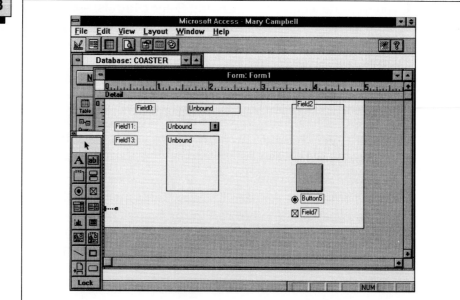

To add several of the same type of controls, such as the controls you put into an option group, Access has a shortcut. Click the Lock button, which is the bottom button in the toolbox. When Lock is on, the same tool in the toolbox remains selected so you can continue adding the same type of control repeatedly. Selecting the Lock button again turns it off so when you add a control to the form, the pointer tool becomes selected.

Controls such as text boxes, option buttons, and check boxes may have text that is inappropriate for your form. When you want to change this text, do so by selecting the control and then clicking the current text where you want the insertion point placed. At this point, you can edit the content, which is part of the control, just as if you are editing an entry on a datasheet.

 Tip   Remember to align your check boxes, option buttons, and toggle buttons that you add to a form. You can align controls you select by choosing Align in the Layout menu and then the direction in which you want the selected objects aligned.

Setting the Field That a Control Represents

Now that you have added a control to a field, tell Access which field you want the control to represent. Some controls, such as labels, do not represent fields since they do not change from record to record. For text boxes, toggle buttons, option buttons, check boxes, option groups, list boxes, combo boxes, and bound object frames, you tell Access which field you want to use with the control. Which field a control represents is one of the control's *properties.*

To set the field for a text box, make the change by editing the text box's contents and changing the Unbound to one of the table or query's field names. You can also change the Control Source property that you use for other types of controls.

For all types of controls that represent a field in the table or query, you can change the control's Control Source property. First display the property sheet by choosing Properties from the View menu or clicking the Properties button in the toolbar. The Properties button looks like this:

When you display the property sheet in the form design, the property sheet window looks like the one shown in Figure 10-4. As you click controls or sections in the form design, the properties and the values of the properties change to match the selected control, section, or form. You may need to move this window if it covers the control you want to select. This window remains displayed in the form design until you choose Properties from the View menu or click the Properties button in the toolbar. The left side of the property sheet window contains the property names appropriate for the selected control or section, and the right side contains the properties' values.

The Control Source property is the property that selects which field a control represents. You can either type the field name or use the DOWN ARROW to select one of the fields from the list.

How you select the field for check boxes, option buttons, and toggle buttons depends on whether these controls are part of an option group. When a check box, option button, or toggle button is not included in an option group, the controls behave as an on/off switch that you usually use for your Yes/No data type fields. Set the field for the control by entering the field name for the Control Source property. For example, the

Property sheet window added to a form design

Completed toggle button in Figure 10-5 has its Control Source property set to Completed so the form shows the button pressed down when the coaster is completed and raised when the coaster is still in progress.

The other use of check boxes, option buttons, and toggle buttons is putting them in an option group to indicate which of several values a field equals. Instead of setting the field for the individual check boxes, option buttons, and toggle buttons, you set the Control Source property for the option group and then set the values of each of the check boxes, option buttons, or toggle buttons.

Figure 10-6 shows a form that uses option groups for two fields. On the left half are option buttons in an option group. The Control Source property for the option group is Employee ID. The Control Source property for the option buttons is the numbers 1 through 10. The names are added as the option buttons' text to match their identification number.

The employee names are entered in the order they appear in the Employee table but once they are all entered, the employee names and their accompanying option buttons are rearranged within the option group in alphabetical order to make data entry easier. Access does not care that you have rearranged the option buttons in the option group since the number for the Control Source property and any text that

FIGURE 10-5   Toggle button used for a Yes/No data type

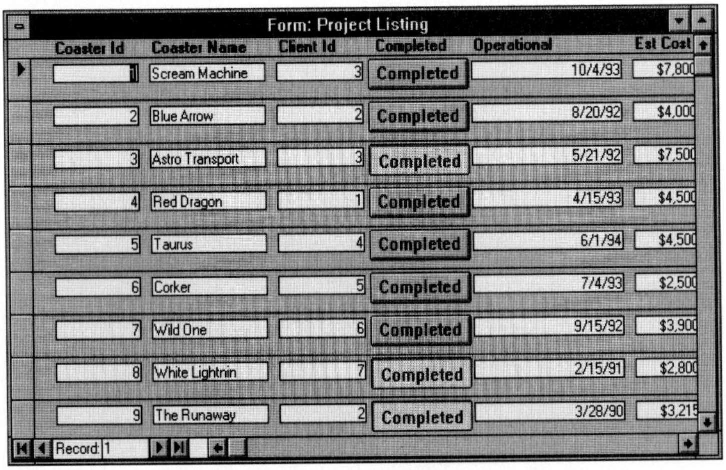

Coaster Id	Coaster Name	Client Id	Completed	Operational	Est Cost
1	Scream Machine	3	Completed	10/4/93	$7,800
2	Blue Arrow	2	Completed	8/20/92	$4,000
3	Astro Transport	3	Completed	5/21/92	$7,500
4	Red Dragon	1	Completed	4/15/93	$4,500
5	Taurus	4	Completed	6/1/94	$4,500
6	Corker	5	Completed	7/4/93	$2,500
7	Wild One	6	Completed	9/15/92	$3,900
8	White Lightnin	7	Completed	2/15/91	$2,800
9	The Runaway	2	Completed	3/28/90	$3,215

Form: Project Listing

Record: 1

FIGURE 10-6   Option buttons and check boxes used as part of an option group

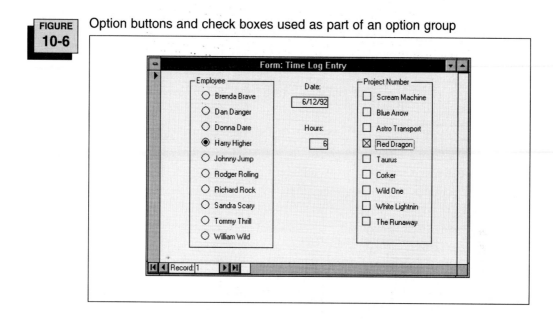

belongs to the option button continues to belong to the option button as you move it in the option group.

On the right side, the Control Source property for the option group is Project Number. The Control Source property for the check boxes is the numbers 1 through 9. The text that belongs to each of the check boxes for the different projects is replaced with the project's name to make data entry easier. With both option buttons and check boxes, you as the form designer, not Access, make the connection between the numbers for the employee and project numbers and the employee and project names.

When check boxes or option buttons are added to an option group, they are numbered sequentially. This means the first check box or option button has the value of 1, the second check box or option button has a value of 2, and so on for all of the check boxes and option buttons in the option group. You can even put the check boxes and option buttons in the same option group, but your form will look more professional when you use only check boxes or option buttons within an option group.

Tip   Remember that the goal of designing a form is to make entering and using the data as easy as possible. When designing your own forms, keep this goal in mind.

Adding Different Controls with the Field List Window

Access has a shortcut for adding fields to a form using different types of controls. Earlier you learned how dragging a field name from the field list window to the form design adds the field as a text box with the field name as an attached label. You can change the type of control you add when you drag a field name from the field list window. By selecting a control from the toolbox and then selecting the field name from the field list window, you add that field as the selected control type.

As an example, you can use this shortcut to create the form shown in Figure 10-6. First, make sure that both the toolbox and the field list window appear. To add the option group on the left, click the option group in the toolbox then drag the Employee ID field from the field list window to the upper-left corner of the form design. For the second option group, click the option group in the toolbox again then drag the Project Number field from the field list window to where you see it in Figure 10-6. Click Lock and the option button in the toolbox to add the option buttons for the employees, and then do the same with the check boxes for the projects.

Working with Form Properties

The form controls, form sections, and the form all have their own properties. You saw some of these properties when you set a control to represent a particular field. As described in the previous section, you can display the property sheet window by choosing Properties from the View menu or by clicking the Properties button in the toolbar. Controls, sections, and the form have many different properties. Access only displays the properties in the property sheet window that apply to the part of the form design you have selected. Access has several properties that specifically apply to controls and other properties that apply to sections such as the Detail, Form Header, Form Footer, Page Header, and Page Footer sections. Finally, a form has overall properties. The following sections describe the various types of properties.

Tip Access has a shortcut to display the property sheet window. If you double-click a control or section that is not currently selected, you open the property sheet window and display the properties for that control or section. The arrow or hand, not the I-beam, must be showing in order for this to work.

Control Properties

Controls have properties that affect how the controls behave and appear in the form. These properties provide many different features. Some of the properties are designed for advanced uses; for example, macros can change the Visible property to display a control when another value, such as a quota, is met. Other controls such as Left, Top, Width, and Height set the control's position and size. You will find it easier to use the mouse to adjust the controls' position and size rather than making entries. Another group, Before Update, After Update, On Enter, On Exit, and On Dbl Click, lets you perform macro instructions when you work with a control on a form. You will learn more about macros in Chapter 16.

Many of the control's properties in the bottom half of the property sheet set the control's appearance. (You will learn in Chapter 14 to create professional-looking forms.) You usually do not need to use these properties because the most frequently used appearance properties are available through dialog boxes and toolbar buttons. The Help Context ID property lets you select which help topic is displayed when you press F1. (This is described fully in the "Form Properties" section later in this chapter.)

You will learn how to use the remaining properties now. These properties include changing the control's name, properties shared with the underlying table, expanding controls to fit long entries, adding scroll bars to a control, changing how the form prints versus how it appears in a window, and how the list box and combo box data appears.

Changing a Control's Name

Most controls have a Control Name property that Access uses to identify the control on the form. Either use the default Access has provided or enter an acceptable object name. You will only care about the control's name when creating an expression that uses another control as described in Chapter 12 or when you are developing macros and programs that modify a control's properties.

 Note You cannot have two controls with the same name.

If using a control for another purpose than having a bound control represent a field, do not use a field name. Label controls have a Caption property in place of a Control Source that other controls use. This is the property that sets the text that appears in the label control. The property is also modified when you edit the text in the label on the form design rather than the property sheet window.

Properties Also Used by Tables

A control has several properties that you are already familiar with since you have used these properties in the tables you have created. When you add controls with the field list window or with FormWizards, the form controls adopt the Format, Default Value, Validation Rule, and Validation Text properties from the underlying table. The controls also pick up the field's description for the Status Line property. If the field uses decimal places, the control's Decimal Places property is Auto to use the same number of decimal places as the underlying table.

You can make another selection to these properties to override the table properties. Changing these properties does not change these same titled properties in the table or query. The entry you make for these properties should match the type of entry you would make for these properties in a table. You will learn more about validation rules and default values in Chapter 12 as you learn about expressions.

The Status Line property sets the text that appears on the status line when the focus is on a field. Use the Status Line property to override the field's description and provide a better description for the type of entry the user should make. This text only appears when the focus is on that control. For example, in Figure 10-6, the text in the status line can switch between displaying information about selecting an employee, entering the date and hours, and selecting one of the projects.

Allowing Changes to a Control

Two of the properties you can use for controls set whether you can move to the controls and make changes to the controls. The Locked property determines whether you can make changes to the control's value. The Enabled property determines whether you can move to the control. The defaults are No for the Locked property and Yes for the Enabled property so you can both move to the control and change its value. The following shows a form where these properties are changed for the four possible combinations.

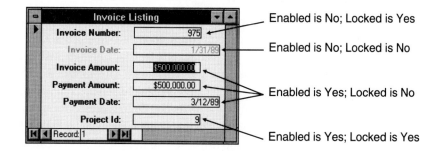

For the Invoice Number text box, Enabled is set to No and Locked is set to Yes so the control displays as normal although you cannot change it or move to it. The Invoice Date control has Enabled and Locked both set to No so the control appears dimmed to indicate that you cannot select it. The Invoice Amount, Payment Amount, and Payment Date fields have the default of Yes for the Enabled property and No for the Locked property so you can change the values of these controls. Finally, the Project ID control has the Enabled and the Locked properties both set to Yes so you can move to the control but you cannot make any changes.

Tip   When you have controls that you cannot move to, make the fields look different so the form's users will not be disappointed by seeing fields that they cannot manipulate. You may also want to comment on those fields that cannot be changed because their Locked property is set to Yes. Do this by adding text that appears in the status line to tell users that specified data cannot be changed. Using colors is also very effective and doesn't depend on users reading the status line.

Adding Scroll Bars to a Control

When you have a larger form displaying in a small window, the form has scroll bars so you can change which part of the form appears in the window. You can display similar scroll bars for text boxes. To add scroll bars to a text box, change the Scroll Bars from None to Vertical. When you display the form, the text box contains the scroll bar only when it contains the focus (the insertion point) as shown in Figure 10-7.

Properties That Affect Printing

Some properties change how a control appears when you print a form. When you have a text or memo field that contains a long entry, you may not want the control large enough to display the entire contents so the entire entry will appear when you print the form. When the Can Grow and Can Shrink properties are set to Yes, the vertical area that the field occupies grows or shrinks to fit the field's contents within the control's width when you print the form. This column extends as far down as the entry needs. Access also adjusts the height of the Detail section to match the size needed for the long entry.

When these two properties are set to No, the field takes up exactly the space set by the control's size. Setting Can Grow to No while setting Can Shrink to Yes expands the field's size as necessary but will not allow it

FIGURE 10-7

Scroll bars in a form

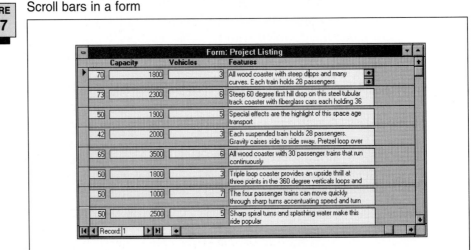

to shrink below the space the control uses. Setting Can Grow to Yes while setting Can Shrink to No means empty spaces will not be used for short field entries but longer entries will be truncated.

Figure 10-8 shows a printed preview of a form that has Can Grow and Can Shrink set to Yes. In this form, the field is designed to take one line. Most of the records have data in this field that is longer than the control on the form. If a record does not have an entry for the Features field or has a short one, the field will only occupy one line and the Detail will shrink to use only one line. The default for these two properties is No. These two properties affect the form's design only when you print the form. When you display the form on the screen, the control is the same size regardless of the properties' settings and the field's contents.

Most controls give you three choices for when they appear: you can have them appear only when you display the form in a window, only when you print the form, or have them always appear. For example, you may want to use one control to represent the Employee ID field when you print the form and have another control represent it when you display it on the screen. When you print the form, you are using the form as a report; when you display the form in a window you may want to use the form to enter data so the controls you select will change.

FIGURE 10-8

Using Can Shrink and Can Grow properties to adjust the sizes of fields

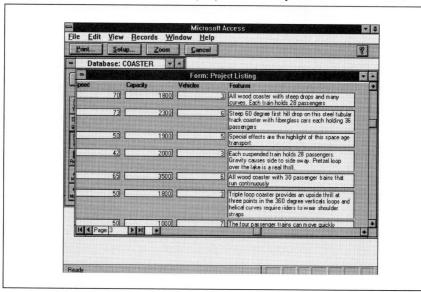

As an example, you might use a combo box for the Coaster Name field to let someone make a selection using the list box but you may want to display the Coaster Name field contents as a text box when you print the form. Make this change by changing the control's Display When property. This property has three choices that let you determine when the control appears: Always, Print Only, and Screen Only.

For the example of using both a combo box and a text box for the Coaster Name field, set the Display When property for the combo box to Screen Only and the Display When property for the text box to Print Only. The default of this property is Always so the controls you add to a form print and appear in a window unless you change the control's Display When property. An example, shown in Figure 10-9, has two controls for the Coaster Id field. The control for the Coaster Id field on the left is a combo box that has its Display When property set to Screen Only. The control for the Coaster Id field on the right is a text box that has its Display When property set to Print Only.

FIGURE 10-9

Controls using different Display When property values

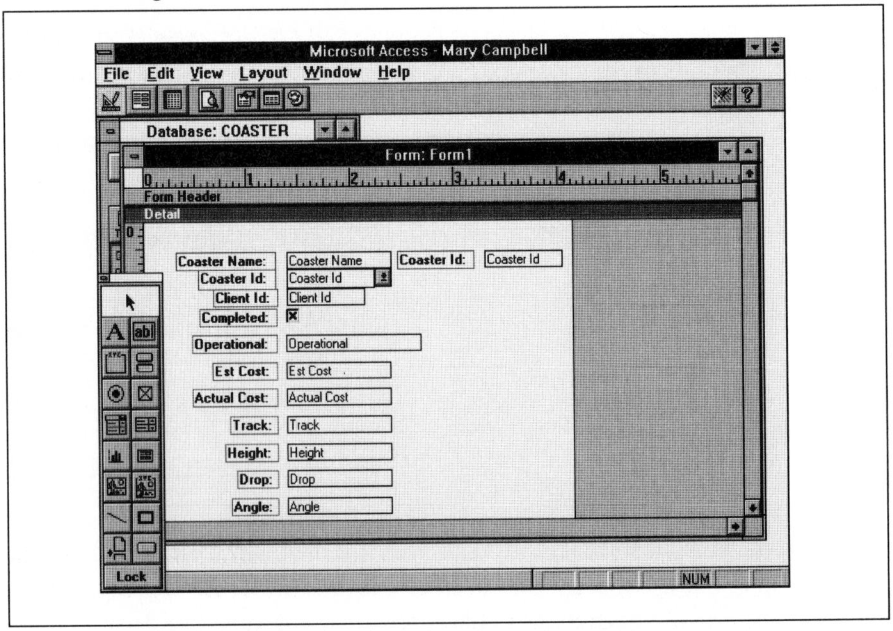

List Box and Combo Box Control Properties

List boxes and combo boxes have several properties that are specific to these two control types. These properties include Row Source Type, Row Source, Column Count, Column Heads, Column Widths, and Bound Column. Combo boxes also have List Rows, List Width, and Limit To List properties.

You have three ways to select what appears in the combo and list boxes: enter the values yourself, take the values from other field names, or take the values from another table or query. To tell Access the source of the data for a list box or combo box, provide the name of the field for the Control Source property. To describe what you want in the list box for these two controls, use the Row Source Type and Row Source properties.

The Row Source Type property has three choices: Table/Query, Value List, and Field List. Table/Query lists the records from a selected table or query. Value List displays the values you enter for the Row Source property, and Field List lists the field names from a selected table or query. For either Table/Query or Field List, you must select the table or query containing the records or field names to use for the list values. For the Value List Row Source Type, you can enter the values you want to appear in the list.

For example, you can use a combo box or list box control to select the department of an employee. In this case, you set this control in one of two ways. You can select Table/Query for the Row Source Type then select the name of the query that you create to contain the unique department names in the table. This method includes new departments in the list box or combo box control as they are added to the table. Figure 10-10 shows the query design for the Unique Department Names query that also has the Unique Values Only property selected.

The second method of including the department names is to select Values List and then enter **Construction;Design;Testing** for the Row Source property. Note that different possible values are separated by a semicolon. You can use this option versus a query to provide the entries for a list box or combo box when you only have a few entries and when they do not change very often.

When you add another department, if you use the department names from a query, the department is included. If you use the department names from the Value List property, you must add the new department

FIGURE
10-10 Query design to list unique departments

to the list of choices. A special option for the Table/Query Row Source Type property is to include an SQL statement that selects the records from the table or query you want to appear in the combo or list box.

A special feature of combo boxes and list boxes is including an entry in the list box that describes the contents of the list as Employee Id, First Name, and Last Name does in the list box in Figure 10-11. This description is a *column head*. To use a column head, change the Column Head property to Yes. When this happens, the field names from the query for the Table/Query Row Source Type, the first field for the Field List Row Source Type, and the first entry in the Row Source property all appear at the top of the list as a column heading as shown in Figure 10-11. This initial entry cannot be selected.

Another special feature is having multiple columns to select your entries. For example, as a list box or combo box lists many items, it may be easier to find the item you want by using multiple columns. You can use multiple columns in a list box or combo box to display a series of entries that the form's user can select as an entire row. For example, in the modified Time Log Entry form shown in Figure 10-11, the two list boxes use multiple columns. The top list box has the Column Count property set to three while the bottom list box has the Column Count property set to two.

FIGURE 10-11 Form using list box controls

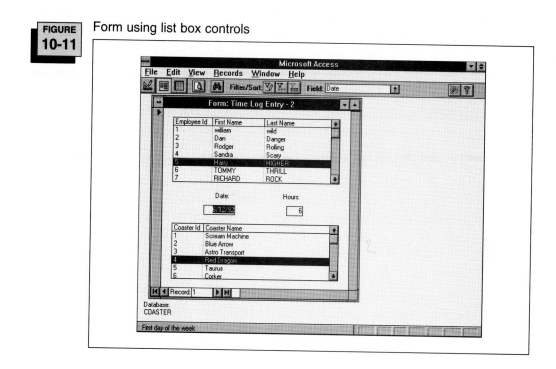

The data that appears in the top list box is in a query named Employee Numbers and Names, which lists the Employee ID, First Name, and Last Name fields from the Employee table. The top list box has the Row Source Type set to Table/Query. The bottom list box also has the Row Source Type set to Table/Query using the Project Numbers and Names query that lists the Coaster ID and Coaster Name fields from the Project table as the Row Source property. When using Value List as the Row Source property, set the values by entering all of the values that appear in a row before entering the next row of values. For the top list box in Figure 10-11, you could enter **1;William;Wild;2;Dan;Danger** as the beginning of the Row Source property.

In multiple column list boxes and combo boxes, the columns have a default width of one inch but you can enter new widths for them using the Column Widths property. For the list box in the top of Figure 10-11, the column widths are set to .75;1;1 for .75 of an inch for the first column and one inch for the other two. For the bottom list box in Figure 10-11, the column widths are set to .6;1.9 for 6/10 of an inch for the Coaster numbers and 1.9 inch for the second column. The last column may be wider or narrower than you set it since its size is adjusted according to the remaining space left in the list box area.

The form in Figure 10-11 knows which value of the fields listed in the list boxes are stored in the field for the control's Control Source property by looking at the Bound Column property. This value ranges from zero to the number in the Column Count property. When the value is zero, the value entered for the control's field is the same as the record number of the selected line in the list. When the value is more than zero, the value entered for the control's field is the value in the column number selected. For example, in Figure 10-11, the Bound Column property for both list boxes is 1 so the list boxes return the employee number for the Employee Id field in the Employee Time Log table and the coaster or project identification number for the Project number field in the Employee Time Log table.

A combo box also has additional properties that apply only to combo boxes. When you click the down arrow of a combo box, the drop-down list box has room for eight rows and is as wide as the combo box. You can change the number of rows in the list box to display more or fewer choices at once by replacing the default of 8 for the List Rows property with another number. You can make the drop-down list box wider than the combination control by entering the width you want for the List Width property. The default is Auto, which sets the list box to be as wide as the combo box control.

The other special control property for a combo box is whether you are selecting one of the items also listed in the list box or entering a new item into the text box part of the combo box. For example, when creating a table and selecting the data type for a field, you must select one of the available data types. Anything you type is converted to one of the acceptable data types or rejected as an entry.

On the other hand, when you are entering a table or query name for the Row Source property, you can select one of the names listed in the drop-down list box or type the name of a table or query that does not necessarily match one of the listed ones. You can do this when selecting a query for a list box or combo box control but have not yet created the query the list box or combo box control will use.

You can put the same limit on the combo boxes you place into your forms. To set a combo box to accept only one of the valid items listed in the drop-down list box, change the Limit To List property to Yes. The default of No means that for the combo box, you can either select an item from the list or type a new entry in the text part of the control.

Tip If you want the entries in the list box in a particular order and these values come from a table or query, create a query that sorts the records as described in Chapter 6. Then, use the query for the Row Source property.

Section Properties

Sections also have properties. Since sections do not represent field values, the section properties are very different than the ones used for controls. The Detail, Form Header, and Form Footer sections all have the same properties. The Page Header and Page Footer sections have a subset of these properties since these two sections do not use the Force New Page, New Row or Col, Keep Together, Display When, Can Shrink, and Can Grow properties. You can select any one of these sections by clicking part of the section that does not include a control. Figure 10-12 shows the properties for the Detail section.

FIGURE 10-12 Detail section properties

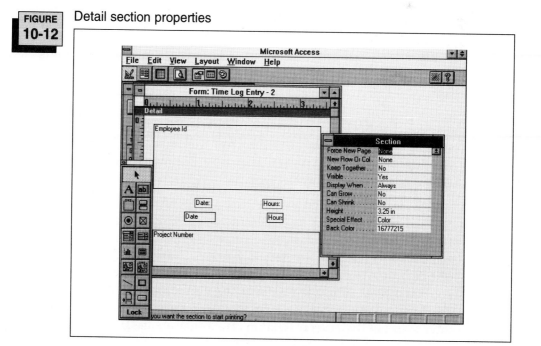

When you print forms, you may want to print the information for each record on a separate page. Rather than adding a page break control to the form design, you can have a new page start at the beginning or end of each section. To add a page break to a section, change the Force New Page property. For example, to have the contents of the Detail section printed using a separate page for each record, select Before & After for the Force New Page Property. The default for the property is None so the form only starts another page after filling the current one. Select Before Section to have the form start on a new page every time the current section is printed. Select After Section to have the form start on a new page after printing the current section. Finally, select Before & After when you want a new page started every time you start and end the current section.

Another result of splitting a form between pages when you print is that part of a section prints on one page and the rest of the section prints on the next page. You can change the form design so if Access cannot fit the entire section on the current page, the section starts on the next page. You may want all of the information about a record printed on the same page so you do not have to flip between pages to look at the record's contents. To make this change to the form design, change the section's Keep Together property from No to Yes. When you print the form, Access moves information to the next page whenever the current page lacks sufficient room to print the entire section.

When you print a form, you can print the data in several columns like the ones you see in a newspaper. When you print form data, you can select whether a section starts at the top of the column or row, or whether the section continues where the previous one left off like a newspaper does for classified ads. Figure 10-13 shows a form that starts each Detail section at the top of the column. You would set up this form for two columns by choosing Print Setup from the File menu, selecting More, and typing **2** in the Items Across box.

The records are filled into the form from top to bottom because the Vertical option button in the Print Setup dialog box is selected. The reason each new record starts in a new column is because, for this form, the Detail section has the New Row or Col property set to After Section. The default is None so when you have a form divided into columns, each column is filled completely before starting another column. You can also set this property to Before Section when you want a new column started after printing the current section. The other choice is Before and After,

FIGURE

10-13

Starting groups in new columns

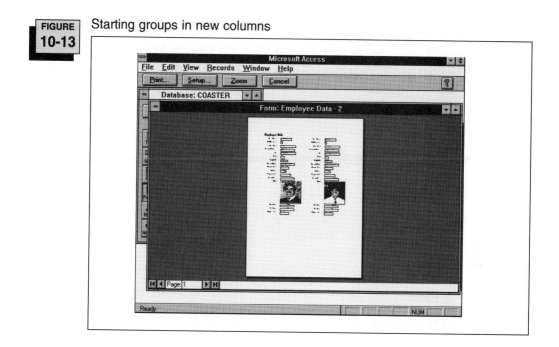

which starts in a new column before the section is printed, and after it is printed as well.

Some of the section properties are identical to properties with the same names that you used for controls. The Visible property sets whether a section appears. You can create macros that select when this section appears based on another criteria. As with controls, you have the same choices for the Display When property (Always, Print Only, and Display Only), which you can select from to determine whether individual sections appear when the form is displayed in a window and printed.

The Can Shrink and Can Grow properties perform the same function in a section as they perform when you apply these properties to individual controls. The default for a section is No for Can Shrink. For Can Grow, the default is No unless you have set one of the controls in the section to have the Can Grow property set to Yes, which also sets the section's Can Grow property to Yes.

The Height property sets the section's height just as you set the section's height by dragging the bottom of the section up or down. You might use this property rather than the mouse when you want to be sure that two sections are the same height or sections appearing in different forms are the same height. The Special Effect and Back Color properties are described in Chapter 14, which tells you how to change the appearance of a form.

Form Properties

Forms also have their own properties. These properties include the table or query the form uses, the grid, the form width, its size, and the views you can switch to. These properties are different than the controls you learned about for controls and sections. You can display the properties for the form in the property sheet window by choosing Select Form in the Edit menu or by clicking an area outside of the form's design. Figure 10-14 shows the properties for the form.

Setting the Form's Title Bar Text

You set the text that appears in the title bar of the form in one of two ways. You can set the text by saving the form; the form will then contain

FIGURE 10-14   Form properties

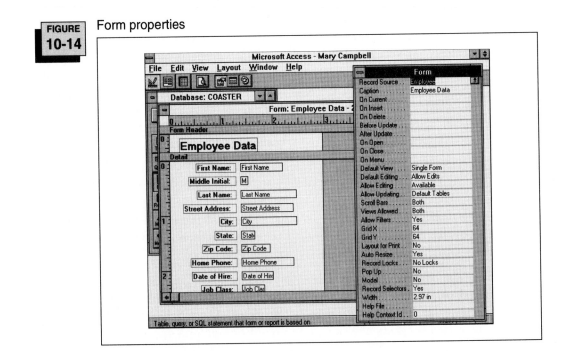

the name of the form in the title bar. The other way is by entering the text you want to appear in the title bar as the form's Caption property. Any text you enter as the Caption appears in the title bar.

Setting the Table or Query for a Form

Usually, you will want to use the table or query you have selected when you first start to create a form. However, if you change your mind or you have selected the Blank Form button from the New form dialog box without selecting a table or query, you will need to select a table or query.

Selecting a table or query controls the fields that are listed in the field list window. To set which table or query the form uses, change the Record Source property. You can select any of the tables and queries available in the database. When you change the table or query, the fields listed in the field list window change to match the new table or query but the fields from the old table or query in the form design do not change. For example, you might change the table or query a form uses when you have copied or imported a form designed to work with one table or query that you want to use with another. You may want to use a form you have created for the names and addresses of the Employee table to list names and addresses of the parks listed in the Client table.

Setting Where a Form Starts

Several of the properties let you select what you will do with the form when you use it. The Default Editing property tells Access whether you plan to use the form for data entry purposes, updating existing information, or just for looking at the data. The choices are Data Entry, Allow Edits, and Read Only. Data Entry starts the form at the end of the table or query so you can start entering data. You cannot look at earlier records without choosing Show All Records in the Records menu. Allow Edits opens the form at the beginning of the table or query and lets you both look at the data and make changes. Read Only lets you look at the data but will not allow changes to be made until you choose Editing Allowed in the Records menu.

You can also turn off and on whether users can make changes to the data with the Allow Editing property. When this property is set to Available, you can choose Editing Allowed in the Records menu to switch between having Access allow changes and not allow them. When this property is set to Unavailable, you cannot choose Editing Allowed in the Records menu. These two properties are often combined. For example, setting Default Editing to Read Only and Allow Edits to Unavailable makes the form read only since you cannot select the command that allows you to change the table's or query's information. You may also want to set Default Editing to Data Entry and Allow Edits to Available when you plan to use the form primarily for entering new records rather than looking at older ones.

Setting the Initial View of a Form

When you look at the forms you create with FormWizards, you may notice that the single-column FormWizard forms only show one record at a time while the tabular form shows as many records as can fit in the window. The reason these two FormWizard types change between displaying one record at a time and many is the Default View property.

The Default View property sets how the form initially appears. You can switch between Single Form, Continuous Forms, and Datasheet using the commands in the View menu or the buttons in the toolbar. When the Default View property is set to Single Form, the default for the single-column FormWizard forms, the form only displays one record at a time as shown here:

When the Default View property is set to Continuous Forms, the default for the tabular FormWizard forms, the form design repeats in the form window to display as many times as possible, as shown in Figure 10-15.

FIGURE
10-15 Continuous Forms as the Default View property

When the Default View property is set to Datasheet, the default for the subform in a main/subform FormWizard form, the table or query's data appears in a table format just as you can see the table or query by opening the table or query.

You can also use the Views Allowed property to limit which views the form's user can switch between. The choices are Form, Datasheet, and Both. Form lets the form's user display only the form without switching to the datasheet. You use Form when a form is designed to display only a few fields so that users don't have to go through all of the fields to find the ones they want.

Datasheet lets the form's users display the table in a datasheet without switching to the form. Both, the default, lets users switch between the datasheet and the form. Regardless of this property's setting, you can still switch to the form's design.

When the view of a form is the Datasheet or Continuous Forms, the window has scroll bars to switch which records appear in the window and which part of the form appears in the window. In a single record form, the window contains scroll bars only when the form design is larger than the form window's area. The scroll bars appear because the Scroll

Bars property is set to Both. This property sets which directions in the form have scroll bars. You can also select Horizontal Only or Vertical Only when you want a scroll bar in just one direction or None when you do not want scroll bars.

The Record Selectors property in a form displays or hides the record selectors. The record selector is the bar containing the small triangle at the left side of the record. These appear because the form has the default of Yes for the Record Selectors property. Select No for this property when you do not want the record selectors to appear.

The following illustration shows a form that has the scroll bars and the record selector removed:

The scroll bars are not needed since the Form Header section has command buttons that let you switch between records, and all of the controls easily appear in the window. Removing the record selectors means you do not have the border on the left side of the record that you can click to select the entire record. In Chapter 16, you will learn how to assign macros to the Next Record, Previous Record, and Done command buttons.

As you work on your form designs, notice that when you open a form, the window is sized to fit the form's design. The Auto Resize property handles this. When the Auto Resize property is set to Yes, every time you open the form, Access sizes the window to fit the Form Header, Detail, and Form Footer sections, if possible. If you set this property to No, the window you open when you open a form is the same size it was when you last used the form. Setting this property to Yes means that as you change the form's size, the window to contain the form also changes. However, once you have finished designing the form, you do not need Access to readjust the appropriate window size. Also, once the form is open, Access does not readjust the window's size until after you reopen it, so changing the size of the form's design does not affect the window's size until after you close the window. When you want to update the form's window size to make it appropriate for the form's design, choose Size to Fit Form from the Window menu.

The Width property sets the form's width just as you can set the form width by dragging the right side of the form to the left or right. You might use this property rather than the mouse when you want the form to be a specific width. Changing the width changes the width of all sections in the form.

Changing the Grid

In Chapter 9, you learned how to use the grid for placement. You can change the size of the grid by selecting the number of grid points per inch that appear vertically and horizontally on the form design. The number of dots per inch is set with the Grid X and Grid Y property. By entering a new number for the Grid X property, you set the number of grid points per inch that fit across the form design. By entering a new number for the Grid Y property, you set the number of grid points per inch that fit up and down the form design. Even when you change the numbers, the grid will not appear until you display it with Grid in the View menu.

Keeping the Form on the Top

As you work with forms you will notice that you can switch easily between windows. You can, however, set a form to prevent users from switching to other windows. To do this, set the Modal property to Yes. When you change the Modal property, the change does not occur until after you close the window and save the changes to the modified form. When you open the form again, the Design View and Datasheet View buttons in the toolbar are dimmed, as are the Form Design and Datasheet commands in the View menu.

When you display the Window menu, the bottom of the window includes only the current form and ignores any other windows on your Access desktop. Also, you cannot click other windows to activate them. You can only activate the windows by closing the form. Continue using the form, and close it when you are finished with it. To change the form's design, select the form name and the Design button from the Database window. When you do not want the form to remain constantly in the front anymore, change the Modal property to No. This change will not occur until you have saved the updated form.

Setting the Fonts That the Form Uses

The fonts the entries in the form use rely on the fonts you have installed for Windows. Windows has some fonts designed for printing and others intended for displaying information on the screen. You select whether you use the screen or the printer fonts for the form. The default for the Layout for Print property is No, which tells the form to use screen fonts. You can select Yes for this property when you want the form to use printing fonts. When you print the form using screen fonts, Windows substitutes a similar printer font. When you use a TrueType font such as the ones available in Windows 3.1 or through accessory packages such as Facelift or Adobe Typeface Manager, changing this property has no effect because TrueType fonts look the same on the screen as they do when printed.

Locking Records

If you are sharing a database with other users, you may want to make sure other users don't change the data that appears in your form. Prevent others from changing your records by selecting All Records for the Record Locks property. When you use the form, all of the records included in the form are locked so other users cannot change the data. The default of No Locks means other users can continue using the data so your use of the form does not prevent them from editing the data; however, the negative aspect of this is that other users do not realize that you are making changes to the record, which could cause errors in their work.

Another choice just for forms is Edited Record. This locks the record or group of records you are working with as soon as you make any change to the current record. Other users will not be able to make a change to the locked records until you have unlocked them.

Other Form Properties

The form has other properties that provide miscellaneous features. Some of these features are covered later in this and in other chapters.

A form has On Current, On Insert, On Delete, Before Update, After Update, On Open, On Close, and On Menu properties that tell Access to perform a macro or user-defined function when certain events occur. These events include moving to another record, inserting a record, deleting a record, updating a field's value, opening the form, closing the form, or attaching a custom menu to the form. You will learn about macros in Chapter 16.

In Chapter 13, you will learn about using multiple tables and popups in a form. Having multiple tables in a form means you can change the Allow Updating Form property to select which tables from the multiple tables you can edit (Chapter 13 describes this fully). In that chapter, you will also learn about using the Popup property when you create popup forms.

Later in this chapter, you will learn about filters. Filters use the Allow Filters property to set whether Access applies the filters you have created for the form.

Sorting and Selecting Records in a Form

When you use a form, you can select the order in which records appear and whether the data in the form contains all of the records. Sometimes you will want all of the records in a table or query but at other times you will prefer to work with only a subset of that data. Sorting and selecting the records from a table or query is done by applying a filter. A filter selects the records and the order in which you see them. You can create a filter and apply it when you want the effects of a filter to be used on a form; you can turn the filter off when you want all the records in the order they appear in the table or query.

You set the order of the records in a form according to the values of one or more fields. You can also change whether the records are sorted according to the field's values in ascending or descending order. Changing the order does not change the order of the records in the table or query. Sorting only changes the order of the records as they appear in the form. A filter can also provide the features of a query in a form.

To change the order of the records and to select which records appear, you need to create a filter. The filter is created from the form view rather than the form's design view. The first step is displaying the Filter, which looks like this:

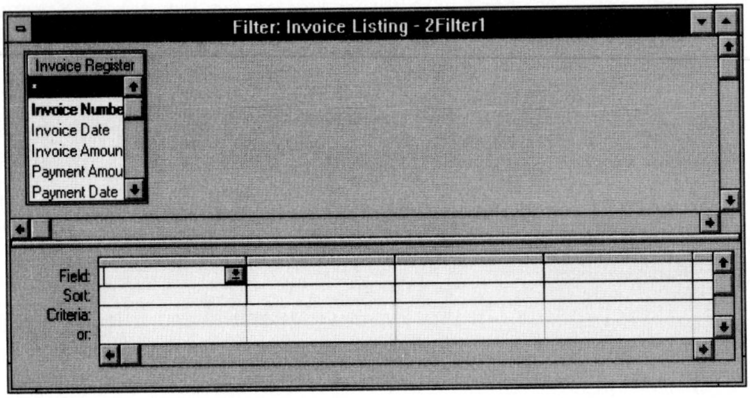

To display this window, either choose Edit Filter/Sort in the Records menu or click the Edit Filter/Sort button, which is the second button in the toolbar, and looks like this:

When the Filter window appears, notice that it looks just like the window you used to create a query—with one exception. The Show check boxes do not appear since whether to display the fields in the form is decided by the form design rather than the filter. In this window, enter the fields you will use to organize the records and the fields you will use to select which records from the table or query that will appear in the form. Once you create the filter, you are ready to use it.

Filter Window

The Filter window has field list windows at the top and the QBE grid on the bottom. The top of the Filter window contains the tables that are part of the data that the form displays. Usually, the top only contains one field list window when the form is for a table but when the form is for a query, the top of the Filter window contains as many field list windows for different tables as the query's definition does. Like the field list window in a form design, you can select one field by clicking it or all of them by double-clicking the title bar. The field of the table's primary index appears in bold in the list. You also have the same table name followed by an asterisk to add all of the fields and have the fields updated as you change the underlying table's design.

In the Field row, enter the field names that will select and organize the records by typing the field name, selecting a field name from the drop-down list box, or dragging a field name from one of the field list windows at the top. You can also drop fields you have added to the bottom by selecting them in the Field row and pressing DEL. The entries you make for the Sort row and for the Criteria row are the part of the window where you select the order and the records that appear when you apply a filter.

When finished creating a filter, close the window to return to the form by choosing Close from the window's Control menu, double-clicking the window's Control menu box, or pressing CTRL-F4. The filter is not yet applied. The filter is only in effect when you apply it.

 Tip You can include fields from the table or query that are not part of the form design. For example, you can create a filter for a form for the Invoice Register table that sorts by the Invoice Amount field even when the field does not appear as part of the form's design.

Sorting Data with a Filter

To sort records with a filter, you need to make entries in the Sort row under the field names you want to use for the sort. This means that if you want to sort the employee records in a form by employee last name, you need to add the Last Name field to the Field row in the QBE grid. Then, under the field name in the Sort row, select between Ascending, Descending, and (not sorted). When you choose Ascending or Descending to order the records according to that field, Access uses that field and any other fields that you have chosen a sort order for to organize the records. The records are sorted according to the field values of the fields you select.

When you have more than one field selected for sorting in a filter, the fields are sorted in the order the fields are selected, from left to right. First, Access organizes all of the records according to the values of the first field you select in ascending or descending order as you have selected. When two or more records have the same entry for the first field, then Access looks at the second field to determine the placement of those records. When two or more records have the same values for the first and second fields, Access sorts those records by the value of the third field. This sorting process continues for up to the number of fields you select to use for sorting.

An example of sorting with a filter is shown in Figure 10-16, in which the records are initially sorted by the date. Next, the records are sorted by employee identification numbers. To create this filter, in the Filter window, add the Date and Employee Id fields to the Field row and then under each of them, change the entry in the Sort row to Ascending.

Tip If you are sorting your records in a form, you may want to index the fields in the underlying table or query. Indexing the fields that you will use to order the records will make the form operate faster.

FIGURE
10-16

Records sorted by the Date and Employee ID fields

Date	Employee Id	Project Number	Hours
6/12/92	1	4	12
6/12/92	1	1	20
6/12/92	1	7	8
6/12/92	2	2	35
6/12/92	2	3	5
6/12/92	3	5	40
6/12/92	4	5	40
6/12/92	5	3	18
6/12/92	5	8	13
6/12/92	5	4	6
6/12/92	6	4	2
6/12/92	6	5	38
6/12/92	7	2	40
6/12/92	8	6	25
6/12/92	8	5	15
6/12/92	9	2	40
6/12/92	10	2	40
6/19/92	1	5	36
6/19/92	1	1	4
6/19/92	2	2	28

Selecting Records with the Filter

Besides using the filter to sort the records that appear in the form, you can also use a filter to select which records appear. Selecting the records to appear in a filter is just like selecting the records to appear in a query. In the Field row, select the fields that you will use as the basis for the decision for whether the record matches the criteria you enter in the rows below. You can enter the same criteria you learned how to enter for queries in Chapter 6. The criteria are expressions (which you will learn about more in Chapter 12).

Here are a few pointers about the entries you can use as criteria. You can enter text numbers and dates directly under the field names when looking for records with the same value for the selected field as in Design under Department to find all employees in the Employee table. You can also use relational operators such as < and > to perform comparisons as in > Total Payments under the Total Invoices field in a filter for the Client table when you want to find clients who still have amounts due (invoices are greater than payments). When you have more than criteria entered on the same row in QBE grid, a record must match all criteria in the row to match the filter. When you have criteria entered on separate rows in the QBE grid, a record must match one of the rows of criteria to match the filter.

The following shows an example of a filter with several entries:

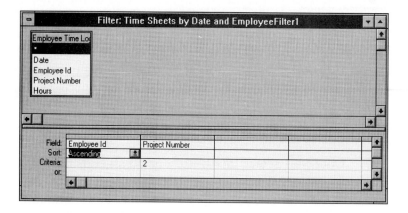

In this filter, the records are sorted according to the Employee ID field. Only the records that contain 2 for the Project ID are included because the filter includes Project ID with a 2 below it.

Creating a Filter with a Query

When you have a query that selects the records you want the filter to use, creating a filter is easy. To have a filter adopt the record selection and sorting choices of a query, choose Load from Query from the File menu while displaying the Filter window, select the name of the query you want to use from the list box, and select OK. Access only lists the potentially available queries that you can use with the form. The query you select must be a select query that is based on the same table or query as the form you are using. It may not include other tables or queries and it may not include totals. When you select OK, the filter picks up the filter type information from the query. Like the filters you create, you have not applied it. The filter is not in effect until you apply it using the same procedure for filters you have created from scratch.

You will want to load a query for a filter to temporarily use the subset of records the query selects. To permanently use the records a query selects, change the form's Record Source property to use the query rather than the underlying table or query.

Applying the Filter

The filter you create with your entries in the Filter window does not change the records that appear in the form immediately. To see the effects of the filter, you must apply it. Applying the filter is as simple as choosing Apply Filter/Sort from the Records menu or clicking the Apply Filter/Sort button in the toolbar. The Apply Filter/Sort button looks like this:

Once you select this button or command, the filter is applied. The status line now contains "FLTR" to indicate that a filter is in effect. At this point, you only see the records that fill the conditions created by the filter. For example, a form displaying the records of the Invoice Register table will change from showing 28 records to 5 records when you add the condition that the Payment Date field is empty. This criterion is added by adding the Payment Date field to the Field row and Is Null to the Criteria row below it.

When you are adding and editing records, the filter is not reapplied until you choose Apply Filter/Sort from the Records menu or click the Apply Filter/Sort button in the toolbar again. You can make subsequent changes to the filter by editing it again. You may notice that some of your entries are rearranged but the effect of the filter is the same.

When the filter is applied, you can remove the effects of it at any time. To remove the effects of the filter, choose Show All Records from the Records menu or click the Show All Records button in the toolbar. The Show All Records button looks like this:

Once you select this button or command, the filter is removed and all of the records appear. You can switch between applying and removing the filter as many times as you want. Before you close the form, however, consider whether you want to keep the effects of the filter for a future use. If you want to keep the filter, save it as a query as described in the next section.

Saving the Filter

A filter is not saved as part of a form. To keep the effects of the filter for future uses of the form, save the filter as a query by first opening the Filter window as if you want to make changes to the filter. Next, choose Save As Query from the File menu. Then, just as you have saved a query on other occasions, type the name you want to use for the query and select OK. At this point, the filter is saved as a query but the form is still set to use the table or query you originally used to create the form. To make a permanent change to the form, change the form's Record Source property from the table or query name you used when you created the form to the name of the query you have just created. You do not need to make any additional changes to the form's design.

Preventing Filters in a Form

If you are creating a form that you want solely used with all of the records in a table or query, you will want to prevent a form's user from applying a filter to the form. If you are designing a form that you don't want to be used with a filter, you can prevent a filter from being applied. To prevent a filter from being created and applied, change the form's Allow Filters property from Yes to No. Once you change this property and return to the form view, the three buttons for the filters on the toolbar are dimmed, as are the Edit Filter/Sort, Apply Filter/Sort, and Show All Records commands in the Records menu.

Using Multiple Pages in a Form

When you have many fields that you wish to include in a form, you may find using the form easier by dividing the Detail section into pages. Each page can show a different related group of controls. For example, when adding another roller coaster project, the table has 17 fields for you to fill in. Rather than having a single crowded window that contains all of the information you need, divide the form into pages and have each page process a smaller, manageable chunk of the information.

To divide a form into pages, add page breaks to the Detail section where you want the section divided. Since the form's window size is set by the size of the first page of the Detail section plus the form's header and footer, if any exist, you will want each page to be the same size. Ensure that each page is the same height by adding the page breaks and entering the values for the Top property so they are an even increment. For example, for the form design in Figure 10-17, the first page break is set at 1.75 and the second page break is set at 3.5. These page break controls appear as a series of six dots next to 1.75 and 3.5 along the vertical ruler of the form design. Once you make this change, choose to Fit Form Size in the Window menu when you display the form view.

When using multiple pages in a form, include information that serves as a reminder for the record you are using. For example, in the form shown here, the coaster name and identification number are repeated in the Form Header section:

Also, the three pages are identified so users know where they are as they use the form. The label controls containing the page numbers have their Display When property set to Screen Only so when you print the form, they do not appear.

When you use a form with multiple pages, switch between pages by using PAGE UP and PAGE DOWN or clicking the scroll bar.

Tip Leave a border of empty space at the beginning and end of the pages. The empty space ensures that information from one page does not accidentally appear on the next or previous page. Also, leaving the empty

FIGURE 10-17 A form design that uses multiple pages

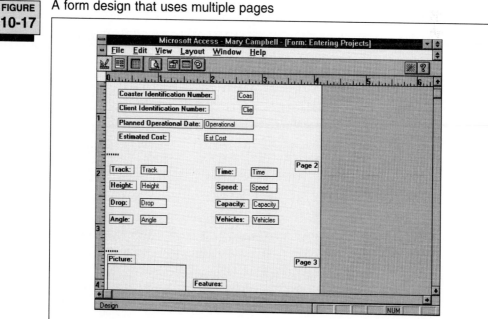

space before and after the page break ensures that a page break control does not divide any other controls in the middle.

Saving a Form as a Report

Some of the forms you create will be exactly what you want to use as reports in Access. Rather than re-creating them in a report's design, you can save a form as a report. First, display the Form Design window for the form you want to convert. Next, choose Save As Report in the File menu. Access prompts for a name for this report using the form's name as a default. Either use this name or replace it with another before you select OK to complete the command. After selecting OK, Access creates a report with the same appearance as the form.

When you look at the reports in your database, you will see the one you have just created. Once this new report is created, use it and make design modifications just as you do for the reports created from scratch. You will learn more about customizing reports in Chapter 11. As an

FIGURE 10-18   Report created from the form design in Figure 10-17

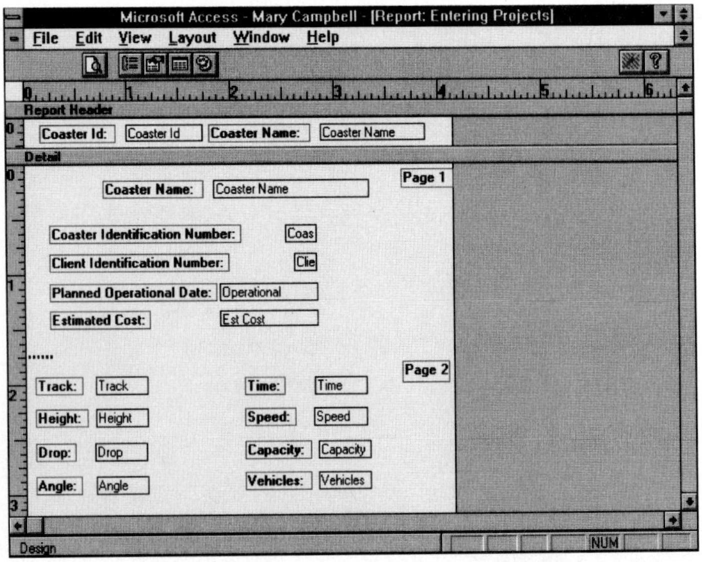

example of saving a form as a report, Figure 10-18 shows the report design created by saving the form design shown in Figure 10-17 as a report.

Quick Reference

To Add a Control to a Form   Display the toolbox by choosing Tool Box from the View menu. Click the tool for the control you want to add then click the form design where you want the control placed.

To Set a Control's Properties   Display the property sheet by choosing Properties from the View menu. Click the control whose properties you want to change in the form design. Click the property you want to change in the property sheet. Type the new entry for the property or select one of the choices available by clicking the down arrow.

To Sort Records in a Form   Display the Filter window by choosing Edit Filter/Sort from the Records menu. Select the field you want to use for sorting in the Field row. Select Ascending or Descending in the Sort row. Repeat adding fields and sort orders in the order you want the records sorted.

To Select Records for a Form   Display the Filter window by choosing Edit Filter/Sort from the Records menu. Select the field you want to use for selecting records in the Field row. Type the criteria for the fields in the Criteria row. Apply the filter by choosing Apply Filter/Sort from the Records menu. Remove the filter by choosing Show All Records from the Records menu.

To Create Multiple Pages in a Form   Add page controls where you want each page break. You will want to add some enhancements such as making the pages the same size and identifying information in the page header and footer.

To Save a Form as a Report   Display the Form Design window for the form you want to convert. Choose Save As Report in the File menu. Modify the report name from the default of the form's name if you want. Select OK.

CHAPTER

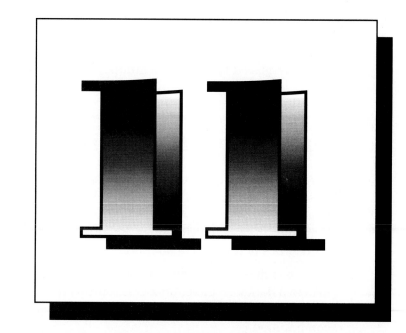

Customizing Reports with Controls, Sorting, and Grouping

*J*ust as with forms, the reports you create with ReportWizards might meet your exact needs or you may have to make some changes. Instead of starting with a complete new design you can often make adjustments to the report created with ReportWizards—by adding controls, for example. The techniques with which you modify a report by adding controls are the same techniques that you use to build a report from a blank report to contain exactly what you want. When you add the controls, you can change their properties to alter how the control's information is presented.

You can also customize reports by organizing the records in the report in a different sequence. Changing the order of records is referred to as *sorting*. With sorting you can create different reports just by reorganizing the records in a new way. You can combine the effects of sorting with *grouping*, in which the records that have the same values for one or more fields are placed together in a group.

Adding Controls to Reports

As you created reports with the ReportWizard in Chapter 9, a control was added to the report for every field that you selected. If you have forgotten a field or two you can add more of these text box controls rather than start over again with a new ReportWizard design. You also can add other types of controls to a report.

Access divides controls into three groups: *bound* controls refer to a field in a database table, *unbound* controls refer to other objects such as lines or text that you have added, and *calculated* controls perform a computation.

Regardless of the type of control that you add you will use the toolbox shown in the lower-left corner of Figure 11-1. Some of these controls do not apply to reports. The Toolbox can appear anywhere within the Access window and remains in the same location unless you move it. With reports, you usually will use label, text box, option group, option button, check box, and page break controls. Controls such as list boxes are available for use with reports but are used more often for forms.

FIGURE

11-1

A report design showing the Toolbox

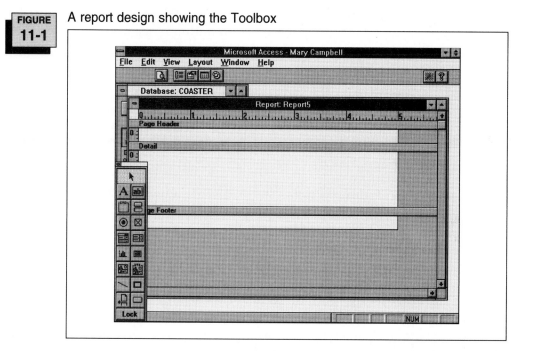

When you add controls to a report, you usually use one of six types of controls:

☐ *Label* Adds text that does not change from record to record. Labels are often used for other sections such as the Report Header, Report Footer, Page Header, and Page Footer.

☐ *Text box* Adds a box that contains the value of a field that changes from record to record. Text boxes can contain other types of entries such as the totals you will learn about later in this chapter and in Chapter 12 when you learn about expressions. A text box that contains the result of a computation is a calculated control.

☐ *Option group* Adds a box that you can subsequently fill with option buttons or check boxes. When option buttons or check boxes are in an option group, only one of them is selected.

☐ *Option button* Adds an option button either to an option group or separately. When option buttons are in an option group, only one option button of the group is selected. When option buttons are not in an option group, each option button is separate from the others and functions as a check box.

☐   *Check box*   Adds a box that is selected or cleared with an X. This control is used just like option buttons. In a report design, check boxes and option buttons can be used interchangeably since they are treated the same. You decide which you want to use based on whether you prefer the appearance of a check box or an option button.

☐   *Page break*   Adds a page break when you have several pages within the report design.

This chapter focuses on these six controls. The label and page break controls are unbound because they do not change from record to record. The other controls are bound because their values are set by the values of fields in the current record. Chapter 13 shows you how to use subform/subreport controls to add subsidiary forms and reports to a report. In Chapter 14 you learn about the controls to add lines and boxes and Chapter 15 shows how to add pictures and graphs to your reports. The other controls in the Toolbox are not used in reports.

Adding a Control to a Report Design

In Chapter 9, you learned how to add a control that represents one of the fields from the table or query by dragging the field name from the field list window. Dragging fields from the field list window adds text boxes for the field and adjoining labels that describe the field's contents. To add other types of controls, use the Toolbox window. You can also combine the Tool Box window and the field list window to quickly create controls of different types that represent the different fields.

To add a label, text box, option group, option button, check box, and page break control, first display the Toolbox by choosing Toolbox from the View menu. Next, select the type of control you want to create from the Toolbox. These controls are identified in Figure 11-2. Then click the part of the report design where you want the control you are adding to begin. This adds the control using the default size of the control. Access will change the control's size of labels and option groups as their contents

FIGURE 11-2

Tools in the report design Toolbox

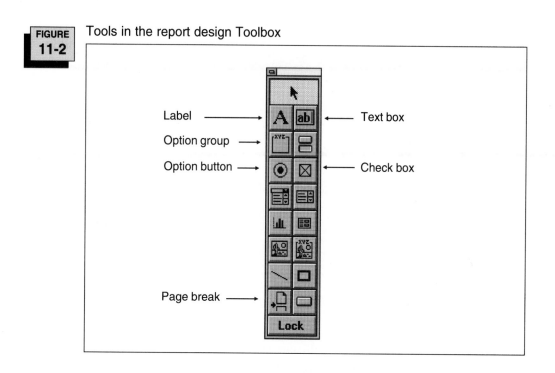

change. Another option for any control is to select the size yourself by dragging the mouse from where you want the control to start to where you want the opposite corner of the control. When you add these controls, Access puts an empty control in the location like the ones shown in Figure 11-3. When adding a label, you can immediately start to type the text you want to appear in the label.

When you add an option group, you are creating a group to which you will subsequently add other check box or option controls. When you add these controls to the option group, the option group reverses its colors to indicate that you are pointing to where you can add the control to the option button. When you add check boxes or option buttons to an option group, you do not have to worry about whether the box will fit the controls you are adding. When you move one of the check box or option button controls beyond the boundary of the option group, the option group is resized to fit where you have moved one of its controls. When you move an option group, you move all of the check boxes and option buttons in the group.

FIGURE
11-3

New controls added to a report design

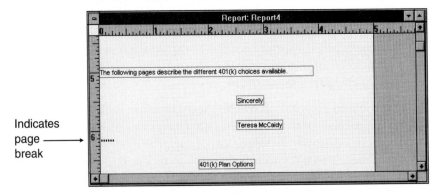

When you add a page break, the page break symbol is added on the left edge of the report design. This page break control lets you divide lengthy reports into multiple pages. A multiple-page form letter, for example, uses page break controls to divide the Detail section into multiple pages. The following shows part of the design of a report that breaks the Detail section into pages.

Indicates
page ——→
break

Controls such as text boxes, option buttons, and check boxes currently have text that is inappropriate for your report. Change this text by selecting the control and then clicking the current text where you want the insertion point placed. At this point, you can edit the contents that is part of the control.

Tip   Remember to align the check boxes and option buttons that you add to a report. You can align controls that you select by choosing Align in the Layout menu and then the direction that you want the selected objects aligned.

 Tip   You can add multiple controls of the same type by clicking Lock in the Toolbox (the bottom button). When Lock is on, the same tool in the Toolbox remains selected. Selecting Lock again turns it off so when you add a control to the report, the pointer tool becomes selected.

Setting the Field That a Control Represents

Once you have added a control to a report, tell Access which field the control will represent. Some controls, such as labels and page breaks, do not represent fields since they do not change from record to record. With controls such as text boxes, option buttons, check boxes, and option groups, you tell Access which field you want to use with the control. The field a control represents is one of the control's *properties*.

To set the field for a text box, make the change by editing the text box's contents and changing Unbound to one of the table's or query's field names. You can also change the Control Source property that you use for other types of controls.

For all types of controls that you want to represent a field in the table or query, you can change the control's Control Source property. First display the property sheet by choosing Properties from the View menu or clicking the Properties button in the toolbar, which looks like this:

When you display the property sheet in the report design, the Property Sheet window looks like the one shown in Figure 11-4. As you click different parts of the report design, the properties and values of the properties change to match what you select. You may need to move this window if it covers the control you want to select. This window remains displayed in the report design until you choose Properties from the View menu or click the Properties button in the toolbar. You can also use the Control menu box in the property sheet window to close this window.

The Property Sheet window added to a report design

The property sheet is just like the property sheet for forms. The left side contains the property names appropriate for the selected control or section and the right side contains the properties' values.

The Control Source property is the property that selects which field a control represents. You can either type the field name or you can use the down arrow to select one of the fields from the list.

How you select the field for a check box or option button depends on whether the check box or option button is part of an option group. When a check box or option button is not included in an option group, the check box or option button is an on/off switch that you usually use for your Yes/No data type fields. Set the field for the check box or option button control by entering the field for the Control Source property. For example, the Completed check box shown in Figure 11-5 has its Control Source property set to Completed so the report shows the check box with an X when the coaster is completed and an empty box when the coaster is still in progress.

FIGURE 11-5

Check boxes and option buttons used separately and as part of an option group

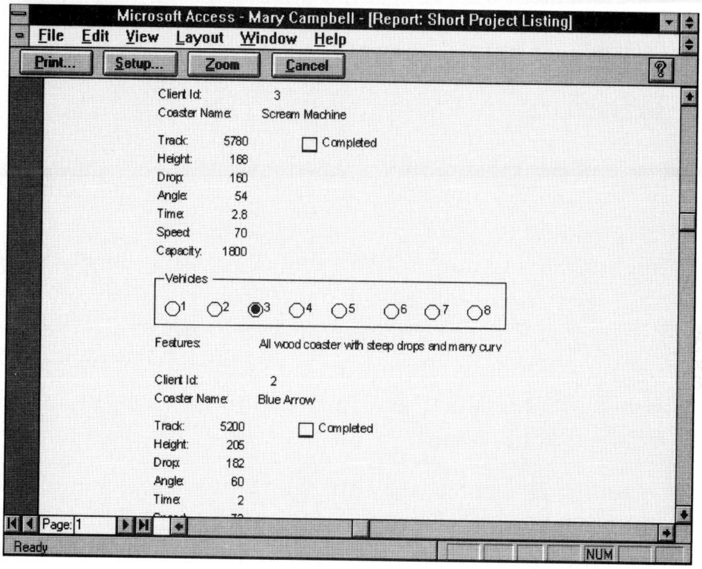

The other use of a check box or option button is for showing the value of a field; this happens when you put several check boxes or option buttons in an option group. Instead of setting the field for the individual check boxes and option buttons, set the Control Source property for the option group and then set the values of each of the check boxes or option buttons. Figure 11-5 shows a report that does this. The box marked Vehicles is the text at the top of the option group. The option group's Control Source property is set to the Vehicles field. Each of the option buttons has numbers for its Control Source property. For example, for the Scream Machine, the 3 option button is selected.

When check boxes or option buttons are in an option group, they are numbered sequentially. This means the first check box or option button has the value of 1, the second check box or option button has a value of 2, and so on for all of the check boxes and option buttons in the option group. You can even put the check boxes and option buttons in the same option button, but your report will look more professional when you use only check boxes or only option buttons within an option group.

Adding Different Controls with the Field List Window

Access has a shortcut for adding fields to a report using different types of controls. Earlier you learned how dragging a field name from the field list window to the report design added the field as a text box with the field name as an attached label. You can change the type of control you add when you drag a field name from the field list window. By selecting a control from the Toolbox and then selecting the field name from the field list window, you add that field as the selected control type. This shortcut changes the Control Source property of the control to the selected field name.

As an example, use this shortcut to add the check box control and option group for the report shown in Figure 11-5. First, make sure that both the Toolbox and the field list window appear. To add the check box, click the check box in the Toolbox and then drag the Completed field from the field list window to the right of the text box for the Coaster Name field. For the option group, click the option group in the Toolbox then drag the Vehicle field from the field list window to below the Capacity field.

Working with Report Properties

The report controls, report sections, and the report each have their own properties. You saw some of these properties when you set a control to represent a particular field. As described earlier, you can display the Property Sheet window by choosing Properties from the View menu or clicking the Properties button in the toolbar. In the Property Sheet window Access displays only those properties that apply to the control, section, or report you have selected. Access has several properties that apply specifically to controls and others that apply to sections such as the Detail, Report Header, Report Footer, Page Header, and Page Footer sections. Finally, the report has properties that apply to the overall report.

Control Properties

Controls have properties that set the appearance of the information that appears in the control. The properties listed in the property sheet include all possible properties a control has.

Most controls have a Control Name property that Access uses to identify the control separately from the other controls in the report. The default is the name of the field a control represents or the name of the type of control followed by a number (for example Text8) depending on how you add the control and whether the report already has the field you selected in the report. Use the default or enter an acceptable object name. You will only care about the control's name when creating an expression that uses another control as described in Chapter 12 or when developing macros and programs that modify a control's properties.

Label controls have a Caption property in place of the Control Source that other controls use. The Caption property sets the text that appears in the label control. The property is also modified when you edit the text in the label on the report design rather than the Property Sheet window.

Controls such as Left, Top, Width, and Height set a control's position and size. You will find it easier to use the mouse to adjust a control's position and size rather than making entries. Usually, the only reason to make entries for these properties is when you want to make several controls the same size by entering the values for the Height and Width properties.

Two of the properties, Format and Decimal Places, will look familiar from your earlier work designing tables. Format is initially set to whatever the field's Format property is in the underlying table. Decimal Places, which only appears when the data type uses digits after the decimal point, is initially set to Auto. These default settings mean that the report uses the Format and Decimal Places properties of the report's table or query.

You can make another selection to override how the values appear in the report. Changing the Format and Decimal Places properties does not change the Format and Decimal Places properties of the table or query. For the Format property, select from all of the choices you have for the formats of different data types (but do select a format that is appropriate for the data displayed in the control).

When you have a field in a report that you want to emphasize when its value changes, emphasize it by only showing the field's value when the field value changes. For example, in Figure 11-6, the report shows the value of the Completed field only when the value switches between Yes and No. Hiding the duplicate field values is done by selecting the control you want to hide the duplicate values, Completed in this case, and changing the Hide Duplicates property from Yes to No. When hiding duplicate values, sort the records by the field in which you are hiding the duplicates so all of the records with the same value for that field are together.

When a text or memo field contains a long entry, you do not have to guess how much vertical space the field needs to display the entire contents. When the Can Grow and Can Shrink properties are set to Yes, the entire entry is wrapped to fit a column within the control's width. This column extends as far down as necessary to include the entire entry. Access also adjusts the height of the Detail section to match the size needed for the long entry. When these two properties are set to No, the field takes up exactly the space set by the control's size.

FIGURE 11-6 Hiding duplicate values in a report

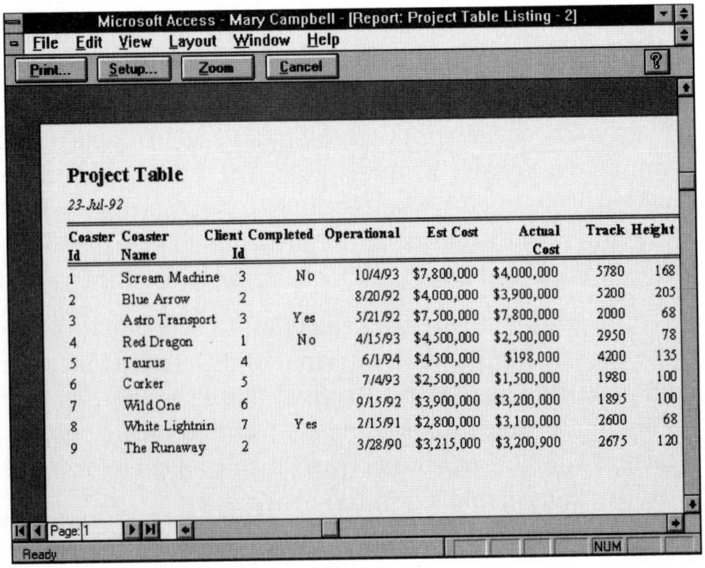

You can also set Can Grow to Yes while setting Can Shrink to No when you want the field's size to expand to fit the entry but not to shrink below the space the control uses. Set Can Grow to No while setting Can Shrink to Yes when you want to skip using empty space for short field entries but want to truncate the longer ones. Figure 11-7 shows a report that has Can Grow and Can Shrink set to Yes. In this report, the field is designed to take two lines. Most of the records use more than two lines so the Detail section expands to fit the entries. If a record does not have an entry for the Features field or has a short one, the field occupies only one line and the Detail section shrinks to only use one line. The default for these two properties is Yes for Memo data type fields and No for Text data type fields.

Some of the properties are designed for advanced uses such as using Visible to create a message that only appears when another value, such as a quota, is met. Many of the control's properties in the bottom half of the property sheet set the control's appearance. Chapter 14 shows you can change the appearance of controls to create professional-looking reports. You usually do not need to use the controls because the most

FIGURE 11-7

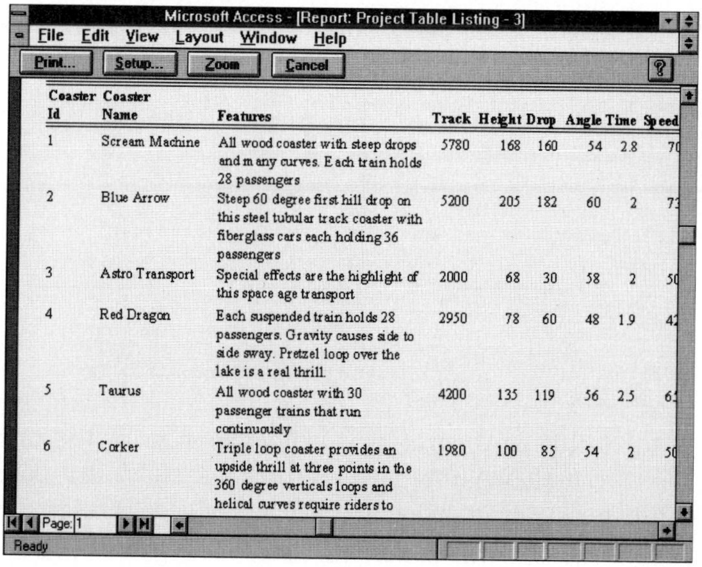

Using Can Shrink and Can Grow properties to adjust size of fields

frequently used appearance properties are available through dialog boxes and toolbar buttons.

The Help Context Id property determines which help topic from the help file appears when the user presses F1. The number entered for this property is between 0 and 2,147,483,647 for the number of slots for help topics available. Usually, you will only change this number when creating a custom help file using the Microsoft Windows Help Compiler, which is separate from Access. When you use a custom help file, you select the help file for the Help File report property and then enter the help topic numbers for the Help Context Id properties of the different controls. This feature is more frequently used with forms than reports.

Section Properties

Sections also have properties. Since sections do not focus on field values, the properties are very different than the ones used for controls. The Detail, Report Header, Report Footer, and the group headers and footers you will learn about later in this chapter all have the same properties. The Page Header and Page Footer sections have a subset of these properties since these two sections do not use the Force New Page, New Row or Col, Keep Together, Can Shrink, and Can Grow properties. You can select any one of these sections by clicking part of the section that does not include a control. The following shows the properties for the Report Header Section:

Section	
Force New Page .	None
New Row Or Col .	None
Keep Together . .	No
Visible	Yes
On Format	
On Print	
Can Grow	No
Can Shrink	No
Height	0.59 in
Special Effect . .	Color
Back Color	16777215

With some reports, you will want to print the information for each record on a separate page. Rather than adding a page break control to the report design, you can have a new page start at the beginning or end of each section. For example, say your Report Header, Report Footer, Page Header, and Page Footer are empty and you want the contents of the Detail section for each record printed on a separate page. To add a page break to a section, change the Force New Page property. The default for the property is None so the report only starts another page after filling the current one. You can select Before Section so the report starts on a new page every time the current section is printed. You can select After Section so the report starts on a new page after printing the current section. Finally, you can select Before & After when you want a new page started every time you start and end the current section. With the example of wanting to put each Detail section on a separate page, you would select Before & After.

Splitting a report between pages can also result in part of a section printing on one page and the rest of the section printing on the next page. You can change the report design so if Access cannot fit the entire section on the current page, the section starts on the next page. You may want all of the information about a record printed on the same page so you do not have to flip between pages to look at the record's contents. To force a report to do this, change the section's Keep Together property from No to Yes. When you print the report, Access moves information to the next page whenever the current page lacks sufficient room in which to print the entire section.

Later in this chapter, you will learn how you can create groups that divide the records in a report into collections of records with the same value for a field. The report in Figure 11-8 shows an example of this. Notice from Figure 11-8 that the report uses three columns. You can use three columns by choosing Print Setup from the File menu, selecting More, and typing **3** in the Items Across box. The records are filled into the report from top to bottom because the Vertical option button in the Print Setup dialog box is selected.

Also, each time the Client Id value changes, the report starts again in the next column even if the report leaves empty space in the current column. The report starts in the next column in this report because the Group Header section, which starts each group of projects for the different clients, has the Keep Row or Col property set to Before Section. The default is None so when you have a report divided into columns, each column is filled completely before another column is begun.

FIGURE 11-8 Starting groups in new columns

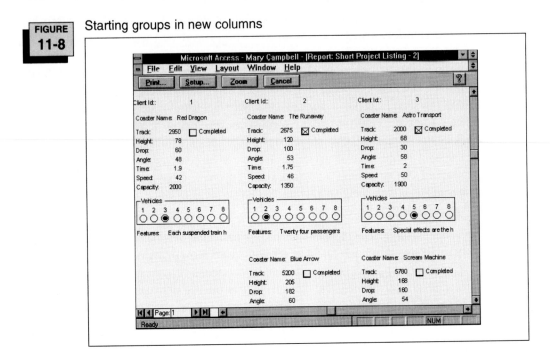

You can also set this property to After Section (which has been done to the Group Footer section in the report later in this chapter in Figure 11-10). The report then prints all records with the same Client Id value. The other choice, Before & After, starts a new column before and after the section is printed. When the report fills the columns and the Item Layout is set to Horizontal, starting a new column causes the report shown in Figure 11-8 to put all of the records for the first client in the first row of records, all records for the second client in the second row of records, and so on.

A section also has On Format and On Print properties. These properties tell Access to perform a macro or user-defined function whenever the report is formatted or printed. Reports are formatted when Access is setting up the information to appear in the report when you print or preview the report. You will learn more about macros in Chapter 16.

Some of the section properties are identical to the control properties having the same name. The Visible property can set whether a section appears. You can create macros that select when this section appears based on another criteria. The Can Shrink and Can Grow properties perform the same function in a section as they perform when you apply them to individual controls.

The default for a section is No for Can Shrink. For Can Grow, the default is No unless you have set one of the controls in the section to have the Can Grow property set to Yes, which also sets the section's Can Grow property to Yes. The Height property sets the section's height just as you can set the section's height by dragging the bottom of the section up or down. You might use this property rather than the mouse when you want to be sure that two sections are the same height or sections appearing in different reports are the same height. The Special Effect and Back Color properties are described in Chapter 14, which tells how to change the appearance of a report.

Report Properties

Reports also have their own properties. These properties include the table or query the report uses, the grid, the report width, and when page headers and footers print. These properties are different than the properties you learned about for controls and sections. Display the properties for a report in the Property Sheet window by choosing Select Report in the View menu or by clicking an area in the Report Design window that is not part of the report design. The following shows the properties for the report:

Report	
Record Source	Project
On Open	
On Close	
Grid X	10
Grid Y	12
Layout for Print	Yes
Page Header	All Pages
Page Footer	All Pages
Record Locks	No Locks
Width	1.9 in
Help File	
Help Context Id	0

In Chapter 9, you learned how to use the grid for placement. Change the size of the grid by selecting the number of grid points per inch that appear vertically and horizontally on the report design. The number of dots per inch is set with the Grid X and Grid Y properties. By entering a new number for the Grid X property, you set the number of grid points per inch that fit across the report design. By entering a new number for the Grid Y property, you set the number of grid points per inch that fit up and down the report design. Even when you change the numbers, the grid will not appear until you display it with Grid in the View menu.

The Width property sets the report's width just as you can set the report width by dragging the right side of the report to the left or right. You might use this property rather than the mouse when you want the report to be a specific width. Changing the width changes the width of all sections in the report.

The fonts used in the entries in the report rely on the fonts you have installed for Windows. Windows has some fonts that are designed for printing and others meant for displaying information on the screen. Select whether you use the screen or the printer fonts for the report with the layout for Print property. The default for reports is Yes so the report uses printer fonts. Select No for this property when you want the report to use screen fonts. When you print the report using screen fonts, Windows substitutes a similar printer font. When you use a TrueType font such as the ones available in Windows 3.1 or through accessory packages such as Facelift or Adobe Typeface Manager, changing this property does not affect the fonts because TrueType fonts look the same on the screen as they do when printed.

If you share a database with other users, you may want to prevent others from changing the data that appears in your report. Protect your records by selecting All Records for the Record Locks property. When you generate the report, all of the records included in the report are locked so other users cannot change their data. The default of No Locks means other users can continue using the data so your generation of the report does not prevent them from editing data.

Usually, you will use the table or query you have selected when you first start to create a report. However, if you change your mind or you have selected the Blank Report button from the New Report dialog box without selecting a table or query, select a table or query to control the fields that are listed in the field list window. To set which table or query the report uses, change the Record Source property. Select any of the tables and queries available in the database.

When you change the table or query, the fields listed in the field list window change to match the new table or query but the fields from the old table or query in the report design do not change. You may want to change the table or query in a report when you have copied or imported a report designed to work with one table or query that you want to use with another—for example, to use a report you have created for the Employee table to print names and addresses with a roster you have in a database that keeps track of your bowling league.

The default for page headers and footers is to print on every page but you may not want to include page headers and footers on pages that already have a report header or footer. To change whether the page header prints on every page, change the Page Header property, and to change whether the page footer prints on every page, change the Page Footer property. The default is All Pages, which prints the page header or page footer on every page. When you select Not with Rpt Hdr, the page header or footer prints on every page except the one that has the report header. When you select Not with Rpt Ftr, the page header or footer prints on every page except the one that has the report footer. When you select Not with Rpt Hdr/Ftr, the page header or footer prints on every page except those that have a report header and report footer. As an example, you may want to change the Page Header property to Not with Rpt Hdr and the Page Footer property to Not with Rpt Ftr when you do not want to print the page header on the first page and the page footer on the last.

A report also has On Open and On Close properties. These tell Access to perform a macro or user-defined function whenever the report is created or when Access is finished creating and printing the report. You will learn more about macros in Chapter 16.

Finally, a report has Help Contents Id and Help File properties to select which help topic appears when the user presses F1 and the help file containing the help topics as described for control properties. When the Help File property is empty, the report uses the same help file as that Access uses.

Sorting the Report's Output

When printing a report, you usually want records to appear in a different order from how they appear in the table or query. You'll often want each report to present information differently. Set the order of the records in a report according to the values of fields. Use the values of one or more fields to organize the records in the table or query. You can also change whether the records are sorted according to the field's values in ascending or descending order. Changing the order does not change the order of the records in the table or query. Sorting only changes the order of the records as they appear in the report. Sorting, unlike filters in a form that you learned about in Chapter 10, is done from the report design.

To change the order of the records in the table or query for the report you are designing, tell Access that you want the records sorted. The first step is to display the Sorting and Grouping box shown here:

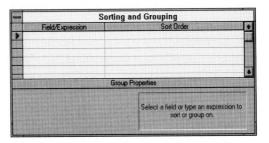

To display this box, either choose Sorting and Grouping in the View menu or click the Sorting and Grouping button, which is the second button in the toolbar, shown here:

When the Sorting and Grouping box appears, enter the fields and expressions you will use to organize the records in the report. In the Field/Expression column, enter the field names that will organize the records by typing the field name or by clicking the down arrow to list the field names that you can pick from the list. Besides selecting the field names, you can select whether the values of the field are sorted in ascending or descending order. In the Sort Order column, select from Ascending or Descending to select the order of the field's values.

Select up to ten fields to sort the records. Access uses the selected fields in the order you enter them. First Access organizes all of the records according to the value of the first field you select in ascending or descending order as you have selected. When two or more records have the same entry for the first field, Access looks at the second field to determine the order of those records. When two or more records have the same values for the first and second fields, Access sorts those records by the value of the third field. This sorting process continues for up to the ten fields you select to sort.

After selecting the fields, close the box. Select Close from the box's Control menu, double-click the box's Control menu box, or press ALT-F4. When you return to the report's design, you will not notice a difference in the report's design. When you preview or print the report, Access will generate the report using the records in the order you select. Later, in Chapter 12, you will learn to create expressions whose values are used to sort the records in the report.

 Note You cannot use Memo, Picture, or OLE objects as a field to sort the records in a report.

 Tip If sorting your records in a report, you may want to index the fields in the underlying table or query. Indexing the fields that you will use to order the records speeds up generating the report.

Grouping Report Records

Grouping records in a report is just like sorting records except the report has breaks in between each group of records. Grouped records can have header and footer sections that start and end each group of records. You have been introduced to groups in records with the groups/totals ReportWizard report type. Figure 11-9 shows a report that uses groups. The department name appears as the header for the groups. The subtotals appear in the footer sections for the groups. The records are ordered by the value of the Department field and are divided into groups when the value of the Department field changes.

Think of using multiple layers of grouping as a way of organizing the report records into an outline. When you have an outline of the records in a report like the one shown in Figure 11-10, the records are divided into groups according to three values. The first set of headings divides the report's records according to their values for the first field. Within each first-level heading, the report is further divided into second-level

FIGURE 11-9

Records grouped by the Department field

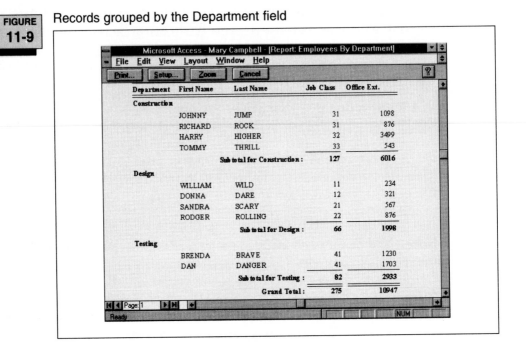

FIGURE 11-10

An outline showing different levels of grouping

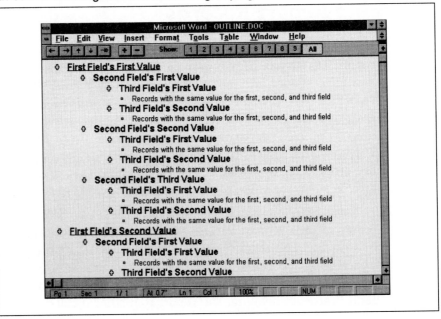

headings according to their values for a second field. Within each second-level heading are third-level headings that further divide the records by their values of a third field. It is only after the third-level headings that the report contains the records. These records can be organized within the section so you can alphabetize the records or put them into numerical order according to some field. A difference between the report outline shown in Figure 11-10 and a report in Access is the report in Access can have a footer section at the end of a group. For example, if you have Number data type fields in a report, you may want to total them at the end of every group.

Grouping and sorting records for a report are done together. When you want to group records, display the Sorting and Grouping box by clicking the Sorting and Grouping button in the toolbar or choosing Sorting and Grouping in the View menu. Access organizes the records to present them in the report according to the fields that you enter in the Sorting and Grouping box. Next, Access adds breaks between the records depending on which fields in the Sorting and Grouping box you select to group the field values. Access only divides the records in groups by the fields that you select to be grouped.

The first step toward grouping records in a report is selecting the fields that you want to order the table or query's records. From the Sorting and Grouping box, select the fields that you want to organize the records for the report. This is the same as sorting. When you want the report to have groups, the first field you use for grouping will be the first field in the Sorting and Grouping box. If you have groups within other groups, select the field for the second set of groups as the second field in the Sorting and Grouping box. You can also select additional fields when you want to divide the records by more than two fields. You can use up to ten fields to sort and divide the records into groups.

For example, in the report in Figure 11-11, the records are grouped by the Client Id field. The records are also sorted according to coaster name. Both Client Id and Coaster Name are included in the Sorting and Grouping box.

The difference between grouping and sorting records is the changes you make to the group properties in the bottom of the Sorting and Grouping box. Once you have selected the fields for organizing the records and selected between ascending and descending order, you are ready to change the group's properties.

Records grouped by Client ID and sorted by Coaster Name

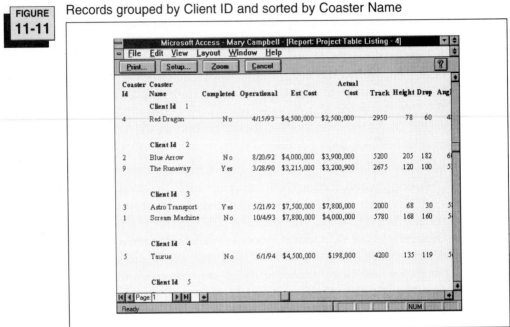

Tip If you want the records in a group to be in a specific order, add the field at the end of the field list in the Sorting and Grouping box but do not change the Group Header or Group Footer property to Yes.

Setting Group Properties

When grouping records, you create the groups and set how the groups are divided by changing the group properties. These group properties are listed at the bottom of the Sorting and Grouping box. Each field in the Field/Expression list can have separate group properties. When you create groups by changing the field's group properties, you are creating groups by working from the top of the list of fields.

When finished selecting the fields to group by, close the Sorting and Grouping box to continue working on the report's design. Select Close from the box's Control menu, double-click the box's Control menu box, or press ALT-F4. This time, when you leave the box, you will notice a difference in the report design. If you have selected Yes for the Group Header or Group Footer properties, the report will have two sections. The header section has the name of the field used to group the records followed by Header. The bottom new section has the name of the field used to group the records followed by Footer. Figure 11-12 shows the report design for the completed report shown in Figure 11-13 (after the groups are added).

Adding Header and Footer Bands

The feature that makes grouping special is that groups can have header and footer sections that mark the beginning and end of each group. You can add these group sections and Access will put them into the report design. Once these sections are part of the report design, you can add controls to them. Usually in a header, you introduce the group the report will display. A footer often contains sections that summarize the records that are part of a group.

FIGURE 11-12

A report design for using a group's header and footer sections

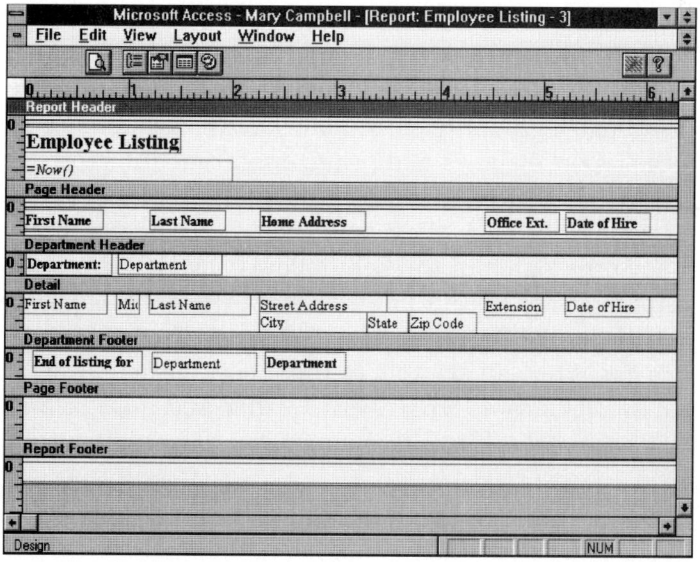

FIGURE
11-13

A report created from the report design in Figure 11-12

To add a header or footer to start or end a field's group or records, select the field from the Field/Expression column. Next, change the Group Header or Group Footer in the group properties section from Yes to No. Once you change either of these properties, you have changed from sorting to grouping since now you are including a special section that the report displays and prints every time the value for the selected field changes. You can even see in the background behind the Sorting and Grouping box how the report's design has new sections. The new sections have the name of the field followed by Header or Footer (whichever is appropriate). Figure 11-12 shows a report design where the Department field has the Group Header and Group Footer group properties changed to Yes. You can see this in the report design because the report design now includes a Department Header and a Department Footer section. Department is the field or expression that divides the records into groups.

The order in which Group Header and Group Footer sections are added to the report design is determined by the order of the fields in the Sorting and Grouping box. Think of the groups as organized starting from the Page Header and Page Footer sections and working in to the Detail section. The first field at the top of the list in the Sorting and Grouping box is the first Group Header and Group Footer section in the report design. The next field in the Sorting and Grouping box that has the Group Header and Group Footer properties set to Yes is the next field that has a Group Header and Group Footer section in the report design. This continues through the list of fields in the Sorting and Grouping box, where each group's header and footer section are added to the report in the order the fields are listed. Finally, after the Group Header and Group Footer sections for the last field in the Sorting and Grouping box that has the Group Header or Group Footer property set to Yes, is the Detail section.

Setting How Records Are Divided into Groups

When you created reports with ReportWizards in Chapter 9, you learned that you can divide groups according to field values different ways depending on the field's data type. For example, text fields can be divided into groups according to their unique values or by the first few characters in the field entries.

The groups you create from the report design can have the same types of divisions. Setting how the records are divided into groups is done with the Group On property and the Group Interval property.

For the Group On property, you are selecting whether you want to start a new group every time the value in the selected field changes or by some other criteria. The default for this property is Each Value, so every time the value for a field that has the Group Header or Group Footer property set to Yes changes, the report starts a new group.

What other choices you have for this property depend on the field's data type. For Text data types, you can group according to the first several characters. To do this, change the Group On property to Prefix Characters and type the number of characters you want to use for each group in the Group Interval property. The default of 1 for the Group Interval property means that unless you enter a new number, when you select Prefix Characters for the Group On property, you will start a new group every time the first letter of the selected field changes.

For Counter, Currency, Number, and Yes/No fields you choose between Each Value and Interval. Interval lets you group the records into sets. When you create a groups/totals ReportWizard report type that creates a group based on one of these field types, you have the choice of Normal and values such as 10s, 50s, and 100s. These numbers are the same types of numbers you can enter for the Group Interval property. For example, if you enter **25** for the Group Interval property, the first group has records with values for the field of 1 to 25, the second group has records with values for the field of 26 to 50, the third group has records with values for the fields of 51 to 75, and so on for all of the values the field has.

For Date/Time fields you have the choices Each Value, Year, Qtr, Month, Week, Day, Hour, and Minute. When you select one of the choices other than Each Value, you can use the Group Interval property to create groups of the selected date or time interval. For example, entering **30** for Group Interval when Group On is set to Minute groups the records by 30-minute intervals for the Date/Time field. As an example, the report design in Figure 11-14 groups the projects by the year of the Operational field. The Operational field is shortened in the Operational Header section so only the year shows. When you use this report design to create the report, the report looks like Figure 11-15, which shows the part of the report for the projects completed in 1992. In the next section, you will learn how to add the formulas that total the estimated costs and actual costs.

Using Groups in a Report Design

Once you have added Group Header and Group Footer sections to your report, you are ready to fill these sections. Filling the section uses the same report design features you use for the Detail section. The Header section often introduces the group. You might include the field name for which all of the records in the group have the same value (as shown in the Operational field in Figure 11-15). When you put a field name in a Group Header section setting, the field value is the field's value of the first record within the group. When you include a field name in the group footer section, the field value is the field's value of the last record of that group. The Group Footer section indicates that the report has listed all

FIGURE 11-14

A report design that combines records for the same operational year

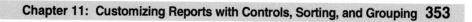

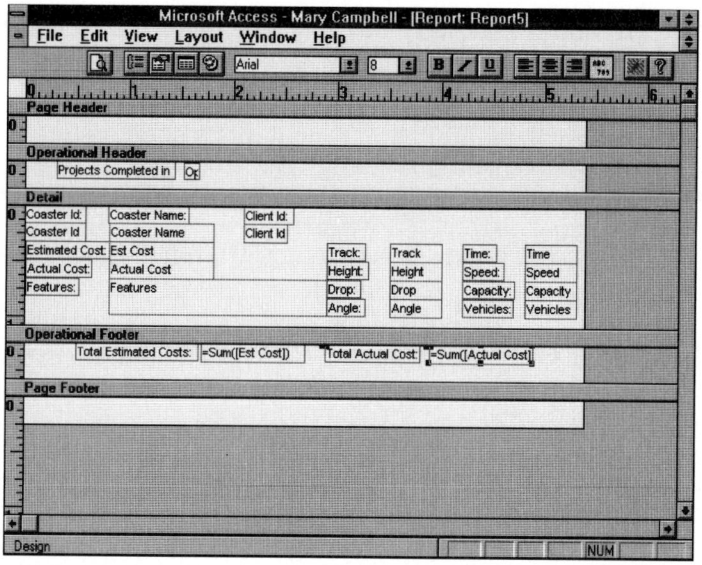

FIGURE 11-15

A report created from the report design in Figure 11-14

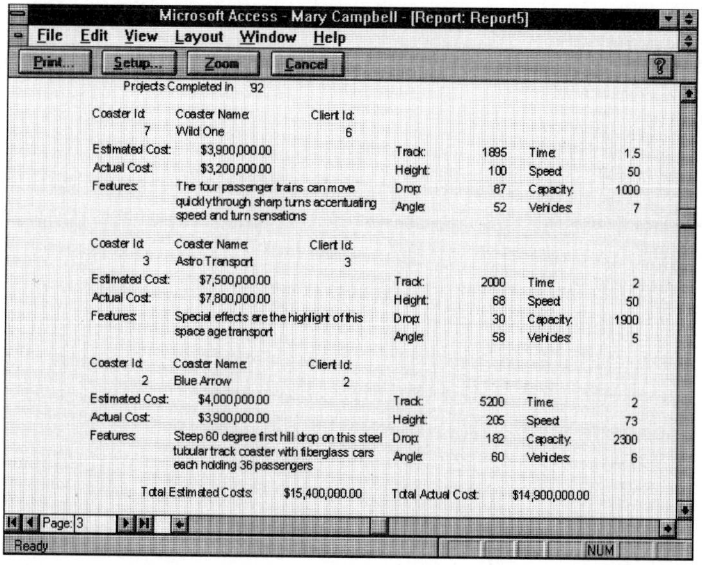

of the records for that group. This section often includes summary information.

To add a summary field like the one for the report in Figure 11-15, you need to add a text box control. In place of the field name for the control's Control Source property, you need to tell Access that you want to put a calculation here. Calculations such as totals, page names, and dates are called expressions. You will learn more about expressions in Chapter 12.

When you create groups, you will often use expressions that total field values so learning to create these types of expressions can help you now. A function is a special type of expression. You will often use functions such as SUM and COUNT when you include an expression in a Group Header or Footer section. A function as an expression starts off as an equal sign followed by the function name and parentheses, which enclose in brackets ([ ]) the field name or other information the function needs to perform. For example, if you want to sum the estimated cost and actual cost for the roller coaster projects you have grouped by Client, the expressions are =SUM([Est Cost]) and =SUM([Actual Cost]). You can either type these expressions in the text box or display the property sheet, select the text box control, and enter the expression for the Control Source property. While this maneuver may seem new, actually, you created reports that use summary fields when you created a groups/totals ReportWizard report in Chapter 9. This report type automatically summarizes all of the Number, Currency, and Counter data type fields.

When you use a function to total the values in a report, where you place the function determines when the calculation is restarted. When you put a summary function into a Group Header or Group Footer section, Access recalculates the function every time you switch between groups created by the selected Group Header or Footer. When the summary function is in the page header or footer section, Access recalculates the function every time you start a new page. When the summary function is in the report header or footer section, the function is only calculated once at the end of the report. Chapter 12 shows you how to change where the function is reset.

Quick Reference

To Add a Control to a Report   Display the Toolbox by choosing Toolbox from the View menu. Click the tool for the control you want to add, then click the report design where you want the control placed.

To Set a Control's Properties   Display the Property Sheet window by choosing Properties from the View menu. Click the control whose properties you want to change in the report design. Click the property you want to change in the property sheet. Type the new entry for the property or select one of the choices available by clicking the down arrow.

To Sort Records in a Report   Display the Sorting and Grouping box by choosing Sorting and Grouping from the View menu. Select the field you want to use for sorting in the Field Name/Expression column. Select Ascending or Descending in the Sort Order column. Repeat adding fields and sort orders for up to ten fields in the order you want the records sorted. Close the box with ALT-F4 or Close from the Control menu.

To Group Records in a Report

Display the Sorting and Grouping box by choosing Sorting and Grouping from the View menu. Select the field you want to use for grouping in the Field Name/Expression column. Select Ascending or Descending in the Sort Order column. Add Group Header and Footer sections by changing the Group Header and Group Footer properties for the fields from No to Yes. You can also change how the values of the fields are grouped by making changes to the Group On and Group Interval properties. After closing the box, add controls to the group's header and footer sections to supply the contents of these sections. Close the box with ALT-F4 or Close from the Control menu.

CHAPTER

Using Expressions in Reports and Forms

Besides using field contents and fixed text entries, you can add *expressions* to your forms and reports. An expression is a formula where you tell Access what you want placed at a specific location in your form or report. You have already used expressions. The queries you created used expressions to select which records would match the criteria you set. Also, many of the reports you created with ReportWizards have expressions added to supply the date, page number, and totals of Number, Currency, and Counter data field types. You will often use expressions to provide information not directly supplied in a table or query. For example, if you want to combine the city, state, and ZIP code for your employees' addresses in a report or form, create an expression that combines the three fields and adds the commas and spaces that you want.

Expressions in a form or report can perform several different functions. An expression can put a calculation's result in a form or report. Expressions can set the default value of a field. Use expressions to check the validity of an entry or total field values for groups of records. You also can use expressions to calculate totals or averages in a report. Access has several predefined functions you can use in a form or report's expression to return information such as the current date or page number.

Think of expressions in reports and forms as entries you might make on a calculator. The imaginary calculator Access uses has many more buttons than you would find in any hand-held model. For example, this imaginary calculator includes the field names used by the report or form. The calculator also includes keys for different functions that return information otherwise not available or works with data you have stored in a field. Figure 12-1 shows some of the features Access's imaginary calculator contains.

Expression Rules

Expressions have several rules. These rules let Access know what types of data and information you are using. Expressions usually start in forms and reports with an equal sign followed by a description of what you want the expression to equal. The types of entries that follow the

FIGURE
12-1

Imaginary Calculator representing expressions you can enter in Access

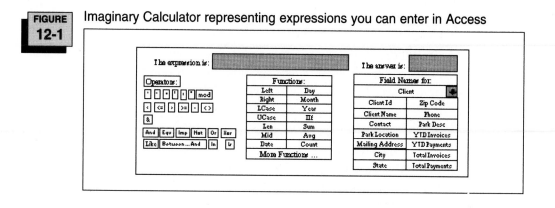

equal sign include controls such as field names, operators such as < and +, and function names.

Some expressions use names of controls. For example, you might have expressions in a report that totals actual and estimated costs of roller coasters. These control names include field names and other controls you add to a form or report.

In an expression, Access needs to know where a control name starts and ends. Since you can have up to 64 characters in a control name, you enclose them in special characters to let Access know when you have finished entering a control name. For example, field names are enclosed in brackets as in [Last Name]. Form and report names also use brackets as in [Clients and Their Coasters]. You will want to include a form name as part of an expression when you are using subforms in Chapter 13.

To separate a field name from a report name, use an exclamation point (!) as in [Employee Data]![Last Name]. If you are providing the form name for an expression, you may need to tell Access that the name is for a form as in Forms![Employee Data]![Last Name]. If you need to include a property name after the control name, separate the control name and property name with a period as in [Last Name].Format.

Expressions also contain *literals*, which indicate text, numbers, or dates to be used exactly as you enter them. Text literals must be enclosed in quotes as in "This is text". Dates must be enclosed with number signs as in #06/03/93# but you can enter the date in any of the acceptable date formats between the number signs. Numbers do not need any special characters. Access assumes the remaining characters in an expression are function names and other expression operators.

Data Types in Expressions

Like fields, expressions have data types. Some of these data types are just like field data types. These include Integer, Long, Short, Double, and Currency. Access has three other types: String, Variant, and User-defined. String contains characters just like the characters you store in Text and Memo data type fields. Variant stores any type of data.

The special feature of the variant data type allows you to flip between storing different data types. User Defined is a data type that you can use in expressions when you are programming using Access Basic. Access Basic is the programming you use for Access. Most of the time, when you add expressions to queries, forms, and reports, you do not use user-defined data types. Usually you do not need to worry about data types since most of the expressions you create are the Variant type; Access adjusts the data type to the results returned by the expression. For example, in some products if you want to combine the text "Phone Number" with a phone number stored as a number, you would have to perform the additional step to convert the text and the phone number to the same data type.

Expression Operators

Expressions can have operators. The operators are like the buttons on a calculator that tell the calculator the function you want to perform with the numbers you have entered or will enter. Access has six categories of operators: arithmetic, comparison, concatenation, logical, pattern matching, and miscellaneous.

Unlike other products where additional spaces cause formulas using the same types of operators to be incorrect, you can include spaces before and after the expression operators. Access will even add them for you after you enter the expression so the expression is easier to understand.

Several of the operators return true or false results. This means Access looks at the expression and decides whether it's true or false. True expressions have the numeric value of -1 and false expressions have the numeric value of 0. As an example, Access looks at an expression such as =3>5 and decides it is false. When an expression that is evaluated contains field names, Access substitutes the field's value of the current record into the expression.

Arithmetic Operators

The easiest expressions to understand are the ones that use the basic arithmetic operators. These operators include many of the mathematical functions you find on the smallest calculators such as addition, subtraction, multiplication, division, exponentiation, and modulo.

Exponentiation raises a number to another power. An example is raising 2 to the third power as in 2*2*2 or 8, which you can write as 2^3.

Modulo performs division except it returns the remainder so when you divide 11 by 5, the result is 2 with a remainder, or modulus, of 1.

Access has two operators for division. The slash key (/) is the standard division symbol but if you are dividing two integers, you use the backslash key (\) instead so Access performs the division faster.

The symbols Access uses for the arithmetic operators include + for addition, – for subtraction, * for multiplication, / for division when both entries are not Integer data types, \ for division when both numbers are Integer data types, ^ for exponentiation, and mod for modulo.

Figure 12-2 shows an example of the results of an arithmetic operator used for calculating the differences in the form. In this form, the formula for the entry after Amount Still Due is =[Total Invoices]–[Total Payments].

Comparison Operators

Comparison operators are also easy to use. The comparison operators include < (less than), <= (less than or equal to), > (greater than), >= (greater than or equal to), = (equal), and <> (does not equal). You use these operators when you want to use one of two values. For example, if you want to show whether all invoices are paid, you use the expression =[Total Payments] = [Total Invoices]. This expression is the expression used by the check box in Figure 12-2.

In Figure 12-2, for the first record where the Amount Still Due control has the value of 200,000, the check box is cleared. For a record where

FIGURE
12-2

Results of expressions used for a text box and a check box control's value

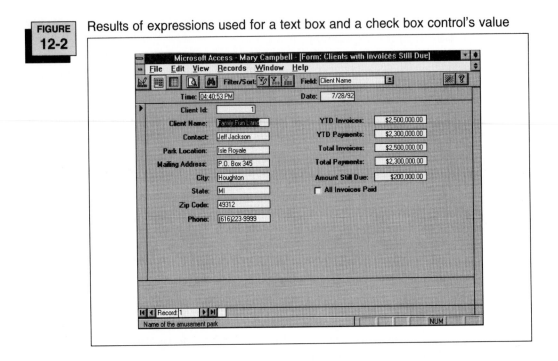

all of the invoices are paid, the check box is selected. When the expression containing the comparison operator is true, the check box, toggle button, or option button is selected. When the expression containing the comparison operator is false, the check box, toggle button, or option button is false. If you used this comparison operator expression in a text box, the text box will display –1 or 0 to indicate true or false.

The other use of comparison operators is to use the value of true or false for subsequent calculations. For example, if you want to add a late fee to overdue invoices, you create an expression that compares the current date to the invoice date. If the invoice date is 60 days ago, you add a late fee. You can add a late fee by multiplying the –1 or 0 the comparison operator returns by the amount of the late fee. The late fee is a negative number so when you multiply it by –1, the late fee becomes a positive number. This expression looks like this:

=([Invoice Date]+60<Date( ))*–.01*[Invoice Amount]

This expression tests if the invoice date plus 60 days occurred before today's date. When the invoice is still current, the rest of the expression equals zero since the 0 from the comparison operator part of the expression is multiplied by the other values. When the invoice is overdue, the comparison part of the expression equals –1, which is multiplied by –1 percent of the invoice amount. The parentheses tells Access to perform the comparison before multiplying the values.

Sometimes you will run into situations using comparison operators where the data type of what you are comparing matters. Access decides how it will compare the data by looking at the data types of the data you are comparing. When the data types are both Number and Currency types, Access determines which number is larger or smaller than the other. When you compare text, Access compares the text left to right, one character at a time. When you use comparison operators, you will want to use them with data that it makes sense to compare.

The Concatenation Operator

Access has only one concatenation operator, the ampersand (&). The ampersand joins two entries as if they are one. For example, when you add an address to a report, you do not want a big gap between the city and the state. Instead of leaving the space between the city and the state, put the state right next to the city by using an expression that uses the concatenation operator.

You have already seen this operator in use when you use the mailing label ReportWizard report type. When you add fields and text to a line in a mailing label, the mailing label ReportWizard report type builds expressions that combine the text and fields you select. For example, in Chapter 9, the example of the mailing label ReportWizard report type using the Client table creates the line containing the city, state, and ZIP code with the expression of =[City] & ", " & [State] &"" & [Zip Code]. To use the concatenation operator, put the ampersand between the two entries you want to combine. Usually, you do not have to worry about the type of data you are combining; you can combine Text data types with Number data types without converting the data as you do with other products.

Figure 12-3 shows a report design that uses this operator to produce the report shown in Figure 12-4. The expressions combine text with some of the values in the Project table so the report presents them as complete sentences. Rather than having gaps between the text and the field values, the text boxes contain expressions that combine them into a stream of

FIGURE
12-3

Expressions that combine text and field values

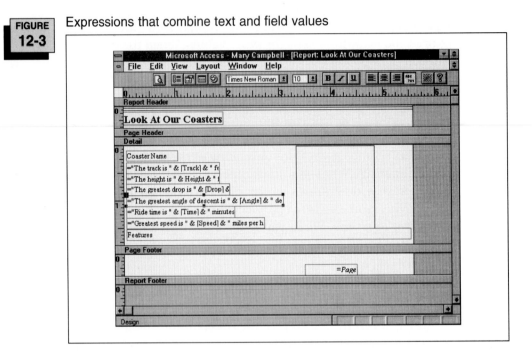

FIGURE
12-4

The report created from the design shown in Figure 12-3

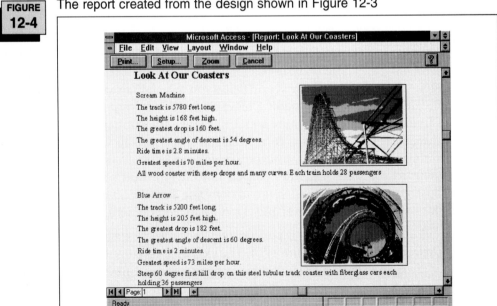

characters with no extra spaces. These are some of the formulas used in the report:

```
="The track is " & [Track] & " feet long."
="The height is " & Height & " feet high."
="The greatest drop is " & [Drop] & " feet."
="The greatest angle of descent is " & [Angle] & " degrees."
="Ride time is " & [Time] & " minutes."
="Greatest speed is " & [Speed] & " miles per hour."
```

Logical Operators

Another type of comparison you will want to make is comparing two true and false values you have from other calculations. For example, you can have comparisons that check both whether an invoice is overdue and, if so, whether the amount is over 100,000. With this example, you may want a true response when both conditions are true or a false response when either or both of the conditions are false.

To make this type of evaluation, you use logical operators. Most of the logical operators compare two true or false conditions placed on either side of the operator. These conditions may use the comparison or other types of operators. Only the Not operator uses a single condition, which is placed after the operator. Here are the logical operators and their results:

And　　Returns true only when the conditions before and after the And are true and returns a false on all other occasions

Eqv　　Returns true when the conditions before and after the Eqv are either both true or both false, and returns a false when either condition is true while the other one is false

Imp　　Returns a true or false value depending on whether the first condition implies the second condition

Not　　Returns true when the condition after Not is false and returns false when the condition after Not is true

Or　　Returns true when either one condition or both conditions are true

Xor　　Returns true when either of the conditions before and after Xor is true and returns false when the conditions before and after Xor are both true or both false

As an example, when you want a check box in a form or report for the Invoice Register table to be selected when both the invoice is over 60 days old and the invoice amount is over $100,000, you can enter the expression =([Invoice Date]+60<Date( )) And [Invoice Amount]>100000.

Only when the results from both comparisons are true will the entire expression be true and the check box selected. When either or both conditions are false, the check box is cleared.

Pattern Matching Operators

When an entry must match a certain pattern, you use the Like pattern matching operator to test that an entry meets a particular pattern. For example, a part number may have a specific pattern of digits and characters. A form can easily tell when you enter a part number incorrectly if the pattern of numbers and letters does not match the pattern you have set up. To use this pattern operator, use the entry you are comparing, then Like followed by the pattern in quotes. The expression equals true when the entry before Like matches the pattern after Like and false when the pattern does not match the entry preceding Like.

The pattern entered after Like is how you tell Access which characters are allowed in the pattern. A pattern uses ? to represent any single character, # to represent any digit (0–9), and * to represent zero or more characters. You can also include characters directly as in (###) for the beginning of a phone number so the phone number has parentheses around the area code. Another option is to include a group or range of characters by including the characters or range of characters in brackets ([ ]). An example of several characters is [abc] and an example of a range of characters is [A–Z].

 Note Access distinguishes between uppercase and lowercase characters in the brackets so [abc] is not the same as [ABC].

One requirement of a range is that the characters be in ascending order so you can use [A–Z] but not [Z–A]. You can also use the brackets to exclude characters by putting an exclamation point after the opening bracket as in [!A–Z] to not match an uppercase letter. You do not want to use [ ] with only a space in between the brackets since Access only ignores that combination. You can include a space when other characters are in the brackets as in [abc].

An example of this operator is used in Figure 12-5. In this form, the phone number is entered with the area code in parentheses and a hyphen after the exchange (three digits after the area code). The expression [Home Phone] Like "(###)###?####" tests whether the home phone number is entered correctly. The ? is used in place of a hyphen since a hyphen in the pattern indicates a range of characters. The form uses this expression by using Like "(###)###?####" as the control's Validation Rule property. The Validation Rule property does not need [Home Phone] since it is implicitly provided.

Miscellaneous Operators

Finally, Access has some miscellaneous operators that provide many different features. These features test if one entry is in a range, whether an entry is a member of a set of entries, or whether an entry is empty. These operators make working with an expression easier since they often combine the features of comparison operators and logical operators.

FIGURE 12-5

A form using the Like operator to check for a pattern

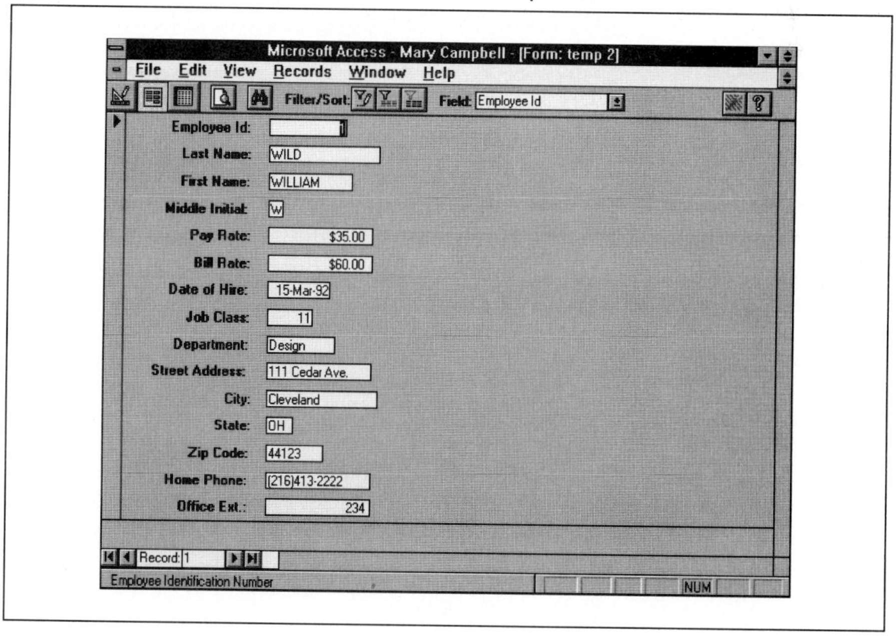

When you need to test whether an entry falls inside or outside of a range, you can combine the logical and comparison operators or you can use the Between ... And operator. This operator tests whether the value before Between is within the range set by the entries before the And and after the And. When the tested entry is in the range, this operator returns a true value. When the tested entry is outside of the range, this operator returns a false value. You can always flip the result of this operator by putting the Not logical operator before the entry so a true value becomes false and vice versa. As an example, you can have an expression =[Height] Between 2000 And 3000 in place of the expression =[Height] > 2000 And [Height] < 3000.

If you need to test whether an entry is part of a group, use the In operator. For example, if you have a Health field in your Employee table to indicate which of four health insurance plans each employee participates in, this field might contain the letters A, B, C, and D. One method of testing that an entry is made correctly is to create an expression such as = [Health] = "A" Or [Health] = "B" Or [Health] = "C" Or [Health] = "D" that checks whether Health is one of these four letters. A better alternative is to use the In operator in an expression like this: = [Health] In ("A", "B", "C", "D"). This expression equals true when Health equals one of the four letters and false when it equals something else.

The last miscellaneous operator, the Is operator, combines with Null to test if an entry is empty. For example, if you are entering amounts paid on invoices for the Client table, you do not want to add payments until you add invoices. Use an expression for total payments that tests whether Total Invoices has an entry. The expression = [Total Invoices] Is Null returns a true value when Total Invoices does not contain an entry and a false value when Total Invoices has an entry. This operator is often combined with the Iif function (which you'll learn about later in this chapter) to return another value depending on whether the expression you are testing contains an entry.

Operator Precedence

When you have several operators in an expression, Access makes decisions for the order it uses to evaluate them. Earlier you saw an example of combining different operator types in the second example of a comparison operator that combined a comparison operator with an arithmetic operator. In that example, the expression included parentheses to tell Access to make the comparison before multiplying the numbers. If you did not include the parentheses, Access would multiply the numbers and then use the resulting values for the comparison. Access does this because in Access's precedence order, multiplication is evaluated before comparison operators. By including parentheses, the comparison is performed first. Anything in parentheses is evaluated before the other parts of the expression. When you have several sets of parentheses, Access works from the inside out. For example, if you have this expression,

```
(5*(3+8))^2
```

Access first adds 3 and 8 in the inside set of parentheses then multiplies the result of 11 by 5. Once Access multiplies 5 by 11 for 55, Access then raises it to the power of 2 (55 X 55) for the result of 3025. The order Access evaluates operators is shown in Table 12-1. Access evaluates operators starting from the top of the table and working down. All operators at the same level are evaluated from left to right.

 Tip Where you place the expression determines where the field values the expression uses are reset. For example, when you put the expression in the Detail section, the expressions are updated for every record. When

TABLE 12-1 Operators and Their Operator Precedence

Operator	Function It Performs
()	Grouping
	Exponentiation
–	Negation (makes a number a negative number)
* /	Multiplication and division
\	Integer division
Mod	Modulus
+ –	Addition and subtraction
&	Concatenation
< <= > >= = <> Like	Comparison and pattern matching
Not And Or Xor Eqv Imp	Logical

you put an expression in a header for a group in a report, the expression is recalculated when you start a new group. You can change when an expression is reset by changing the expression's Running Sum property as described later in the chapter.

Functions

Functions are included in expressions to provide ready-made formulas and return information that is not readily available. Functions are used for forms, reports, and other advanced Access features such as macros and modules. Some of the functions are not often used with forms and reports. This section focuses on some of the functions most frequently used in forms and reports.

Functions have the format of the function name followed by its arguments surrounded in parentheses. The function's argument(s) is the information you must supply for the function. The arguments a function uses depends on the function since each function may need different information. Function arguments are often field names, or literals such as a number, date, or a string. Appendix B lists all of the available functions with the arguments they use and the results the functions provide.

 Tip   If you have used spreadsheet applications such as Excel, Lotus 1-2-3, or Quattro Pro, you may already know about many of the functions available through Access. Functions such as Left, Right, and Npv perform the same function in both Access and these spreadsheet products although the format for entering them differs.

Using Functions to Return Part of a String

Access has several functions that return part of a section of text. If you want to create mailing labels to your employees that use the first letters of their first and middle names, you can use a function to return only one character out of the first name. You can also use other functions to return the last few characters or a section of characters from the middle of a string or text field. The Left function returns a selected number of characters starting from the left side of the text and the Right function returns a selected number of characters starting from the right side of the text. The Mid function returns a selected number of characters starting from a position in the text that you select.

An example of using one of these functions is if you want to combine the first letter of the first and middle name with the last name for mailing labels. For this purpose, the expression that creates the name looks like this:

```
= Left([First Name],1) & ". " & [Middle Initial] & ". " & [Last
Name]
```

The Left function returns the first character from the First Name field because the function has a 1 as the second argument. The ampersands join the field names and the strings containing the periods and spaces. When you use this expression in a form or report for the Employee table, the results for the first two records are W. W. Wild and D. D. Danger.

Two other functions you may want to use with text and strings are the LCase and UCase functions, which convert text to lowercase and uppercase, respectively. For example, the Format property for the Last Name, First Name, and Middle Initial fields in the Employee table is >, which displays the entries entirely in uppercase. If you want to display these names, such as in a report in proper case where the first letter is uppercase and the rest is lowercase, use the LCase, UCase, and Len functions to do so. The Len function returns the number of characters in a string. This is the expression you will use for the Last Name field:

```
= UCase(Left([Last Name],1)) & LCase(Right([Last Name],Len([Last
Name])-1))
```

This expression uses the Left function to return the first character of the field and convert it to uppercase. This uppercase letter is combined with the lowercase letters created by the second half of the expression. In the second half, the LCase function converts the letters into lowercase. But before that happens, the Right function returns the remaining number of characters. To decide how many characters the Right function uses, the second argument is the Len function to return the number of characters in the field less one for the letter the UCase function turns into uppercase. This example is only for the Last Name field but it can be repeated for any field you want presented in proper case as it has been for the Last Name and First Name fields in the report in Figure 12-6. The

FIGURE 12-6 Using functions to change the case of text

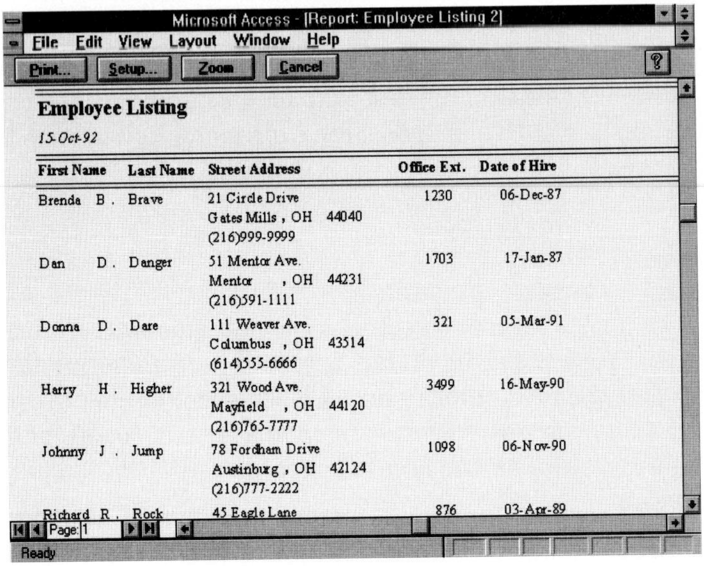

Microsoft Access - [Report: Employee Listing 2]

File   Edit   View   Layout   Window   Help

Print...   Setup...   Zoom   Cancel

Employee Listing

15-Oct-92

First Name	Last Name	Street Address		Office Ext.	Date of Hire
Brenda B .	Brave	21 Circle Drive		1230	06-Dec-87
		Gates Mills , OH	44040		
		(216)999-9999			
Dan D .	Danger	51 Mentor Ave.		1703	17-Jan-87
		Mentor , OH	44231		
		(216)591-1111			
Donna D .	Dare	111 Weaver Ave.		321	05-Mar-91
		Columbus , OH	43514		
		(614)555-6666			
Harry H .	Higher	321 Wood Ave.		3499	16-May-90
		Mayfield , OH	44120		
		(216)765-7777			
Johnny J .	Jump	78 Fordham Drive		1098	06-Nov-90
		Austinburg , OH	42124		
		(216)777-2222			
Richard R .	Rock	45 Eagle Lane		876	03-Apr-89

Page: 1

Ready

only problem this function has is with a name like McMillian that has two uppercase letters.

A special feature of this example is how you can put one function inside another. The functions are evaluated from the one furthest inside the expression outward. Putting one function inside another is called *nesting*. When you nest functions, each function must be entirely inside the other. This means that the Right function is entirely contained within the LCase function.

Using Functions to Return Part of a Date

Access has many functions that work with dates. You have already seen the Date function since this is the function that ReportWizards adds to single column and groups/totals report types in the Report Header section to add the current date. Access has other date functions that work with dates. The Day function returns the day part of a date, the Month function returns the month part of a date, and the Year function returns the year part of the date. These three functions require a date entered in the parentheses.

In Chapter 11, you saw an example of a report that grouped records by date. By changing the group interval, Access grouped the records by looking at the date and ignoring the day and month portion. However, when you put the date in Operational in the Operational Header section, the only reason that the report omitted the day and month was because the text box was shortened so only the year appeared.

You can use the Year function so the text box can be as large as you want without the day and month appearing. The Year function requires that the date be entered in the parentheses. Figure 12-7 shows the same report after modifying the design. In this report, the text box after Projects Completed In contains the expression = Year([Operational]). When the report is generated, the text box shows only the year.

The date and time in the upper-right corner of the report in Figure 12-7 is created by the Now function in a text box in the Page Header section. When you generate the report using the Now function, you

FIGURE 12-7

Using a function to return the year from a date

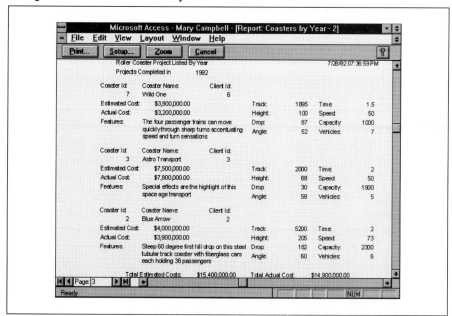

always know the date and time it was created. The Now function does not use any arguments so the parentheses are optional.

Using Functions to Return More Than One Value

The values for most controls are simply plugged in from fields and then calculated. You can use functions that change the value the expression returns depending on another expression's value. One of these functions is the IIf function. This function returns one value when another expression is true and another value when the same expression is false. The other function is the Choose function, which returns one of several values depending on the result of the first argument.

The IIf function is used for switching between two expressions at once depending on another expression's value. The format of this function is IIf(expression,truepart,falsepart). This formula evaluates expression and decides whether it is true or false. The value this function equals when the expression is true is truepart. The value this function equals when the expression is false is falsepart. As an example, suppose you are creating a form that includes a text box indicating whether the invoice is overdue. When the invoice date is more than 30 days past, you want the text box to display "Invoice is overdue." When the invoice date is less than 30 days ago, you want the text box to display an empty string (" "). This is the expression you would use:

```
= IIf([Invoice Date]+30<Date(), "Invoice is overdue", " ")
```

You can see the text box this expression creates in Figure 12-8, which shows the form for two records of which the first invoice is overdue and the second one is current. If you need more than two choices, nest the IIf functions. For example, if you only want to display different messages for overdue invoices depending on the invoice amount, you might have an expression like this:

```
= IIf([Invoice Date]+30<Date(), IIf([Invoice Amount]>50000,
"Send copy of invoice to collections","Invoice is overdue"), " ")
```

Access evaluates the outer IIf function to test whether the Invoice Date is more than 30 days past. When the invoice is overdue, then Access

FIGURE
12-8

Using the IIf function to display different text

evaluates the truepart argument of this expression. For this example, the truepart argument is another expression that Access must evaluate. Access then evaluates the second IIf function to compare the amount of the invoice with 50,000. When the invoice is more than 50,000, the entire expression equals the truepart argument of the inner IIf function, Send copy of invoice to collections. When the invoice is less than or equal to 50,000, the entire expression equals the falsepart argument of the inner IIf function, Invoice is overdue. When the invoice is not overdue, the outer IIf function evaluates to a space.

Using Functions for Statistics

Access has several functions that provide statistical information about the values in a record or the values in several records. You have already seen the Sum function used for totaling the records in a group of records on a report. Besides the Sum function, Access has functions that calculate the average, count the entries, find the smallest or largest entries, and calculate how much the values vary from the mean. These statistical functions use the same format of a function name followed by parentheses enclosing the expression on which they perform their statistical evaluation.

You can use these functions to calculate statistics among the values in a record. If you have a table that contains salespeople's sales for three products, you can average the sales for the projects for each salesperson with a formula such as this: =Avg([Product 1], [Product 2], [Product 3]).

You are more likely to include the statistical functions in different locations than the Detail section. For example, by including one of these functions in the Form Footer, Report Footer, or Group Footer sections, you can summarize the records for an entire form, report, or group. The following shows a form that uses the Sum function in the Form Footer section to total the value of the Invoice Amount field:

The expression for this text box is =Sum([Invoice Amount]). The results are calculated for all of the records in the selected table or query. This total is updated as you change the Invoice Amount field's values. Figure 12-9 shows a report that uses several statistical functions to summarize each group or records for a particular project. The four expressions in the Project Id Footer section are shown here:

```
="Subtotals for Project " & [Project Id] & " : "
=Count(*) & " Invoices"
=Sum([Invoice Amount])
=Sum([Payment Amount])
```

FIGURE
12-9 Using functions to generate statistics for a group of records

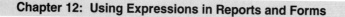

Invoice Number	Invoice Date	Invoice Amount	Payment Amount	Payment Date
Project: 1				
1057	6/30/91	$500,000.00	$500,000.00	7/28/91
1062	10/31/91	$1,200,000.00	$1,200,000.00	12/20/91
1078	3/31/92	$1,700,000.00	$1,700,000.00	5/3/92
1092	5/31/92	$600,000.00	$300,000.00	7/15/92
Subtotals for Project 1 :				
	4 Invoices	$4,000,000.00	$3,700,000.00	
Project: 2				
1073	2/29/92	$400,000.00	$400,000.00	6/1/92
1094	5/31/92	$1,500,000.00	$1,500,000.00	7/17/92
2011	7/31/92	$2,000,000.00	$0.00	
Subtotals for Project 2 :				
	3 Invoices	$3,900,000.00	$1,900,000.00	
Project: 3				
1021	12/31/90	$250,000.00	$250,000.00	2/16/91
1058	7/30/91	$2,750,000.00	$2,750,000.00	9/7/91
1063	10/31/91	$3,000,000.00	$3,000,000.00	12/21/91

The Count function counts the number of records in the group. Since it counts any type of data, Access does not care which field you place in the parentheses. Since you want to count all records for the group—even ones that do not have an entry for the Payment Date field—use * as the function's argument as in =Count(*).

Resetting an Expression

When Access calculates the value of an expression, it must decide when the expression is reset. Resetting an expression sets its value to zero so the next time it is calculated, it does not include the value from the previous calculation. The location of an expression determines when Access recalculates the values. When an expression is included in the Detail section of a form or report, the expression is usually calculated for each record. When you switch to another record, Access clears the expression's value and recalculates it for the next record. For Page Header and Page Footer sections, these expressions are reset every time you start a new page. For Form Header, Form Footer, Report Header, and Report Footer sections, these sections are reset and recalculated when you start using the form or report. Of course the expressions are also updated when the values the expressions use change.

In reports, you can override when an expression is reset. To change where an expression is reset, change its Running Sum property. The default is No so the expression is reset according to the expression's location. Expressions in the Detail section are reset every record, expressions in a group's Header or Footer section are reset every time the group changes, expressions in the Page Header and Page Footer sections are reset every page, and expressions in the Report Header and Report Footer sections are reset every report.

The other choices are Over All and Over Groups. Over All tells Access to restart the function's calculation only at the beginning of the report. Over Groups tells Access to restart the calculation when the group level above the one with the expression changes groups. This means that if you have a report that groups time log records first by project and then by date, an expression in the Date Footer section that totals the hours and has the Running Sum property set to Over Groups, resets when you change project groups but not when you change date groups. The expression keeps a running total within each project even as you change date groups.

Using Expressions in Forms and Reports

So far you have seen the types of expressions you can create. This section focuses on how you use them in forms and reports. Reports and forms use expressions for many reasons. These reasons include calculating the value of a control, setting the default value of a field in a form, validating data in a field, and using expressions to group and sort records in a report.

You have already seen several expressions added to reports you have created. For example, the reports you create with ReportWizards often include expressions for dates and page numbers. Also, the groups/totals

ReportWizard report type totals the values of data types containing numbers.

Where you enter an expression into a form or report design is based on what you want the expression to do. Expressions can be entered as the value of the Control Source property and as the Default Value property of a control. When you use an expression to check the validity of an entry in a form, you will enter the expression in the Validation Rule property.

 Tip An easy way to add an expression to a form or report is to modify one of the existing controls. When you do so, change the Control Name property from the field name the control previously represented to another name. If you do not change the name, the expression won't be properly calculated.

Setting the Default Value of a Field

The Default Value property for a field in a table sets the default value for that field when you add records onto a datasheet. This Default Value property is adopted in forms that you create by the controls you add through the FormWizard or by dragging the field name from the Field List window in the form design. You can override the table's default value by entering a different expression for the Default Value property in the field's control on the form. For example, when entering invoices you have billed, you may want the current date as a default for the invoice date. To do this, the Default Value property for the Invoice Date control is =Date(). As you add new invoices, the current date is placed in this field.

Using Expressions for Validation Rules in a Form

In Chapter 3, you learned about adding validation rules to a table. You can also use validation rules for a form. A form's validation rules are separate from the validation rules of a table. The table's validation rules apply when you enter data to the table through the datasheet. The form's validation rules apply when you enter data to the table through the form.

When you add a control for a field by dragging the field name from the Field List window onto the form design or add the field to the form through FormWizards, the control in the form picks up the validation rule the field has in the table. You can subsequently modify the validation rule to add one, delete one, or modify it. When you enter a validation rule as a control's Validation Rule property, you do not need the equal sign to tell Access you are entering an expression since Access assumes the entry for the Validation Rule property is an expression.

One of the uses of a validation rule when you are entering new records into a form is to provide an entry in fields. The form in the following illustration has the controls for the First Name, Last Name, and Date of Hire fields using the validation rule of Is Not Null:

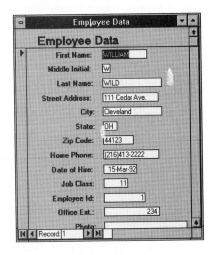

This rule prevents the form's user from leaving these four fields empty. For these controls, you can also enter this validation rule using the IsNull function as in Not IsNull([First Name]) for the First Name field.

Another example of using expressions for the Validation Rule property is the validation rule used for the home phone number. The Home Phone control uses the validation rule of Like "(###)###?####" so the area code is surrounded by parentheses and the number has a character between the first three digits and the last four digits of the phone number. You do not need the field's control name, Home Phone, before the Like operator since the field name is implied by the expression's location.

In Chapter 16, you will learn about using macros for data validation. Most of the time you will enter an expression for the Validation Rule property. You will find macros helpful when you want to perform data validation that is more complex than the expressions can handle. You can also use macros to convert data you have entered as in converting text to proper case.

Setting a Control's Value with an Expression

Besides using field values for a control, you can use expressions in controls. When you use expressions for a control's value, you are adding a control for one of three purposes. First, use an expression for a control's value to provide information that is not otherwise available from the table or query's data such as the page numbers and date. You can also use expressions for calculated values that operate on the values stored in the table or query. The third reason to use expressions is to create summary calculations that involve more than one record in the table or query.

When you use an expression for a control's value, enter the expression for the Control Source property. In the form or report design, Access displays as much as possible of the expression but when you display the form or report, the control displays the current value of the expression.

A control that contains an expression rather than a field value cannot be edited. With the controls in Figure 12-10, the time and date cannot be changed so the Status Line property is set to tell the user this. Also, when one expression depends on the value of another record, the expression is immediately updated as the value it depends on changes.

Setting a Control's Value from Another Source

When you create reports with ReportWizards, the report contains controls that print the page number and report date. Controls like the one for the date use a function to create the value that appears in the report. Access has more functions that you can use such as Time for the current time. You can create expressions that use function results as the control's value.

Another special value you can have in a form or report is the Page property. When included in an expression, this property is replaced by

Including controls in a form that you cannot modify

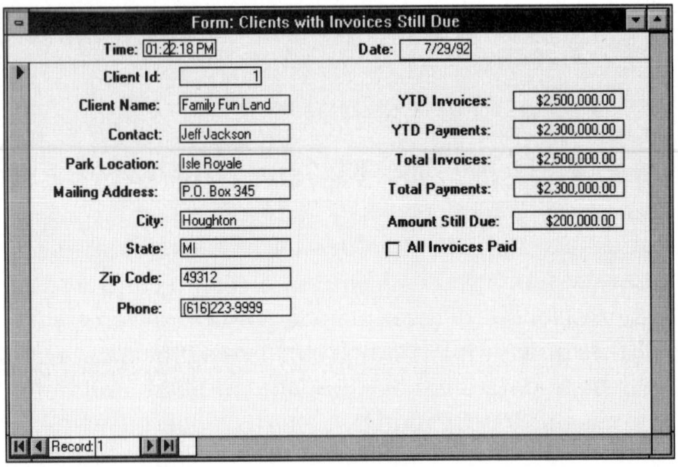

the current page number. Page is not a function so you do not want to include any parentheses. You can combine Page with other parts of an expression so you can include the word Page or whatever text you want to place next to the page number.

Figure 12-10 shows a couple of fields that are created using values that do not appear in the underlying table or query. In this form, the date and time at the top are added with the expressions =Date() and =Time(). You can also see these expressions in the report design shown in Figure 12-11.

Calculated Controls

In Chapter 2, when you designed your database, the chapter mentioned how you do not want to include fields in a table that contains values that can be calculated. For example, if you offer a two-percent reduction in account receivables when they are paid promptly, you do not want to include a field in your accounts receivable table that calculates the potential discount of every account receivable. Simply calculate these values whenever you need them so you do not have to consume disk space to store values that are readily available. You can

FIGURE
12-11

The form created from the design shown in Figure 12-10

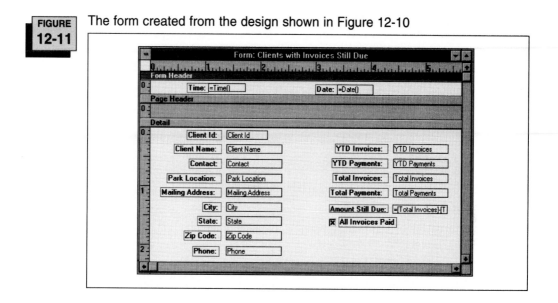

create calculated controls that work with the data from a single record or with the data from multiple records, which is described later in this chapter.

A calculated control in a form or report often uses the field names of the table. For example for the form shown in Figure 12-10, the control after Amount Still Due is the result of subtracting Total Payments from Total Invoices. This calculated control uses the expression of =[Total Invoices]–[Total [Payments]. This field has the Enabled property set to No so you cannot move to this field. Chapter 14 tells how to change the colors of controls and sections in a form so the user will realize that calculated fields are different from the other ones.

When you have a control that relies upon another control that does not directly contain one of the table's or query's fields, you have two choices for how to refer to that calculated control. For example, suppose you have a form like the one shown in Figure 12-12. The control below Difference contains the expression =[Bill Rate]–[Pay Rate]. The control below Percentage Markup contains the amount of the difference divided by the Pay Rate. You can enter this expression in one of two ways. You can use the expression =([Bill Rate]–[Pay Rate])/[Bill Rate]. Another option is to use the name of the control below Difference. This control

An example showing the result of expressions that use values of other expressions

```
┌─────────────────────────────────────────────────────────────────┐
│  Microsoft Access - Mary Campbell - [Billing And Pay Rates]       │
│  File  Edit  View  Records  Window  Help                          │
│                         Filter/Sort:        Field: First Name     │
│                                                                    │
│  First Name  Last Name   Department    Pay Rate  Bill Rate  Difference  Percent Markup │
│  WILLIAM     WILD        Design        $35.00    $60.00     $25.00      41.67%          │
│                                                                    │
│  First Name  Last Name   Department    Pay Rate  Bill Rate  Difference  Percent Markup │
│  DAN         DANGER      Testing       $30.00    $50.00     $20.00      40.00%          │
│                                                                    │
│  First Name  Last Name   Department    Pay Rate  Bill Rate  Difference  Percent Markup │
│  RODGER      ROLLING     Design        $33.00    $55.00     $22.00      40.00%          │
│                                                                    │
│  First Name  Last Name   Department    Pay Rate  Bill Rate  Difference  Percent Markup │
│  SANDRA      SCARY       Design        $31.00    $50.00     $19.00      38.00%          │
│                                                                    │
│  First Name  Last Name   Department    Pay Rate  Bill Rate  Difference  Percent Markup │
│  HARRY       HIGHER      Construction  $6.50     $10.00     $3.50       35.00%          │
│                                                                    │
│  First Name  Last Name   Department    Pay Rate  Bill Rate  Difference  Percent Markup │
│  TOMMY       THRILL      Construction  $7.00     $10.00     $3.00       30.00%          │
│                                                                    │
│  First Name  Last Name   Department    Pay Rate  Bill Rate  Difference  Percent Markup │
│  RICHARD     ROCK        Construction  $8.00     $10.00     $2.00       20.00%          │
│                                                                    │
│  First Name  Last Name   Department    Pay Rate  Bill Rate  Difference  Percent Markup │
│  DONNA       DARE        Design        $35.00    $75.00     $40.00      53.33%          │
│  Record: 1                                                         │
│  Browse                                                       NUM  │
└─────────────────────────────────────────────────────────────────┘
```

has the default name of Field followed by the next unused number. You can give it a better name by entering a new name for the control as the control's Control Name property. You can use up to 64 characters just as you have with other objects that you've named in Access.

If you have named the control that subtracts the two rates as Difference, enter the other expression as **=[Difference]/[Bill Rate]**. Using the control names instead of repeating the formula makes the calculations easier to understand and giving descriptive names to the controls makes it easier to use the control names.

Using Expressions for Controls in Other Sections

So far, many of the examples have focused on adding expressions to the Detail section of forms and reports. Expressions are often used in other form and report sections. You can also include expressions in the

Form Header, Form Footer, Report Header, and Report Footer sections when you want an expression to appear at the top or end of a report. For example, the form in Figure 12-10 includes controls to display the time and date in the Form Footer section. Page Header, Page Footer, and Group Headers and Footers are other sections that you can add controls to. For example, you can include controls in the Page Header or a Group Header section to summarize the reports on the page or group.

Using Expressions to Sort and Group Records in a Report

In Chapter 11, you learned how you can sort records using the values of fields but you can also create expressions whose values for the records determine the order of the records in the report. To use an expression to sort the records in a report, enter the expression in place of the field name in the Sorting and Grouping box. Just like when sorting records by field contents, you can select whether the sorting is performed in ascending or descending order, and whether to divide the records into groups based

FIGURE 12-13   Using an expression to sort records in a report

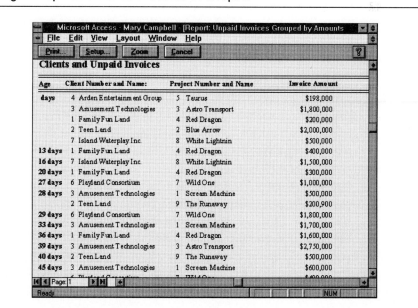

on the expression's values. Think of using an expression for organizing records in a database as having a temporary field in the table or query that contains the values of the expression. Other than the fact that you enter the expression in place of a field name, sorting and grouping records in a report using an expression is just like using a field name to sort and group records.

As an example of using an expression to sort and group records in a report, the report in Figure 12-13 uses the expression = [Invoice Date] – [Payment Date] to sort the records. The entries in the first column are the result of the expression =[Payment Date]–[Invoice Date] &" days" with its Hide Duplicates property set to Yes.

Quick Reference

To Enter an Expression Type an equal sign (=) followed by the control names, field names, operators, and functions you want the expression to evaluate.

To Use an Expression as a Control's Default Value Enter the expression in the control's Default Value property.

To Use an Expression to Validate Entry in a Form's Control Enter the expression in the control's Validation Rule property.

To Enter an Expression as a Control's Value Enter the expression in the control's text box or as the control's Control Source property. The control cannot be altered in a form.

To Use an Expression to Sort Records in a Report Display the Sorting and Grouping box by choosing Sorting and Grouping from the View menu. Type the expression you want to use for sorting in the Field Name/Expression column. Select Ascending or Descending in the Sort Order column. Repeat adding fields or expressions and sort orders for up to ten fields in the order you want the records sorted.

CHAPTER

Using Multiple Tables in Reports and Forms

While the reports and forms you have created thus far have focused on one table or query at a time, you also can use data from multiple tables or queries in a report or form. In Chapter 8, you learned how to do this using the FormWizards to create a main/subform form type. You can create other types of multiple table reports and forms. One option for creating multiple table reports and forms is inserting a form or report inside another report or form. A second option is to create a query that provides the data from the multiple tables you want to combine.

Combining Tables with Subforms and Subreports

You can actually combine forms and reports when combining multiple tables in a form or report. You can put one form inside another, a report inside another report, and a form inside a report. You can also make one form a pop-up form to another one. You do this by adding a subform/subreport control to your form or report design. This control shares many of the same properties as other controls in forms and reports that you have learned about in earlier chapters. When you make these combinations, the principal form or report is the *main form* or *main report*. The form or report contained within the main form or report is a *subform* or *subreport*.

Adding a Subform to a Form

The main/subform form types you created with the FormWizards create a main form that contains a subform inside of it. You can also create these types of forms without using the FormWizards.

The first step in creating a main/subform form is creating the two forms you will later combine. Decide in advance which will be the main form and which the subform, and then create the two separately. When you finish designing your main/subform form, you will have two separate forms listed in the database window. Ideally, you would complete one of the two forms before starting the other but realistically, you probably will switch between designing the two forms. You can continue making enhancements to either form's design after you add a subform/subreport control.

Usually, you leave an area in the main form in which you will later place the subform. For best results, make the subform as small as practical. Figure 13-1 shows three form designs. The form designs on the bottom and top right will be added as subforms to the form designs on the top left. The Invoice Generation form uses the Project table as its record source. The Form 1 for Invoice Generation form uses the Client table as its record source that matches the records in the Project table by the Client Id field in both tables. The Form 2 for Invoice Generation form uses a query that combines the Employee Time Log table with the employee names from the Employee table. The records in the query match the records in the Project table by the Project Number field in the query and the Coaster Id field in the Project table.

Tip   When creating a subform that you intend to use as a datasheet, don't worry about the size of the form or the placement of the controls in the form. However, make sure the tab order of the controls matches the order in which the fields are to be listed as part of the subform.

FIGURE 13-1   Form designs to be combined into one form

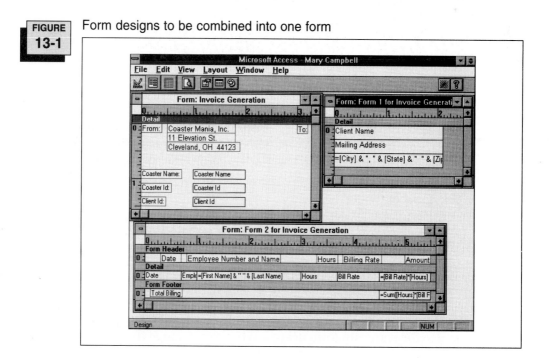

Once you have both forms designed, you can add one form to the other. Select the main form and switch to the database window. Since you will drag the form from the database window to the form design, make sure the window is not maximized. Next, display the forms in the database window and highlight the subform. Drag this form name from the database window to the form design window of the main form.

When you drag the form name, the pointer changes to a form icon. When the icon is where you want the subform, release the mouse. If the Default View property of the form you are pointing at is set to Continuous Forms, Access warns you that it is changing this property to Single Form. Select OK to continue adding the form as a subform. Access adds a subform control to the form's design that is the subform's size. This control also has text above the control that is the same as the subform's name. At this point, switch to the main form's design and make changes to the main form. You can also change the subform control by moving and sizing it. Figure 13-2 shows a form design after adding two subform controls.

You also have another method of adding the form as a subform to the current form you are designing. When you display the toolbox, select the subform/subreport control that looks like this:

When you select a location in the form design, Access adds an unbounded subform control. You can move and size the control and change the text that appears above the control just as you have with other controls. To tell Access which form you want to appear in the subform control's location, display the Property Sheet window and then type the form name after Source Object or use the down arrow to select the name of the form.

Tip   Before you create forms to use as a main form and subform, look over your existing forms. You can save yourself time by finding an existing form to use as a main form or subform or that will serve as the basis for the form, which you can subsequently modify to meet your needs.

Once you add the subform to the main form, the main form continues to use the same subform design. When you change the subform's design

FIGURE
13-2

A form design with subform controls added

with the main form open, tell the main form to refresh its memory of the subform's design. You can tell Access to update the current form for a subform's design by clicking the form name in the subform control when the control is already selected then pressing ENTER or clicking another part of the form design. You can also display the list of form names with the Source Object property in the Property Sheet window and select the same form again. If you double-click a subform control when it is not selected, you will open a form window containing that form's design.

The link between the main form and the subform selects the records from the subform's table or query that appear as you change records in the main form. This link means that when you switch clients in a main form when the subform displays the projects, the projects change to show only the projects for the currently displayed client.

Depending on how you added the subform to the form, Access either will create the link between the main form and the subform or you will have to create this link. When you add a subform to a form by dragging the form's name from the database window to the main form's design, Access first checks to see if you have already established a relationship between the two tables. If you have not, and the tables for the two forms have fields using the same name and data type, Access creates the link that way.

When you select a subform for the Source Object property of the subform, if the underlying tables of both forms use a field with the same name and data type, Access creates the link that way. In other cases, you must define the link. The link between the main form and the subform is created with the Link Master Fields and Link Child Fields properties of the subform/subreport control. The Link Master Fields contains the name of the field in the main form that matches a field in the subform. The Link Child Fields contains the name of the field in the subform that matches a field in the main form.

Once you have created both forms, added one form as the subform to another, and established the link between the two tables or queries, you are ready to use this main/subform form. Display the main/subform form by switching to the form view of the form window just as you do for other forms you have created. Figure 13-3 shows the form created by the form design in Figure 13-2.

 Tip The fields that you use to link the main form and the subform (as well as main reports and subreports described later in this chapter) do not need to be included in the design. Since the linking fields are still part of the underlying tables or queries the forms and reports use, Access can link the two tables without the linking fields appearing in the form or report design.

Using a Main/Subform Form

While you are using the main form and subform, you can switch between the main and the subform parts of the form. To switch the focus to the subform, click any area of the subform. To switch the focus to the main form, click one of the controls in the main form. If you click the main form's background, you will not reposition the focus. You can switch back to the two parts of the form to add, edit, and delete records in either part. If the subform is a query, you may need to reapply the query so you are only seeing the applicable records. You can apply the query while the focus is on the subform by pressing SHIFT-F9. Any filter you use only applies to the main form and does not affect the subform.

FIGURE 13-3

The form using subforms

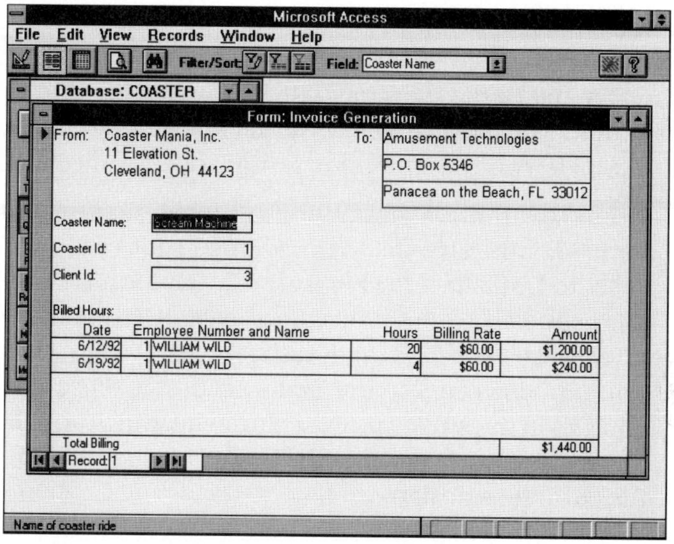

You can switch subforms that can appear as either a form or datasheet by choosing Subform Datasheet in the View menu. When this command has a check mark by it, the subform data appears as a datasheet view. When this command does not have a check mark by it, the subform's data uses the form. This command is only available when the focus is in the subform. This command can be disabled by changing the properties of the subform.

Properties in a Main/Subform Form

When you are using a main/subform form, the main form and subform have their own properties. You are familiar with most of these properties because you have used them in other forms. Some of these properties are particularly useful for a main/subform form. You can use them to effect the kind of changes that are made to the records and how the data appears in the subform. These changes are made by displaying the subform's form design and modifying the properties for the overall form.

In a subform, you select whether the data appears as a datasheet or uses the form design. Change whether the subform can use one or both of these views by changing the Views Allowed property. The default is Both but you will want to change it to Datasheet or Form if you only want the subform to appear using either the datasheet view or the form view. When you have selected Datasheet or Form, the Subform Datasheet command in the View menu is not available. When Views Allowed is set to Both, you can also select the default view by changing the Default View to Single Form, Continuous Forms, or Datasheet.

For example, the main/subform forms you create with the FormWizards have the Views Allowed set to Both while the Default View is set to Datasheet. In Figure 13-3, the form for the subform has Views Allowed set to Form so you cannot switch between displaying the subform in a form view and a datasheet view. Also, Default View is set to Continuous Forms so the Detail section is repeated for each record that appears in the subform. The column headings and the total at the bottom of the subform are part of the Form Header and Form Footer sections in the subform's design.

You might also want to change whether edits are allowed. You can prevent editing in specific parts of the form. For instance, prevent edits in the main/subform form shown in Figure 13-3 by changing the Default Editing property of the subform's form design to Read Only. Also, Allow Editing is set to Unavailable and Allow Updating is set to No Tables so you cannot use menu commands to change the contents of the subform. The subform in Figure 13-3 differs from the one shown in Figure 13-4, where the subform allows entries as you can see by the empty values in the third row of data in the subform.

Pop-up Forms

A special type of main/subform form is when the subform is a pop-up form. A pop-up form does not appear as part of the main form. For example, in Figure 13-5, the New Roller Coasters is the main form. If you click the New Client command button, the New Clients pop-up form appears as shown in Figure 13-6. Pop-up forms can be used to display a message or prompt for more information. In the examples in Figure 13-5 and 13-6, the pop-up form lets you add a new client to your Client table at the same time you add a new roller coaster to your Project table. Pop-up forms use macros, which you will learn about in Chapter 16.

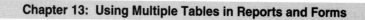

FIGURE 13-4

A form that lets you add data to the subform

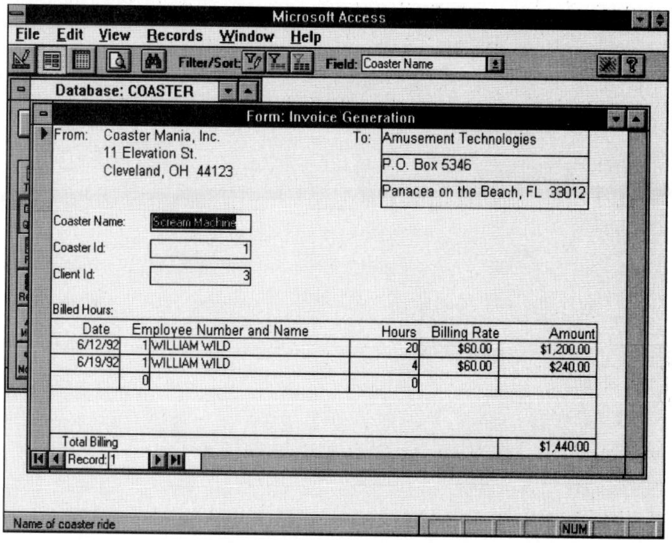

The examples of pop-up forms shown in Figures 13-5 and 13-6 are very easy to create. The New Roller Coasters form contains the fields

FIGURE 13-5

A form that invokes a pop-up form

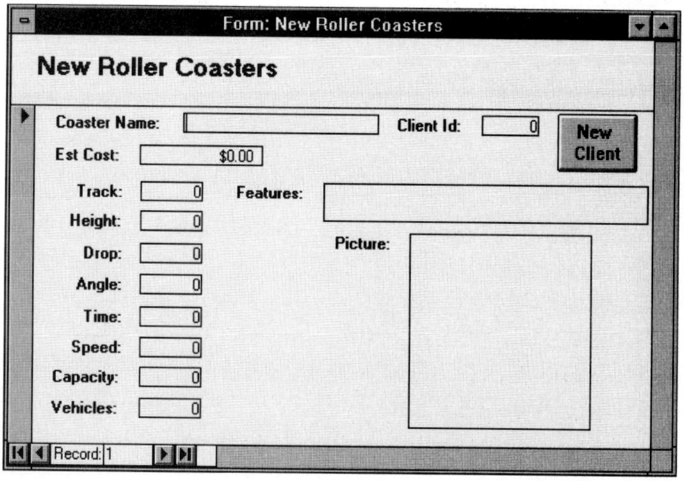

FIGURE
13-6

A popup form

shown and has a command button added. This form does not let you move to the Coaster Id field since Access will assign the next unused number for this counter field and you do not need to know the number it is assigned. The command button is added just as you would add a toggle button, which you learned about in Chapter 10.

The only properties changed are the Caption property to New Client and the On Push property to Open New Clients Form, a macro name. The On Push property tells Access which macro to perform when you click the button. The macros are a set of instructions that are contained as a separate object. The New Clients form is created using the fields shown. The Client ID has the Enabled and Locked properties set to No so the form's user cannot make changes to it. Also, this form has the Done command button that is added just like the New Client one in the New Roller Coasters form. This command button has its On Push property set to perform the Close New Clients Form macro.

The only other special feature about this form is a few changes of the form's properties. The Pop Up and Modal properties are set to Yes so the form always remains on top of all other Access windows and you cannot switch to the design or datasheet view. Also, the On Close property is set to perform the Back to New Roller Coasters Form macro. These three macros, Open New Clients Form, Close New Clients Form, and Back to New Roller Coasters Form contain macro instructions like the ones you will learn about in Chapter 16 and subsequent chapters. The New Clients form is a pop-up form because the Pop Up property is Yes.

The macro instructions these forms use open the pop-up form, close the pop-up form, and copy the new Client ID from the Clients table to the Projects table. In Open New Clients Form, the macro contains the instruction with an action of OpenForm and arguments of New Clients for Form Name and Add for Data Mode. In Close New Clients Form, the macro contains an instruction with an action of DoMenuItem and arguments of Form for the Menu Bar, File for the Menu Name, and Close for the Command. In Back to New Roller Coasters Form, the macro contains an instruction with an action of SetValue and arguments of Forms![New Roller Coasters]![Client Id] for Item and Forms![New Clients]![Client Id] for Expression. This last macro sets the new Client Id number for the record you have just added with New Clients form to the record you are entering in the New Roller Coasters form. In a macro, the actions tell Access what you want the macro to do and the arguments are the information Access needs to complete the action.

Tip   Change the Display When property of the command buttons you use to display the popups to Screen Only since you do not want these buttons to appear when you print the form.

Adding a Subreport to a Report

Just as you can create a form that contains another form, you can create a report that contains another report. You can use the combined reports to create unique-looking reports you could not otherwise create.

Just as with main/subform forms, the first step of creating a main/subreport report is creating the two reports you will later combine. You may already have reports you want to use for these purposes. These two reports are separate reports that are listed separately in the database window. Expect to make changes to both reports as you work on them since what makes a report look good by itself may not be attractive when you combine it with another. Usually, you leave an area in the main report in which you will place the subreport. Figure 13-7 shows the report that will become the main report. Figure 13-8 shows the report that will become the subreport.

Once you have designed both reports, you are ready to add one report to another. Select the report that will be the main report and then switch to the database window. Since you will drag the report from the database

FIGURE 13-7

A report to be used as a main report

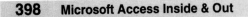

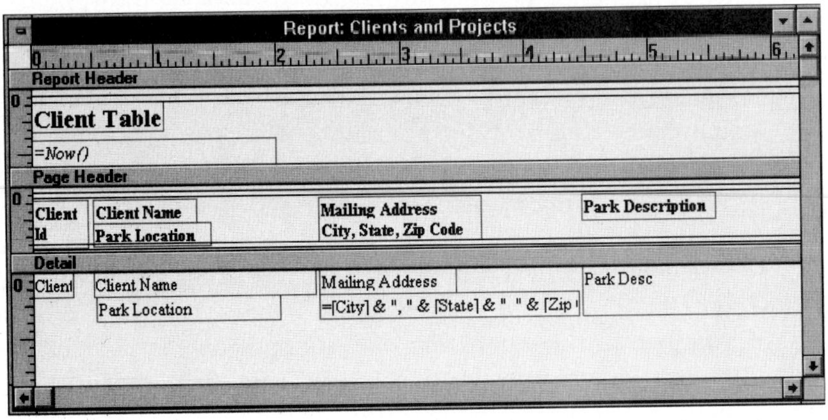

window to the report design, you do not want the windows maximized. Next, display the reports in the database window and highlight the report you want to use as the subreport. Drag this report name from the database window to the report design window of the main report.

FIGURE 13-8

A report to be used as a subreport

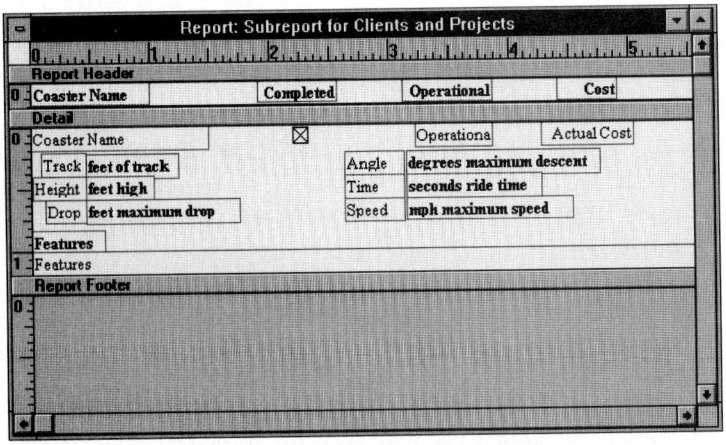

When you drag the report name, the pointer changes to a report icon. When the icon is where you want the subreport, release the mouse. Access adds a subform/subreport control that is the size of the subreport to the report's design. The report's size is the total of the height of the Report Header, Report Footer, Detail, and any group header and footer sections. The subform subreport Can Grow property has the default of Yes so the subreport's size adjusts according to the number of records printed by the subreport. This control also has text above the control that is the same as the subreport's name. At this point, switch to the main report's design if you need to make any changes to the main report. You can change the subreport control by moving and sizing it. Figure 13-9 shows a report design after adding a subform/subreport control and changing the text above it.

You also have another method of adding the report as a subreport to the current report you are designing. From the toolbox, select the subform/subreport control and then select a location where you want the subform/subreport control placed. When you select a location, Access adds an unbounded subform/subreport control. As with other controls, you can move and size the control and change the text that appears above the control. To tell Access which report you want to appear

FIGURE
13-9

A subreport added to a main report

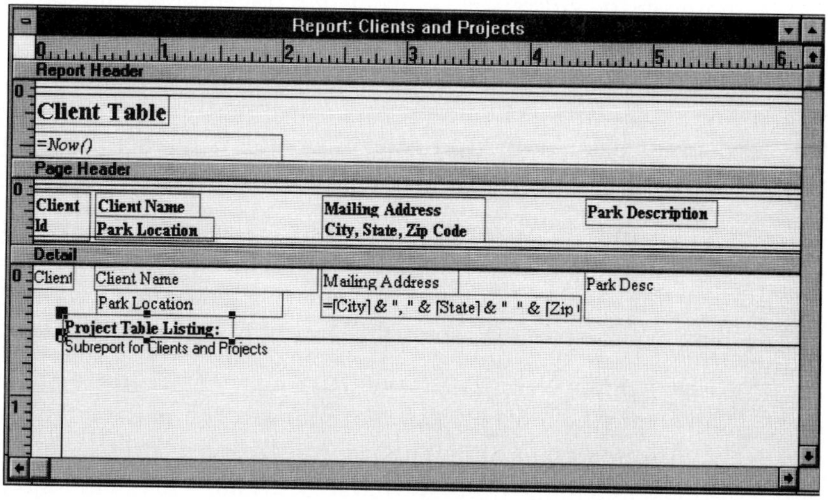

in the subreport control's location, display the Property Sheet window and type the report name after Source Object or use the down arrow to select the name of the report.

Notice that the list for Source Object now includes both reports and forms with each preceded by Form or Report and a period. Also, when you edit the control's Source Object property by editing the text that appears in the subform/subreport control, the name of the form or report has the same Form or Report and a period to distinguish whether the control's contents are a form or report.

Tip   When you create a subreport, you may want to make some changes to where you place controls in the report design. Remove the date from the Report Header section of the subreport and the page number from the Page Footer section since this information should be part of the main report. Also, any information in the Page Header or Page Footer sections that you want to appear in the subreport should be moved to another section. Page Header and Page Footer sections will never appear in a subreport.

Once you add the subreport to the main report, the main report continues to use the same subreport design. When you change the subreport's design and the main report is open, you need to tell the main report to refresh its memory of the subreport's design. Tell Access to update the current report for a subreport's design by clicking the report name in the subreport control when the control is already selected then pressing ENTER or clicking another part of the report design. You can also display the list of report names by using the Source Object property in the Property Sheet window and selecting the same report again. If you double-click a subreport control when it is not selected, you will open a window containing that report's design.

The link between the two reports selects the records from the subreport's table or query that appears for each record in the main report. This link means that for each client in a main report when the subreport displays the projects, the subreport only includes the client's projects.

Depending on how you added the subreport to the report, either Access will create the link between the main report and the subreport or you will have to create this link. When you add a subreport to a report by dragging the report's name from the database window to the main report's design, Access first checks to see if you have already established a relationship between the two tables. If you have not, and the tables for the two reports have fields using the same name and data type, Access creates the link that way. Also, when you select a subreport for the Source Object property of the subreport, if the underlying tables of both reports use fields with the same name and data type, Access creates the link. In other cases, you must define the link.

The link between the main report and the subreport is created with the Link Master Fields and Link Child Fields properties. The Link Master Fields contains the name of the field in the main report that matches a field in the subreport. The Link Child Fields contains the name of the field in the subreport that matches a field in the main report. Once you have created both reports, added one report as the subreport to another, and established the link between the two tables or queries, you are ready to use this main/subreport report just as you would use any other report. Figure 13-10 shows the part of the report for the third client with the information from both of the client's projects created by the subreport.

Tip If you only want the subreport to display summary data, change the subreport's Detail section's Visible property to No. The report will

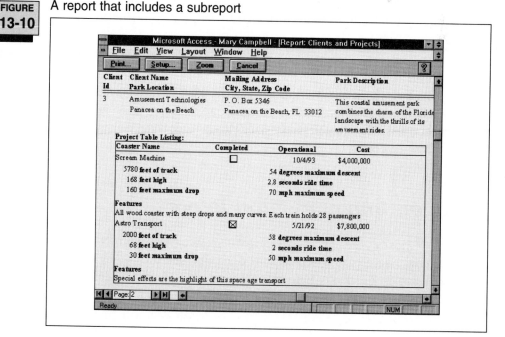

FIGURE 13-10

A report that includes a subreport

continue to create the Detail section and perform any calculations required but the Detail section is not included in the report.

Adding a Subform to a Report

Another possible combination for using multiple tables in a report is adding a subform to a report. This is just like adding one form to another or adding a report as a subreport to another report. When you use a subform in a report, you are not using the form to enter and edit data; you use a subform in a report strictly to affect how the data in the other table or query appears. You can end up with a report/form combination like this when you have a main/subform form that you subsequently save the main form as a report using Save As Report in the File menu. The new report continues using the same subform even though the main form is now the main report.

Most of the steps are identical to creating main/subform forms or main/subreport reports. First, create the main report and the subform. Next, add the form to the report by either dragging the form from the database window or by adding a subform/subreport control and changing the control's Source Object property to the name of the form. This time the form name is preceded by the word Form and a period.

Next, check the link between the Link Master Fields and Link Child Fields properties. These two properties link the data in the main report and the subform so the subform contains related information to the record shown in the report. Figure 13-11 shows the designs of a form and report. When the form is added to the report as a subform/subreport control below the Department field control, the resulting report looks like Figure 13-12.

Using an Unbound Main Report

Most of the reports you create are based on some table or query. You can also create a report that does not use a table or query. You might want to do this when you want to print a report that contains other reports or forms as subreports or subforms. For example, you may want

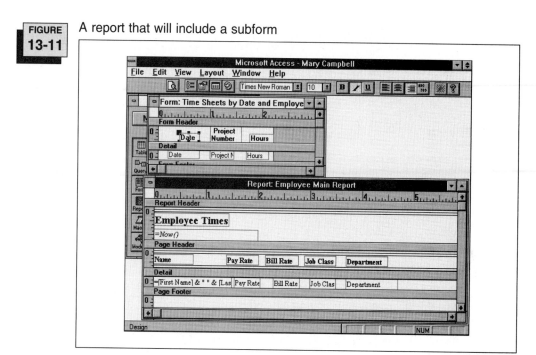

FIGURE
13-11

A report that will include a subform

FIGURE
13-12

The report and subform

a report that prints both the contents of the Employee table and the contents of the Employee Time Log table for a specific week. To create this report, create a report that does not use a table or query, and then add the subreports for the scparate reports you want combined into a single report. Since the Page Header and Page Footer sections from a subform or subreport do not appear in the main report, you probably only want to use this feature on reports that are less than a page in length or do not use headings.

Figure 13-13 shows a report design created for this purpose. The Main Report - Coasters and Clients report is created by choosing New from the File menu and then choosing Report and selecting the Blank Report button without selecting a table or query in the Select a Table/Query drop-down list box. Next, after the controls that appear in the Report Header and Report Footer sections are added, add the subform/subreport controls. The first one is for the Look At Our Coasters report. This is added the same way you added other subreports, as described earlier in this chapter. The second one is for the Coaster Mania Client List - Plain form. This is added just as you add other subforms, also described earlier in this chapter. Reports can have both subforms and subreports.

FIGURE
13-13

A report design for a report without an underlying table or query

Tip You can have nested subforms and subreports. A subform can contain other subforms and a subreport can contain other subforms and subreports. Use this feature to create composites of several tables.

Queries to Combine Data from Different Tables

Another option for combining multiple tables into a single form or report is creating a query that combines the data from the tables for you. You can use a query as the basis for any form or report, including one you use as a main form or report or as a subform or subreport.

Using a query over a subform has several advantages over subforms and subreports in different circumstances. Sometimes using a query is better than using a subform or subreport and other times the reverse is true. Using a query for a form or report has these advantages:

☐ *A query can be more selective about the data from the selected tables that appears in the reports or forms.* For example, if you want a form or report to include information from the Client table for a particular client and all their invoices for the current year from the Invoice Register table, use a query. In a subform or subreport, you would display all of the invoices for the particular client. Subforms or subreports do not use filters to limit the records that appear.

☐ *A query can have calculated fields that you use either as the basis for selecting which records appear or the basis for linking two or more tables.* For example, you can have a query that combines the Project and Invoice Register tables. In this query, you can create a calculated field to determine when the Payment Amount and Invoice Amounts are different, and then only show those records.

☐ *A form or report using a query is faster than a main/subform form or a main/subreport report using the same tables when the table for the main form or report has a many-to-one relationship with the table for the subform or subreport.* For example, a query that joins the Employee Time Log and Employee tables performs faster in a single form than using Employee Time Log for the main form and Employee for the subform.

☐ *A form using a query creates a single datasheet versus the two separate datasheets that you have in a main/subform form.* If your intended form uses the datasheet view rather than the form view, you will see all of the fields from both tables using a query.

☐ *A form or report using a query lets you put fields from any of the tables anywhere in the design.* When you have a main/subform form or main/subreport report, the fields from the main form or main report are not placed where the subform or subreport control is located and the fields from the table of the subform or subreport only appear within the subform/subreport control's boundaries. Using a query lets you intermingle the fields from both tables.

☐ *Creating a form or report can be quicker when you already have a query that combines the two or more tables you would otherwise combine with forms and reports.*

Figure 13-14 shows a report using a query that combines the data from the Employee and Invoice Register tables. The fields from the two

FIGURE 13-14

A report created with a query

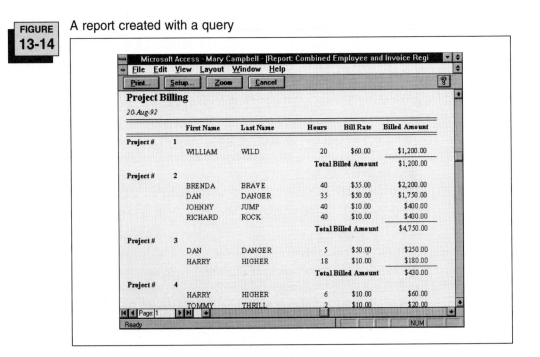

tables are placed among each other. Also, the records are grouped according to project number and only the records from the Invoice Register table with a Date field of 6/12/92 are included.

Using a Crosstab Query as a Subform

One particular time you may want to use a query as a subform is when you want the results from a crosstab query combined with another table. In Chapter 7, you learned how to create these crosstab queries that calculate totals of groups of records. You can create a crosstab query that totals the values for groups in a table then use that query in a subform or subreport when you want the totals in another form or report.

Figure 13-15 shows two versions of the same crosstab query. This query groups the records in the Invoice Register by project number then totals the project's invoices for each year. You can see how the project numbers label each of the rows in the resulting dynaset. The column headings of the crosstab query are created by extracting the year from the invoice dates. This query uses Fixed Column headings created by choosing Query Properties from the View menu. The fixed column headings are necessary when you plan to use the query in a report. If you do not have fixed column headings, they will constantly change and the form or report design will not adjust for the altered headings.

The form that this example uses (you can do the same thing with a report) is shown in two copies in Figure 13-16 so you can see the design and the resulting form at the same time. This form is the design that will be used as the subform. The form is created using the tabular FormWizard and making a few changes to the design.

The report design is shown in Figure 13-17. In this design, the subform/subreport control has the Source Object property set to Yearly Invoices, the Link Master Fields property is set to Coaster Id, and the Link Child Fields property is set to Project Id. Other than the subform/subreport control, the rest of the report is created with the groups/totals ReportWizard report and then moved closer together. Also, the control for the Completed field is replaced with an option button. When this report's design is complete, the finished report looks like Figure 13-18.

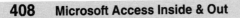

FIGURE
13-15

A crosstab query design and data

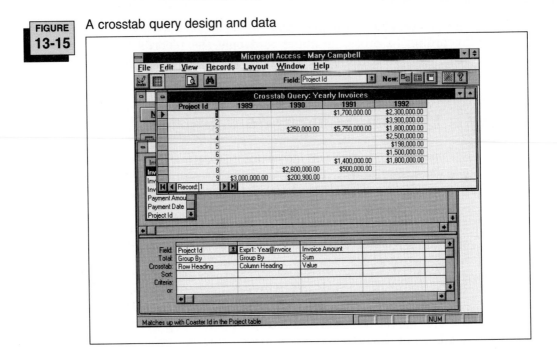

FIGURE
13-16

A form using a crosstab query

FIGURE
13-17

A report design to include a form

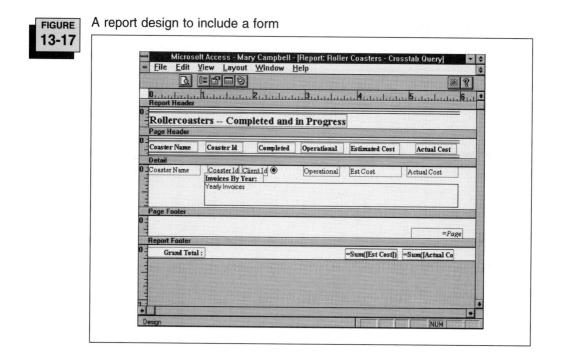

FIGURE
13-18

The report using a subform of a crosstab query

FIGURE
13-19 A report with a subform to calculate subtotals

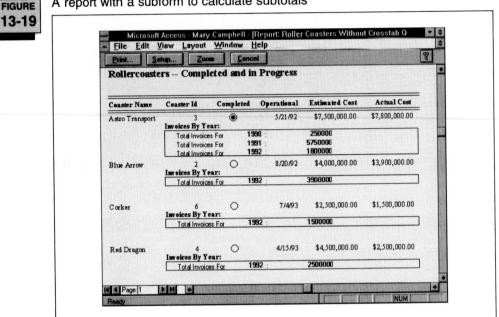

In this case, you can present the same information using groups in a subreport. Figure 13-19 shows a report that uses the subreport shown in Figure 13-20. In this report, the report groups the records together according to the year since the expression for grouping the records is =Year([Invoice Date]). The =Year([Invoice Date]) Footer section contains label and text box controls that display the total as in Total Invoices for 1991: 9350000.

The other special feature of the subreport is that the Detail section's Visible property is set to No. Hiding the Detail section means that the report only produces the =Year([Invoice Date]) Footer section for each year. When you combine this report with the report in Figure 13-19, the yearly totals are calculated for the invoices of each of the products separately. Figure 13-19 shows the beginning of the resulting report. You can see that the year's total invoices are listed vertically instead of horizontally but the results are the same.

FIGURE

13-20 A subreport design for the report shown in Figure 13-19

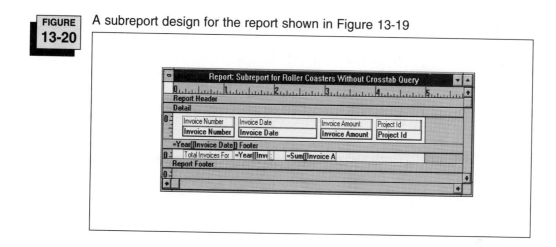

Quick Reference

To Add a Subform or Subreport to a Form or Report   Drag the form or report name from the database window to where you want the subform or subreport to start in the main form or report. You can also select the subform/subreport tool from the toolbox. Point to where you want the subform or subreport to start then change the Source Object property for the control to the name of the form or report.

CHAPTER

Using Color and Effects in Reports and Forms

*T*he features you have learned about so far let you choose the information you want to present. This chapter shows how to adjust the appearance of the information. You can add boxes and lines to add emphasis and separate different parts of a form or report. You can also enhance forms and reports by changing alignment and fonts and adding three-dimensional effects, colors, and borders. While all of these features can be applied to both forms and reports, some features are used more often with forms and others are used more often with reports.

The features described in this chapter—adding lines and boxes, using different font styles and sizes, and adding color or shading—improve your form's appearance without changing its contents. Think of these features as similar to those that distinguish a a Mercedes-Benz from a pared-down budget-oriented car. Both cars will get you where you are going but the Mercedes-Benz has features that make the drive more pleasant. The enhancements that you add to your forms make using it easier and more pleasant.

Figure 14-1 shows a very simple form. This same form can be enhanced to look like Figure 14-2 using the features described in this chapter.

Besides changing the appearance of your forms and reports through style enhancements, you can set the appearance of your forms and reports by changing the defaults. You change the defaults for a single

FIGURE 14-1 A plain report showing the contents of the Client table

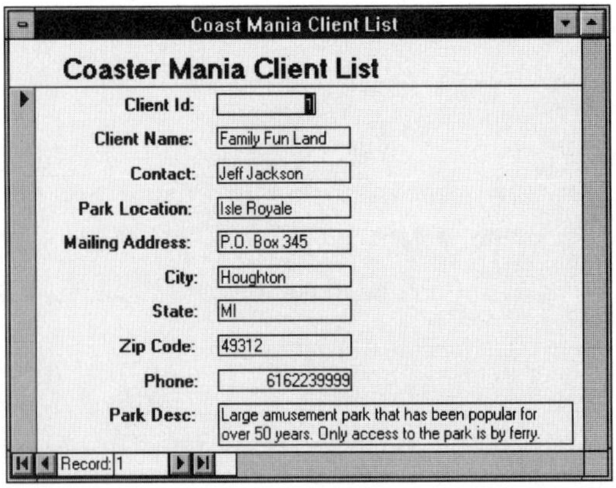

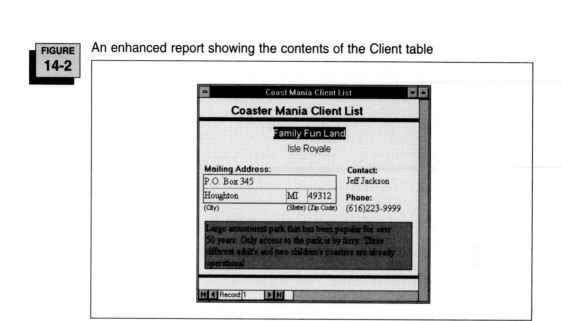

FIGURE 14-2

An enhanced report showing the contents of the Client table

form or report by changing the default properties of the controls you plan to add. You can also change the default form and report appearance by using a *template*, which is a model that sets up how the form or report appears (more about this later in this chapter).

Adding Lines and Rectangles to Forms and Reports

The forms and reports you create using AccessWizards use lines to separate sections and indicate totals. The lines and rectangles you add to forms and reports can emphasize portions of the form or report or separate one part from another.

You add lines by selecting the Line tool in the toolbox, which looks like this:

Next, point to where you want the line to start and drag the pointer. The Line tool draws a straight line from where you start dragging the pointer to where you release the mouse. You also can add a default line by clicking a location in the form or report design. This line is a horizontal line starting at the location you select and continuing for one inch.

Adding a rectangle is just as easy. First, select the Rectangle tool in the toolbox. The Rectangle tool looks like this:

Next, point to where you want the rectangle to start and drag the pointer to where you want the opposite corner. The Rectangle tool draws a rectangle using the spot where you began dragging the pointer and the spot where you released the mouse as the two opposite corners of the box. You also can add a default rectangle by clicking a location in the form or report design. This rectangle starts at the location you select and is one-half inch tall and wide.

Figure 14-3 shows an example that uses several lines and boxes. In this report, the boxes group different pieces of data. The lines are added

FIGURE 14-3   A report after adding lines and boxes

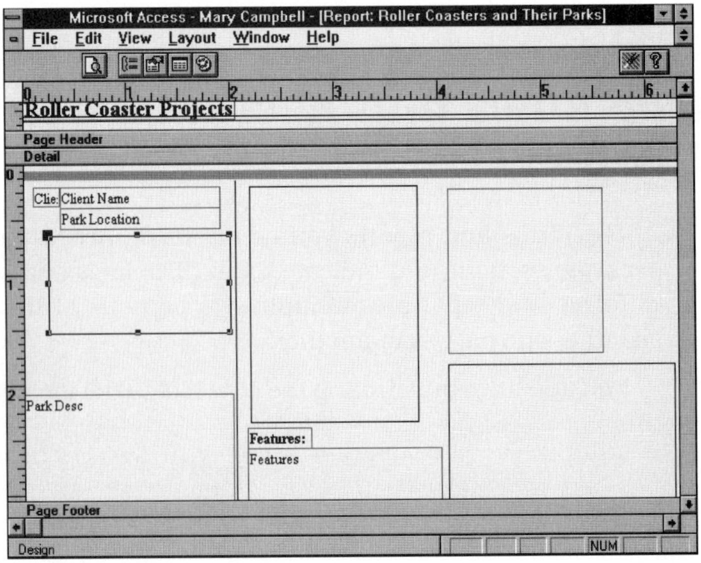

to the Report Header section to emphasize the report's title and in the Detail section to separate records and separate the park information from the coaster information. When you add boxes like the ones in Figure 14-3, they are initially placed on top of any other controls. For example, the box in the upper-left corner of Figure 14-3 is covering other controls that lie beneath it. The next section shows how to change a control from being on the top layer to the bottom layer. Later in the chapter, you will learn how to change the thickness and color of the lines and rectangles.

A line has one property not found with the other controls. The Line Slant property changes whether a line slants down or up. Select \ to have the line slant from upper left to lower right or / to have the line slant from the upper right to lower left. Use this property to quickly change the direction of a line's slant. To change the angle of a line, drag one of the ends of the line with the mouse to a new location.

Changing Control Layers

Each of the controls you add to a form or report is placed on top of whatever was there before. This is like creating a collage out of the controls in the form or report design. When children create a collage, they glue one item on top of another without concern for what they are covering. With a form or report, you may need to see what you are covering. You can take one control and put it behind another—for example, move a rectangle behind other controls that it was covering. You can also move the other controls on top—for example, move controls hidden by a rectangle on top of the rectangle.

To move a control from the front to below the other controls, choose Send to Back from the Layout menu. For example, when you select the rectangle chosen in Figure 14-3 and then choose Send to Back from the Layout menu, the report design changes to show the mailing address, phone, and contact fields shown in Figure 14-4. When you use the report design shown in Figure 14-4 after putting the rectangles behind the other controls, the report looks like Figure 14-5. Now the rectangle is behind the controls it previously covered so you can see them. Conversely, you can take a control from behind other controls and put it on top by choosing Bring to Front from the Layout menu.

FIGURE
14-4 Moving controls to the bottom layer

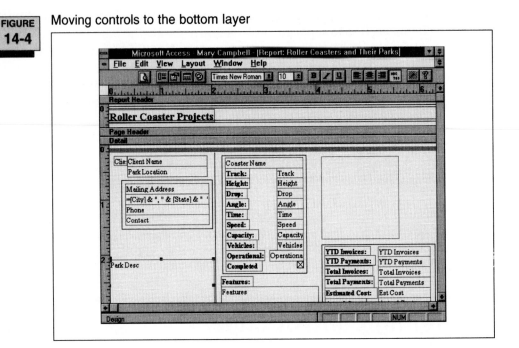

FIGURE
14-5 A report created from the report design in Figure 14-4

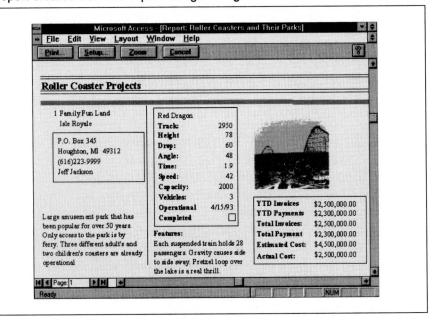

Adding Style to Your Forms and Reports

The style enhancements you can make to controls include alignment, color, three-dimensionality, fonts, and borders. These properties are listed in the bottom half of the Property Sheet window. Access also has buttons in the toolbar to make these style enhancements even easier to use. You add styles to a form or report by changing the properties of the control either through the Property Sheet window or through the toolbar. When you select a control that uses many of the style enhancements described in this section, the middle and right sections of the toolbar change to look like this:

These new toolbar boxes and buttons let you easily change the font, font size, weight, italics, underlining, and alignment of the selected control. Also, when you change the style of a control, the control in the form or report design appears with the alignment, font, color, three-dimensional effect, and borders that you have added or changed.

Setting Alignment

You can change the alignment of any control that uses text. Alignment determines whether the characters that appear in the control start at the left side of the control, end at the right side of the control, or are centered in the control's position. The default for alignment is to right-align data fields that contain numbers and dates and left-align all other controls. Change the alignment of a control by clicking one of these four buttons:

The first button left-aligns the text in the control, the second button centers the text in the control, the third button right-aligns the text in the control, and the fourth button sets the control to use the default alignment. You can also change the alignment by changing the Text Alignment property in the Property Sheet window and selecting from General, Left, Center, and Right.

Figure 14-6 shows a report that uses different alignments. The controls for the Employee Id column and the Hours column use general alignment. The label and field for Project Number use center alignment. The control for the Date field uses left alignment, and the controls for the Employee Id and Hours labels use right alignment.

Tip   Set the headers to use the same alignment as the entries below them. Your forms and reports look more professional when the column headings align with the data. Usually, you will change the alignment of labels that are used for column headings of date and numeric fields to right alignment so the text aligns with the numbers and dates.

Setting the Font for Controls

Using the same font for all the text in a form or report is dull. Using several kinds of type not only enlivens your form or report, it also lets you emphasize important information. For our purposes, a *font* is a collection of features that describe how the text appears. The name of a font tells you the font's general appearance but a font also has size and weight. (*Weight* is simply the boldness of the type—a very thin lightweight

A report using different control alignments

Time Records

07-Aug-92

Date	Employee Id	Project Number	Hours
6/12/92	3	5	40
6/12/92	5	3	18
6/12/92	5	8	13
6/12/92	6	4	2
6/12/92	1	4	12
6/12/92	6	5	38
6/12/92	1	1	20
6/12/92	1	7	8
6/12/92	5	4	6

Report: Employee Time Log - New Alignments

Page: 1

type is useful for copy that you don't want to stand out; a heavy, very bold type draws the reader's attention to text you really want to emphasize.) The fonts you use can have other features such as italics and underlining. Each control has its font properties set separately so changing the font of one control does not affect the others.

A font's name sets the style of the characters in a form or report. The default is MS SanSerif or Helv in Windows 3.0 and Arial in Windows 3.1 depending on whether the Layout for Print property of the form or report is Yes or No. To change the font name, select one of the font names from the Font Name list box in the Property Sheet window or from the Font box in the toolbar, which looks like this:

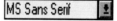

The list of names includes all of the fonts available to Windows. These fonts include the fonts installed as part of Windows, the fonts available through your printer, and any fonts you have added to Windows. If you do not see a font style that you think should be available, check the Windows Control Panel program to see if the font is available.

Figure 14-7 shows a few of the font names you can use. Some of these are available through Windows 3.1 so if you are using Windows 3.0, you will have different font names. Also, the Lucida fonts shown in Figure 14-7 are provided through a separate package. Several companies make additional fonts that once installed are available to Access as well as other Windows applications.

When selecting a font for a control, keep two ideas in mind. First, don't use more than two or three fonts since too much variety focuses attention on the different fonts rather than the information you are trying to present. Second, select the font that fits the purpose of the form or report. For example, the calligraphy font in Figure 14-7, while pretty, is inappropriate for almost every business situation.

Which font names are listed depends on the Layout for Print property of the form or report. The default for this property is No for forms to use screen fonts and Yes for reports to use printer fonts. When this property is set to Yes, the font names list includes all of the screen fonts and any installed scalable fonts. When this property is set to No, the font names list includes all of the printer fonts and any installed scalable fonts.

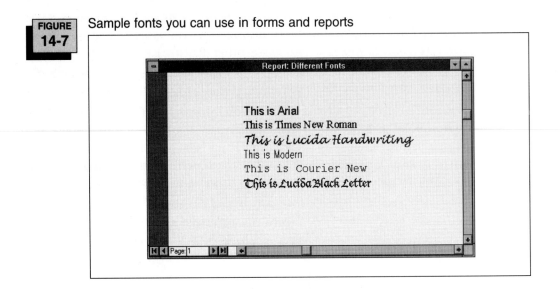

FIGURE
14-7

Sample fonts you can use in forms and reports

When you use a screen font to print or a printer font to display the information on the screen, Windows makes the closest substitution possible. Since the substitution is not exact, you'll see differences between how the form or report appears on the screen and on paper.

Tip   If you have TrueType fonts, use them. These fonts look the same displayed on the screen and printed. Also, Access does not have to make substitutions depending on whether you are looking at the form or report on the screen or printing it. When you use them and preview the output, the preview matches much more closely what you get when you print the form or report.

You can also select the size of the font for a control. The font size is set by the Font Size property in the Property Sheet window or from the Fontsize box in the toolbar, which looks like this:

The list of sizes includes many of the font sizes available for the selected font name. Not all font names have every size possible. One of the advantages with scalable fonts such as TrueType fonts is that you can use any size. Use the Windows Control Panel program to check if the selected font name is a scalable font. When setting the size of a scalable font, you can type the size of the font you want so you can have other font sizes than the ones listed.

The remaining features seem more like those you would expect from a word processor than a database product. The Font Weight property sets how heavy or light the characters appear. Select between Extra Light, Light, Normal, Medium, Semi-bold, Bold, Extra Bold, and Heavy in the Font Weight drop-down list box. A shortcut to quickly change the Font Weight property of a control to Bold is to click the Bold button in the toolbar, which looks like this:

You can also italicize the text in a control by changing the Font Italic property from No to Yes. A shortcut for changing this property is clicking the Italic button in the toolbar, which looks like this:

You also can underline the text in a control. Note that you underline the *text* in the control rather than underlining the control. (If you want a line under the control itself, add it using the Line tool.) To underline text in a control, change the Font Underline property from No to Yes or use the shortcut of clicking the Underline button in the toolbar, which looks like this:

Use these properties to draw attention to the important parts of a form or report. The following shows a form that is enhanced with various font properties:

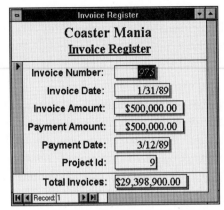

In this form, the controls for the fields use the Times New Roman font while the controls for the field names use Arial. The font size for the fields and their labels is 14 points while the font size for the two label controls in the Form Header section is 16 points. Also, the Invoice Register label is underlined and the control for the invoice number field is italicized.

Access remembers the printer that is currently selected when you create a form or report. Access does this because the form or report may use fonts that are specific to the selected printer. For example, if you switch from printing a report that uses the CG Times font available on a Hewlett-Packard LaserJet Series III to printing the report on a Hewlett-Packard LaserJet Series II, Access must substitute the CG Times font selection with another one.

Setting Dimensions, Colors, and Borders

Forms and reports can look bland without something to liven them up. You can make a control look three-dimensional. You can use colors to brighten the forms (and also to separate sections of a form or report). You can use different colors for different forms so the users know immediately that they are using the correct form. Since most printers do not print colors, you will primarily use colors for forms. Borders for controls can be set to different widths so you do not have to use the default hairline border, which you have seen up to this point.

While you can make entries for a control's colors and borders when you change a control's properties, Access has a better way. Select Palette from the View menu or select the Palette button to have the dialog box shown here displayed:

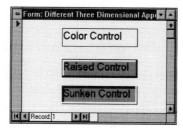

This dialog box sets the color of a control, the border's width, and the three-dimensional appearance of the control.

Adding Dimensions to Controls

You can give controls a three-dimensional appearance in one of three styles. These three types—Color, Raised, and Sunken—are exaggerated here:

Set one of these by selecting one of the option buttons in the Color Palette window shown previously or change the control's Special Effect property (your three choices there will be Color, Raised, and Sunken). Color is the default for most controls. Raised has the white border on the top and left sides with the dark gray border on the bottom and right sides while Sunken has the dark gray border on the top and left sides with the white border on the bottom and left sides. When you select Raised or Sunken for a control's appearance, the control uses the same colors as buttons in the toolbar and command buttons. These colors are set by the Control Panel program. Also, when a control's appearance is Raised or Sunken, changing the border as described later in the chapter has no effect.

Tip Command buttons, toggle buttons, and raised and sunken control colors are set through the Control Panel. The Button Face, Button Highlight, and Button Shadow screen elements set the front, top, and bottom appearance of these controls. When you change the button colors with the Control Panel, you also change several other colors in Access as well as changing the button colors used by all Windows applications.

Setting Colors of Controls

Using the Palette window you can set the color of text, the border around controls, and the background color of a control. Once you select the control, the Palette window indicates the selected colors of the object although when the selected color is black, you will not see it since the black border blends with the black color. A control can have separate colors for text, fill, and border.

Not all of the options are available for all controls. For objects that have a raised or sunken appearance, you can only change the text color since other changes have no effect. Several controls use the fill color to select the colors that fill the control. Option groups, rectangles, and labels also use the Clear check box at the end of the fill color. When you select the Clear check box, the control is transparent so the control shows whatever controls are behind it. When this check box is cleared, which is the default, the control is filled with the selected color even if the color is white.

You can also set colors through properties using the Property Sheet window. The Fore Color property matches the text color. The Back Color matches the fill color. The Border Color matches the border color. The Back Style property matches the Clear check box after the fill color in the Palette window. Notice how the color properties contain numbers. Since you do not want to have to remember the color code for each color, it's easiest to select colors using the Palette window.

The following shows a form that has the colors of several controls (that appear as shades of gray) and sections altered:

In this form, the color of the Form Header section is changed to cyan and the Form Footer section is changed to black with the text in the Form Footer section changed to white. When you print a form or report with colors, how colors print depends on how your printer converts colors into shades of gray.

 Tip Do not use the Fore Color, Back Color, and Border Color properties in the Property Sheet window to change color. The numbers do not indicate the colors they represent. Using the Color palette lets you see the color you are selecting.

 Tip When adding color to a form or report, choose a light color. The people who read the forms and reports will find it easier to read characters against a light background rather than a dark one.

Changing the Border of a Control

All controls have borders that you can adjust. Some controls, such as the labels for check boxes, option buttons, and text boxes, have as a default not to display any border. Other controls, such as option groups, list boxes, and combo boxes, have as a default to display a thin black border. You can set the border displays, its thickness, and its color.

To select whether a border appears around a control, clear or select the Clear button to the right of the colors for Border in the Palette window. You can also change the Border Style property in the Property Sheet window. When the check box is selected or the Border Style property is Clear, the control does not display the control's border in the form view or report. In the form's design, you will still see the thin border although it is dimmed to indicate that it will not appear. When the check box is cleared or the Border Style is Normal, the control's border appears in the form or report. Also, any color and border width setting appears on the form's or report's design.

Select the border's width with the buttons at the bottom of the Palette window or with the Border Width property. You can visually select the border's width by clicking one of the controls. If you use the Border Width property in the Property Sheet window, select between Hairline and 1 pt through 6 pt, which matches the seven buttons available in the bottom of the Palette window.

The border's color is set by the color button selected for Border in the Palette window or through the Border Color property in the Property Sheet window. Selecting a border's color is just like selecting the color for text and the fill color of an object.

Figure 14-8 shows a report that uses different border styles. The Employee Id and the Last Name boxes use thicker borders than the remaining fields. The labels that identify the fields have borders and appear since the Clear button in the Palette window for the border is not selected.

Setting the Default Properties of Form and Report Controls

You can set the properties as you add controls to a form or report or before you add them. Set the default for controls by changing the

FIGURE
14-8

A report that uses different border styles

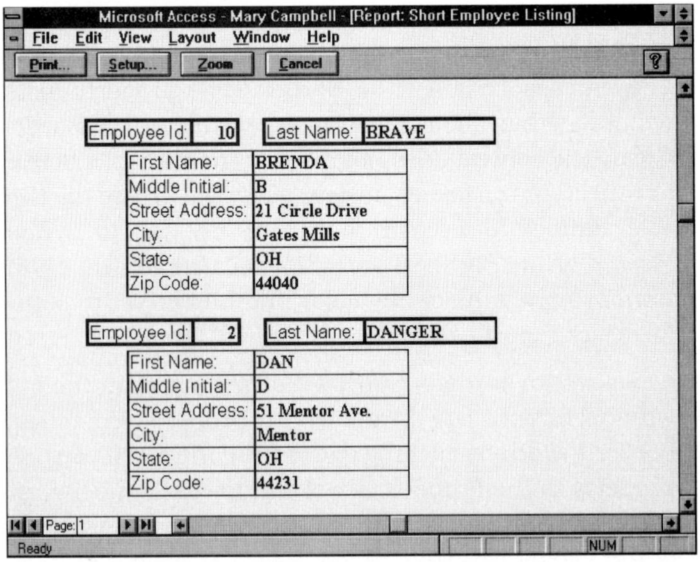

properties of the tools in the toolbox. The default properties apply to all of the controls of that type that you add to the current form or report. When you want to use a set of default control properties for multiple forms or reports, you can create templates that store default settings. Use these templates whenever you create forms and reports.

Setting Property Defaults

Setting property defaults for a form or report is just like setting property settings for a control added to a form or report. Simply click the tool in the toolbox while the Property Sheet window appears. The Property Sheet window changes to show only the properties you can set as the default for controls of the selected type. The following shows the Property Sheet window displaying the default properties for a text box in a report:

Default Text Box	
Visible	Yes
Can Grow	No
Can Shrink	No
Width	1 in
Height	0.17 in
Special Effect	Color
Back Color	16777215
Border Style	Clear
Border Color	0
Border Width	Hairline
ForeColor	0
Font Name	Arial
Font Size	8
Font Weight	Normal
Font Italic	No
Font Underline	No
Text Align	General
Help Context Id	0
Auto Label	Yes
Add Colon	Yes
Label X	-1 in
Label Y	0 in
Label Align	General

You can see that the title bar changes to Default and the name of the object. Most of the properties you see listed are a subset of the properties you can set for the individual controls. You have learned about these properties in prior chapters; later you will learn about the properties that are specifically default properties. At this point, change the properties in the Property Sheet window just as you change the properties for specific parts of forms and reports. Any control of that type that you subsequently add to the form or report uses the new settings you have made to the control.

Figure 14-9 shows a report created by changing the default properties. Changing text font and size is easier if you change the default properties since you make the change to the tool in the toolbox, which applies the change to all controls of that type that you subsequently add. When you create forms and reports using FormWizards and ReportWizards, each Wizard changes the default properties of the controls it adds such as labels, text boxes, and check boxes. By changing the default properties, all of the controls added with the FormWizards and ReportWizards have the same appearance.

Tip You can change the appearance of several settings at once using the toolbar and the Palette window. When you select multiple controls in a form or report design and then select buttons in the toolbar, make your selections from the boxes in the toolbar, or make your changes in the Palette window. The changes affect all selected controls. You cannot use

 A report created by changing the default properties

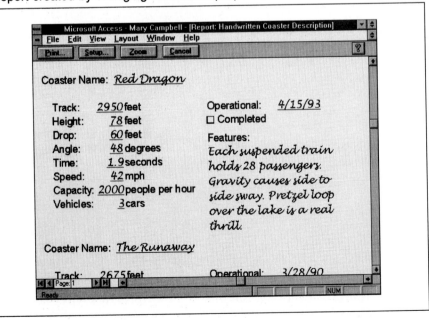

the Property Sheet window since it appears empty when you have multiple controls selected.

Control Properties Specific to Default Control Settings

When you set default settings for different types of controls, you will notice as many as five new properties that you have not seen before: Auto Label, Add Colon, Label X, Label Y, and Label Align. These properties can only be set as part of the default settings.

Auto Label

When you have added controls up to this point, you have seen controls with a label control attached to the control with text ending in a colon. These labels appear with the control because the Auto Label default control property is set to Yes. This property is set to Yes for text boxes, option groups, option buttons, check boxes, combo boxes, list boxes, and subforms. This property is set to the default of No for toggle buttons and command buttons. Change this property when you want toggle buttons and command buttons to add the label controls as part of the control or you do not want to add the label controls as part of the other control types.

Add Colon

When these labels are added, they have a colon after them when the Add Colon property is Yes (the default for text boxes, option buttons, check boxes, combo boxes, list boxes, and subforms). Changing this property to No omits the colon when you add that type of control to the form or report.

Label X and Label Y

When you create a form with the FormWizards, notice that the Boxed look for the form (as described in Chapter 8) puts field names above the fields. When you create a report with the ReportWizards, notice that the labels added for the fields using the Ledger look puts the labels closer to the text box controls than the other report looks and the labels are right-aligned. These labels are added at different relative positions to the field controls because the Label X and Label Y properties that you can set as default control properties set the relative distance from the upper-left corner of the selected control.

Label X sets how much to the left or right the label is placed relative to the control, and Label Y sets how much above or below the label is placed relative to the control. The number is positive to have the label to the right or below the control and negative to have the label to the left or above the control. The distance is measured in inches or centimeters just like the other parts of the form or report.

Label Align

The position of the text is set by the Label Align property. You have the same choices of General, Left, Center, and Right that you have for the Text Align property. The difference between Text Align and Label Align is that Label Align sets the alignment of the label control added next to a control and Text Align sets the alignment of the characters that appear in the control.

The following shows a form created by changing these default settings:

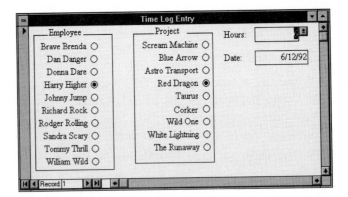

In this form, the Label X and Label Y properties are changed so the labels are added to the left of the option buttons rather than to the right. Also, the Label Align property is changed to Right so the employee names and project names are right-aligned.

Creating a Template

When you want several of your forms or reports to have a similar appearance, you can create a template. The template determines the default settings for form, report, section, and control properties, section sizes, and whether the form or report includes headers or footers. A template is really nothing more than using an existing form or report as the basis for a new form or report.

To create a template, create a form or report in which the settings for the different types of controls are set as you want them to be. (You may already have a form or report that contains all of the settings that you want to use as defaults. If so, use this for the template; you do not need to create another one just for this purpose.) Display the form or report header and footer and the page header and footer if you want these sections to be included as the default. Set the section sizes to determine their default size if you want. When you have created this form or report, save it just as you would other forms or reports.

When your form or report is ready to serve as a template, choose Options from the View menu. In the Category list box, select Form & Report Design. Next, after Form Template or Report Template in the bottom of the dialog box, enter the name of the form or report you want to use as a template. Once you select OK, you have changed the form or report design that is used as a template. The default form and report templates are Normal. When you do not have a form or report named Normal, the form or report uses the default settings.

Using a Template

To use the template, create a form without using the FormWizards. The form you create uses the same default settings for all of the controls you add through the toolbox. Also, the form or report has the same headers and footers as the template as well as the same section sizes.

The new form you create does not have any of the controls added to the form or report you are using as a template. That is why you can use an existing form or report as a template without the individual controls from the template form or report affecting the current form or report. The new form or report does not have any of the property settings of the individual controls in the template form or report. As an example, if you have all of the controls in a form using the Courier font by changing the Font Name property of the individual controls of text boxes, using the form as a template does not set the Font Name property of all text boxes to Courier in the new form unless you also have set the Font Name property for the default text box.

Tip If you want to use the same template for both forms and reports, create the template for the form then save the form as a report. Both the form and report template will have the same settings.

Figure 14-10 shows a report created using the report in Figure 14-9 as a template. In Figure 14-10, the text boxes automatically use the same Lucida handwriting font used in Figure 14-9. The labels also use the same Arial font in both reports. These settings are not altered in the report

**FIGURE
14-10**

A report created using the report in Figure 14-9 as a template

Microsoft Access - Mary Campbell - [Report: Handwritten Park Descriptions]

File Edit View Layout Window Help

Print...   Setup...   Zoom   Cancel

Client Name: *Family Fun Land*
Park Location: *Isle Royale*
Mailing Address: *P.O. Box 345*
City: *Houghton, MI 4931*
Park Description: *Large amusement park that has been*
                     popular for over 50 years. Only access
                     to the park is by ferry. Three different
                     adult's and two children's coasters
                     are already operational

Client Name: *Teen Land*
Park Location: *Ashtabula Park*
Mailing Address: *P.O. Box 786*
City: *Ashtabula, OH 4432*
Park Description: *Turn of the century amusement park*

Page: 1

Ready   NUM in Figure 14-10 because the text boxes and labels have these properties set by the report in Figure 14-9.

Quick Reference

To Add a Line or Rectangle to a Form or Report   Select the line or rectangle tool from the toolbox. Point to where you want the line or rectangle to start, and then drag the mouse to where you want the line or rectangle to end.

To Change the Layer of a Control   To put a control on the bottom layer of the form or report, select Send to Back from the Layout menu. To put a control on the top layer of the form or report, select Bring to Front from the Layout menu.

To Set the Alignment of a Control   Click the Left, Right, Center, or General alignment buttons in the toolbar or change the Text Alignment property in the Property Sheet window to Left, Right, Center, or General.

To Set the Font of a Control   Change the font name by selecting another font from the Font Name box in the toolbar or from the Font Name property in the Property Sheet window. Change the font size by selecting a size from the Fontsize box in the toolbar or from the Font Size property in the Property Sheet window. Add effects such as boldface, italics, and underlining with the Bold, Italic, and Underline buttons in the toolbar or by selecting Yes or No for the Italic and Underline properties and the thickness for the Font Weight property in the Property Sheet window.

To Display the Palette Window   Choose Palette from the View menu or click the Palette button in the toolbar.

To Set the Color, Border, and Three-Dimensional Appearance of a Control   Select the three-dimensional appearance you want for the control by selecting between the Color, Raised, and Sunken buttons in the Palette window or Color, Raised, or Sunken for the

Special Effect property. Select the color you want for the text, fill, and border from the Palette window. You can also select Clear on the first check box or Clear for the Back Style property in the Property Sheet window to select whether the control is transparent (if it is, it displays the controls behind it). To select the width of the border, select one of the border width buttons in the Palette window or select a width for the Border Width property in the Property Sheet window. You can also select Clear on the second check box in the Palette window or Clear for the Border Style property in the Property Sheet window to select whether the border even appears.

To Set the Default Properties of a Control   Display the Property Sheet window and then click the tool in the toolbox. The properties listed in the Property Sheet window are the properties you can set for the defaults for all controls of that type you subsequently add to the form or report.

To Create a Form or Report Template   Choose Options from the View menu. Select Form & Report Design from the Category list box. After Form Template or Report Template, enter the name of the form or report that you want to use as a template for all forms or reports you subsequently create without using the FormWizards or ReportWizards. The form or report adopts the control properties, default size, and settings.

CHAPTER

Adding OLE Objects to Forms and Reports

Access is one of the many Windows applications that support OLE (Object Linking and Embedding). OLE lets you add pictures, charts, and other data created in other applications to your tables, forms, and reports. OLE adds the functionality of other packages to the one you are presently using.

You can either link or embed objects into Access. Windows 3.1 allows both linking and embedding but Windows 3.0 only allows linking. To use OLE objects in Access, first decide whether you want to link or embed the data from the other applications into Access. After deciding, you add these objects to your database.

You use the linked and embedded objects you add to a database either in tables or in forms and reports. The embedded and linked data can be part of the table's data such as pictures of employees or projects. The embedded and linked data added to forms and reports can be graphics such as a company logo. You can continue to edit these objects. A graph like the ones you created in Chapter 8 for the graph FormWizard form, is a special type of OLE object that you will learn about in this chapter.

Embedding Versus Linking

When you want to take data from another application and put it into your tables, forms, and reports, you first must choose whether to embed or link the data. (You choose between linking and embedding only if using Windows 3.1—if using Windows 3.0, the choice is made for you since Windows 3.0 only supports linking.) You decide based on where you want the data stored and whether you plan to use the data in other applications besides Access.

Figure 15-1 shows a diagram of how embedding and linking differ. Embedded data is stored in the database file along with other objects such as tables, forms, and reports. This data is still in the format that the other application can use. When you use the other application to edit the embedded data, the application gets the data to work with from the database. The embedded data is not available for sharing between other applications.

When you link data, the data is stored in the other application's format but the data is in its own file, which the application uses to store the data

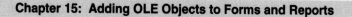

FIGURE 15-1 Differences between embedded and linked objects

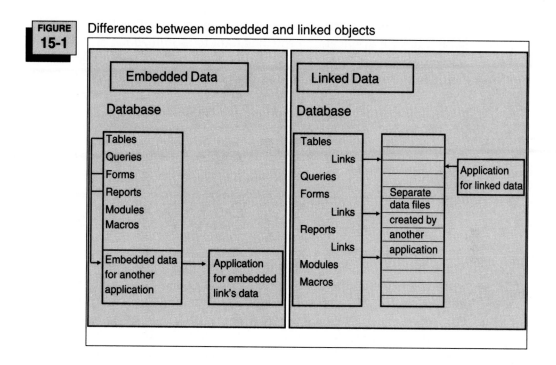

it works with. The tables, forms, and reports that use that data store links to the files rather than storing the actual data. When you use the other application to edit the linked data, the application gets the data from the separate file—not from the Access database. Also, other applications can continue using the file. For example, a Paintbrush file containing a company logo can still be linked to Excel worksheets and word processing documents.

If you plan to use the data solely in an Access database, embed the data. This keeps the data in the database that uses it even while the data is used by another application. If you plan to use the data in another application, link the object. Linking keeps the data in the other file's format, which other applications can use for their own links.

An application must have the capability to link or embed objects before you can link and embed objects from that application into Access. Some applications can only make data available for linking and embedding in another application, some applications can only link and embed data from other applications, some applications can do both, and some can do neither. The application accepting data to embed or link is a *client application*. An application providing data to be embedded or linked is a *server application*. While Access can be a client or server application, it provides two applications that can only be server applications. Microsoft Graph creates graphs like the ones you made with the graph FormWizard in Chapter 8. This is the same program available with Word for Windows 2.0. Paintbrush, which replaces an older version provided with Windows, gives you graphic drawing and editing capabilities.

Adding Embedded and Linked Objects to Forms and Reports

In a form or report, OLE objects are either bound or unbound object frame controls. The controls for OLE objects are bound controls when they represent an OLE Object field in the underlying table. These controls are unbound controls when you add OLE objects directly to a form or report design. Just like the labels you have added to form and report designs, these controls are static and do not change from record to record.

Figure 15-2 shows a form that includes both bound and unbound object frame controls. The person's face in the form is a bound control since the face changes to match the employee described. The tracking at the top of the form is an unbound control since it always appears in that position regardless of which record is displayed. The text in the Form Header section is composed of separate label controls that appear on top of the Paintbrush drawing because the Send to Back command in the Layout menu was used on the unbound object frame control.

Bound controls are chosen as embedded or linked when you use the form in a form view. Unbound controls are chosen as embedded or linked when you add the control to the form or report design. You can tell whether the unbound controls are embedded or linked by looking at their properties since linked objects have an Update Method property that embedded objects do not have. Also, linked objects may look different than embedded objects that use the same application. This difference in appearance varies by application. When you initially add an unbound OLE object to a form or report design, the control appears empty. When you look at the form or report design after displaying the form in a form

FIGURE 15-2 OLE objects in a form

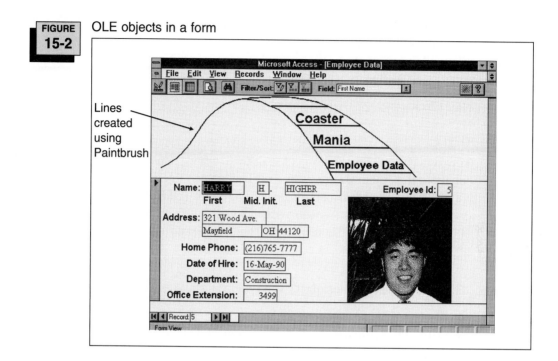

view or previewing or printing the report, the control displays the last displayed contents of that OLE object. Bound controls always look empty in the form or report design since they are filled by the data from the underlying table.

Adding New Data as an Embedded Object

You can add data from another application as you work with the form or report design. You use this method of adding an embedded object when the data to be embedded is copied to the Clipboard and you want to paste it into one of the applications that support linking and embedding. You can create the data that appears as an OLE object while you embed the data. For example, you can use Microsoft Paintbrush to quickly draw the picture you want to use. To add an unbound object frame control to contain a new embedded object, follow these steps:

1. From the toolbox, select the unbound object frame control, which looks like this:

2. Click where you want the object to start.

Besides using the default object size, you can also drag the pointer from where you want the object to start to where you want the lower-right corner of the object. Access displays the Insert Object dialog box. Another way to do this is by choosing Insert Object in the Edit menu. When you use this command rather than steps 1 and 2, the embedded object starts at the upper-left corner of the currently selected section in the form or report design.

3. Select the application for the type of data you want to add from the Object Type list box.

4. Create the data you want to appear as the embedded object.

5. Choose Exit or Return from the File menu. When prompted about updating or saving the changes, select Yes.

You can see the OLE object on your screen. Figure 15-2 shows the results of following these steps using the Paintbrush application to the Form Header section of the drawing.

Adding Existing Data as an Embedded Object

If you already have the data you want to embed in one of the other application's files, using that data is easy. You can add an entire file from one of the acceptable formats as the embedded object.

Remember Existing objects must have been created by an application that supports OLE.

To add an unbound control for an existing file as an embedded OLE object to a form or report design, follow these steps:

1. Select the unbound object frame control from the toolbox.

2. Click where you want the object to start.

Besides using the default object size, you can also drag the pointer from where you want the object to start to where you want the lower-right corner of the object. Access displays the Insert Object dialog box. As with adding a new embedded object, you can use the Insert Object command in the Edit menu to add the control in the upper-left corner of the currently selected section instead of following steps 1 and 2.

3. Select the File button.

4. Select the type of file you want to display from the List Files of Type drop-down list box. This list includes all of the file types for applications that support linking and embedding.

5. Select the name of the file that you want to use and OK.

You will be able to see the selected object on your screen. Figure 15-3 shows an example of a report design that has a Paintbrush file embedded. This graphic was created originally with CorelDRAW to take advantage of CorelDRAW's extensive clip art. Then this image was exported to a .PCX file that Paintbrush and other graphic programs can use. When this image is embedded and the File button is selected in step 3, Paintbrush Picture (*.pcx) is selected and the file COASTER.PCX is selected. You would want to link rather than embed a logo like this if you plan to use it in several locations or if you plan to change it later.

 Tip When creating a graphic for an OLE object, if the graphic is small keep it simple. A complex drawing becomes a blur when it is scaled down. For example, the gentlemen in the Coaster Mania logo in Figure 15-3 originally had more detail on their faces and clothes but the details were removed since the facial expressions were obscured due to competing details.

Adding a Section of Existing Data as an Embedded Object

When you want to embed only a section of data rather than an entire file into an unbound object frame control, you use different steps than

FIGURE
15-3
A Paintbrush file embedded in a report

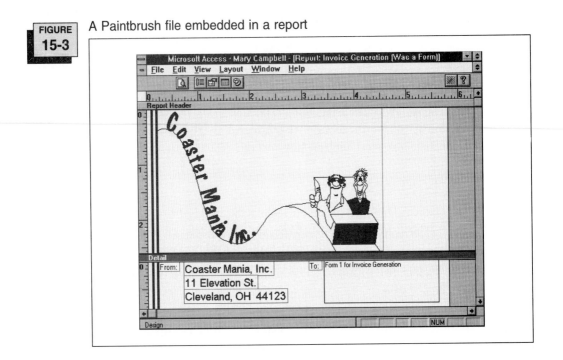

you do when embedding a new object or an entire file. When you embed only a section of a file, the object contains the entire file but only displays the section you select. To embed a section of data, use the Clipboard. To add an unbound control for a section of data from another application to a form or report design, follow these steps:

1. Switch to the application that displays the data you want to embed in an unbound form or report control.

2. Select the data you want to embed.

3. Choose Copy from the application's Edit menu to copy the selection to the Clipboard.

4. Switch to Access and the form or report design where you want to embed in an unbound form or report control.

5. Choose Paste from the Edit menu.

If the data can be embedded, Access creates an unbound object frame control containing the selected section of data as an embedded object. If the type of data cannot be embedded, Access tries adding the Clipboard's contents as a label or as a picture that you cannot edit. This object is added as a control in the upper-left corner of the currently selected section.

Figure 15-4 shows a form that has a section of an Excel worksheet embedded. The cells A1:C11 are selected in Excel then copied to the Clipboard. After switching to Access, this data is pasted to the form's design. The entire worksheet is embedded even though only part of it appears on the form's design.

These steps also work for copying data from other applications that do not support OLE. You can use these steps as another way to put the logo shown in Figure 15-3 into the report design. This logo is originally created in CorelDRAW 2.0, which does not support OLE but does support the Clipboard (CorelDRAW 3.0 does support OLE objects). You can copy the logo from CorelDRAW to the Clipboard then paste it into the report. The difference is that the pasted image from the Clipboard cannot be edited with the Paintbrush as it can with the embedded .PCX file.

FIGURE 15-4

A section of an Excel worksheet embedded in a form

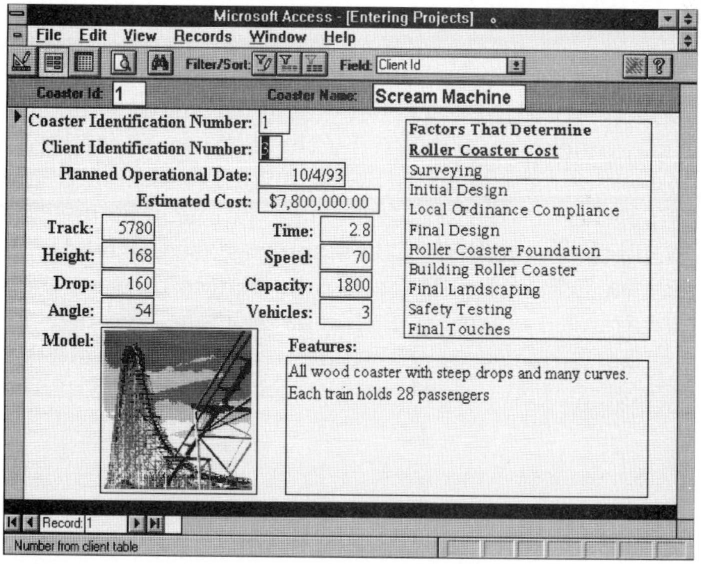

Linking Objects to a Report or Form

Linking data to an unbound control in a form or report design is a lot like embedding a section of data. To link data to a control in the form or report, you use the Clipboard. To link data to an unbound control from another application, follow these steps:

1. Switch to the application that displays the data you want to link.

2. Select the data you want to link.

3. Choose Copy from the application's Edit menu to copy the selection to the Clipboard.

4. Switch to Access and the form or report design where you want the linked unbound form or report control.

5. Choose Paste Link from the Edit menu.

This command is only available when the data in the Clipboard is from an application that you can link to Access. The Paste Link dialog box displays the name of the file containing the link and a check box for selecting when the link is updated.

6. Select OK.

The data may look different than if you embedded it. For example, in Figure 15-5, the Excel data includes the row and column borders that may otherwise be omitted if the data was embedded. The difference in how the data looks between linking and embedding depends on the application. This form is just like the one in Figure 15-4 except the Paste Link command in the Edit menu was used instead of the Paste command in the Edit menu. The other differences between the two forms are the rearranged entries to fit the larger embedded object. The worksheet is still separate so you can continue to use the worksheet when you start Excel, and other applications can have links to this worksheet.

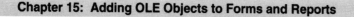

FIGURE
15-5

Part of an Excel worksheet linked in a form

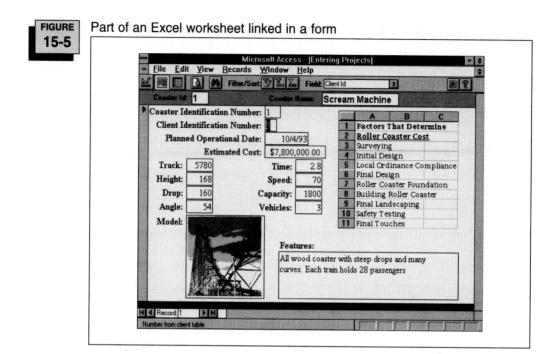

Adding a Bound Object Frame Control to a Form or Report

When you add a bound object frame control to a form's or report's design, you do not care if the data that will appear in the control's location is linked or embedded. A bound object frame control in a form or report only selects where the OLE object data from the underlying table or query is placed. It is the data in the table or query, or the data that is entered as you use a form, that determines the linked or embedded data that appears in a certain location. To add an bound object frame control to a form or report design, follow these steps:

1. From the toolbox, select the bound object frame control, which looks like this:

2. Click where you want the object to start.

Besides using the default object size, you can also drag the pointer from where you want the object to start to where you want the lower-right corner of the object. Access displays the Insert Object dialog box.

3. Click the Properties button in the toolbar or select Properties in the View menu to display the Property Sheet window.

4. Select the field name you want to appear in the object frame for the Control Source property.

Another option for selecting the field to appear in the bound object frame control is to click the control a second time. With the insertion point in the control, you can type the name of the field you want to display just as you can with text boxes and other bound controls. Typing the field name in the text box replaces the contents of the control's Control Source property to become the field name you have entered. This control appears empty because it will be filled when you use the form or report with the table's data.

Using the field list window you can add a bound object frame control for a table's field that is an OLE Object data type. This is the same shortcut you learned about for adding other types of controls to a form or report design with the field list window. With the toolbox and the field list window displayed, select the bound object frame control from the toolbox and the OLE Object data type field from the field list window. Then click on the field design where you want the control for the selected field added.

Setting How an OLE Object Is Created

You also have the option of adding an OLE object as an unbound control to a form or report as you paste the Clipboard's data to the form or report design. Select between embedding the data, linking the data, or saving it in a picture or bitmap format. To select how Clipboard data is copied to an unbound object frame control, follow these steps:

1. Switch to the application that displays the data you want to link.

2. Select the data you want to link.

3. Choose Copy from the application's Edit menu to copy the selection to the Clipboard.

4. Switch to Access and the form or report design where you want to embed an unbound form or report control.

5. Choose Paste Special from the Edit menu to display this dialog box:

Under Data Type, select which of several formats the Clipboard data is stored in. You can also select the Paste or Paste Link buttons to select when you want to copy the data to the field. Paste pastes either the embedded data or the image of the Clipboard's contents. Paste Link links the data in the selected format. Paste Link is only available when the selected data type supports linked OLE objects.

6. Select the data type you want to paste.

7. Select Paste or Paste Link.

The OLE object is added in the upper-left corner of the currently selected section.

In step 6, you may want to select Text when you want to link to the text in another application without linking to how that application presents the data. For example, you may want to use text from a Word for Windows document that omits the formatting. In that case, you would paste the link using the Text data type so the text appears in the form or report but the character formatting does not appear.

Form and Report Properties for OLE Objects

Bound and unbound object frame controls have additional properties you have not seen with other types of controls. Bound and unbound controls have the Scaling property. Unbound controls have an OLE Class property. Unbound controls containing embedded objects also have the same Row Source Type, Row Source, Link Master Fields, and Link Child Fields properties you saw for list and combo box controls. Unbound controls containing linked objects also have Source Object, Item, and Update Method properties.

When the area you have selected for a bound or unbound object frame control is smaller or larger than the size of the image, you can select how the image is reduced to fit in the area or how the extra area is used. How the object fits in the control is set by the Scaling property. When this property is set to Clip, Access fits as much of the image as possible in the area provided. When this property is set to Scale, the height and width is altered to fit the area provided although the height-to-width proportion of the original object is altered. When this property is set to Zoom, the height and width is altered to fit the area provided while retaining the original height-to-width proportion. Figure 15-6 shows the three different scaling choices operating on the same original object. You can always return the OLE object control's size to the size of the OLE object by selecting Size to Fit in the Layout menu. This command expands or contracts the control's size to that of the OLE object.

Tip   You can use the Palette window to add a border around a bound or unbound object frame control. Choose Palette from the View menu or click the Palette button in the toolbar to display the Palette window.

With unbound controls in a form or report, the controls have properties that select the source of the object appearing in the control. OLE Class selects the application that you use to work with the object. The control's current setting matches the choice you have made from the Object Type list box. This property is read-only so you cannot change the setting. When the object is linked to a control, the control includes the Source Object and Item properties.

The Source Object property selects the file the link uses and the Item property selects the part of the file that appears in the control. When you are linking an entire file to a control, the Item property is empty. When you are only linking a section, the Item property describes the section of the file displayed according to the format the application uses to describe a section of data. For example, for the link to an Excel worksheet shown in Figure 15-5, the Item property is R1C1:R11C3 to indicate that you want to link the range that starts from the first row and column to the eleventh row and third column.

FIGURE
15-6

Different scaling options on the same OLE object

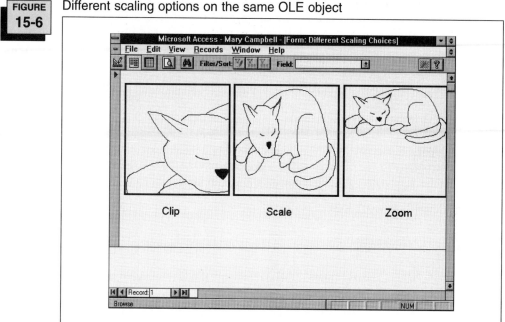

The remaining property that is specific to linked controls is the Update method, which selects when the object in the control is updated. Your choices are Automatic and Manual. Automatic, which is the same as when the Auto Update check box in the Paste Link dialog box is selected, updates the object displayed in the control as the object changes in the application that created it. Manual, which is the same as when the Auto Update check box in the Paste Link dialog box is cleared, updates the object only when you choose *OLE Class* Object from the Edit menu and Update Now. *OLE Class* is substituted with the name of the application the object is created with.

Using OLE Objects in a Form and Datasheet View

Working with OLE objects in a form or datasheet view is slightly different than using them in a form or report design view. When you add

OLE objects to a table from a datasheet or form view, these objects are part of the table's data. The difference between adding OLE objects in a datasheet versus a form view is how the OLE object appears. In a datasheet, the field's location identifies the source of the OLE object. This is the same information shown by the Object Source property if the same object is added to a form or report design. In a form view, the contents of the OLE object appear.

In either view, you can edit, add, or remove the OLE object. The only exceptions are unbound OLE objects, which you can modify in the form design rather than the form view, and pictures that are no longer OLE objects, which you can remove but not edit.

Adding New Data as an Embedded Object

You can add data from another application as you work in a datasheet or form view. Use this method of adding an embedded object when the data you will embed is copied to the Clipboard and you want to paste it into one of the listed applications. You can create the data that appears as an OLE object while you embed the data. Use the Microsoft Paintbrush to quickly draw the picture you want to use. To add an embedded object for a field that has the OLE Object data type, follow these steps:

1. Choose Insert Object in the Edit menu to display the Insert Object dialog box.

2. Select the application for the type of data you want to add from the Object Type list box.

3. Create the data you want to appear as the embedded object.

4. Choose Exit or Return from the File menu. When prompted about updating or saving the changes, select Yes.

You can see the selected object on your screen in a form view while in a datasheet the object appears as the name of the application you have selected in step 2.

Adding Existing Data as an Embedded Object

If you already have the data you want to embed in another application's files, embedding that data is easy. You can add an entire file from one of the acceptable formats as the embedded object. Existing objects must be created by an application that supports OLE. To add an OLE object to a OLE Object data type field in the form or datasheet view, follow these steps:

1. Choose Insert Object in the Edit menu to display the Insert Object dialog box.

2. Select the File button.

3. Select the type of file you want to display from the List Files of Type drop-down list box. This list includes all of the file types for applications that support linking and embedding.

4. Select the name of the file that you want to use and OK.

In form view, you will see the selected object on your screen. In a datasheet view, you will see the name of the selected object.

Figure 15-7 shows the preview of a report after adding several roller coaster pictures to the Project table. These pictures are stored as separate .PCX Paintbrush files.

Adding a Section of Existing Data as an Embedded Object

When you want to embed only a section of data rather than an entire file as an OLE object, paste the data to the OLE Object data type field. When you embed only a section of a file, the object contains the entire file but only displays the section you select. To embed a section of data, use the Clipboard. To add an embedded OLE object that contains a section of another file, follow these steps:

1. Switch to the application that displays the data you want to embed in a table.

2. Select the data you want to embed.

3. Choose Copy from the application's <u>E</u>dit menu to copy the selection to the Clipboard.

4. Switch to Access and move the pointer to where you want to embed the selected data in the table.

5. Choose <u>P</u>aste from the <u>E</u>dit menu.

If the data can be embedded, Access adds the embedded data as the OLE object for the field. The data appears in the form view and the object's application appears in the datasheet view. If the type of data cannot be embedded, Access tries adding the data as a label or as a picture that cannot be edited.

FIGURE 15-7   A form with OLE objects added to a table

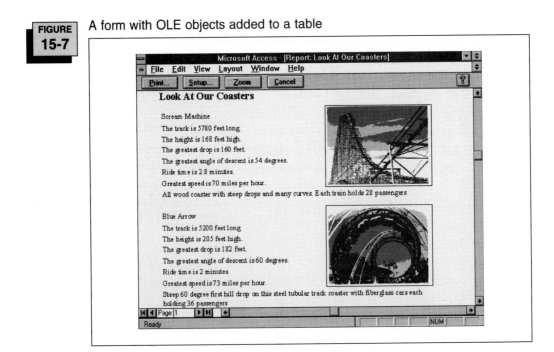

Linking Objects to a Report or Form

Linking an OLE object for a field's value keeps the reference to the original file, so as changes are made, the OLE object data is updated. To link data to a field in a table, use the Clipboard. To create an OLE object for an OLE Object data type field in a form or datasheet view, follow these steps:

1. Switch to the application that displays the data you want to link.

2. Select the data you want to link.

3. Choose Copy from the application's Edit menu to copy the selection to the Clipboard.

4. Switch to Access and the part of the table or form where you want to link the selected data.

5. Choose Paste Link from the Edit menu.

This command is only available when the data in the Clipboard is from an application that you can link to Access. The Paste Link dialog box displays the name of the file containing the link. The check box for selecting when the link is updated is dimmed because the link is updated as the record containing the link becomes the current record.

6. Select OK.

The linked data may appear different when embedded. For example, linked Excel worksheet data does not include the row and column borders that appear when the same data is embedded. Figure 15-8 shows a report that includes the beginning of different Paintbrush files. As you add each Paintbrush file to the disk, you copy it to the Clipboard and then link the file in Access. As the Paintbrush files change, the report is updated.

Setting How an OLE Object Is Created

A final option for putting an OLE object into an OLE Object data type field is selecting how Clipboard data is copied to a field as you copy the

FIGURE
15-8

Linked Paintbrush files in a form

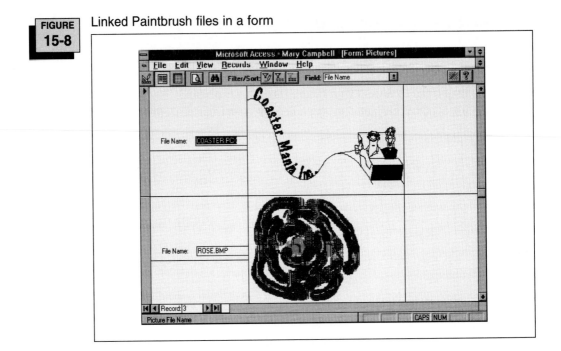

data. You can select between embedding the data or linking the data as text or in a picture or bitmap format. To select how Clipboard data is copied to an OLE Object data type field in a form or datasheet view, follow these steps:

1. Switch to the application that displays the data you want to link.

2. Select the data you want to link or embed.

3. Choose Copy from the application's Edit menu to copy the selection to the Clipboard.

4. Switch to Access and the field where you want to add the OLE object.

5. Choose Paste Special from the Edit menu.

Under Data Type, select which of several formats the Clipboard data is stored in. You can also select the Paste or Paste Link buttons to select when you want to copy the data to the field. Paste pastes either the embedded data or the image of the Clipboard's contents. Paste Link links the data in the selected format. Paste Link is only available when the selected data type supports linked OLE objects.

6. Select the data type you want to paste.

7. Select Paste or Paste Link.

In step 6, you may want to select Text when you want to link to the text in another application without linking to how that application presents the data. For example, you may want to use text from a Word for Windows document that omits the formatting. In that case, you would paste the link using the Text data type so the text appears in the form or report but character formatting does not appear.

 Tip In the Paintbrush application, change a picture from color to black and white by copying the color picture to the Clipboard, changing the image attributes to black and white, and then copying the Clipboard's contents back into Paintbrush.

Working with OLE Objects

As you work with OLE Objects in tables, forms, and reports, some of the features you use with these objects stay the same. These features include converting an OLE object into a picture, editing the picture, and changing the file of a linked OLE object.

Making an OLE Object Unchangeable

If you have finished changing an OLE object either in a form or report design or in a table, you can freeze the object so nobody else can edit it. Access can switch between records in a form or datasheet view faster when the records contain objects that can no longer be edited. To make the OLE object uneditable, choose *OLE Class* Object from the Edit menu and Change to Picture. *OLE Class* is the name of the application the object is created with.

After you select this command, you cannot edit the picture of the data that displays in that location. This is a one-time event for the OLE object because once you use this command, you cannot remove its effect. You cannot even use the Undo command in the Edit menu if you change your mind. When you convert an OLE object to a picture when the OLE object appears in a form or report design, you may notice that the control no longer has OLE Class, Source Object, and Item properties. These properties are no longer in use since you cannot edit the object.

Having a picture as an OLE object occurs in two other situations. One is when you paste the contents of the Clipboard using the Paste Special command in the Edit menu and you select Picture for the data type. The other is when you paste the Clipboard's contents to an OLE Object data type field or form or report design and the Clipboard's contents cannot be copied in an embedded format. For example, with the Coaster Mania logo created in CorelDRAW 2.0, copying the logo from CorelDRAW and pasting it into the form or report design pastes an uneditable picture. Another example is if you copy the screen's image to the Clipboard, such as copying pictures of the structure of your tables to a field. The report in Figure 15-9 is created by copying pictures of the table's design window. The picture of each table's design is captured by pressing PRINT SCREEN. Once the picture is in the Clipboard, switch to the report design and choose Paste in the Edit menu.

Modifying OLE Objects

When you want to change the data that is part of the OLE object, you can edit the data directly from the design, form, or datasheet view.

 Note   Unbound controls for OLE objects can only be edited in design views. Bound controls for OLE objects can only be edited in a form or datasheet view.

You can change the OLE object by double-clicking it. Access opens the application for the object and puts the data in that application. When the OLE object is linked, you will notice the object's filename as part of the application's title bar or in its own title bar depending on the application and the window sizes. When the OLE object is embedded, the title bar for the application or the document indicates that the data belongs to

FIGURE 15-9

Uneditable pictures added to a report

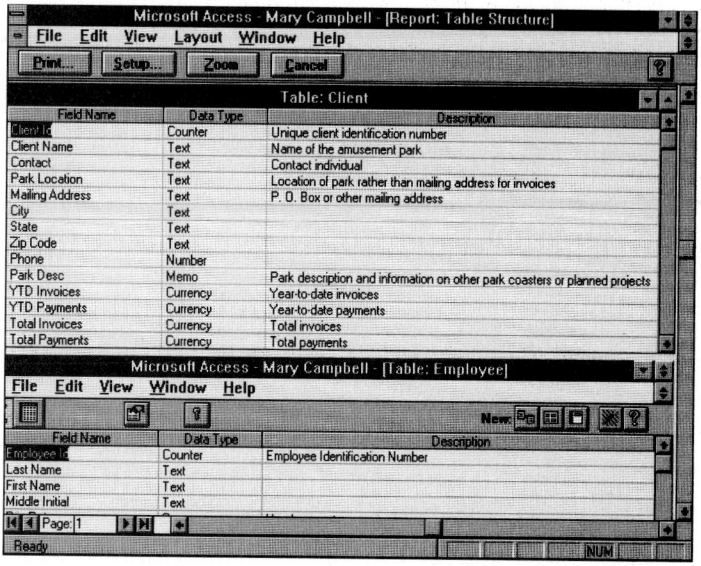

Access. For example, an embedded Paintbrush drawing displays Paint-brush Picture in Microsoft Access in the title bar when you edit this object. When you finish, select Save from the application's File menu. When the OLE object is linked, saving the file saves the file that is separate from the database. Next, select Exit or Update from the application's File menu (the exact command depends on the application) to leave the application and return to Access. Select Yes when given the confirmation message box asking whether you want to update the object in Access.

Modifying Linked OLE Objects

With both the linked OLE objects you add to a form or report design and those you add to field contents, you can change the file used by the link. Choose *OLE Class* Object from the Edit menu and Change Link. *OLE Class* is the name of the application the object is created with. From the Change Link dialog box, you can select another file. You may need to make this change when you have renamed the file the link uses. You can also change the source of the link of an OLE object used in the link by changing the control's Source Object property. If you want to change the section of the object displayed in an unbound object frame control, change the Item property for the control. If you want to change the section of the object displayed as a field's value, you must re-create the link.

Adding Graphs to Forms and Reports

You can create graphs that are separate controls in your forms and reports. These graphs are OLE objects created with the Microsoft Graph program that accompanies Access. This is the same program that accompanies Word for Windows. When you create a graph FormWizard form, you have already created these controls. The graphs you create take the data from a table and query. Also, the graphs can add or average the values of one field by groups created by another. You can also use the Microsoft Graph program to create graphs that use data from other sources.

Adding a Graph Control to a Form or Report

A graph is added to forms and reports by adding a control for the graph just as you did for other parts of a form or report. After you add a graph control to a form or report design, Access prompts you for the graph type and the data that will appear in the graph. These are the same prompts you see when you create a graph FormWizard form. Figure 15-10 shows a report design that includes a graph control. This control is added to the Report Header section so it appears at the beginning of the report. Figure 15-11 shows the beginning of the report this report design creates. Every time you print or preview that report, Access recalculates the values the graph displays.

To add a graph control to a form or report design, select from the toolbox the graph tool, which looks like this:

FIGURE 15-10

A report design containing a graph control

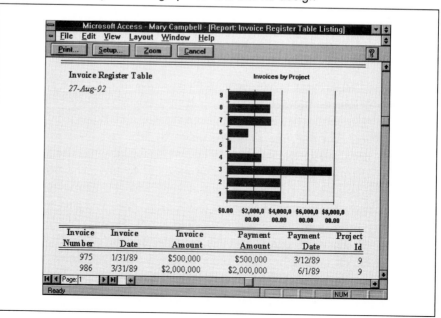

FIGURE 15-11

A report that incorporates a graph control into its design

Next, select where you want the graph to start. As with other controls, you can drag the pointer from one corner to another of the area you want the graph to fill. Clicking one location adds a graph of the default size that you can later move and size.

At this point, Access starts prompting you for the information to include in the graph. Change the table or query used for the data in the graph by choosing another table or query from the drop-down list box at the top of the dialog box. Choose which type of graph you want to create by selecting one of the 11 buttons representing the different graph types. These are the same types you saw with the FormWizard. Six of these are actual different graph types while the remaining five are three-dimensional versions of the first five graphs. Besides selecting the type of graph, you can select whether you are graphing the total or average of the values for each point along the X axis. When the table or query, graph type, and summary operation are selected, choose the Next button.

At this point you select the fields to appear in the graph just as you did with the single column and tabular form. The first field you select is usually the field or the fields containing the values you want along the X axis. This can be a field that contains text, values, or dates. Adding fields for this form type is just like adding fields for other FormWizards forms and ReportWizards reports. Most of the fields you select to include in the form contain numbers.

 Tip   You do not have to include all of the fields used by a form or report in the graph. Include only those fields you want to see in the graph.

When you select Next, Access looks at the Data Type property of the fields you have selected. At this point Access may need more information. If one of the fields is a Text data type or if all fields are Number data types, you can use one or more fields to label the X axis. The FormWizards prompts for the selected fields to use for labeling the points on the graph. Usually, you will select a single field to have the points along the axis labeled with the entries in that field. Select multiple fields when you want those field names to label the X axis. For example, in Figure 15-10, the contents of the Project ID field label the X axis. You can also select whether a legend appears by selecting or clearing the Display legend check box. When you have finished selecting fields in response to this prompt, select Next. Depending on the data types of the remaining fields, you may be prompted for the fields you want to use for the legend. Select one field to use the contents of the field as the legend entries or select multiple fields to use the field names as the legend entries.

If one of the selected series is a Date/Time data type, Access assumes you want the dates or times to identify the different points along the X axis. You have two options when one of the fields contains dates or times. You can choose how the dates or times in the Date/Time data type field are grouped by selecting a term in the Group [*field*] By drop-down list box. This drop-down list box lets you group dates or times by years, quarters, months, weeks, days, hours, or minutes. You can also select whether to use all the dates and times or only use the dates and times within a range. The default is to use all of the dates and times but you can select the Use Data Between Radio button and modify the dates and times to select the range of dates and times you want to use. The range of dates and times select which records from the table or query the form uses for the graph. When finished selecting options for the Date/Time data field, select Next.

At this point, how you proceed differs from the steps you used when creating the graphs produced with the graph FormWizards form. Access displays a confirmation message box asking if you want to link the graph with one of the fields in the form or report. Select Yes when you want only the records selected by the current record in the form or report to be included in the graph.

For example, if you want separate graphs for each of the projects, select Yes since you will use the records only for specific projects that change as the project numbers change. Select No on other occasions. If you select No, enter the graph's title and then select the Design button to display the form or report design after the graph control is added.

If you select Yes in the confirmation message box, Access needs to know how to link the fields in the graph with the fields in the form or report using the dialog box shown in Figure 15-12. If the graph uses the same table or query as the form or report, you usually are connecting the same named fields. If the graph uses a different table or query as the form or report, you are often connecting the same fields you use to link the two tables or queries if you used them in a main/subform form or main/subreport report.

FIGURE
15-12

The Microsoft Access GraphWizard dialog box

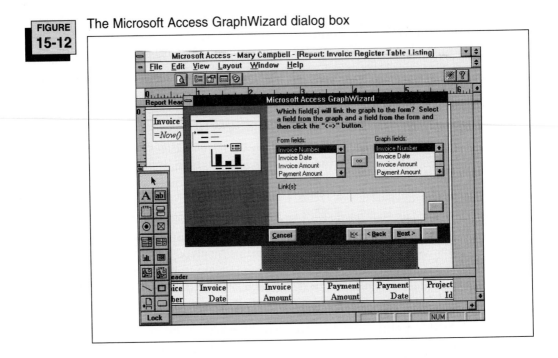

Under the Form Fields and Graph Fields list boxes, select the fields you want to link and then select the <=> button. The link you have just created appears in the link list box below. You can create one or many links. In a report that uses groups, you may want many links for each of the different groups the report uses. After the links are created, select Next. Now you can enter the graph's title and then select the Design button to display the form or report design after the graph control is added.

After the graph is added, the control appears on the form or report design. It is empty until you display the form view or preview or print the report. When you look at the properties for this control, notice that OLE Class is Microsoft Graph, Row Source Type is Table/Query, and Link Master Fields and Link Child Fields are set to create any link. The Row Source property contains an SQL statement. This statement selects the data from the selected table/query that appears in the graph. You will learn more about SQL statements in Appendix D. The GraphWizard creates the SQL statement for you using the selections you have made. The graph control may appear shaded.

Adding a Graph Using Other Data

When the data you want to appear in a graph is not part of a table or query, you create a graph differently. You can create a graph for a form or report that does not use data from a table or query. A graph that does not use data from a table or query is added to forms and reports by adding an unbound object frame control that you fill with the Microsoft Graph OLE object. Adding this unbound control adds an embedded Microsoft Graph object. All of the data that is part of the graph must be entered in the Microsoft Graph program. Using Microsoft Graph is like using other OLE object programs since you are creating the object you want to appear in the form or report.

Tip   When the data for a graph is in Access, do not use Insert Object in the Edit menu to add a graph from the Microsoft Graph application to a form or report. Using the graph control to add a graph to a form or report lets Access handle putting the data from the form's or report's table or query into Microsoft Graph.

To add a graph control to a form or report design, choose Insert Object in the Edit menu just as if you are adding another OLE object. From the list of object types, select Microsoft Graph. The Microsoft Graph application window looks like Figure 15-13. Microsoft Graph has two windows: the datasheet window contains the data displayed by the graph and the Chart window contains the graph. Switch between the two windows by pressing F6 or clicking the other window.

In the datasheet window, the top row lists the data to appear along the X axis, and the data in the left column makes up the entries that appear in the legend. The rest of the datasheet window contains the data that is graphically displayed in the graph. You can type entries in each of the cells of the datasheet. You also can paste data from other applications that you have copied to the Clipboard. Since you are copying the values of the Clipboard entries, if the values change in the other applications, the values in the graph are not updated. As you change the entries in the datasheet window, Microsoft Graph updates the chart in the Chart window. When finished adding the data, choose Exit and Return to Microsoft Access in the File menu then choose Yes from the confirmation message box to update the changes in Access. The graph

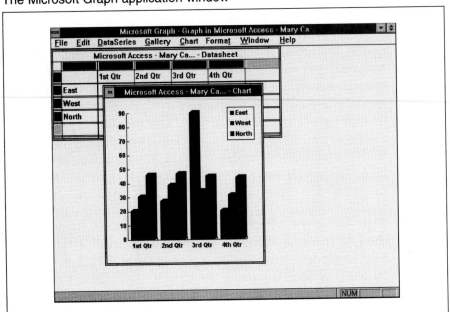

FIGURE
15-13
The Microsoft Graph application window

looks just like the graphs you have added to the forms and reports using the graph control.

Tip   If you want to use values from another application's file that you want updated in Access as the data changes, attach the data from the file into a table in Access as described in Chapter 5. This works for all the formats supported by attaching tables including Excel, dBASE, Btrieve, and SQL databases.

Making Changes to the Graph

You can make several changes to the graph you create for your forms and reports. The best way to change the data from the table or query that appears in the graph is to create a new graph control as a replacement for the old one. Creating a new graph control means you do not have to decipher the SQL statement that selects the table's or query's data to use in the graph. If the graph contains data that is not stored in a table or query, you can start Microsoft Graph and then change the data that needs to be updated.

Make other changes to the graph's appearance using the Microsoft Graph program. Some of the changes you can make include color selection, adding labels to identify data points, and grid lines. To do this, first double-click the graph in the form or report design. To change the size of the graph the control represents, drag the boundary of the graph window to the size you want for the report.

Once in Microsoft Graph, you can use the menus to change the graph's appearance. Select Data Labels in the Chart menu and then select the option button for how you want the data labels to appear. Figure 15-14 shows a graph in a report that displays the data labels and has the legend removed.

Change the graph's type by selecting another type from the Gallery drop-down menu. Once you click part of the graph to select it, you can use several commands in the Format drop-down menu to change how the selected graph object appears. For example, when you select a series,

FIGURE 15-14   The graph after changes using Microsoft Graph

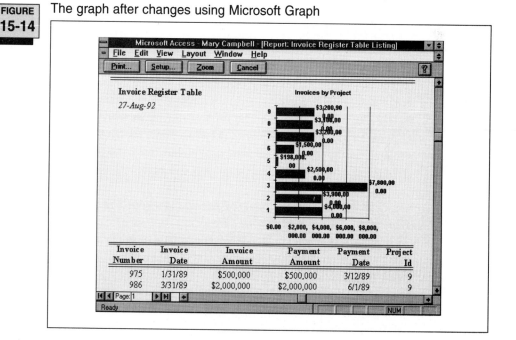

choose Patterns from the Format menu to change the color and pattern of the series. A *series* is a set of values that use the same color or pattern.

You can also set the font of a selected graph object with Font in the Format menu. As you work with the Microsoft Graph program, try out the different features. You can always return to Access without saving the changes you have made to the graph by selecting No from the confirmation message box when you leave Microsoft Graph. Update the graph in Access as you work on it in Microsoft Graph by choosing the Update command in the File menu. When finished with your changes, choose Exit and Return to Microsoft Access in the File menu, and then choose Yes from the confirmation message box to update the changes in Access.

The graph title will probably be the only change you make by modifying the SQL statement. If you look at the graph's current title then look at the SQL statement, you can see which part of the SQL statement you need to change. When you look at the Row Source property, you can see the entire SQL statement by pressing SHIFT-F2 to display the statement in a Zoom dialog box.

Quick Reference

To Add an Unbound Control for a New Embedded OLE Object to a Form or Report Design Select the unbound object frame control from the toolbox. Click where you want the object to start. Select the application for the type of data you want to add from the Object Type list box. Create the data you want to appear as the embedded object. Choose Exit or Return from the File menu. When prompted about updating or saving the changes, select Yes.

To Add an Unbound Control for an Existing Embedded OLE Object to a Form or Report Design Select the unbound object frame control from the toolbox. Click where you want the object to start. Select the File button. Select the type of file you want to display from the List Files of Type drop-down list box. Select the name of the file that you want to use and OK.

To Add the Clipboard's Contents as an Embedded OLE Object to a Form or Report Design Move to the section of the form or report design where you want to embed an unbound form or report control. Choose <u>P</u>aste from the <u>E</u>dit menu.

To Add a Linked OLE Object to a Form or Report Design
Copy the data you want to appear in the linked OLE object to the Clipboard. Switch to Access and move to the section of the form or report design where you want the linked unbound form or report control. Choose Paste <u>L</u>ink from the <u>E</u>dit menu and select OK.

To Add an Unbound Control for a New Embedded OLE Object to a Form or Report Design Select the bound object frame control from the toolbox. Click where you want the object to start. Change the Control Source property of this control to the name of the field you want to appear in the object frame.

To Add a New Embedded OLE Object to a Field Choose Insert Object in the <u>E</u>dit menu. Select the application for the type of data you want to add from the <u>O</u>bject Type list box. Create the data you want to appear as the embedded object. Choose <u>E</u>xit or <u>R</u>eturn from the File menu. When prompted about updating or saving the changes, select <u>Y</u>es.

To Add an Existing Embedded OLE Object to a Field Choose Insert Object in the <u>E</u>dit menu. Select the <u>F</u>ile button. Select the type of files you want to display from the List Files of <u>T</u>ype drop-down list box. Select the name of the file that you want to use and OK.

To Add the Clipboard's Contents as an Embedded OLE Object to a Form or Report Design Move to the OLE Object data type field and choose <u>P</u>aste from the <u>E</u>dit menu.

To Add a Linked OLE Object to a Field Copy the data you want to appear as the linked OLE object to the Clipboard. Switch to Access and move to the field where you want the linked OLE object. Choose Paste <u>L</u>ink from the <u>E</u>dit menu and select OK.

To Make an OLE Object Uneditable Choose OLE Class <u>O</u>bject from the <u>E</u>dit menu and <u>C</u>hange to Picture.

To Edit an OLE Object Double-click the OLE object in the table or form view. OLE objects that are part of a form's or report's design must be edited from the design view.

To Add a Graph Control to a Form or Report Click the graph button in the toolbar then click where you want the graph to start. For each of the subsequent dialog boxes, select the information it is prompting for such as the fields the report includes, its style, and its title. When you select the Design button from the final dialog box, the graph is created. You can also add a graph by adding an unbound object frame control and selecting Microsoft Graph as the application. When you create the graph this way, you must enter the data the graph charts.

IV

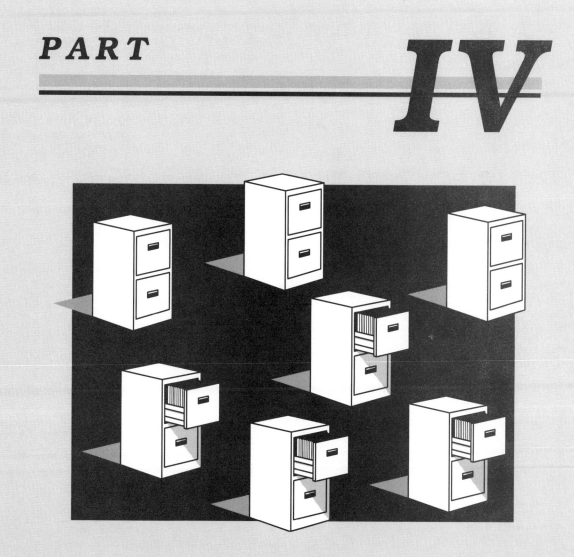

Macros

CHAPTER

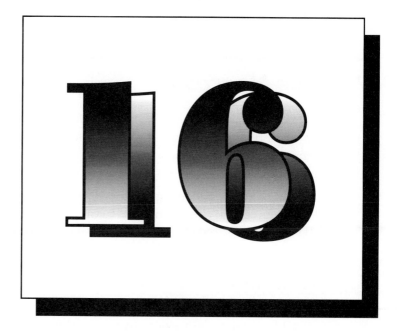

Macro Basics

Access makes it easy to create macros to automate any task. You can either select from a list of actions or drag the appropriate object to the Macro window to record the action that you want to perform. Once created, you execute the macro to perform the action. Each time you use the macro, you are guaranteed the same results. Since Access macros are so easy to create, they do not require the attention to detail required in earlier macro products.

Macros are especially suited to creating your own custom menus and controlling the use of forms and reports. These topics are covered in Chapters 17 and 18. This chapter addresses a few quick basics that will work with macros regardless of where you decide to use them. Master these building blocks and you will be ready to look at more sophisticated examples of their use.

Why Use Macros?

Increased productivity is the most important reason to use macros. You can record the steps that compose a task that you perform often. When you need the task performed, simply run the macro, often by pressing only a few keys.

Macros also provide capabilities that are not possible without them. For example, you can use macros to validate data entered on forms before the record is saved. You can also update a second form based on the values entered and saved in the first form. You can attach macros to command buttons that you add to forms to make it easy to select a task. You can also create a custom menu bar and pop-up forms for the collection of information, and customize your workspace in other ways with macros.

Access macros are easier to record than macros in other packages. Most other macro capabilities require a significant amount of typing on your part and have required entries where a slight mistake results in a syntax error and failed macro. This is not the case with Access since everything is menu selectable.

Creating and Using Macros

Access macros consist of a series of actions that can be selected from a list to make up each macro instruction. You can add comments to your macro to explain the need for each step. Actions can have *arguments*, which define the objects that will be used with each action.

You enter macros in the Macro window that is displayed when you click the Macro button in the database window and then click the New button. Macro windows have different sections to organize the entry of actions, comments, and arguments as shown in Figure 16-1.

The entries in the Action column tell Access what you want to do. The entries in the Comment column document your selection of different actions. Arguments in the bottom half of the Macro window further specify how an action works. Arguments do not display until you have selected an action. The list of arguments that displays within the window depends on which action has the focus, the insertion point that indicates the macro action you are working with. The toolbar is different since the toolbar now contains the Macro Names, Conditions, Run, and Single Step buttons.

FIGURE 16-1

The Macro window

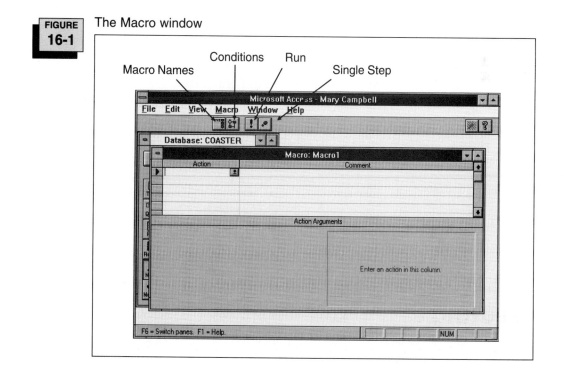

Recording the Macro

You must record the actions that you want a macro to perform before you can use it. Macros are always recorded in a special Macro window. At a minimum this window has two columns at the top for actions and comments and a bottom section for the arguments associated with each action. Optionally you can display two additional columns in the top part of the window as you learn to show macro names and conditions that affect whether or not actions are executed. The display of these sections and the entries that you place in them are discussed later in this chapter. With all the help that Access provides, the process is really quite easy once you have created a few macros.

You enter actions in the top part of the window by typing them or using the drop-down list box to select the action you want. To supply values for arguments use F6 to move to the bottom of the window and complete each argument entry. Use F6 when ready to move back to the top part of the window.

To record a macro you must open the Macro window as your first step. From the database window, follow these steps:

1. Click the Macro button in the database window.

2. Click the New button shown in Figure 16-2.

A Macro window that looks like Figure 16-1 will appear. Record macro actions in the order in which you want them to execute.

3. Click the arrow to display the action list shown here:

4. Select the action you want or type the name of the action.

FIGURE
16-2 The database window with the Macro button chosen

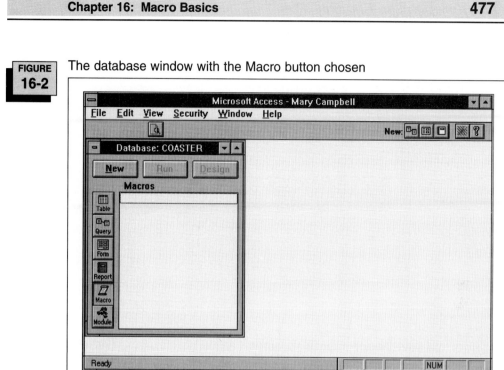

The Hourglass action selected in the example will display an hourglass while the action runs.

5. Type a comment in the Comments column as shown in Figure 16-3, where the comment reflects the Hourglass action.

Comments are optional but do include them. Comments let you know how a macro works months after you create it. If a complex macro does not have comments, the macro will not be used since nobody will be able to understand what task the macro performs.

6. Press F6 to move to the arguments or click the argument that you want to change.

7. Complete the argument entries.

Figure 16-4 shows the argument entries for the Print action. Access initially set the Print Range argument to All, which means the Page From

FIGURE
16-3 A comment entered for the Hourglass action

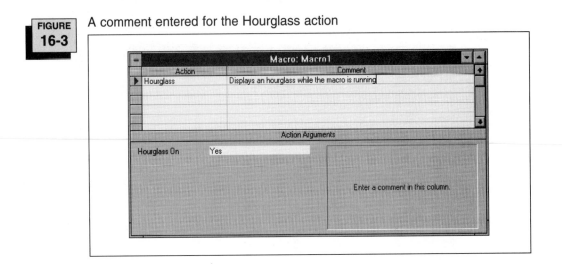

and Page To arguments are empty. After Print Range is changed to Pages, complete these arguments by typing **1** after each of them. The other actions, Hourglass and OpenTable, have their arguments set separately.

8. Press F6 to move to the top and use the DOWN ARROW or TAB to move to the next row and select another action.

Figure 16-5 shows the macro with another action. This one requires that you specify an object type and name.

FIGURE
16-4 Argument entries for the Print action

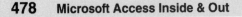

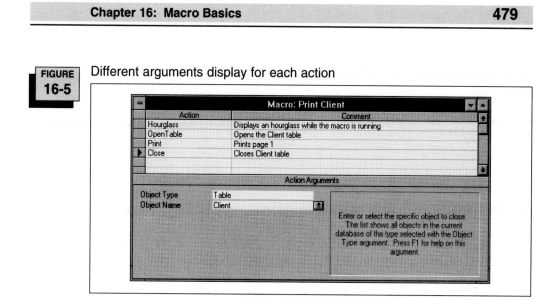

Different arguments display for each action

With the macro entries complete, save the macro, close the Macro window, and try executing the macro.

Saving the Macro

Use the Save command in the File menu to save the macro. You will need to supply a name for the macro if you have not saved it before. Restrict your entry to no more than 64 characters. Leading spaces and control characters are not acceptable in macro names.

Close the Macro window after saving by choosing Close from the File menu. The name that you assign to the macro displays in the database window. Notice that two new buttons are now available: Run and Design. Use the Run button to execute the macro from this window and the Design button when you want to modify your entries. You also can double-click a macro's name to run the macro or double-click the macro's name using the right mouse button to open the Macro window and make changes to the macro's design.

Executing the Macro

You can run a macro from the Macro window or from other locations. To run a macro from the Macro window, simply click the Run button in the toolbar (the Run button has what looks like an exclamation point on it, as shown in Figure 16-1). To run a macro from the database window click the Macro button, select the macro, and click the Run button. From other locations, choose Run Macro from the File menu, select the macro to run, and select OK.

Actions and Arguments

An action is nothing more than an instruction that tells Access to perform a task for you. The task might be opening a table, saving a report design, displaying an hourglass, or closing a table. So you don't have to worry about the syntax of action entries, they are all prerecorded for you in a list that you can select from. Many actions are specified as two words with no space between them where initial capital letters are used for each word, such as OpenTable.

Categories of Actions

Access categorizes actions into five different groups depending on how they are used. These groups are Data in forms and reports, Execution, Import/export, Object manipulation, and Miscellaneous.

Actions in forms and reports either restrict data or move from record to record. The ApplyFilter action restricts data. The FindNext, FindRecord, GoToControl, GoToPage, and GoToRecord actions all move you from one record to another.

Actions in the Execution category either perform or stop a task. You can use the DoMenuItem to execute a menu command. Macro procedures can be executed with either OpenQuery, RunCode, RunMacro, or RunSQL. You can even run another DOS or Windows application with the RunApp action. To stop execution you can use CancelEvent, Quit, StopMacro, or StopAllMacros.

The Import/export action category transfers data between Access and other applications. The actions are TransferDatabase, TransferText, and TransferSpreadsheet.

Object manipulation actions are the largest category. You can use SetValue to set the value of a field, property, or control. To update objects use the RepaintObject, Requery, and ShowAllRecords actions. To select an object use the SelectObject action. Objects can be copied or renamed with CopyObject and Rename. You can open or close an object with OpenForm, OpenQuery, OpenReport, OpenTable, DoMenuItem, and Close. You can use the Print action to print an object once you open it. To work with windows use the Minimize, Maximize, MoveSize, and Restore actions.

The Miscellaneous actions are those that do not fit into the other categories. Echo, Hourglass, MsgBox, and SetWarnings all display information. SendKeys generates keystrokes and Beep sounds a beep noise. The AddMenu action creates a custom menu bar.

Sets of Arguments

Each action has its own set of arguments. These arguments define the data that should be used for the action or how it is to take place. Think of arguments as the specifications for the action. For example, if you wanted to have a tailor make a suit, the making of the suit is the desired action and the measurements of the individual it needs to fit are the arguments. When you use the OpenTable action, the arguments are the table to be opened, the view that you want the table to display in (datasheet or design), and the Data Mode with the default being Edit.

Just as you can pick actions from drop-down list boxes, many arguments have drop-down list boxes providing a choice of options. You can click the arrow or press ALT-DOWN ARROW to see the list of possibilities if an arrow displays at the right side of the argument entry area. Table 16-1 shows the arguments for each of the actions supported by Access.

Speeding the Process with Shortcuts

If you choose Tile from the Window menu, you can see the Macro window and database window on the desktop at the same time. With the database objects in view you can drag them to the Macro window to supply both actions and arguments. Create an OpenTable, OpenQuery, OpenForm, and OpenReport action by dragging the object listed in the name of the action to a blank action row. Dragging a table from the database window creates the OpenTable action quicker than you can

TABLE 16-1 Macro Actions and Arguments

Action	Arguments	Use
AddMenu	Menu Name Menu Macro Name Status Bar Text	Adds a drop-down menu
ApplyFilter	Filter Name Where Condition	Restricts or sorts an underlying table or query
Beep	No arguments	Sounds a beep
CancelEvent	No arguments	Cancels the event that caused Access to run the macro
Close	Object Type Object Name	Closes the active window or the specified window
CopyObject	Destination Database New Name	Copies a database object
DoMenuItem	Menu Bar Menu Name Command Subcommand	Executes an Access menu command
Echo	Echo On Status Bar Text	Determines whether or not the screen is updated
FindNext	No arguments	Finds the next matching record
FindRecord	Find What Where Match Case Direction Search As Formatted Search In Find First	Finds the record specified by the arguments
GoToControl	Control Name	Moves the focus to the field or control specified
GoToPage	Page Number Right Down	Moves the focus to the specified page

**TABLE
16-1
(cont.)**

Macro Actions and Arguments *(continued)*

Action	Arguments	Use
GoToRecord	Object Type Object Name Record Offset	Move to the specified record in the table, form, or query
Hourglass	Hourglass On	Changes the mouse pointer to an hourglass to indicate the macro is running
Maximize	No arguments	Maximizes the active window to fill the Access window
Minimize	No arguments	Minimizes the window to an icon
MoveSize	Right Down Width Height	Moves or resizes the window
MsgBox	Message Beep Type Title	Displays one of several styles of message boxes
OpenForm	Form Name View Filter Name Where Condition Data Mode Window Mode	Opens a form in the specified view
OpenQuery	Query Name View Data Mode	Opens a crosstab or select query
OpenReport	Report Name View Filter Name Where Condition	Opens the specified report
OpenTable	Table Name View Data Mode	Opens a table

TABLE 16-1 (cont.) Macro Actions and Arguments *(continued)*

Action	Arguments	Use
Print	Print Range Page From Page To Print Quality Copies Collate Copies	Prints the active object
Quit	Options	Exits Access
Rename	New Name	Names the selected object
RepaintObject	Object Type Object Name	Updates the screen
Requery	Control Name	Updates the data in a control
Restore	No arguments	Restores a window to previous size
RunApp	Command Line	Runs another application
RunCode	Function Name	Executes an AccessBasic function
RunMacro	Macro Name Repeat Count Repeat Expression	Executes a macro
RunSQL	SQL Statement	Runs an SQL query
SelectObject	Object Type Object Name In Database Window	Select a database object
SendKeys	Keystrokes Wait	Sends keystrokes to an application
SetValue	Item Expression	Sets the value of a control, field, or property
SetWarnings	Warnings On	Turns the system messages on or off
ShowAllRecords	No arguments	Removes all filters
StopAllMacros	No arguments	Stops all macros
StopMacro	No arguments	Stops the current macro

TABLE 16-1 (cont.)	Macro Actions and Arguments *(continued)*		
Action	**Arguments**	**Use**
TransferDatabase	Transfer Type Database Type Database Name Object Type Source Destination Structure Only	Imports or exports data
TransferSpreadsheet	Transfer Type Spreadsheet Type Table Name File Name Has Field Names Range	Exports or imports data
TransferText	Transfer Type Specification Name Table Name File Name Has Field Names	Exports or imports data

select it from the drop-down list box. If the row is not blank, Access inserts a blank row for the new action. If you drag another Macro object, Access adds a RunMacro action.

When you drag objects to macro actions, Access fills in several of the arguments for you. You can supply arguments for some actions by dragging objects to the arguments. For example, when the acion is Close, you can drag the table, query, or form you want closed to supply the Object Type and Object Name arguments. The commands and arguments that support this dragging action are shown in Table 16-2.

Modifying a Macro

You can modify macros once they are created by adding and deleting rows and changing the values of arguments. To choose a replacement selection for any entry, all you have to do is make another selection.

TABLE 16-2

Arguments Supplied by Dragging Objects

Action	Argument	Object Dragged
AddMenu	Menu Macro Name	Macro
Close	Object Type Object Name	Any Object
GoToRecord	Object Type Object Name	Form, Table, Query
OpenForm	Form Name	Form
OpenQuery	Query Name	Query
OpenTable	Table Name	Table
RepaintObject	Object Type Object Name	Form, Table, Query
RunMacro	Macro Name	Macro
SelectObject	Object Type Object Name	Any Object

Copy and Paste techniques that you have used elsewhere in Access will work in macros. Everything attached to an action—including arguments, comments, macros, and conditional expressions—remain attached to the copy or relocated action after the Copy or Cut and Paste operation.

The strategy you use for entering new actions depends on where in the macro the new action should be added. If it's to go at the end of the macro all you need to do is move to the blank row at the end of the macro and add the new action. If you need to insert an action in the middle of the macro, click the action below where you want the new action and choose Insert Row from the Edit menu. A blank row is inserted above the selected action, and you can add a new action and complete the argument entries.

To delete an action, click the action and press the DEL key. The action, its optional comment, and any arguments are removed. Macros and conditional statements attached to the action are also deleted.

Adding Sophistication

You can create many useful macros by following the basic techniques described in the first section of this chapter. As you become experienced with the process you might refine these techniques to create more sophisticated macros. This section teaches some of the other options available to you such as creating a group of related macros and allowing Access to check conditions before executing an action. You can assign a key combination for quick access to a macro.

Using Conditions

A *condition* allows you to alter how a macro works depending upon the condition of your data. A condition is an expression Access evaluates to be either true or false. The macro will behave differently when a condition is true than it will when the condition is false.

Conditions are entered in the Conditions column of the Macro window. This column is displayed as shown in Figure 16-6 when you click the Conditions button in the toolbar or choose Conditions from the View menu.

Conditions are recorded as expressions that can be evaluated as true or false. You must follow Access rules for recording expressions, constructing them carefully from allowable components and following syntax rules when referencing database fields or controls. You have already used expressions for entering query criteria, constructing validation rules, and recording calculated controls. Since conditional expressions are essential to recording macro conditions we will look at each component of these expressions in detail before looking at examples of their entry.

FIGURE 16-6

The Conditions column displayed

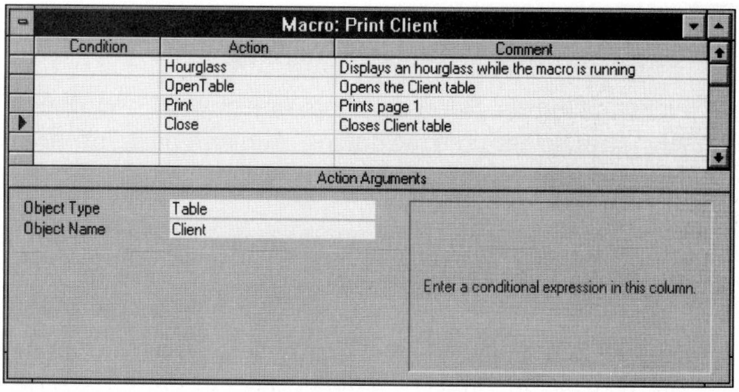

Components of an Expression

Like other expressions, conditions can contain operators, identifiers, functions, literals, and constants. A quick look at each component will show you how many options there are for each component of a valid expression.

Operators tell Access which operations must be performed on the elements of an expression. They can specify a comparison operation that can be evaluated as true or false and can require other operators before the expression is fully evaluated. Allowable operators in a conditional expression include the comparison operators =, <>, <, >, <=, and >=. Other types of operators such as arithmetic operators (+ – * / ^ \ and Mod), the concatenation operator (&), logical operators (And, Eqv, Imp, Not, Or, Xor) and other operators (Between, In, Is, Like) can also be used as part of these expressions.

Identifiers are used to reference forms, reports, fields, controls, or properties. Each identifier can have several elements with the ! and . symbols used as separators between the components. The ! is used after the name of a system object that tells what kind of object you are referring to. You will use Forms, Reports, and Screen as system object entries. The Screen object lets you refer to whatever is on the screen without identifying it by name.

Following the Forms or Reports system objects, you will enter the name of the report or form followed by the name of the field, control, or property. If you want to refer to a field, control, or property that is currently on the screen you can omit the two qualifying entries for the system object and object. The *qualifiers* are the Forms or Reports and the field or control name that appears at the beginning of the identifier. You must use brackets around these names if they contain a space and another ! between the name of the form or report and the field or control. An example is Reports![Coasters by Year]![Coaster Name]. If a property is specified the . is used as a separator.

Following the Screen system object you enter one of the three properties supported: ActiveControl, ActiveReport, or ActiveForm. Here are some examples:

Forms![Employee Data]![First Name] to refer to the First Name control on the Employee Data form

Reports![Coaster Projects]![Completed] to refer to the Completed control on the Coaster Projects report

Screen.ActiveReport to refer to the active report on the screen. The . is used because ActiveReport is a property.

Field names that are used as part of the expression to be evaluated must be qualified. If you are checking an entry in the Pay Rate field on a form called NewEmp, an example of your condition entry might be Forms![NewEmp]![Pay Rate] <= 7.

Functions can be used within an expression to return a value. Access has many functions to perform mathematical or financial calculations. Avg, Count, and Date are three examples. You can also create your own function definitions through Access Basic. The available functions are listed in Appendix B.

Literals can be character strings, dates, or numbers. Numbers are entered without any special symbols to enclose them. Character strings used as part of the expression must be enclosed in quotes as in Forms![NewEmp]![Last Name]= "Smith". Number signs are used around dates as in Forms![Employee Data]![Hire Date] < #1-Jan-90#.

Constants represent values that do not change. True, False, Yes, No, and Null are examples of constants that can be used in expressions.

You will not use all possible components in every expression that you record. The variety of options is meant to provide flexibility. The following represent some conditions that might be entered in the Conditions column:

[Contact Name] = "John Smith"
Forms![Employee Data]![Last Name] = "Jones"
[Last Name] Is Null
[Last Name] In ("Smith", "Jones", "Walker")
LEN([Last Name]) > 1
[Park Location] = "Isle Royale" Or [City] = "Houghton"

The conditions in the previous list without system objects or form or report names all refer to the current form or report.

Processing Conditions

If Access does not encounter a condition for an action, it executes the action. When a condition is present, Access first evaluates the condition. If the condition evaluates as true, the action is performed.

Access also performs any actions that follow as long as an ellipsis (...) is included in the Conditions column for the actions. You can enter the ellipsis by typing three periods. Encountering another expression, the end of the macro, a blank condition entry, or a macro name will all halt the execution. If the condition evaluates as false, the action is skipped. Subsequent actions are skipped until another condition, a blank row, or a macro name is encountered. Figure 16-7 shows a condition entry that causes three additional actions to be performed if the condition is true. The condition; [Park Location] Is Null; is true only when the Park Location control is empty. If the condition is false, only two actions are performed.

Creating a Macro Group

A *macro group* is a macro that contains more than one macro. It is really no different than any other macro except the Macro window has multiple macro names displayed when you show the Macro Name column. Think of a macro group as a library of macros and you can execute any macro within the group. It is a great solution when you have macros attached to several command buttons on a form to place all of these macros in the same group.

FIGURE 16-7

Conditions control macro actions

Condition	Action	Comment
[Park Location] Is Null	MsgBox	Display a message box if there is no entry in the park location
...	GoToControl	Go to the Park Location control
...	StopMacro	End the macro
	RunMacro	Run a macro to print this record
	Close	Close the table

Macro: Macro1

Action Arguments

Enter a conditional expression in this column.

Creating macros within a group is no different than creating a single macro in a window except you must display the Macro Name column in the Macro window and name each macro. To display the Macro Name column, click the Macro Names button or choose Macro Names from the View menu. Figure 16-8 shows a macro with two macro names, Print client and Print employee. Each named macro starts in the row containing the macro name and continues until the row before the next macro name.

You save the Macro window the same way you save a single macro except that the name that you assign actually refers to the group. You can execute any macro in the group by typing the macro group name, a period (.), and the macro name that you want to execute. For example, execute the Print client macro in the Print macros group by typing **Print macros.Print client** as the macro name when you want to run the macro.

Assigning a Macro to a Key

To be able to execute a macro quickly, assign it a key combination. This lets you execute the macro just by pressing a key.

You can create one macro group that contains all of the macros that you want to assign to keys. The name of this macro group must be AutoKeys. The key combinations must be entered in the Macro Name

FIGURE 16-8

Macro group with three macros

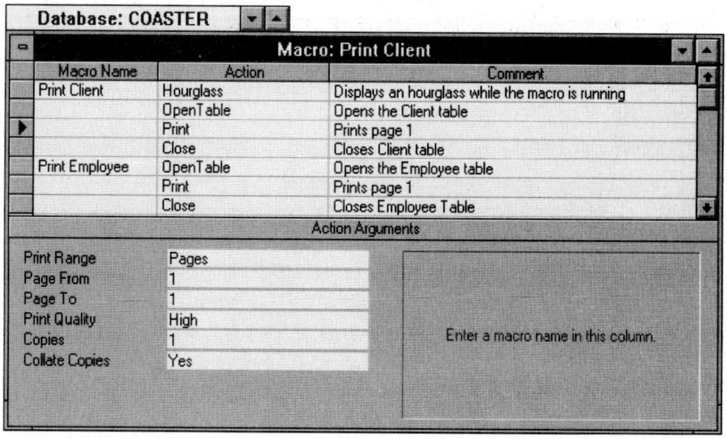

column using the same representation as the SendKeys action. For the SendKeys representation, a single letter is represented by the letter itself, such as h. If you want to specify that the key be pressed in combination with SHIFT, CTRL, or ALT, use the symbols +, ^, or %, respectively, to represent these keys. For example, CTRL-H is represented by ^h. To use other keys such as F2 enclose the special representation in braces such as {F2}. The macro must be saved as AutoKeys. After you save the macro, when you press the key combination, these key combinations will execute the assigned macros.

Calling One Macro from Another Macro

You can branch from one macro to another. Branching means performing another macro before the current macro has finished. To do this you include the RunMacro action in the macro that you want to branch to a second macro. You must supply the Macro Name argument. You can also use Repeat Count to specify how many times the called macro will execute, and Repeat Expression if you want an expression evaluated with each execution until the expression evaluates as No. Branching from one macro to another is often used in conjunction with conditional expressions. The condition can decide whether the RunMacro action is performed. If a RunMacro action is performed, after Access performs the actions in the other macro, Access returns to performing the macro actions in the original macro.

Solving Problems

At times a macro will not behave as expected. In some instances you get a different result than you expect and in others the macro actually fails during execution.

When a macro actually fails an error message displays in a dialog box that only provides the Halt option. The action causing the error is listed. After choosing Halt you can correct the action from the Macro window and try the macro again.

Walking through a macro one step at a time can help identify the cause of a problem. After opening the macro choose the Single Step button to execute one action at a time. A Macro Single Step dialog box appears. Choose Step to execute the next action, Halt to suspend execution, and Continue to execute without the single step operation as shown here:

In the next chapter, you see application examples using macros in forms and reports. You will see many of the components discussed in this chapter used in longer application examples there.

Quick Reference

To Record a Macro   Click the Macro button in the database window. Click New. Select the desired actions from the drop-down list box in the Action column. Use F6 to move to the arguments after selecting each action and completing it. Use F6 to move up and select the next action in the top part of the window.

To Run a Macro   Choose Run Macro from the File menu or from the database window when it displays macros, select the macro, and then select Run.

To Delete an Action   Select the action and then press the DEL key.

To Insert an Action   Move the focus immediately below where you want to add the action. Choose Insert Row from the Edit menu.

CHAPTER

Using Macros for Forms and Reports

Macros can be used with forms and reports to save time and add flexibility to your applications. The macros you add to a form or report are performed as you use the form or report. Macros that you add to a form are performed regardless of whether you use the form in a form or a datasheet view. You use the events that occur when you use a form or report to determine when a macro is executed.

In this chapter, you first learn about the events to which you can attach macros. Next, you will get some insight into the different purposes for macros in your forms and reports by looking at a few examples. You will see how to use macros to perform data validation, data entry, changes to the report layout, or synchronization of multiple forms.

When Macros Are Performed in Forms and Reports

While you use forms and reports, Access constantly checks what you are doing to see when Access should perform any macros you have added. Each check that Access does to see whether it should perform a macro is called an *event*. Events occur frequently so you have many opportunities to tell Access when you want to perform a macro.

Think of events as shopping in a mall. A mall has many stores but you do not have to go into every one of them. Also, you can go into stores and not buy anything, while in other stores, you will enter and make purchases. Similarly in forms and reports, although there are many events, you select only those events to which you want to attach a macro. You only need to supply macros for the events where you want a macro performed. The rest of the events will pass by without any indication that Access is checking for macros.

How often events occur depends on the focus' location. (Remember that the focus is another name for the insertion point or the indication of where you are in a form.) If you placed your finger on the screen for your current location, your finger would represent the focus.

 Tip Sometimes you will see event names as a single word as in OnOpen. The Property Sheet window where you enter macro names to occur at events displays these event names as two words. In the text, you will usually see the macro names spelled as two words.

Report Events

The order of events in reports is simple since a report has only four events. The first event is the On Open event that occurs when you open the report but before Access determines the data that appears in the different sections. The second event, the On Format event, occurs for each section of the report. The On Format event occurs just before Access takes the data that it knows will appear in the section and lays it out as it will appear in the final printed report. The third event, the On Print event, is performed for each of the sections just before the section is printed. The fourth event, the On Close event, occurs when you are closing the report.

The report has properties that let you select macros to perform when the On Open and On Close events occur. Each section of the report has properties that let you select macros to perform when the On Format and On Print events occur. Each section can have different macros.

To better understand when these events occur, imagine printing the report previewed in Figure 17-1. When you select Clients and Projects in the Database window, the On Open event occurs. In the background, Access determines which data appears in the different sections. As Access decides on the data that appears in each section, the On Format event occurs. After the On Format event, Access decides the layout of the report. If you are previewing the report, no events occur. When you print the report that Access has prepared, before Access sends the information to Windows Print Manager for later printing, the On Print event occurs as each section is prepared for printing. When you leave the Preview window of the report or Access has finished printing the report when you are not displaying the preview, the On Close event occurs.

Form Events

The order of events is more complex in forms simply because a form has more events to which you can attach macros. Both the form and the

FIGURE 17-1

A report illustrating when events in a report occur

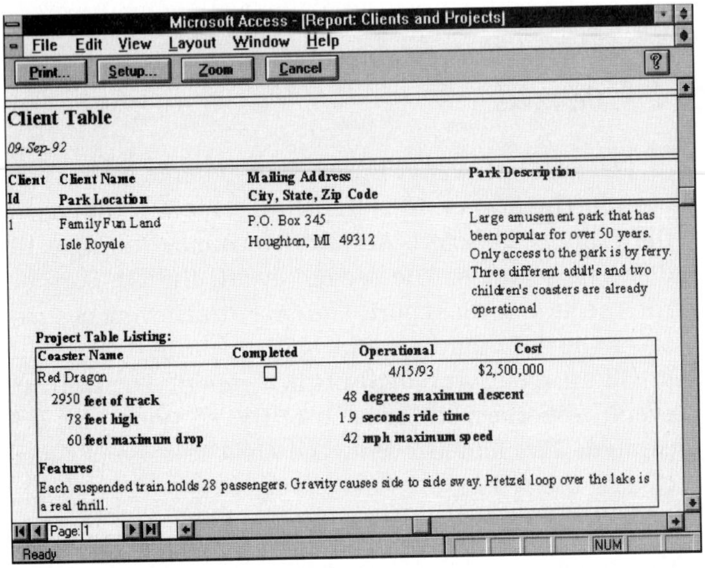

individual controls can have events. Unlike reports, form sections do not have events. To get an idea of the possible events, first look at the events that occur that affect the overall form rather than the individual controls.

When you open a form, the first event is On Open. Next, since you have made a record the current record, the On Current event occurs. At this point the focus is now in the controls of the forms so the events of the form's controls are occurring. When you are finished with the current record, the Before Update event occurs. Access knows this event occurred because you have done something to leave the current record. This might be switching to another record, closing the window, or clicking the current record's record selector to finish any changes you have made. After the Before Update event occurs, Access updates any changed data for the current record. Next, the After Update event occurs.

At this point, you have updated the record for one of three reasons. If you are leaving the current record because you are closing the form, Access performs the On Close event. If you are leaving the current record because you are switching to another record, the On Current event will occur as soon as you've switched to the next record. (Each time you move to another record, the On Current event occurs again.) The third possible reason you have updated the current record is that you have selected Save Record in the File menu. After the After Update event, no events occur until you leave the current record or make further changes.

As an example of the events that occur in a form, suppose you are using the form in Figure 17-2 (William Wild's photo was copied from Andrew Fuller's photo in the NWIND database that accompanies Access). When you select Employee Data - 3 in the database window, the On Open event occurs. After the window is open, the On Current event occurs as Access displays the current record in the form. After you make changes to the record, you may finish this record and then switch to the next one. As you move to the next record, the Before Update event occurs. Next, Access updates the data saved for that record. After the updated record's data is saved, the After Update event occurs. Finally, since you have made a different record current, the On Current event occurs.

A form has other events that occur as you use a form. When you delete a record, just before the data is actually deleted, the On Delete event occurs. Often the On Current event occurs just before the On Delete event

FIGURE 17-2 A form illustrating when events in a form occur

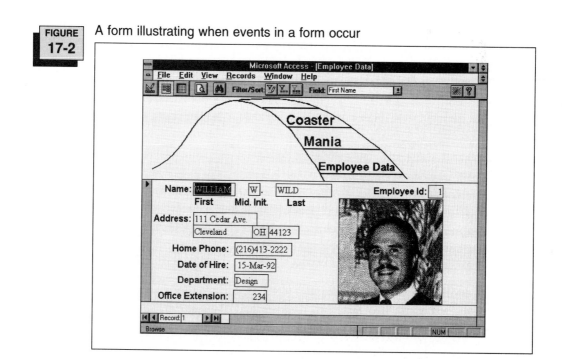

since you are selecting the record you will delete. After you delete the record, the next record is displayed and the On Current event occurs. When you insert a record, just as you type the first character for any field in the record, the On Insert event occurs. The On Insert event occurs after the On Enter event for the control you are entering the data into (the On Enter event will be described shortly). Finally, the other event that occurs with forms is the On Menu event that occurs at the same time as the On Open event. This event is solely for substituting another menu for the menu you would otherwise see in the menu bar.

While you are editing the data of a record in a form, the events that are occurring are the ones created by the controls in the form. Each control can have its own separate events. The controls that trigger events include text boxes, option groups, toggle buttons, option buttons, check boxes, combo boxes, list boxes, and command buttons.

All of these controls have an On Enter, On Exit, and On Dbl Click event. Except for the command buttons, these controls also have a Before Update event and an After Update event. Command buttons have an On Push event.

When you first move to a control, the On Enter event occurs. When you double-click a control, the On Enter event occurs if it has not already done so for the control, and then the On Dbl Click event occurs. When you switch to another control, which event occurs next depends on whether you have changed the data in the control. If the data has changed, the Before Update event occurs, the data in that control is updated, the After Update event control occurs, and then the On Exit event occurs. If the control's data has not changed, only the On Exit event occurs.

When the control is a command button on which you have put the focus by pressing TAB or ENTER, the On Enter event occurs. If you click the command button, the focus moves to the command button to make the On Enter event occur for the command button—after which point the On Push event occurs in response to clicking the control. If you double-click the command button, the focus moves to the command button to make the On Enter event occur for the command button—after which point the On Push event occurs in response to clicking the control, the On Dbl Click event occurs, and then the On Push event occurs again. Events for controls occur for each control you switch to. The control events usually occur in between the events for overall records.

As an example of the events that occur as you use a form, suppose you open the form in Figure 17-2, change the First Name field to Bill, switch to the Last Name text box, and then close the form window. When you open the form window, the On Open event and then the On Current event occur. Next, the On Enter event for the First Name text box occurs as the focus is added to the First Name text box. After you type **Bill** for the new value, you can press TAB or ENTER or click Wild to switch to the Last Name text box. Since you have changed the data in the First Name text box, the Before Update event for the First Name text box control occurs, the data is updated, and the After Update event occurs for the First Name text box control. Before Access moves the focus to the Last Name text box, the On Exit event occurs for the First Name text box control. Now, as the focus moves to the Last Name text box control, the On Enter event occurs for the Last Name text box control. At this point, when you close the form window, the On Exit event for the Last Name text box control occurs. Then since you changed the record's data, the Before Update event occurs, Access updates the record's data, and the After Update event occurs. Finally, since you have closed the window, the On Close event occurs.

 Remember   The On Enter and On Exit events occur for a control each time it contains the focus even if you do not change the data. This means that if you use TAB or ENTER to move from one control to another, these two events occur for each control you move through.

Adding Macros to Events

To add a macro to any one of the macro events, you need to add the macro name to the form or report design. Specifically, when you display the form or report design, select the form or report, the section, or the control that the event you want to assign the macro belongs to. Next, if the Property Sheet window is not present, select Properties from the View menu or click the Properties button. Then, move the insertion point in the property sheet to the name of the event when you want the macro performed. For that property, type the name of the macro. Remember that if the macro is part of a macro group, you must enter the macro group name, a period, and the macro name. When you use that form or report, the macro is performed when the selected event occurs. Now that you know how to add macros to forms and report events, find out more about macros by looking at several examples.

Adding Command Buttons to a Form

Command buttons are designed to use macros because the only action these controls perform in a form is the macro that you have assigned to the different events for the command button. Command buttons offer a quick method of automating the use of forms and reports because by selecting command buttons you can select predefined choices that perform an action for you. An example of a form that does this is one that lets you select the report you want to print and then prints that report. A form like this might look like Figure 17-3.

To create a form like the one in Figure 17-3, you need to create the macro instructions that you want the different command buttons to perform. In this macro, which looks like Figure 17-4, the various reports the form will print are dragged to the different lines of the macro. Later,

FIGURE 17-3   A form using multiple command buttons to run macros

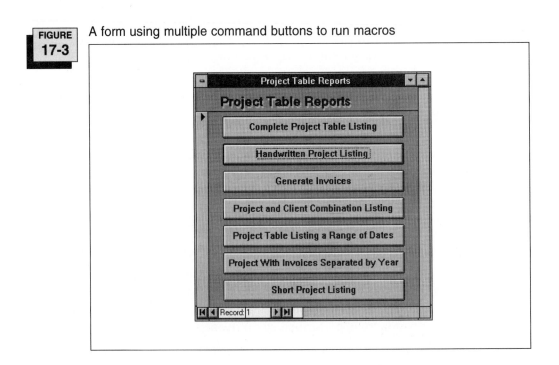

FIGURE
17-4   Macros used to print reports

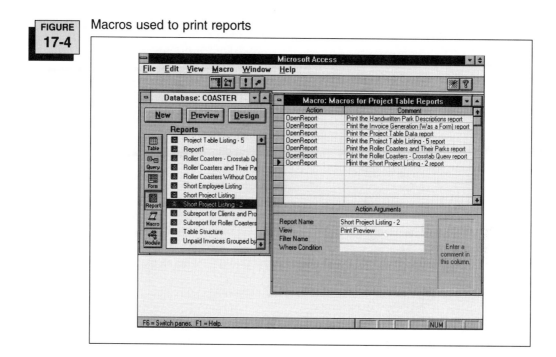

when you know that all the reports print correctly without any changes, you can change the View arguments for each of the actions from Print Preview to Print.

Now you are ready to add the command buttons to a form design. These buttons are added using the command button tool in the toolbox, so they look like the ones shown in the left half of Figure 17-5. Next, the text in the buttons is replaced by text that describes the report each button will print. The buttons are sized with the Size to Fit command in the Layout menu, and then the Width property is set for all of the buttons to the width of the widest button.

Once you have the command button names entered as shown in the left half of Figure 17-5, copy the Caption properties for each of these command buttons to the macro name for the action in the macro window the command button will perform. For example, for the first button, Complete Project Table Listing is copied from the button's Caption property. After switching to the macro window, you can move to the action that prints the report of the entire Project table and paste the Clipboard's contents.

FIGURE
17-5

Command buttons in form design and macro names added to a macro group

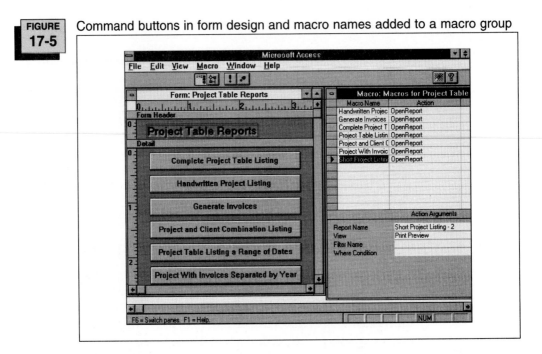

The only task left for the command buttons in the form design is to tell Access which macro to perform each time you select one of the command buttons. In this example, you only want to print the selected report when you double-click the command button. For these command buttons, you enter the macro names for the On Dbl Click property.

Since all of the macros are part of the same macro group, you want the macro group's name, a period, and the macro name for the On Dbl Click property. For this example, you can quickly add this information by typing the macro group's name, **Macros for Project Table Reports**, for the On Dbl Click property of one command button and copying the macro's group name to the On Dbl Click property of the other command buttons.

Next, for each of the command buttons, copy the Caption property that is also the name of the macro in the macro group. Move to the On Dbl Click property, press F2 or click the current entry (the macro group name), move to the end of the entry, type a period, and paste the caption to the end of the macro name. For example, the first command button has an On Dbl Click property of Macros for Project Table Reports.Complete

Project Table Listing. Once this is completed, when you display the form, the form looks like Figure 17-3.

Using Macros to Hide and Display Data

One purpose for macros is selectively deciding whether other data is displayed. Most controls in forms and reports have a Visible property. When this property is Yes, the control appears; when this property is No, the control does not appear. To see how you can use macros to change this property, suppose you have a form like the one shown here:

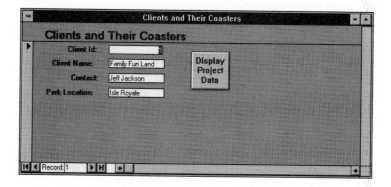

In this form, you only want to display the Project Table's Data for a client in a subform when the Display Project Data button is selected. You also want to be able to hide the subform. You can use command buttons that change the subform's Visible property when selected. This example uses two command buttons—one displays the subform and the other hides it. Since the command buttons are in the same location, the command buttons look like they are the same one with the text changing as the buttons are selected.

For the preceding form, you need to add the command button that will display the subform. This command button is added with the command button tool in the toolbox. The Control Name for the command button is Display, the Caption property is Display Project Data, and the On Push property is Macros for Clients and Their Coasters - 2.Display Project Data. In this example, the On Push property has the macro name rather than On Dbl Click so you only need to click the command button rather than double-click it to perform the macro.

At this point, the form design only has one command button. To add the second one, select the button and copy it to the Clipboard by choosing Copy in the Edit menu. Choose Paste from the Edit menu to make a second copy of the command button. Use the Clipboard to duplicate the command button so the second command button is the same size and has most of the same properties as the first. Once you have the second command button, change the Control Name to Hide, the Caption property to Hide Project Data, and the On Push property to Macros for Clients and Their Coasters - 2.Hide Project Data.

You'll see the two command buttons slightly apart from one another. Leave them this way for now because you will find it easier to make any other necessary changes, since you can select one without selecting the other. The only other change you should make to the form's design is to set the Visible property for the subform control to No so the default property setting is to not display the subform. This subform control has the Control Name property of Subform.

For the macro this form uses, the macro group looks like the one in Figure 17-6. You need one macro to display the subform and another to hide it. The actions for these two macros have only one or two arguments. These are the macro names, actions, and arguments:

Macro Names	Actions	Arguments	
Display Project Data	SetValue	[Subform].Visible	Yes
	SetValue	[Hide].Visible	Yes
	GoToControl	Subform	
	SetValue	[Display].Visible	
Hide Project Data	GoToControl	Client Name	No
	SetValue	[Subform].Visible	No
	SetValue	[Hide].Visible	No
	SetValue	[Display].Visible	Yes

In each macro, the macro hides or displays the Display Project Data command button, the Hide Project Data command button, and the subform controls. Also, the GoToControl action moves the focus to either the subform control or the Client Name control. The focus must be moved because you cannot hide a control that has the focus. Save the macro since you cannot run the macro until you save it.

FIGURE
17-6
Macros to hide and display subform control

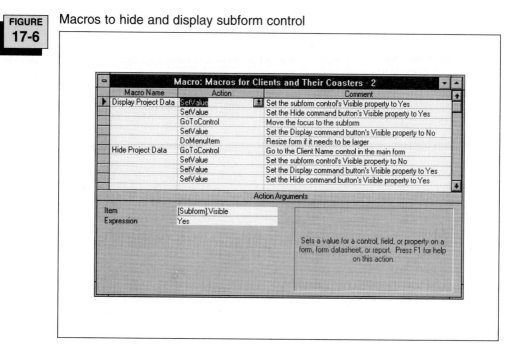

Now try the macros. Switch to the form and display the form view. The form looks like the preceding illustration. Select the Display Project Data command button. The subform appears; the Display Project Data button disappears and is replaced by the Hide Project Data button, as shown here:

When you select the Hide Project Data button, the subform disappears and the Hide Project Data command button disappears as it is replaced by the Display Project Data button. When the two command buttons and their macros perform correctly, you will want to switch to the form design and set the Top and Left properties of the two command buttons to the same value so they are in exactly the same location.

When you create macros like this for your own forms, remember that you can add conditions that let the macro decide whether or not a control is hidden or displayed. The preceding example used command buttons to determine whether the subform appeared but you can create conditions that determine this instead. Also, this example used forms but report controls also have Visible properties for which you can use macros to hide and display controls. For example, you can use macros for the On Format property of a control that hides or displays controls depending on another field's value.

Tip Use a macro group to contain all of the macros used by the same form or report. Putting the macros in a central location lets you quickly find all of the macros a single form or report uses. Give the macro group name the same name as the form or report so you easily know which macro group contains the macros a form or report uses.

Using a Macro to Synchronize Form Data

Besides using main/subform forms to show data in two formats at once, you can use two separate forms and then use a macro to synchronize the data between the two forms. Each form is separate just like the other separate forms you use in Access. This example shows how you can synchronize two forms as well as using a shortcut to add a macro.

To use a macro to synchronize two forms, suppose you have a form like the Clients and Their Coasters form used earlier, except the subform control is removed, the command buttons are removed, and the form is resized to fit its new size. In this form, you want the Project Listing form to display the projects for just a particular client when the Display Project Data command button is selected.

For this example, create the macro first since you will only use one. (You'll see later how to use a special shortcut to add a macro as a command button to a form.) The macro in this example is named Display

Project Data. This macro only has one action, OpenTable, with Project Listing as its Form Name argument.

The only other argument of this macro is the Where Condition. This argument selects which records appear in the second form. This macro uses [Client Id]=Forms![Clients and Their Coasters - 3]![Client Id] as the Where Condition argument. The first [Client Id] matches one of the controls in the Project Listing form, the one the OpenTable action opens. The rest of the argument sets the value from the original form that you want to match. Since this control's value is for the Project Listing form, you must supply the full identification.

Using a Shortcut to Create the Command Button

When the macro is completed, you can create the command button using a shortcut. Display the form design and then switch to the Database window and list the macros. With both the Database and the form design windows in view, drag the macro name from the Database window to where you want the command button to start. Access adds a command button of the default size to the form and gives this button the Caption property of the macro name. This shortcut does not work when you want to add a macro in a macro group since the command button you create will include only the macro group's name without the individual macro in the group that you want to create.

Figure 17-7 shows the Database window and part of the form design after adding the command button. You can use the Size to Fit command in the Layout menu to quickly adjust the command button's size to fit the text of the Caption property. The On Push property for this command button is Display Project Data. Access will perform the Display Project Data macro when you click or move to this command button and then press ENTER.

Now try the form with this command button. When you click the Display Project Data command button or move the focus to this command button and press ENTER, Access performs the Display Project Data macro. After opening the Project Listing form and setting the form to only display

FIGURE 17-7 Dragging a macro to a form design

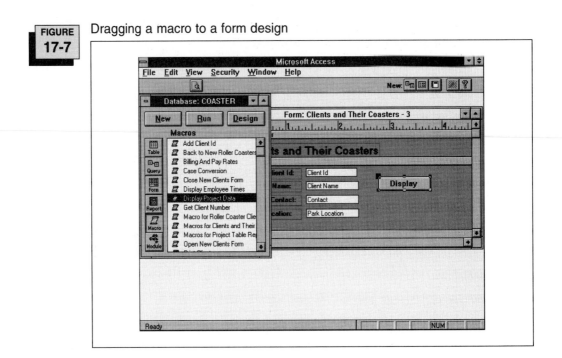

the records for the same client as the one displayed in the Clients and Their Coasters - 3 form, the two forms look like Figure 17-8.

Tip Use the dragging method to add command buttons to a form when the macro is stored separately rather than as part of a group.

Using Macros for Data Conversion

You can use macros to convert an entry in a control to another entry. For example, you may want to convert the names in your Employee table into uppercase. Another example is a part number for an inventory table to which you want to add characters such as hyphens in specific locations.

The macros you create for this purpose are performed at the On Exit or On Update events for a specific control. Whether you add the macro

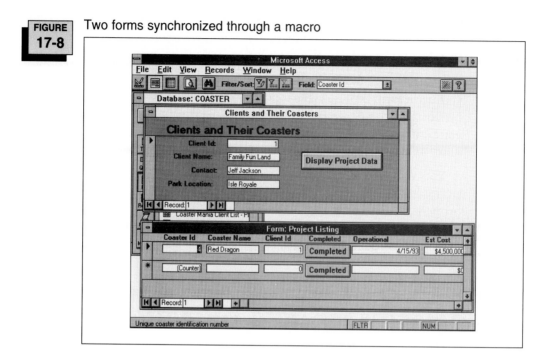

FIGURE 17-8

Two forms synchronized through a macro

to the On Exit or On Update event depends on if you want the data conversion performed based on whether the data in the control has changed. If you want the data conversion performed on a control's entry regardless of whether you change the field's entry, add the macro to the On Exit event. If you only want the conversion performed when you have changed the data, add the macro to the Before Update event. To see an example of using macros to convert the format of data, create macros for a form using the Employee table that converts the entry to uppercase.

As an example, suppose you want to convert a state entry into uppercase so data is stored in the table as uppercase regardless of whether uppercase or lowercase letters are used to enter the data. To do this conversion, add a macro to either the On Exit property or the Before Update property, depending on whether you want to convert existing data and new data or only convert new data. This macro contains a single SetValue action. The Item argument for this action is the field you want to convert. For the state example, it is [State]. For the Expression argument, you want this data converted into uppercase using a function. For the state example, the Expression argument is UCase([State]).

This example works for both the Client and the Employee tables. When you use a form that has this macro added to the On Exit or Before Update property of the State field control, before the data is actually updated your entry is converted into uppercase. Then Access uses this converted entry when Access updates the record's values.

You can use all sorts of functions to convert data in a form. For example, you can create a module for a function that converts text into proper case (that is, the first letter is uppercase and the rest is lowercase). Once you have a function like this, you can use it in place of the UCase example just described.

Using Macros for Data Validation

Besides using the Validation Rule property for a field in a table definition to check whether a correct entry is in a field, you can use macros to check data validity. Use macros for data validation when the conditions to check if the entry is correct are more complex than you can enter for the validation rule. Here are some examples of when to use macros for data validation:

☐ The correct entry on the field depends on the entry of another field. For example, the billing and pay rate of your employees depends on which department they are in.

☐ You want to make sure the user leaves an entry on the field. For example, in a form for the Employee Time Log table, you want to be sure every field in every record has an entry.

☐ You want to display different messages that vary according to the incorrect entry made in a field.

☐ You want to let the user make decisions about whether the entered data is accepted even if it goes against a validation rule.

☐ The condition for testing whether an entry is valid has several parts.

❏ You want to share the validation checking between several forms.

❏ A form has multiple validation checks that you want checked simultaneously.

For each of these cases, add the macro to check a control's entry for the control's On Exit or Before Update property. Use On Exit when you want the entry validated even if the entry has not changed. Use Before Update when you only want to check whether the entry is valid when the user has changed the entry.

As an example, suppose you have the following form:

	Billing And Pay Rates					
First Name WILLIAM	Last Name WILD	Department Design	Pay Rate $35.00	Bill Rate $60.00	Difference $25.00	Percent Markup 41.67%
First Name DAN	Last Name DANGER	Department Testing	Pay Rate $30.00	Bill Rate $50.00	Difference $20.00	Percent Markup 40.00%
First Name RODGER	Last Name ROLLING	Department Design	Pay Rate $33.00	Bill Rate $55.00	Difference $22.00	Percent Markup 40.00%
First Name SANDRA	Last Name SCARY	Department Design	Pay Rate $31.00	Bill Rate $50.00	Difference $19.00	Percent Markup 38.00%
First Name HARRY	Last Name HIGHER	Department Construction	Pay Rate $6.50	Bill Rate $10.00	Difference $3.50	Percent Markup 35.00%

Record: 1

This form has the same validation rule as the underlying table that checks whether the entry in the Pay Rate field is between 4.25 and 35 and whether the entry in the Bill Rate is 10 percent more than the amount of the Pay Rate field. For this form, you may want to add some additional checks. Each department has a different range of what is valid for the pay and billing rates. You can add these validation checks and display different messages depending on the department. This example has separate macros for the Bill Rate and the Pay Rate controls.

Figure 17-9 shows the macros this example uses. The conditions test whether the value of the Department control is Construction, Design, or Testing and whether the value of the Bill Rate or Pay Rate is in a range. The values in the Bill Rate or Pay Rate controls only meet one of the conditions when its value does not match the range for the particular department. When a condition is met, Access displays the message set by the MsgBox action and then cancels the updating. For each of the MsgBox actions, the Message describes the appropriate range and the

FIGURE 17-9 Macros that validate the Bill Rate and Pay Rate control values

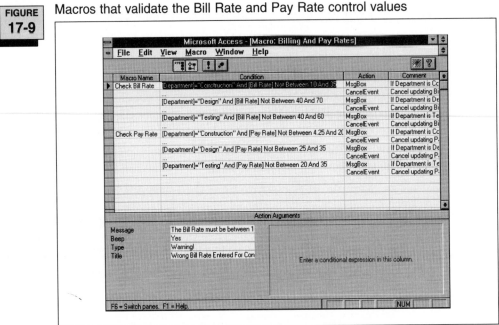

title bar indicates that the wrong value is entered. The CancelEvent action halts the updating process so the form's user can make a new entry.

To make creating the two macros easier, copy the entries to the Clipboard and then paste them back, changing only the department names, ranges of valid values, and whether you are testing the Bill Rate or the Pay Rate. The ellipsis is necessary to continue the condition above them. If you omit the ellipsis, every time you make an entry in the Bill Rate or Pay Rate controls, they would not be updated because the CancelEvent action cancels the updating even when the entry is within the range appropriate for the department. The form has the Before Update properties changed to Billing And Pay Rates.Check Bill Rate for the Bill Rate control and Billing And Pay Rates.Check Pay Rate for the Pay Rate control.

When you use the form with the macros, every entry is checked by the form's Validation Rule and then by the macro that you have entered for

FIGURE

17-10

A message box displayed in response to an invalid entry

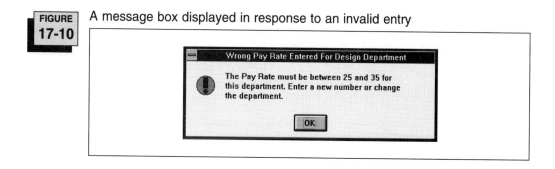

the Before Update property. Figure 17-10 shows the message one of the MsgBox actions displays when you enter the wrong number for an employee. In this case, 5, which is entered for the Pay Rate field, is not in the range of valid entries for the Design department. Since this entry is incorrect, the condition of [Department]="Design" And [Pay Rate] Not Between 25 And 35 is met. The MsgBox action displays the message box that you see in Figure 17-10. The ! icon appears because the Type argument is set to Warning!.

The message box in Figure 17-10 also shows the text that is entered for the Title and Message arguments. When the form's user selects OK, the message box disappears and the updating of the control is canceled by the CancelEvent action. At this point, the form is ready for you to make another entry for this control. If you typed **3** for the Pay Rate control, you would see the Validation Text property's entry in a message box because a control's Validation Rule is checked before any On Exit and Before Update macros are performed.

When you create macros like this for your own forms, the only difference is the condition entered in the Condition column of the macro and the text the MsgBox action displays when the condition is met. You may also want to enter the macro names for the On Exit property of controls when you want the validation performed on the controls for those fields that you do not change.

Using a Macro to Add Data for You

You can create macros that present another form to make additional selections while you are working on a form. For example, you can create a form for adding new roller coaster projects that lets you select the name of the client and have the macro supply the client identification number. Using a macro for this means you do not have to remember a client identification number.

The form in Figure 17-11 lets you enter new roller coaster projects. The Coaster Id and Client Id controls have their Enabled properties set to No so you cannot move to these controls. The Client Name control is an unbound text box control so it will contain whatever you enter in it or whatever macro commands you want to enter data into it. This unbound text box also has the Get Client Number macro assigned to its On Enter event. Every time you move to this control, Access performs the Get Client Number macro.

The Select a Customer form, shown in Figure 17-12, lists just the client names and park locations for all of the records in the Client table. The Client Name controls can be selected although the entries cannot be edited because the Locked property for this control is Yes. This form only has one macro, Add Client Id. This macro is attached to the On Dbl Click property of the Client Name text box control. Access performs this macro whenever you double-click any of the customer names.

FIGURE
17-11

A form that uses a macro to get a value from another form

Form: New Roller Coasters - 2	

New Roller Coasters

Coaster Name:	Free Wheeler	Coaster Id:	
Client Name:		Client Id:	0
Features:			
Est Cost:	$0.00	Picture:	
Track:	0		
Height:	0		
Drop:	0		
Angle:	0		
Time:	0		

Record: 1

FIGURE 17-12

A form that selects the data to add to the other form

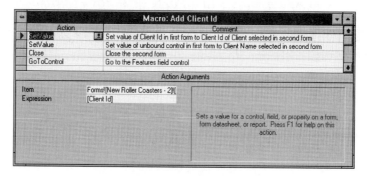

The Add Client Id macro, shown next, is the part of each of the two forms that performs the most work:

This macro sets the value of the Client Id text box control in the New Roller Coasters - 2 form to the client identification number of the client selected in the Select a Customer form. The first SetValue action sets this value. Access does not care that the value you are setting is in a different form than the one that is active when you run the macro. The second SetValue action sets the unbound text box control in the New Roller Coasters - 2 form, called Client Name, to the name of the client chosen in the Select a Customer form. Next, the macro closes the Select a

Customer form. Since you are closing the form, you do not need to move the focus to another location the way you do when you hide controls. Finally, Access moves the focus to the Features control in the New Roller Coasters - 2 form.

When you use the New Roller Coasters - 2 form, after you enter the name of the roller coaster, the focus moves to the Client Name unbound text control. This triggers the On Enter event so the Get Client Number macro performs and opens the Select a Customer form. When you double-click a client in the Select a Customer form opened by the macro, Access performs the Add Client Id macro. The only effect you will see from the macro is that the Select a Customer form is closed, the client name you have just selected is in the Client Name text box control, the client's identification number is in the Client Id text box control, and the focus is in the Features text box control.

Quick Reference

To Add a Macro to a Form or Record Event   Display the form or report design. Select the control that has the event to which you want to attach the macro. Display the Property Sheet window and enter the macro name for the property name of the event for which you want the macro to occur.

To Add a Macro as a Command Button   Display the form design and then switch to the Database window. Drag the macro name from the Database window to where you want the command button to start.

CHAPTER

Creating Custom Applications with Macros

Chapter 17 showed how adding macros to forms and reports can make using forms and reports easier. You can use macros for other purposes—for example, to design applications. When you use macros to design applications, you want the macros to guide the user through each step, from selecting the data through presentation of the final output.

In this chapter, you will learn about creating macros that run every time you open a database, macros that create popup forms, macros that set the menus and commands available through the menu bar, and macros that run with special key combinations.

Creating a Macro that Performs When You Open a Database

When you open a database in Access, Access opens the database window for that database, displaying the tables stored there. Using a macro, you can change how a database is presented. This type of macro, called AutoExec, is executed whenever you open a database. Every time you open a database, Access checks if any of the macros in the database's list of macro names is AutoExec. If Access finds a macro named AutoExec, Access runs the macro.

AutoExec macros can provide two functions. First, an AutoExec macro can set up a different interface, or way of selecting the data you want to use other than through the database window Access provides. Second, an AutoExec macro can provide daily reminders of tasks you need to perform.

As an example of an AutoExec macro, you can create a macro that minimizes the database window and displays a form from which users can choose the tasks they want to perform. A form for this purpose looks like the form in Figure 18-1. You can produce this form using the Project Table Reports form created in Chapter 17 and changing the command buttons and the text the form uses.

Each of the command buttons in the form have an On Dbl Click property of Macros for Autoexec.Command button name. For example, when you double-click the Current and Prospective Customers button,

FIGURE
18-1 The opening screen displayed by an AutoExec macro

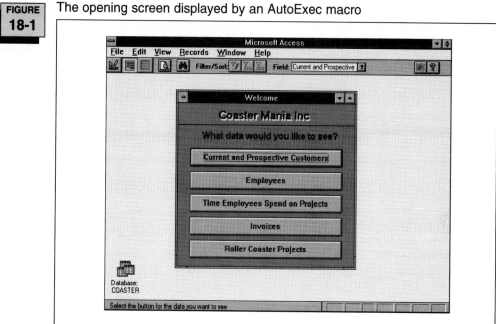

Access performs the Macros for Autoexec.Current and Prospective Customers macro. This form displays because the database has an AutoExec macro. This macro has only two actions. The first is Minimize, which minimizes the database window (see the icon in the lower-left corner of Figure 18-1). The second action is OpenTable with Initial Form as the table argument (the form shows Welcome in its title bar because the form's Caption property is set to Welcome). This simple macro executes every time you open the COASTER database.

From the form in Figure 18-1, you can select command buttons. These command buttons display other forms, which let you select exactly the data you want to see and the format in which you want the data presented. Using these command buttons means you will not need to use other keystrokes and mouse selections to choose the object you want to display. You can continue to use macros throughout the application—how you use them is limited only by your imagination. Having all of these command buttons in various forms also means that someone who doesn't know how to use Access can use the data in the database.

Tip With a macro such as AutoExec, you may want to have a keystroke combination that also executes the macro so that every time users need to return to the initial form, they can press the key combination to have AutoExec execute again.

 Tip To open a database and *not* run the AutoExec macro, hold down the SHIFT key while you open the database.

Adding Macros to Create Popup Forms

You can add popup forms with macros. These forms remain at the top of your Access window just as if you are using a command's dialog box. Popup forms can serve a variety of purposes including these:

- ❑ Prompt for confirmation that you want to override the validation rules.

- ❑ Prompt for information used by other actions. The information you get can be used for selecting which records appear in a form or report. The popup form can also prompt for entries for other fields not included in the main form.

- ❑ Display another form for data entry depending on the value of a field in the current form. For example, as you add invoices to the invoice register, a macro can check that the project number you entered matches a project number stored in the Project table. When you enter a project number that does not match, the macro displays a popup form to add the project information for the new project.

- ❑ Display messages that look different from the message box created by the MsgBox action.

In Chapter 13, you learned about using a popup form in place of a subform. You can see two additional examples by looking at popup forms used to override the validation rules set by another macro and popup forms used to prompt for additional information when an entry does not match a field's value in another table.

A Popup Form to Override Validation Rules

In Chapter 17, you learned how to use macros for validation rules, which prevent entries that do not match criteria. Sometimes you want users to be able to override a rule. Since you still want the validation rule present, you want the user to be aware that their entry does not fit the validation rule and give them the choice of continuing with the entry or canceling the entry.

As an example, in the Billing and Pay Rates form shown next, the Pay Rate and Bill Rate field controls have validation rules just like the ones added in Chapter 17.

The difference here is, when users make an entry in one of these fields, the fields Before Update macro validates the entry. The macros for the Before Update of these two fields are shown in the top of Figure 18-2. These OpenForm actions in both the Check Bill Rate and the Check Payrate macros use the Dialog window mode for the form they open so the opened form behaves as if the Pop Up and Modal properties are set to Yes regardless of the setting the form has saved as part of its design.

The Override? form opened by entering an inappropriate pay or bill rate is shown here:

This form has two command buttons. The OK button runs the Billing and Pay Rates - 2. Override macro that closes the form and continues

FIGURE
18-2 Macros to run popup forms

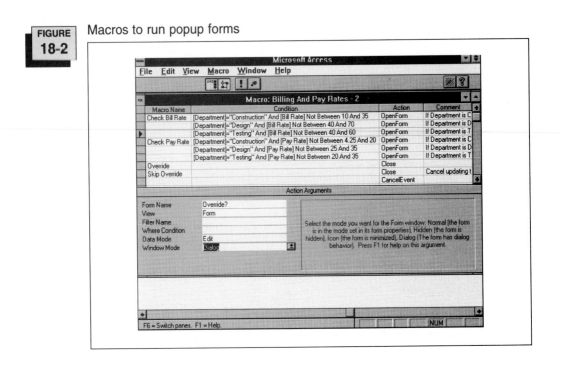

with the updating process in the Billing and Pay Rates form. The Cancel button runs the Billing and Pay Rates - 2. Skip Override. This macro closes the form and cancels the updating occurring in the Billing and Pay Rates form. Initially the OK button has the focus because of the Override? form's tab order. If you want the Cancel command button to have the focus when the form opened, edit the form design and use the Tab Order command in the Edit menu to change the tab order of these command buttons.

A Popup Form Activated by Data Entry

When you make an entry in a field that is linked to the values of a field in another table, you want to know that both tables have the appropriate records. For example, before you enter a new project, you want to know that you have the client's information entered into the Client table. Also, before you enter an invoice for a project, you must have a record in the Project table that provides information about that project. You can create a macro that checks whether the data you enter for a field in a form matches the data in another form. When the data does not match, have the macro display a popup form to supply the information added to the other table.

The following shows a form used to enter invoices:

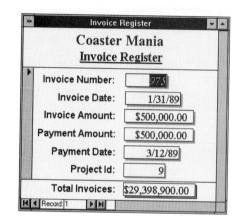

The Project Id control has an After Update macro that checks if the entry in this control matches one of the projects in the Project table. This macro has this entry in the Condition column of the macro's design:

```
IsNull(DLookup("[Coaster Id]","Project","Form.[Project
Id]=[Coaster Id]"))
```

The DLookup function returns a field's value (Coaster Id) from a record in the selected table (Project) that matches the condition set by the criteria (Project Id in the current form matches the Coaster Id field in the Project table). This function returns a null or empty value when the DLookup function does not find a matching record. The IsNull function returns a true value when the DLookup function cannot find a matching record and a false value when the DLookup function finds a matching record.

In this example, when the macro's condition is met, the action to the condition's right, OpenForm, displays a form like the one in Figure 18-3. This form has the Window Mode set to Dialog so you cannot continue doing other changes in Access until you close the popup form.

The form that appears when you enter a new project number

Macros to Define New Menus

Access has a defined menu that appears at different points as you work with your data. You can change the menu that you see when you look at a form in the form view. You can remove commands you do not use and add commands to perform macros. You can add commands that normally appear in menu bars other than the form view. The macros that define the menu structure run when you open a form. When you open a form, the On Menu event occurs so you can attach a different menu structure to the form menu bar of Access.

When you replace a menu, the menu replacement completely removes the previous menu. For example, when you replace a menu by supplying a macro's name for the form's On Menu event, all of the commands you previously used for the menu are absent. You see only those commands that you selected through the macros that define the menu.

A macro that runs during the On Menu event is special because this macro can only contain AddMenu actions. Also, the AddMenu action is used solely for macros run during the On Menu event. You will use the AddMenu event only to create custom menus.

Tip The easiest way to create your own menu system is by using the copy of the menu system included with the NWind database. These macros can be added to your own database with the Import command in the File menu. Once you have a copy of the macros in your own database, you can change only the parts of the menu system you want to change.

Setting Up the Macros for a Menu

Creating macros for a menu is done in several steps. First, create the macro that defines the menu bar to replace one of the existing ones. Figure 18-4 shows a menu for this purpose. In this macro, the AddMenu actions add the titles of the selections you want to appear across the menu bar. For each of these actions, the Menu Name argument includes the text to appear in the menu bar.

FIGURE 18-4   A macro to set up a custom menu bar

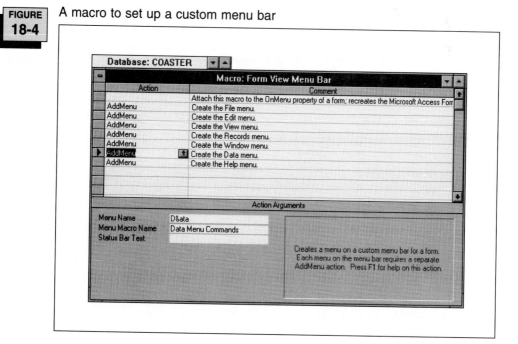

For example, the default form view menu bar uses File, Edit, View, Records, Window, and Help as the arguments for the different AddMenu actions. The ampersand (&) is placed before the letter to be underlined so for the menu bar item shown in Figure 18-4, the item appears as Data. For the Menu Macro Name argument of each of the AddMenu actions, the argument is the name of the macro group that defines the commands that appear in the drop-down menu. For example, the macro in Figure 18-4 tells Access that the Data Menu Commands macro group contains the information Access needs to determine which commands appear in the Data drop-down menu.

Finally, you can supply the Status Line argument that sets the text to appear in the status line when you select the drop-down menu. If you do not supply this text, the text that appears in the status line of the commands is the text you enter for the macro's comment that defines the command.

To list the commands that appear in a drop-down menu, list each of the commands as a separate macro name in the Macro Name column of the macro group. Each drop-down menu named in the menu bar macro has its own macro group. These macro group names match the Menu Macro Name arguments supplied for the different drop-down menu names. The macro name is also the name of the command. Figure 18-5 shows the macro group for the Data Menu Commands macro group.

For the Data Menu Commands macro group, the commands that appear in the Data drop-down menu are Client, Employee, Invoice Register, Project, and Time Log. Like the items in the menu bar, the ampersand (&) indicates which letter is underlined. Next to the macro name is the action or actions Access performs when you choose the command in the menu bar. The actions you select for a command are the actions you want Access to perform when you select the command from the drop-down menu. For example, if you choose Project in the Data drop-down menu, Access performs the OpenForm macro action that opens the Project Table Reports form.

To have a menu perform one of the existing commands when you use the same or different name, use the DoMenuItem action. This action uses the menu bar name, the menu name, the command name, and any subcommand selection as arguments. For example, to have a command open another database, the Menu Bar argument is Database for the

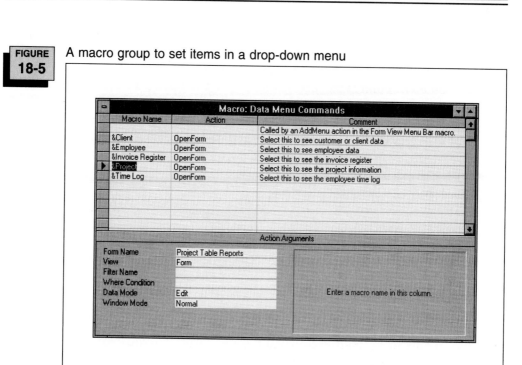

FIGURE 18-5 A macro group to set items in a drop-down menu

database window, the Menu Name argument is <u>F</u>ile for the File menu, the Command is <u>O</u>pen Database, and the Subcommand is empty.

Tip To create lines in a menu like the lines on either side of the three printing commands in the File menu, create a macro name of - (a hyphen). This macro has no action.

Tip Be sure to include a command to close the form. Without a command for this purpose, you can only close the form using the form window's Control menu box.

Using Your New Menus

When you complete the macros that will create the menus, try out your menu by displaying a form's design and changing the On Menu property of the form. The macro name you supply for this property is the name of the macro that defines the menu bar. In turn, this macro selects the other macro groups that select the commands to appear in the drop-down menu. The macros in the macro groups are run as the different commands are selected. For example, you can change the On Menu property of the Initial Form form that the AutoExec macro uses to Form View Menu Bar. When you display this form, by opening a form that has Form View Menu Bar entered for the On Menu property, the menu bar includes a Data drop-down menu, which looks like this:

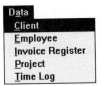

The macro that creates the menu must be added to every form that you want to use the new menu. For example, you may want the Data menu to be included in your other forms so you can quickly switch between the data you are viewing. To do this, enter **Form View Menu Bar** for the On Menu property of every form you want to use the modified menu. Forms that do not have Form View Menu Bar as the On Menu property use the standard form view menu when you open them.

Creating Macros that Perform with Key Combinations

You already have developed a group of commands that you can perform by pressing one or two keys. For example, you can press F11 in place of selecting the database window from the bottom of the Window menu. You can create other key combinations that perform any macro action you assign them.

To create macros that perform when you press a key combination, name the macro group AutoKeys. This macro group contains macros named by the key combinations that perform them, like this one:

The key combinations are the same key combinations the SendKeys action uses. For numbers and letters, the keys are represented as entered. The SHIFT key is presented as + and the CTRL key is presented as ^. Most of the remaining key combinations are the name of the key in braces as in {F11} or {INSERT}. For the macros entered in the preceding illustration, the key combinations are CTRL-D, CTRL-F, CTRL-R, and CTRL-S.

Each of these macros is followed by the macro action Access performs when you press the different key combinations. For the CTRL-D, CTRL-F, and CTRL-S macros, the macro actions switch between the design, form, and datasheet views. For the CTRL-R macro, Access performs the Project Table Reports macro. Once you save this macro, the key combinations are immediately available. When a key combination in the AutoKeys macro conflicts with a key combination Access has assigned, the macro in the AutoKeys macro is performed instead.

Every time you open a database, Access checks whether the database has an AutoKeys macro. When Access finds an AutoKeys macro, the key combinations set in effect by the macro are in force while the database is open. When Access does not find an AutoKeys macro, only the default key combinations are in effect.

Quick Reference

To Make a Macro Run When a Database Is Opened   Simply name the macro (that you want to run whenever the database is opened) AutoExec.

To Make a Form a Popup Form   In the macro that opens the form, for the OpenForm action that displays the form, set the Window Mode property to Dialog or change the form's Pop Up and Modal property to Yes.

To Add a Different Menu to a Form View   Create a macro containing AddMenu actions for each item that you want to appear in the menu bar. Create macro groups for each of the menu bar items that contain macros with the name of the menu command and the actions to perform when the command is chosen. Add the macro to the form's On Menu property.

To Assign Macros to Specific Key Combinations   Name the macro group containing the macros for the key combinations Auto-Keys. For each key combination, name the macro the same as the key combination that, when pressed, runs the macro.

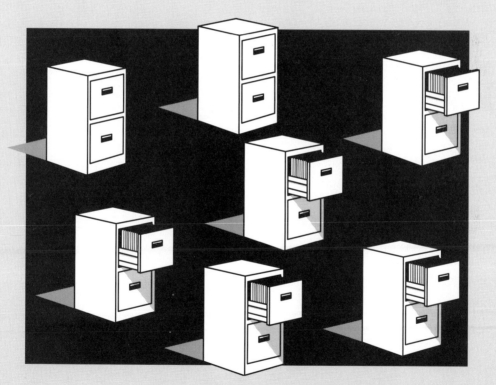

Network and
Administrative Topics

CHAPTER

Special
Considerations for
Network Use

You will use the same techniques to correct the entry in a field whether you are using a database on a stand-alone PC or in a shared environment. You can share data on a file server with other users or attach the same external table to your database that other users have attached to their databases. There are important features that you will want to utilize to ensure data integrity in a shared environment.

In a multiuser environment you have special considerations that do not apply when you are the only user who accesses and updates a database on your own PC. In a multiuser environment, it is possible that two users will want to read or update the same record at a given point in time. If you do not take the proper precautions, both users could update a record simultaneously and one user's changes could overlay the other's. Review this chapter carefully if you are not the sole user of your database to see how this situation can be prevented—and to see how many users can obtain the benefits of shared data access while avoiding the pitfalls.

You will learn how to open a database in a multiuser environment and how to choose a record-locking strategy that meets your needs. You will also learn how to change the design of database objects. This chapter shows you the features that Access provides to ensure your success in this environment.

The Dangers of Lost Data

With the specialization that exists in many organizations today, one user is not always responsible for updating the values in every field of a database table. If you look at the Client table in the COASTERS database, there are fields that might be updated by different departments. The Contact fields may be updated by someone in marketing while the YTD Payments and Total Payments fields might be updated by someone in accounting. If both users happen to request the records and the accounting changes are applied first, they will be overwritten when the marketing change is applied. Follow through this sequence of steps with a hypothetical three-field table to see how important changes can be lost.

Both User 1 and User 2 retrieve a record with the following field entries:

Name	Salary	Job Code
John Smith	29500	54

User 1 changes the salary and saves the record as this:

Name	Salary	Job Code
John Smith	32500	54

User 2 changes the record, overwriting User 1's changes. The record now looks like this:

Name	Salary	Job Code
John Smith	29500	63

When John Smith's record is later retrieved, User 1 will be confused as to why the salary increase entered no longer appears. This type of problem can be prevented by following the recommendations in this chapter.

Opening a Database

You will use the same Open Database command from the File menu to open a database in a multiuser environment. You might need to change the drive to the network drive, and you will need to be able to tell Access when you want to use a database for your own exclusive use.

To open a database for shared usage it is important that the Exclusive check box not have an X in it. If it does, no other users will be able to use the database. If someone else already has a database opened for exclusive use you will not be able to open it until they have closed it.

To open a database that can be shared with other users, follow these steps:

1. Establish the network connection that will be able to use your database.

2. Choose Open Database from the File menu to display the Open Database dialog box shown here:

```
┌─────────────────────────────────────────────────────────┐
│ ⊟                      Open Database                      │
├─────────────────────────────────────────────────────────┤
│ File Name:              Directories:        ┌──────────┐ │
│ ┌──────────────┐        d:\                  │   OK     │ │
│ │ *.mdb        │                             └──────────┘ │
│ ├──────────────┤▲       📁 d:\           ▲   ┌──────────┐ │
│ │ c1.mdb       │        📁 access            │ Cancel   │ │
│ │ coaster.mdb  │        📁 hg                └──────────┘ │
│ │              │        📁 inset                          │
│ │              │        📁 word                           │
│ │              │                        □ Read Only       │
│ │              │▼                    ▼  ☒ Exclusive       │
│ ├──────────────┤                                          │
│ List Files of Type:     Drives:                           │
│ │Databases (*.mdb)│▼   │💾 d: symbol     │▼                │
│ └──────────────┘                                          │
└─────────────────────────────────────────────────────────┘
```

3. Select the network drive from the drive's drop-down list box.

4. Select the filename of the database that you want to open.

5. Remove the check from the Exclusive box if it contains one.

6. Select OK.

The database will be opened as long as it is not already open for exclusive use by another user. Any user who attempts to open it for exclusive use will see an error message since it is already open for shared use.

Altering Database Objects

Once a database is open you can make changes to any of the objects that comprise it. Microsoft Access has some restrictions to prevent problems from occurring. The following rules apply:

☐ Access will not allow a user to make design changes to a table while another user is using it.

☐ Access presents a message if you make a design change to an object that another user has changed since you opened the object.

☐ Access only allows you to look at a table design as read-only if another user has its table open or is viewing a report, form, or query based on the table.

❑   Access presents the most recently saved version of an object if someone opens an object that has been changed.

Altering a Table

If you are going to alter a table design, make sure that the Exclusive check box is checked when you open the database. This allows you to make changes to the database tables and associated objects without a conflict with other users. Stick to your task and complete it as soon as possible as you are preventing others from using the database during this time. Some companies have rules that restrict exclusive use to weekends and after hours to ensure that work throughput is not impeded by removing a database from productive use during normal business hours.

Even if you open a database in nonexclusive mode, once you display the design view for a table no other users will be able to use the table data. Minimize the time that you are in design mode to eliminate the restrictions you are placing on other users.

When you change the design of a table, other database objects may be affected. You will need to update each object to ensure consistency in the database.

Altering Non-Table Objects

When you plan to alter database objects other than the tables, it is best to obtain the database for exclusive use. Although you can modify forms, reports, queries, modules, and macros without doing so, you can encounter some problems.

If you change a macro that someone is using, they may get unexpected and unacceptable results from its use.

Users working with a form, report, or query that you change must close the object and reopen it. Otherwise, they will be using the old rather than the new version.

Dependency between database objects can cause problems unless you are able to modify all the objects before users work with them. If you add fields to a form or a report the underlying query should have the fields added first. Figure 19-1 shows how the query should have fields added before the same fields are added to a report, since the report will get its information from the query results.

Changing Options for a Multiuser Environment

Some of the changes that you can make for a multiuser environment are customizing options available by choosing Options from the View menu to display the Options dialog box shown here:

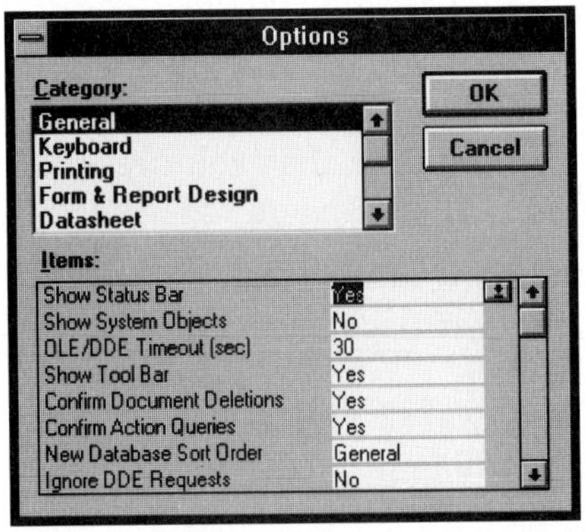

When you select Multiuser for the category, the options presented will match those given here:

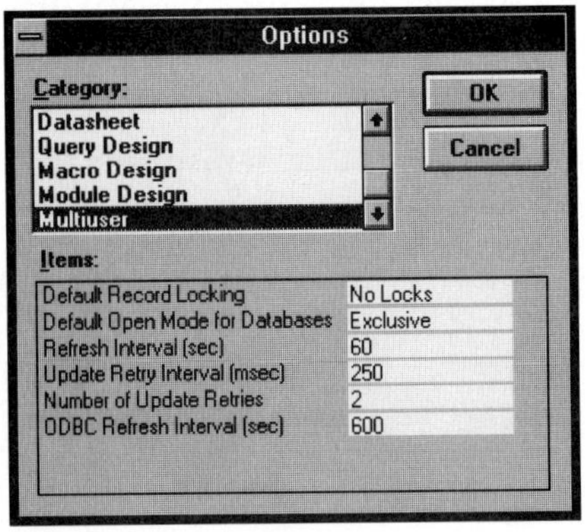

FIGURE
19-1

New fields are added to a query before a report

Last name field must be added here

Database: COASTER

Select Query: Employee Names and Hours

Employee	Employee Time Log
Employee Id	
Last Name	Date
First Name	Employee Id
Middle Initial	Project Number
Pay Rate	Hours
Bill Rate	

Field:	Date	Employee Id	Project Number	Hours	First Na
Sort:					
Show:	☒	☒	☒	☒	
Criteria:	#6/12/92#				
or:					

before it can be added to the report based on the query

Microsoft Access - [Report: Combined Employee and Invoice Register]

File   Edit   View   Layout   Window   Help

Print...   Setup...   Zoom   Cancel

Project Billing

16-Sep-92

		First Name	Last Name	Hours	Bill Rate	Billed Amount
Project #	1					
		WILLIAM	WILD	20	$60.00	$1,200.00
				Total Billed Amount		$1,200.00
Project #	2					
		BRENDA	BRAVE	40	$55.00	$2,200.00
		DAN	DANGER	35	$50.00	$1,750.00
		JOHNNY	JUMP	40	$10.00	$400.00
		RICHARD	ROCK	40	$10.00	$400.00
				Total Billed Amount		$4,750.00
Project #	3					
		DAN	DANGER	5	$50.00	$250.00
		HARRY	HIGHER	18	$10.00	$180.00
				Total Billed Amount		$430.00
Project #	4					
		HARRY	HIGHER	6	$10.00	$60.00

Page: 1

Ready

You can use these options to set the default mode when a database is opened to control the default setting for the Exclusive check box as well as to establish a default mode for locking records and a refresh interval.

 Tip The changes that you make for your system do not affect other users. The network administrator must ensure that certain settings are established for all users as an organizational standard.

Setting Record Locking

Record locking determines whether other users can change the same record that you are editing. You can even use this feature to lock all records in the same table or dynaset. If a record is locked, other users attempting to update the record get a message telling them that you are updating the record or table.

You can choose a default setting for record locking that applies to all tables and queries. You can also set the record-locking feature on forms to override the default setting. The options available to you for record locking are the default setting of No Locks, Edited Record, and All Records. Each option is discussed separately in the following sections.

The No Locks Setting

The No Locks setting allows anyone to edit a record at any time. The No Locks setting means that as you are editing a record, it is not locked from use by other users. If another user changes this record before you save it you will see a message indicating that this has occurred. You can discard your changes, overwrite the other user's changes, or take a closer look at their changes. To look more closely, you need to copy the record to the clipboard and look at the changes.

Another danger of the No Locks setting is that another user can overwrite your changes with their own and you will not know that your changes have been lost (remember the example with User 1 and User 2 earlier in this chapter). If another user locks a record that you are editing you will need to wait until they are finished with the record before you can save your changes.

The Edited Record Setting

The Edited Record setting locks the record being edited until you are finished. Other users wanting to edit the same record will be prevented from doing so until you are finished.

This options prevents one user from overlaying changes made by another user. It can cause delays when many users want to edit the same records but is a necessary precaution to prevent data loss from most users' perspective.

The All Records Setting

The most restrictive option is to lock all the records on the form or datasheet. Other users will not be able to edit or lock any records from the table while you have the table open. You might want to consider this option if you need to work for a short time getting totals of all the records and want to ensure that the totals do not change until you have all the totals that you need.

Setting a Default Mode for the Exclusive Setting

By default a new database is opened as exclusive unless you change the Options command in the View menu. To make the change to Shared, choose the Multiuser category and then select Shared for the Default Open Mode for Databases.

Refreshing the Data Displayed

Access automatically updates records displayed in a form or datasheet every 15 seconds if other users have updated the records. You can change this interval by choosing Options from the View menu, selecting the Multiuser category, and then entering a Refresh interval other than the 15-second default. Any number from 1 to 32,766 seconds is possible.

You can choose to refresh the data at any time. Choose Refresh from the Records menu to refresh immediately. To see added records, deleted records removed, and reordered records, you will need to perform another query on the records.

Retrying Updates

You can tell Access to continue trying an update to a record if it is not able to update the record due to someone else having a lock on the record. The default is two retries but you can choose any number from 0 to 10.

You can also specify an update interval in milliseconds. The default is 250 milliseconds but you can specify any number from 0 to 1,000 milliseconds.

To make the change, choose Options from the View menu, select the Multiuser category, and then specify an Update Retry Interval and a Number of Update Retries. If you are using a table stored on an SQL server, the update interval is set by the number after ODBC Refresh Interval.

Quick Reference

To Open a Database in Shared Mode   Choose Open Database from the File menu. Select the network drive and filename. Be sure that the X is removed from the Exclusive check box, and then select OK.

To Change Multiuser Settings   Choose Options from the View menu. Select Multiuser from the Category list box and then change the appropriate settings before selecting OK.

To Refresh Records Immediately   Choose Refresh from the Records menu.

CHAPTER

Network Administrator's Guide to Access

*T*he tasks in this chapter will interest the individual responsible for data in a shared computing environment. This individual may have the title of network administrator or those functions may be just one part of a myriad of other responsibilities. People using Access in a stand-alone fashion solely on their machine will also be interested in this information since they will want to protect the investment they have in their data.

In a network environment it is not possible to allow each individual user to make his or her own decision regarding the overall system and the security of the data that it contains. These tasks must be the responsibility of the network administrator. In most organizations the network administrator is also regarded as somewhat of a technical guru with the capability to advise users on settings for the best performance. Many organizations have allowed this individual to establish the custom settings for all software used on the system to ensure the highest level of system throughput for all users.

In this chapter you will learn all about the security settings for Access. You implement them to control who can use the system and what tasks they can perform. Backup considerations will be discussed as well as recovery and compaction procedures. If you have had the role of network administrator for some time you will want to focus on the procedures for each task as you are already well versed in the need for them. If you are less experienced as a network administrator, read the entire chapter to find the reasons for these measures.

Access Security

The security that Access provides is designed to supplement the security options in your network software and hardware. It also is useful for users running Access in a stand-alone environment who want to add a measure of security to prevent unauthorized users from logging onto Access or using or changing their databases. Access provides both users and groups to which you can assign permission to perform tasks with various database objects. Each user must belong to at least one group.

Without security options, any user who logs onto the system is considered automatically to be the Admin user. In a secure system, this classification is normally reserved for the network administrator since there are no restrictions on the Admin user. This Admin user is part of the Admins group and any users that you add to this group also will have full permission to use every object in the database in any way they want. This means that a member of the Admins group can review, create, and modify any object in the database including objects created by users in any group.

When you first start Access your system is not secure. You have two additional groups besides Admins: Users and Guests. You also have two defined users: Admin, which belongs to the Admins and Users groups, and Guest, which belongs to the Guests group. Figure 20-1 shows the users and groups that are automatically available when you start using Access.

Despite these categorizations, when starting the system all users begin without the logon procedure and are considered to be Admin users. You can add additional groups and add users to these groups as well as new groups. You can delete the existing users and remove users from any group except the Users group and the last member of the Admins group but you cannot delete the existing groups. Adding new users and groups will not have any effect until you make the system secure with passwords. You also must assign permissions for each object to make your databases as well as your system secure.

To secure your system, first add a password for Admin. This activates the logon procedure the next time Access is started, at which point the password is needed to proceed. Next, set up a new administrator's

FIGURE 20-1   Existing Groups and Users at startup

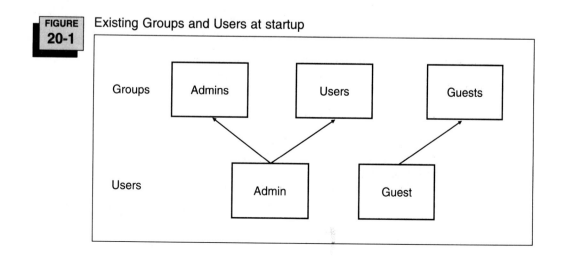

account and an administrator's password and *PIN* (personal identification number). You then will be able to delete the old administrator's account. At this point you will have added a basic level of security to the system that may be adequate if you are the only user. If you operate in a shared environment, the next step is to define groups and users and decide on the level of access you want groups and users to have for each database object.

 Tip Create a database that only the network administrator can use that has all of the user account names, PINs, and passwords in it.

Setting Up the Network Administrator

Your system will not be secure until you have a new administrator's account set up with a password and have deleted the old Admin account that did not need a password. A series of procedures are required since you must activate the logon procedure first by assigning a password to the existing Admin account. Exit Access and log on to see the new dialog box shown here:

Supply a correct user name and its matching password to proceed or you will not be able to start Access. After logging on, create a new administrative account with a password. You must delete the old Admin account as the last step. You will also want to learn how to change your password.

Activating Logon

Access provides a logon procedure, which does not display when you first install the package because no password is assigned. After assigning a password, this Logon dialog box will display every time you start the system.

Since the initial use of the package places you in the Admin user account, when you add a password it will be for the Admin user. The password that you enter is case sensitive, making it especially important to remember not only the word that you use but its capitalization.

The password can be any length from 1 to 14 characters and can include spaces and special characters. The only character that cannot be used is the null character represented as an ASCII 0. Since the password is the lock that protects your data, don't share it with others. You should not choose names or numbers that coworkers are likely to guess, and you should never write down your password and place it on your computer or in a desk drawer. Use acronyms instead of words since they are more difficult to guess. For example, if you took the words "I use Microsoft Access for all my work" and created an acronym such as IuMA4amw, the combination of uppercase and lowercase letters and numbers is not likely to be guessed by coworkers trying to discern your password—yet you are more likely to remember it than you would a random combination of letters.

Here are the steps for adding the password the first time:

1. Open a database and then choose <u>C</u>hange Password from the <u>S</u>ecurity menu.

2. Type a new password in the <u>N</u>ew Password box.

You do not need to type an old password since none exists. As you type the new password, asterisks appear onscreen so anyone happening to glance over your shoulder won't see the characters you're typing.

3. Retype the same password in the <u>V</u>erify box and then choose OK.

A Logon dialog box appears when you start Access again; you will need to supply the password that you just assigned.

Creating an Account for the Administrator

As an administrator you will want to create an account under the Admins group and then delete the Admin user account that was provided just to get you started. You can pick your own name for this account and assign a unique PIN. This command is only available for users who belong to the Admins group.

Your user account name can be as long as 20 characters. Access combines your user account name with your PIN to uniquely identify the account. You can use your name for the user account even if it is the same as another user's name because the PIN will make the two entries unique. Unlike passwords you will find that the user account names are not case sensitive.

To add a user account, follow these steps from the Access database window:

1. Choose Users from the Security menu.

2. Type the new user account name in the Users dialog box and press ENTER or click the New button.

3. Type a four-digit PIN number.

PIN numbers assigned to each user should be placed in a safe place, such as a database that only the administrator can access. To communicate across systems, users will need to know the name and PINs for their recipients.

4. Choose OK to display the Users dialog box.

5. Choose Admins from the Available Group list box, and then choose Add to display Admins in the Member Of list box.

6. Choose Close.

You now have your own account in the Admins group. The password that you assigned to the Admin account is not operational for this account. Add a new password for yourself and delete the old Admin account.

Changing the Password

You must be logged on under the account name for which you want to change the password. If you are logged on as Admin or another user name you must exit Access and restart the system supplying the user name for which you want to add a password when the Logon dialog box appears. As a member of the Admins group you will be called when users cannot remember their password or have other system difficulties. Because you must be able to log on as any user, it is imperative that you have a list of user names and passwords for your reference.

Tip To remove a password, choose Change Password from the Security menu and simply type the old password. Then leave the New Password and Verify boxes empty.

After logging on as the user for which you want to change the password, follow these steps:

1. Choose Change Password from the Security menu to display the Change Password Dialog box shown in Figure 20-2.

2. Type the old password in the Old Password box or leave it blank if the user does not have a password assigned.

3. Type the new password in the New Password box.

4. Type the new password again in the Verify box.

5. Select OK.

FIGURE 20-2   The Change Password dialog box

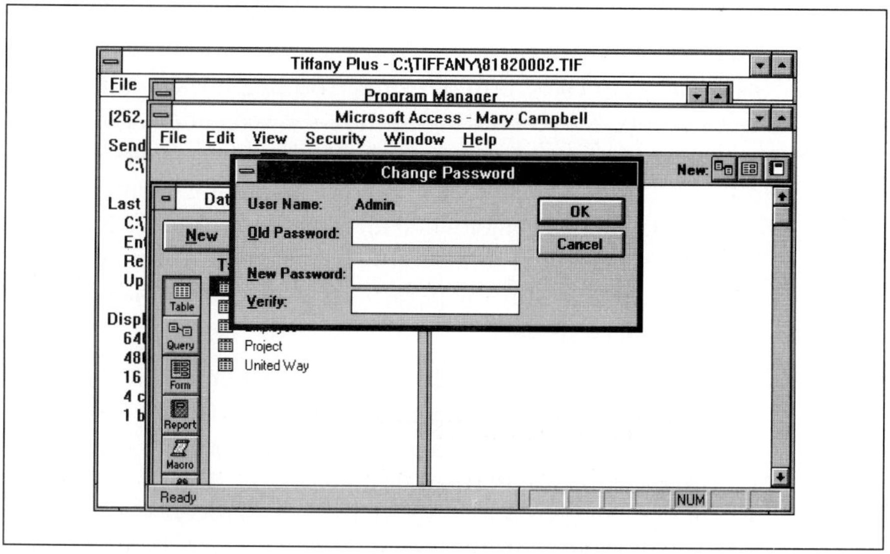

Tip Always change the Guest password after a guest has finished using the system. They will not be able to log onto the system without your giving them the new password at a later time.

Securing Database Objects

Securing your system with a logon and passwords is the first step toward protecting the company's investment in the database system but more is needed. You need to protect the database objects, which consist of tables, forms, reports, macros, and modules. To do this you must establish *permissions* for each object for each group or user.

It is a good idea to establish the permissions for your system as soon as you load Access since the default is to allow all users to work with any object. You will need to set up groups and users and clear the default setting. Next, establish permissions for each database object. A user automatically inherits the permissions assigned to any group that they are a part of. This means that you should make the group permissions as restrictive as necessary and add additional permissions only for users that need them.

Setting Up Groups

Although you can assign permission for objects at the user level, it is more efficient to create groups of users with similar needs and assign permission to the group of users. You might have a marketing group, a sales group, an accounting group, a management group, and a payroll group within your organization. Each group needs to be able to use different forms, reports, and tables. Assigning permission at the group level also makes it easier when an individual changes job responsibilities. You can move them to a group that fits with their new position rather than having to modify the permissions for each of the old and new objects that they need to use.

You can use from 1 to 20 characters when you assign a group name. Avoid leading spaces and control characters (ASCII codes 0 to 31) as well as " ^ [ ] : | < > + = ; , . ? and *. Try to pick names that convey meaning to anyone who selects them.

To create the first group, follow these steps:

1. Choose Groups from the Security menu in the database window.

2. Type a group name in the Name box in the dialog box shown in Figure 20-3.

3. Choose the New button.

The New User/Group dialog box appears with the name you entered in the Name box.

4. Type a 4-digit PIN number in the Personal ID Number box.

5. Select OK to create the group.

6. Continue creating groups until all the groups are entered and then choose Close.

 Tip Do not leave old unused groups in the system. Use Groups in the Security menu to remove them. Select a group name after using this command and then select the Delete button.

FIGURE
20-3

The Groups dialog box

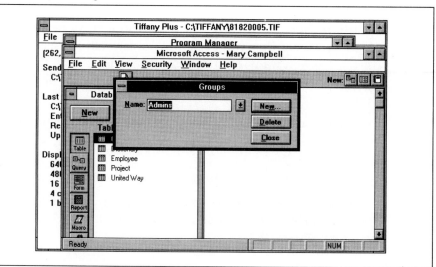

User Accounts

To log on to Access you must have a user name since no one can log on directly as a group. Users are not added to a group until they are set up with a name and a PIN. You also will want to learn how to add users to groups and how to remove them from a group as well as how to delete a user account.

Setting Up New Users You can create a new system user by entering nothing more than an account name and a PIN. Every user that you create will automatically be added to the Users group at the time of creation.

To add a new user, follow these steps:

1. Choose Users from the Security menu to display the dialog box shown in Figure 20-4.

2. Type the new user name in the Name text box.

3. Select the New button to display the new name in the New User/Group dialog box shown in Figure 20-5 and then type a PIN number and select OK.

Choose Close to end without adding the new user to a group or proceed to look at the groups to determine which you want to add the user to. Even if you do not specifically add the user to a group it will be part of the Users group.

Adding Users to Groups At a minimum every new user that you set up is a part of the group Users. You can add a user to as many other groups as you want. An individual supervising both the accounting and the finance staffs might be part of the groups for accounting, finance, and management.

To add a user to an existing group, follow these steps:

1. Choose Users from the Security menu.

2. Select a user name from the list in the Name box.

3. Select the group to which you want to add the user from the Available Groups list box.

4. Select Add and then select Close.

The Users dialog box

The New User/Group dialog box

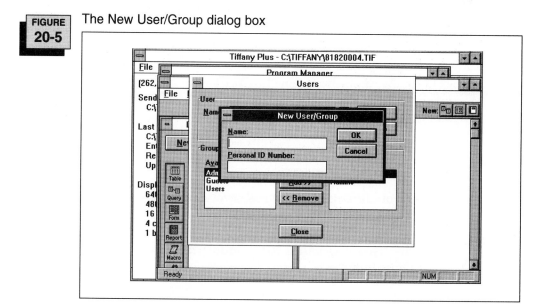

Removing Users from Groups When a user is transferred to another department it is important to remove them from their existing group. If you are not certain as to what permissions they should have in the new workgroup they can remain in the system without a group assignment until you are able to clarify the permissions that they should have.

To remove a user from a group, follow these steps when logged on as a member of the Admins group:

1. Choose Users from the Security menu.

2. Select the user name from the list in the Name box.

3. Select the group you want to remove them from in the Member Of list box.

4. Select Remove and then select Close.

Deleting a User Users who leave the company should be removed from the system immediately. Delete their user account rather than just removing them from a group as you want the account to be inoperable.

Follow these steps to delete a user:

1. Choose Users from the Security menu.

2. Select the user name from the Name box.

3. Select Delete and then select Close.

 Tip During layoffs or other involuntary terminations, users accounts are normally made inoperable at the time the user is being informed to prevent potential malicious damage to the data files by disgruntled employees.

Setting Permissions

When you first install Access, every user that you add has full permission to all objects. This means that they can read and modify data, read and modify definitions for all objects, and execute macros, reports, and forms. This is because the default permission is set to grant full permission to all Access users. You can assign permissions for each database object on your own by choosing Permissions from the Security menu and clearing the check box for Full permissions.

All permissions are defined for each object with some permissions operating on all objects and others restricted to a certain type of object. Table 20-1 shows the objects that are affected by the various permissions.

Some permissions imply another permission. For example, if you allow a user to modify the definition of a report you are implying that he or she can also read the report definition. It is not necessary to implicitly assign permissions that are inherited. These inherited definitions are not shown in the Permissions dialog box. Look at Table 20-2 to see the permissions that are implied with each selection.

TABLE 20-1   Available Permissions for Objects

Object	Permissions Settings Available
Table	All permissions except Execute
Query	All permissions except Execute
Form	All permissions except Read Data and Modify Data
Report	All permissions except Read Data and Modify Data
Macro	All permissions except Read Data and Modify Data
Module	All permissions except Execute, Read Data, and Modify Data

TABLE 20-2   Implied Permissions

Explicit Assignment	Implied Permission
Read Definitions	Execute (Macros only)
Modify Definitions	Read Definitions
Read Data	Read Definitions
Modify Data	Read Definitions
	Read Data
Full Permissions	Read Definitions
	Modify Definitions
	Read Data
	Modify Data
	Execute

Defining the Permissions for an Object Objects in the database consist of tables, queries, reports, forms, modules, and macros. You can assign permission on an object by object basis and specify which users or groups can use them.

To assign permissions, follow these steps:

1. Choose <u>P</u>ermissions from the <u>S</u>ecurity menu.

2. Select the type of object from the <u>T</u>ype drop-down list box shown in Figure 20-6.

3. Select the name of the object.

4. Select the group or user.

5. Select the permissions you want to assign to the user or group for the selected object.

 Warning If you save a database object to a new object with the Save <u>A</u>s command in the <u>F</u>ile menu, the permissions are not retained in the new object. You will have to assign permissions for the new object.

FIGURE 20-6 The Permissions dialog box

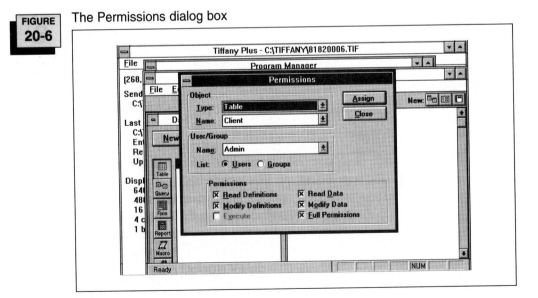

Restricting Access to Less than a Table   Field level security is often desired to more closely control the data that users can see and update. Since Access security is assigned at the object level, the permissions are assigned for an entire table. A solution that fits within the capabilities of the system and effectively provides a more refined security is to define a query or a form that contains only the data elements that a user can see and modify.

Defining a query allows you to let a staff member update every field in the Employee table except the pay rate. Since the pay rate is not part of the query, the user who has permission to use the query object will not be able to see or change it. It is important that you do not give this user permission to use the Employee table or they will be able to read the pay rate field.

Using Encryption to Improve Security

If someone tried to read your database file with a word processor or utility program, it would not display on the screen as it does from Access. Although he or she may be able to discern some information, it is not easy to read. If the database contains confidential information even this level of data availability to unauthorized users may be too much.

Access allows you to *encrypt* databases that you do not want accessible to unauthorized users. An encrypted file is one that is not readable if it is displayed on the screen or printer using a utility package or word processor. Everything in the file is represented by secret codes that only Access knows, and this information is transcribed into a readable format only by Access when you look at it from within the Access system or decrypt the file.

Encryption is an important technique if your database contains confidential sales information or salaries. Although encryption does reduce performance slightly it can be an important technique for protecting your information. This is especially important when you transmit a file over the telephone lines or mail a copy of the information on a disk and are concerned about unauthorized access to its contents.

Encryption is done to an entire database rather than to individual objects. It must be done while the database is closed on your system and the database is not used by any other user. To encrypt your database, follow these steps:

1. Close the database.

2. From the Access window choose Encrypt/Decrypt Database from the File menu.

3. Specify a filename, drive, and directory for the encrypted file in the Encrypt/Decrypt Database dialog box.

   You can use the same name as the database to overwrite it with the encrypted file.

4. Select the OK button.

   Access encrypts the database and compacts it at the same time. You can decrypt the database to remove the encryption using the same dialog box.

 Warning Encryption is best left to the network administrator who has permission for all database objects. If a database is encrypted using the same name as the original file and you do not have permission for these objects, the new file will not contain these objects and will be given a new name by Access. You will not be able to delete the original database since it is the only location with all of the data.

Compacting a Database

As you continue to add to a database, it becomes impossible for the information to be stored in adjacent locations on your hard disk; data becomes fragmented in many places. When data is subsequently retrieved, performance can be degraded. When you *compact* the database you eliminate all the fragments and make the database more efficient.

How often should a database be compacted in order to run efficiently? There is no one correct answer since some users will use a database primarily to look up existing information. A database that consisted solely of a catalog price list or a list of chemical elements is one example of a database that would not require compacting. Since data is not added, fragmenting doesn't occur; compaction would never be necessary after the initial creation. On the other hand, a database that consists of customer orders and a growing base of other information with many new reports would require compaction just about whenever the database was closed.

A database can only be compacted when it is not open on any system. There also must be adequate storage space for the existing file and the compacted version. You must supply a from and to database name for the compact operation but they can be the same. The original file will be replaced after a successful conclusion for the procedure.

Follow these steps to compact a database:

1. From the Microsoft Access Startup window choose Compact Database from the File menu.

   The dialog box shown in Figure 20-7 appears.

2. Select the file that you want to compact from the list of filenames, changing the drive and directory if necessary.

3. Type the name for the compacted database in the Database to Compact Into dialog box

4. Select OK.

FIGURE 20-7   The Database to Compact From dialog box

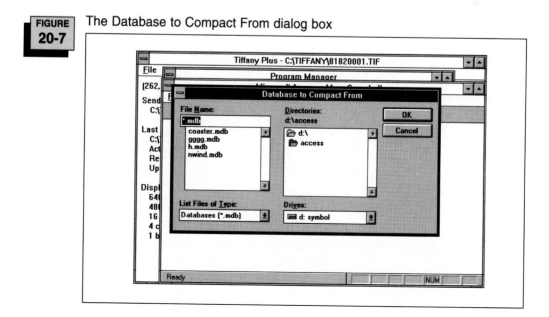

Repairing a Database

Within the database file there are pointers to many interrelated pieces of information. If your system crashes when Access is writing to this file there is the potential for your database to become corrupted. This could mean that some vital data is missing or the pointers between information are not properly updated. You will not be able to open and use a corrupted database unless you correct the situation. If you experience problems with a database, try closing it and using the Repair Database command. You can start the repair procedure either by choosing Repair Database from the File menu or by clicking OK in response to a prompt when you attempt to open, compact, or encrypt a database. After selecting Repair Database from the File menu, specify the name of the database file to be repaired. Select the drive and directory if the current setting is not the correct one.

Backups

The network administrator is responsible for backing up all the shared databases on the network as well as expected to advise users when to back up databases stored on their own systems.

Backups will protect your organization against data loss and the inevitable down time that occurs when a large database is lost. Databases that are updated infrequently will not require daily backups. If many people update a database each day then daily backups are essential.

Backup is easy with Access since all tables, reports, forms, macros, and queries are stored in one .MDB file. You may choose to use the DOS Copy command, the Windows File Manager, or backup software. Most organizations will use more efficient backup software to save time when backups must be done on a daily basis since the database cannot be open and in use during the backup period and it is best to keep this time to a minimum.

You may want to schedule an extra backup immediately following a large important operation or the creation of numerous macros, reports, or forms to ensure that they are available on the backup copy. Make a backup copy of SYSTEM.MDB along with any databases that you are backing up to ensure that your system configuration changes are also retained.

A backup copy should be stored offsite in the event that a fire or other major catastrophe strikes the building where the network is installed. Lock up your backups or use encryption since the value of the data they contain is the same as the database. You may want to keep between three to seven backups to be able to restore the database in the event of a backup also being damaged.

Customizing Access

Access has many different settings that allow you to customize its operation. These changes are all made by choosing Options from the View menu. It does not matter which database is open when the changes are made since they will remain in effect for all databases in the system.

Customizing is an important role for the network administrator since all the individuals who work together will use the same options settings. These individuals are said to be part of a workgroup, and members of a workgroup will all share the settings in the SYSTEM.MDA file for their group.

There are nine different categories of customizing changes that you can make to Access: General, Keyboard, Printing, Form & Report Design, Datasheet, Query Design, Macro Design, Module Design, and Multiuser. A brief look at each category lets you focus on which changes can bring the users in different workgroups the best results possible with Access. Figure 20-8 shows the dialog box that appears when you choose Options from the View menu. You can choose any category from the Category list box and the properties list for that category will replace the properties for the General category displayed initially.

General Options

The General category contains customization options that do not fit into any of the more specific categories. Options in this category allow

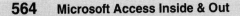

FIGURE
20-8

The Options dialog box

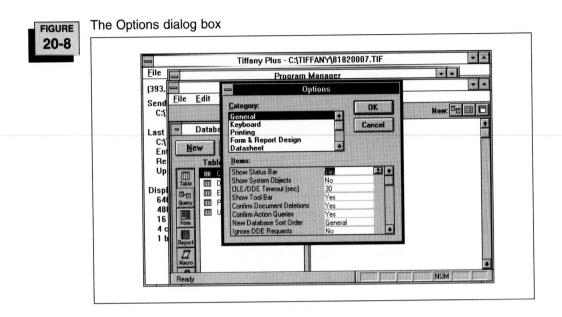

you to customize the display of the status bar and toolbar, the sort order, and provide confirmation of various actions.

Table 20-3 shows each of the General category options, their default settings, and gives a brief explanation of the customizing feature that they provide.

Keyboard Options

The keyboard options let you customize the way certain keys on the keyboard work. It is important that you assess this category of changes before users start working with Access and leave the settings unchanged since they are basic to any typing that you do with the package. The Keyboard category also allows you to specify the name of the macro that you will use for definitions of macro tasks assigned to keyboard keys.

Table 20-4 shows the four Keyboard category options and their default settings.

TABLE 20-3   General Customizing Options

Option	Default Setting	Meaning
Show Status Bar	Yes	Displays or hides the status bar
Show System Objects	No	Displays or hides objects defined by Access
OLE/DDE Timeout (sec)	30	Determines how long Access attempts a failed OLE or DDE task
Show Tool Bar	Yes	Displays or hides the toolbar
Confirm Document Deletions	Yes	Determines whether the "Delete object?" prompt displays
Confirm Actions Query	Yes	Determines whether a confirmation message box displays
New Database Sort Order	General	Sets the sort order for new databases. Other options are Traditional Spanish, Nordic, and Dutch
Ignore DDE Request	No	Determines whether DDE requests from other applications are serviced
Default Find/ Replace Behavior	Fast Search	Determines whether the current field is searched for the whole entry (Fast Search) or whether all fields are searched for any part of the field (General Search)
Default Database Directory	Current Access Working Directory	Specifies the directory to be used for new database files
Confirm Record Changes	No	Determines whether a confirmation message box appears for deleted or pasted records

TABLE 20-4

Keyboard Category Options

Option	Default Setting	Meaning
Arrow Key Behavior	Next Field	Determines whether the insertion point is moved to the next field or character when the arrow keys are pressed
Move After Enter	Next Field	Determines the effect of pressing ENTER on the insertion. Other choices are No to not move the insertion point and Next Record
Cursor Stops at First/Last Field	No	Determines whether the insertion point stops moving at the first or last field
Key Assignment Macro	AutoKeys	Specifies the name of the macro used when macros are assigned to a key

Printing

The Printing options are all very basic to the print operation since they establish the margins on all four sides of the printed output. You can change the default settings to make the printed section of the page either larger or smaller.

Form & Report Design

The Form & Report Design templates allow you to add standard logos or other changes to the basic forms and reports. This category provides settings that make alignment easier and determines whether or not the gird lines should be displayed. Changes do not affect any existing forms or reports, or those that you may subsequently create with FormWizards or ReportWizards.

If you want to see all the options look at Table 20-5, which contains all the settings for the Form & Report category.

TABLE
20-5

Datasheet Category Options

Option	Default Setting	Meaning
Form Template	Normal	The name of the form in the current database that you want to use as a template when creating reports
Report Template	Normal	The name of the report in the current database that you want to use as a template when creating reports
Objects Snap to Grid	Yes	Controls whether objects are aligned with the grids
Show Grid	No	Displays or hides the grid
Selection Behavior	Partially Enclosed	Select whether controls enclosed or intersected by the selection rectangle are included or only the ones that are fully enclosed
Show Ruler	Yes	Displays or hides the ruler in a new form or report

Datasheet

Datasheet category options affect the display of datasheets. This includes new and existing query datasheets and new table and form datasheets. Existing datasheets are not affected. Options include font options, column width, and gridlines. Table 20-6 shows the full set of options.

Query Design

The Query Design Category offers options that let you tailor the query design environment to more closely meet your needs. You can control the field names and table names that display and control permissions for running queries. Table 20-7 shows the options that are available.

Form & Report Design Category Options

Option	Default Setting	Meaning
Default Gridlines Behavior	On	Determines whether gridlines are displayed or hidden
Default Column Width	1 inch	Sets the width of datasheet columns
Default Font Name	MS Sans Serif	Specifies any installed font
Default Font Size	8	Sets the font size from available options for the font selected
Default Font Weight	Normal	Sets the weight with options such as thin, extra light, light, normal, medium, semi-bold, bold, extra-bold, or black
Default Font Italic	No	Displays names and data in italic or non-italic
Default Font Underline	No	Displays names and data in underline or non-underline

Query Design Category Options

Option	Default Setting	Meaning
Restrict Available Fields	Yes	Use only the fields in the QBE grid or all fields when you use the query as the basis for another query, a form, or a report
Run with Owner's Permission	Yes	Decides whether users who cannot view a query's underlying tables can view the data in a new query or run an action query
Show Table Names	No	Controls the display of table names in a QBE grid

Macro Design

The Macro Design category has two customizing options. The Show Macro Names Column determines whether or not the Macro Name column displays in a macro window for new macros. The Macro Names button on the toolbar can also be clicked to change the display status of this option for the current macro. The second category option, Show Conditions Column, determines whether the Condition column appears for new macros within the macro window. You can use the Conditions button on the toolbar to toggle this setting on and off for the current macro. The default settings are No for both options.

Module Design

There are two customizing options for the Module Design category. You can turn syntax checking for your Access Basic code on and off. You also can set the tab stops anywhere from 1 to 30 spaces depending on the level of nesting and indentation you normally use in your programs. Syntax checking is the default and the default tab set is 4.

Multiuser

The Multiuser category provides customizing options that are only of interest in a multiuser environment. You can make changes to features such as record locking, shared versus exclusive access to databases, and refresh intervals. Table 20-8 shows the full set of options and default values.

TABLE

20-8

Multiuser Category Options

Option	Default Setting	Meaning
Default Record Locking	No Locks	You can choose no record, locking all records, or edited record
Default Open Mode for Databases	Exclusive	Selects whether the default open for a database is exclusive or shared
Refresh Interval (sec)	15 sec	Sets the refresh interval from 1 to 32,766 sec
Update Retry Interval (msec)	250 msec	Sets the time interval for trying resave on a record locked by someone else from 0 to 1000 msec
Number of Update Retries	2	Sets the number of retry attempts for saving a changed record from 0 to 10
ODBC Refresh Interval	600	Sets the ODBC refresh rate from 1 to 3600 sec

Quick Reference

To Add or Change a Password   Choose Change Password from the Security menu and then type the old password. Type the new password in both the New Password and Verify text boxes and then select OK.

To Create a New User   Choose Users from the Security menu. Type a user name in the Name text box and then select New. Type a PIN and then choose OK followed by Close.

To Create a New Group   Choose Groups from the Security menu. Type a group name and then select New. Type a PIN and then select OK followed by Close.

To Add a User to a Group   Choose Users from the Security menu. Select a user name and then select the desired group from the Available Groups list box. Select the Add button and then select Close.

To Set Permissions for an Object   Select Permissions from the Security menu and then select the type and name of the object. Select the desired permissions and then select Assign.

To Encrypt/Decrypt the Database   Choose Encrypt/Decrypt Database from the File menu. Select the desired database and then select OK. Supply a name for the encrypted file and then select OK.

To Compact the Database   Choose Compact Database from the File menu. Select the file and choose OK. Complete the Database to Compact Into dialog box and supply the name of the compacted file before selecting OK.

To Change a Custom Setting   Choose Options from the View menu. Choose the category of options that you want to change and then select the particular option and the desired value.

PART VI

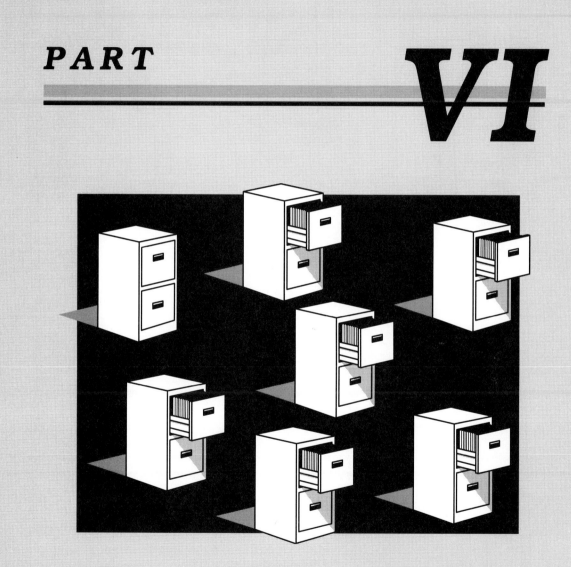

Programming

CHAPTER

Introduction to Access Basic

Most database applications provide the user with a programming language for applications development, and Access is no exception. Access calls its programming language Access Basic. As a programming language, it has many of the same features as Microsoft's Visual Basic. If you have used other database programming languages, you will find Access Basic easy to use since it shares many programming capabilities with them.

Most of the features for which other programming languages require lines of code are handled automatically by the objects that an Access Basic program uses. For example, a dBASE program would have many lines that display the data, get the data, and validate the data. In Access Basic, this is all handled by the form so a program using the form has much less work to do. You use Access Basic when you want customized functions or you want to automate using several objects.

This chapter shows you the basics of using Access Basic to create programs. Access Basic is a full-fledged programming language. Like most programming languages, entire books can be written on how to use it. This chapter's intent is to get you started.

The programs in Access Basic are called *procedures*. These procedures are stored in a database object called a *module*. You can put all of the procedures you use in a database into a single module or you can split the procedures among several modules. This chapter starts with the basics of creating a module and then shows how to add procedures to it. In each procedure, the instructions telling Access the steps to perform are called *statements*. Once you have procedures, you will want to save them, print them, and use them. After learning these basics, you will learn a few of the advanced programming capabilities you can add to your procedures. Finally, you will learn about some of the tools Access provides to help you make your procedures error free.

Modules

To use Access Basic you need to create modules. After creating other Access objects, creating modules will seem like a familiar skill. Once you have created a module, you are ready to fill the module with procedures— the parts of a module you use to perform tasks.

Creating a Module

To create a module, begin by clicking the Module button in the database window and the New button, or select New from the File menu and then choose Module. Access opens a window to contain this module like the one shown in Figure 21-1.

At the beginning of a module is the *declarations section*, which initially contains Option Compare Database when you open a new module. This section may subsequently contain other declarations if needed.

Creating a Procedure

Creating a procedure is easy since Access constantly looks at what you enter in a module window. To tell Access you want to start a new procedure simply begin typing an entry in the module window. This entry is either **Sub** or **Function** followed by the name of the procedure,

FIGURE 21-1

The initial window for working with a module

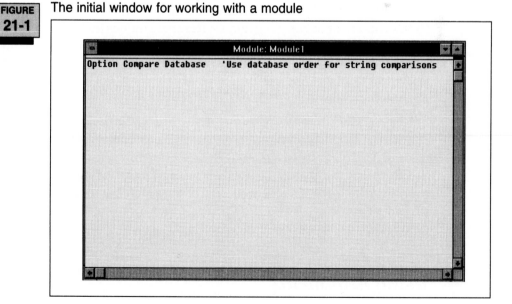

parentheses, and any arguments the procedure uses. Sub or Function tells Access the type of procedure you want to create.

A *function procedure*, like the functions Access provides, takes zero or more arguments and returns a value that you can subsequently use in an expression. A *sub procedure* takes zero or more arguments but does not return a value. Sub procedures are used by function procedures. When creating a new procedure, you have to decide whether the procedure is a function procedure or a sub procedure. The difference between these two procedures is whether you want the procedure to return a value when completed.

For example, when you use an Access function, the function returns a value. When you create a procedure that is to be included in an expression, you want the procedure to be a function procedure. In other cases, when Access performs a procedure, the procedure does not return a value. An example of this is a procedure that changes a control's Visible property without returning information other parts of Access can use. This type of a procedure is a sub procedure.

A procedure name can be up to 40 characters including letters, numbers, or underscores, and must start with a letter. You cannot have more than one procedure in a database with the same name. You cannot name a procedure the same name as global variables or constants (defined later), or as *reserved names*. Reserved names include statements used by Access Basic, function names, operators, and methods (defined later in this chapter). These rules for naming are explicitly for Access Basic, and differ from the database object rules you use for naming objects and controls.

When a procedure is a function procedure, you can add one of several characters as the last character of the name to indicate the data type of the result. These suffix characters are % for Integer, & for Long, ! for Single, # for Double, @ for Currency, and $ for String. If a function procedure name does not use one of these characters, the function procedure returns a Variant data type. Unless you need a specific data type result, use a Variant data type.

Using Arguments

Parentheses surround the arguments the procedure uses. These arguments are like the arguments the Access functions use. When you use the procedure, it expects a specific number of arguments and the information provided by the arguments often must be in a specific order. Argument names are like the names of arguments for Access functions. You want them to describe the data the argument represents. You only need as many arguments as you plan to pass to the procedure. Each of the arguments is separated with commas.

As an example, suppose you want a function procedure that takes a word and converts it to proper case. By using a function procedure for this purpose, you use the custom function procedure every time you want the results without typing the longer formula that the custom function procedure represents. In this example, you tell Access you want to create a function procedure by typing **Function Proper (OldText)**. Function tells Access to create a Function procedure, that Proper is the name of the function procedure, and that OldText represents the single argument that you pass to this function procedure every time you use it.

When you press ENTER, Access recognizes that you want to create a function procedure and adds an End Function line for you two lines below the function, as you can see in Figure 21-2. If you were creating a sub

FIGURE 21-2

The module window after creating a new procedure

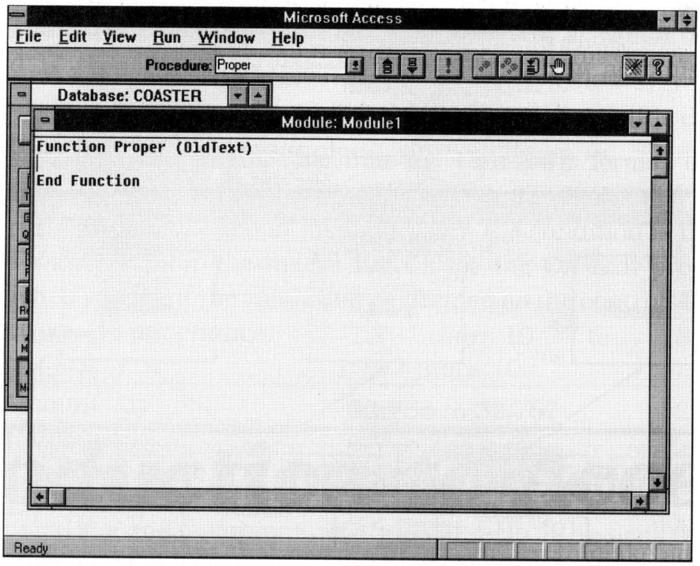

procedure, Access would add End Sub at the bottom of the procedure. The Function or Sub lines start the beginning of the procedure and the End lines end the procedure. The lines in between contain the instructions for Access to perform every time you run this procedure. Also, notice that the procedure name appears in the tool bar.

Tip   You can also start a new procedure by choosing New Procedure from the Edit menu. When you use this command, you can select whether the procedure is a sub or a function procedure and the procedure's name. This adds the top and bottom lines of the procedure without any arguments in the parentheses. You can always fill in the parentheses later as you decide which data the procedure will use.

Changing the Procedure Displayed

You only see one procedure at a time in the window (later you will learn how to see two). Each procedure is like text written on separate pages of a loose-leaf notebook. You have several ways to switch between which procedure appears in the window. You can press CTRL-UP ARROW and CTRL-DOWN ARROW, which is the same as choosing Previous Procedure and Next Procedure in the View menu. You also can click one of these two buttons in the toolbar:

The Previous Procedure button on the left displays the previous procedure and the Next Procedure button on the right displays the next procedure. You also can choose which procedure to display by selecting the name of the procedure or the declarations section from this drop-down box:

An additional method of selecting which procedure you are viewing is to choose Procedures from the View menu or press F2. Access displays a dialog box like the one shown next. You can select the different modules as well as which procedure you want to see.

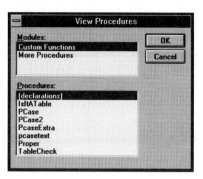

Reminder Access alphabetizes the procedures in a module so the order of the procedures changes from the order you enter them into the module.

Splitting a Module Window

When you want to look at two procedures or a declarations section and a procedure from the same module, you can split the window. Splitting the window is like splitting a window of a query design where you divide the query design window between the field list windows and the QBE grid. To split a module window into two, drag the white bar below the title bar (the mouse will change to a double-headed arrow) to where you want the window split.

You also can choose Split Window from the View menu to divide the module window in half. Once the window is split, switch between the two halves by clicking them or pressing F6. Each window can show a separate procedure or declarations section from the same module. The following shows a module window split in half to show two separate procedures:

```
Module: Custom Functions
Function TableCheck ()
'This function is solely for starting the IsItATable sub procedure
IsItATable
End Function

Function Proper (OldText)
    Proper = UCase(Left(OldText, 1)) & LCase(Right(OldText, Len(OldTe
End Function
```

While a window is split, you can change the position of the split by dragging the white bar up or down. You can return a window to showing a single declarations section or procedure by dragging the bar to the top of the window. You also can remove the split in the window by choosing Split Window from the View menu again to remove the check mark next to the Split Window command.

Editing a Procedure

When you have the beginning and end of a procedure, you are ready to add the statements that tell Access what to do when you use the procedure. Editing in a module window is like editing with the Windows Notepad accessory. The only difference is that Access reviews the statements you enter. When you enter a statement it cannot understand, Access displays a message indicating that the current line has a problem. This review process finds mistakes as you enter statements, catching typing errors and some incorrect entries.

Each of the lines contains a statement. Some of these statements are expressions. For example, the following Proper function procedure contains a single statement:

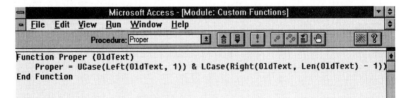

```
Function Proper (OldText)
    Proper = UCase(Left(OldText, 1)) & LCase(Right(OldText, Len(OldText) - 1))
End Function
```

You can see from this example that every time the procedure needs the data that it is sent when the procedure is run, the procedure has the name of the argument. Therefore, every time the Proper function procedure needs the old text to convert, the function procedure contains OldText. The expression that this statement computes is the same expression you saw in Chapter 12 to convert a form or report control's entry into proper case. Access knows what value this function procedure returns because the procedure contains an expression that equates the function procedure's name with a value. In this case, this function procedure returns the text it is sent after changing the first letter to uppercase and the rest of the letters to lowercase.

This function procedure only works with single words. Later you will see a PCase function procedure that handles making each word proper case. The PCase function procedure uses the Proper function procedure to switch individual words to uppercase.

With expressions in a procedure, you must tell Access where you want the result of the expression stored. In the module in the preceding illustration, the expression's result becomes the function procedure's return value. At other times, you will put the expression's result in a variable. Variable names follow Access Basic naming conventions (up to 40 letters, numbers, and underscores).

Saving the Module

Use the Save command in the File menu to save the module. You will need to supply a name for the module if you have not saved it before. Like other database objects, you can use as many as 64 characters in the module name. Leading spaces and ASCII control characters are not acceptable. You are also prompted about saving the module if you try closing the window when the module has unsaved changes. Close the module window by choosing Close from the File menu, pressing CTRL-F4, or double-clicking the window's Control menu box. The module's name displays in the database window. Now you have the Design button available. Later when you want to edit the module, you can select the module and then select the Design button or double-click the module's name using the right mouse button.

Printing a Module

To help you work on the procedures you create, print them out. Printing a module prints the contents of the declarations section and all the procedures in the module. You can preview the appearance of the printout by choosing Print Preview from the File menu. Use Print Setup in the File menu to change how the output is printed. Choose Print from the File menu when ready to print.

Using the Procedures

After you have a procedure completed, you can start using it. Procedures are run through either controls in forms or reports or through a macro. The purpose of the procedure and when you want it performed determines whether you use controls or a macro.

Some of the function procedures you create can be used as part of any expression. You use function procedures in the same locations in which you use the functions Access provides. For example, you can add the Proper function procedure to controls for the First Name and Last Name fields in the report in Figure 21-3.

This report is shown twice so you can see both the report design and the results. The controls that use the Proper function procedure are calculated controls. The control for the first name has =Proper([First Name]) as the Control Source property, and the control for the last name has =Proper([Last Name]) as the Control Source property. Since Access does not have a function of its own named Proper, Access checks for a function procedure in any one of the database's modules for one named

FIGURE
21-3
A report using the Proper function procedure

Proper. Access uses this function procedure to convert all of the first and last names to proper case.

The other time procedures are run is when you use a procedure in a macro. You can use a procedure either as one of a macro's actions or as a condition. To create a macro action that runs a function procedure, select the RunCode action in the Action column and the name of the function procedure for the Function Name argument. If the function procedure uses any arguments, you must supply them in parentheses as well. For example, you might enter **Proper ([Last Name])** for the Function Name argument. The value the function procedure returns when Access performs the RunCode macro action is ignored.

If you use a function procedure as part of a macro action's condition, Access evaluates the condition to decide whether to perform a macro action. Include the function procedure just like you would use any other Access function in a condition. For example, you might have a function procedure that calculates the percentage difference between your employee billing rates and pay rates. To use this function procedure in a macros condition to find records where the markup percentage is more than 25 percent, the condition may look like this:

```
PercentMarkUp([Bill Rate],[Pay Rate])>25%
```

In this case, Access uses the result of the function procedure since the result of the condition that uses the function procedure determines whether a macro action is performed.

Later in the chapter, you will learn how to run a procedure from the module window by using the Immediate window. The Immediate window is a debugging tool Access provides to help you find errors in a procedure. Also, later you will see an example of running a sub procedure. Sub procedures are run from function procedures. Sub procedures do not use parentheses around their arguments, but multiple arguments are separated with commas.

Programming with Access Basic

Programming in Access Basic has many possibilities. You select what a procedure does through the information you place in a procedure. When creating your own procedures, you will want to plan and comment the statements you add to your procedures. Most procedures use variables; you will learn about their types and the different information they can represent shortly. Access Basic has many statements providing repetitive and selective processing that you will incorporate into your own procedures. Access Basic also has methods that you use to work with data stored in the different Access Basic objects. This is just an introduction to programming with Access Basic so as you try to create your own procedures you will be learning about Access Basic features that are beyond the basics presented here.

Planning and Adding Comments to Your Procedures

When creating procedures that are longer than a single line, you will need to plan the statements you will be entering. Rather than focusing on exact tasks, you will make planning procedures easier if you first think of the tasks you want to perform and later convert the tasks into exact statements.

Figure 21-4 shows the PCase procedure that has the tasks the procedure will perform. The text describes these steps as if you are describing these tasks to another person. These tasks also act as placeholders. The task descriptions temporarily fill lines that you know need to contain a statement—yet you are not yet sure what that statement will be. Later, when you know what that statement is, you can add it. Using the placeholder comment lets you know where the statement belongs and is a reminder to prevent you from forgetting a crucial step.

All of the lines of description in Figure 21-4 start with a single quote. The single quote tells Access that the text following is a *comment.* Comments in a procedure are like comments in a macro. They describe the purpose of each of the statements. When you look back later at a procedure, you can quickly determine what each of the statements accomplishes. While Access Basic does not require them, comments are a good idea so your procedures will not be abandoned when you forget what the lines represent. You can use the descriptions of the tasks the procedure completes as the comments after you add the statements to perform the task. Figure 21-5 shows the PCase procedure shown in Figure 21-4 after adding the statements to complete the function procedure.

FIGURE 21-4

Comments in a procedure to lay out the tasks to perform

```
=                    Module: Custom Functions                    ▼ ▲
Function PCase (OldText)
'for 1 to the length of OldText
'    get that numbered character out of OldText & put in CurrentChar
'    Is CurrentChar a space?
'        If so, you have a word
'            Take existing word and make it proper case
'            Add word to NewPhrase
'        If not, add character to CurrentWord
End Function
```

FIGURE 21-5

The PCase procedure after adding statements

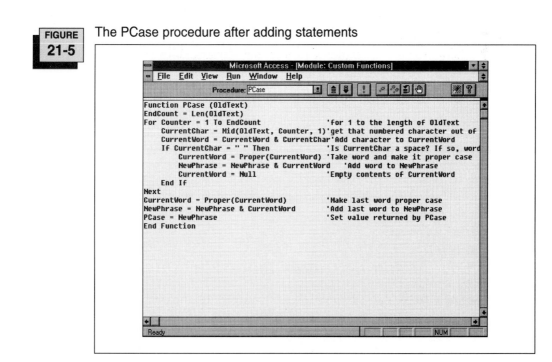

```
=          Microsoft Access - [Module: Custom Functions]          ▼ ▲
= File  Edit  View  Run  Window  Help
         Procedure: PCase
Function PCase (OldText)
EndCount = Len(OldText)
For Counter = 1 To EndCount                 'for 1 to the length of OldText
    CurrentChar = Mid(OldText, Counter, 1)'get that numbered character out of
    CurrentWord = CurrentWord & CurrentChar'Add character to CurrentWord
    If CurrentChar = " " Then               'Is CurrentChar a space? If so, word
        CurrentWord = Proper(CurrentWord) 'Take word and make it proper case
        NewPhrase = NewPhrase & CurrentWord   'Add word to NewPhrase
        CurrentWord = Null                  'Empty contents of CurrentWord
    End If
Next
CurrentWord = Proper(CurrentWord)            'Make last word proper case
NewPhrase = NewPhrase & CurrentWord          'Add last word to NewPhrase
PCase = NewPhrase                            'Set value returned by PCase
End Function

Ready                                                              NUM
```

Variables and Data Types in Access Basic

Variables let you store the data as a procedure performs each of the statements. Variables are temporary storage facilities available to a procedure. Think of variables as Post-it™ notes containing different information. The procedure can create these variable Post-it notes and change the data placed on each one. Usually, when Access is done with a procedure, it takes all of these little Post-it™ notes that it has created and throws them out.

Variable names follow Access Basic naming conventions. This means you can include up to 40 letters, numbers, and underscores. The variable name must start with a letter. Variable names cannot have the same name as a procedure, a global variable, a global constant, an Access Basic statement, a function, an operator, or a method.

When a procedure contains something that looks like a variable name and is in a location where a variable name is allowed, Access creates a variable with that name. To help you keep track of all of the variables in a procedure, use a *Dim statement*. Dim is followed by the variable names and possibly their type. The following is an example of a Dim statement:

```
Dim My_Number As Integer, My_Date as Variant, OldText as String
```

Most of the variables you use are Variant data types. Variant data types have the wonderful ability to accept most types of data. (However, keep in mind that Access can perform procedures more efficiently when it knows the data types of the variables.) Most of the examples in this chapter use the Variant data type because this data type provides the most flexibility. The other available types are Integer, Long, Short, Double, Currency, String (for text), and User-defined (created by defining how the data is formatted). You can define the data types when you want to be sure that only a particular type of data is accepted.

Local, Module, and Global Variables

When you use variables in modules, some are shared by all procedures in a module (global), some are shared with any procedure (module), and some are only available to a single procedure (local). All local and global mean when applied to variables is how long a variable lasts and which procedures can use the values the variables contain.

When you use the different variables in Access Basic, you initially will not have to worry about whether you are creating local, module, or global variables. The only time the variable scope makes a difference is when you try using a module variable and a local variable with the same name or a global variable with either a module or global variable. In either case, the procedure will not work.

Local Variables Most variables in procedures are local variables. When you are done with the procedure, the variable disappears. If the procedure calls another one, the procedure that is called has access to all of its variables as well as all of the ones in the procedure that called it. Local variables are the variables you use within a procedure that are either defined with a Dim statement or are not defined at all.

Module Variables If you want to have a variable that all procedures in a module can share, you want a module variable. To create these variables, use the Dim statement to declare them but declare them in the declarations section of the procedure.

Global Variables Global variables are available in any procedure of any module in the database. To create global variables, declare them in the declarations section of the procedure but use Global in place of Dim. With module and global variables, the current values of these variables remain as long as the database is open.

Global constants are text that represent specific values. Access has defined some of them such as True, False, and Null. You can create your own—for example, if working with circles in several procedures in a module, you might define a global constant of pi that always equals 3.141592. Using the global constant means you use pi in a statement every time you want to use the value of 3.141592.

Object Variables

Besides having variables to represent specific types of data, you can have variables representing objects. For example, instead of having a variable that equals the current value of a client name, you can have a variable that represents the Client Name control in a form or report. Object variables have eight types that select the type of object an object variable represents. These types are Database, Form, Report, Control, QueryDef for the query definition, Table, Dynaset for a table or query containing data you can edit, and snapshot for a table or query containing data you cannot edit. To use an object variable in a procedure, you must define it. For example, you can have a Dim statement in a procedure that looks like this:

```
Dim My_DB as Database, My_Table as Table, My_Client as Control
```

With these variables defined, you subsequently can use My_DB for the database, My_Table for the table the procedure uses, and My_Client for the Client Name control in a form or report. Access also has two other objects that you can use in place of an object variable when you want to refer to these objects. These are like predefined object variables. *Screen* represents the current form, report, and control. *Debug* represents sending output to the Immediate window, which you will learn about later in the chapter.

To assign the object these object variables represent, you use the Set statement. The Set statement is like an expression prefix since you use Set, the object variable to assign, an equal sign, and the description of the object it represents. Often you are supplying an object identifier just like the ones you used for forms and reports. Here are some examples:

```
Set My_DB = CurrentDB()
Set My_Table = Forms![Employee Data - 3]
Set My_Table = Forms(Name_Table)
Set My_Client = Report![Handwritten Park Description]![Client
Name]
Set My_Client = My_Table![Client Name]
```

The difference between the two assignments for My_Table is that in the first example, My_Table represents the Employee Data - 3 form. In the second example, My_Table represents the form with the same name as the entry placed in the Name_Table variable. The contents of Name_Table is either set by a previous statement or it is sent to the procedure as an argument when you use it so the form that My_Table represents changes every time you use it. With the two examples that set the value of My_Client, the first one selects My_Client to represent the

Client Name control of a specific report while the second example selects My_Client to represent the Client Name control of the form represented by the My_Table object variable.

Object Variables that are sent as an argument to another procedure must be identified in the procedure as such. For example, in the NextControl procedure that accepts a control as an argument that NextControl identifies as ThisControl, the first line of the procedure is Sub NextControl (ThisControl As Control). The As indicates that you are providing the data type and the Control identifies the variable as an object variable for a control.

This example purposefully uses a sub procedure because you cannot use object variables as arguments for function procedures. You can send an object to a function procedure, and the function procedure uses the value of that object. For example, you can use the object variable My_Client, which represents the Client Name control of a form to a function procedure, and the function procedure uses the current value of that control.

Nesting Procedures

Besides running a single procedure, you can have one procedure that runs others. This process is called *nesting procedures*. To run a sub procedure, you must use a function procedure that calls the sub procedure. At other times, you will have a group of statements that you want to run repetitively. Put the same statements into a single procedure and then run the procedure every time you want to run the statements the procedure contains. Putting frequently used statements in a procedure that other procedures can use makes creating procedures faster because you have chunks of statements that you know already run correctly.

When one procedure calls another, the procedure that has just been called begins processing. Only when the called procedure is finished does Access continue with the procedure that called the other one.

As an example, suppose you want a function procedure to convert text into proper case but unlike the Proper function procedure you saw earlier, you want each word of the phrase in proper case. A procedure that performs this for you can divide each word in a phrase and then use the Proper function procedure to make each word proper case. Before all of the statements that the PCase function procedure will use are completed, the procedure might look like Figure 21-6.

This PCase function procedure uses the Proper function procedure twice. The first time Proper is used is during the loop. This loop goes through each character of the text it is given. Then, the procedure tests whether the last character of the current word is a space. If it is a space, the procedure sends this current word to the Proper function procedure to let the Proper function procedure convert the word into proper case. Then, after adding the word the function procedure will return to the phrase and the loop continues until the procedure finds the next word. When the PCase procedure gets to the end of the text, the procedure uses the Proper function procedure one last time to make sure the last word is proper case. Using the Proper function procedure in place of the lengthy formula makes the procedure easier to understand.

FIGURE 21-6   A partially completed PCase function to show procedure nesting

```
Microsoft Access - [Module: Custom Functions]
 File   Edit   View   Run   Window   Help
                    Procedure: PCase

Function PCase (OldText)
'Count the number of characters in the text

'Repeat loop for each character of the text
    'Get that numbered character out of OldText and put in CurrentChar
    CurrentWord = CurrentWord & CurrentChar'Add character to CurrentWord

    'If the CurrentChar is a space, do these next three steps:
       'Use the Proper function procedure to convert the current word
       CurrentWord = Proper(CurrentWord) 'Take word and make it proper case
       NewPhrase = NewPhrase & CurrentWord     'Add word to NewPhrase
       CurrentWord = Null               'Empty contents of CurrentWord

'Go to the top of the loop and repeat for the next character

CurrentWord = Proper(CurrentWord)       'Make last word proper case
NewPhrase = NewPhrase & CurrentWord     'Add last word to NewPhrase
PCase = NewPhrase                       'Set value returned by PCase
End Function


Ready
```

Adding Repetitive Processing

Access has five statements you can use in a procedure to have Access repeat a section of code. These five statements have similar control structures in most other programming languages. Access has the For ... Next statement, the If ... Then ... Else statement, the Select Case statement, the Do ... Loop statement, and the While ... Wend statement. Each of these selectively performs a group of statements a specific number of times or the number of times set by a condition you create.

The For ... Next Statement

To use the For ... Next statement, you have a counter variable that varies from one value to another. For the procedure shown in Figure 21-7, the counter is Counter and its value ranges from 1 to the length of the text this function accepts. After the For statement are the statements you

FIGURE 21-7

Using For ... Next and If ... Then ... Else statements in a procedure

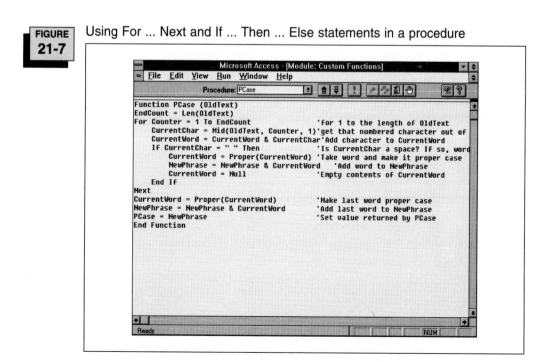

want repeatedly performed each time Access goes through the loop. At the end of these statements is the Next statement, which tells Access the loop is finished and to repeat the loop again if necessary.

For the procedure in Figure 21-7, Access repeatedly performs the statements between the expression that sets the value of the CurrentChar (that uses the value of Counter to select which character to return) and the End If statement.

The If ... Then ... Else Statement

To use the If ... Then ... Else statement, you place a logical condition between the If and the Then. Every time this statement is performed, Access checks whether the condition is true. When the condition is true, Access performs the statements below the If ... Then statement until an Else or End If statement. If the condition is false, Access checks whether the statements between the If ... Then and the End If have an Else statement. If Access finds an Else statement, Access performs the statements between the Else and the End If. If Access does not find an Else statement, Access skips to the statements after the End If statement.

For the procedure in Figure 21-7, the condition is whether the current character is a space. When the current character is a space, Access performs the three statements between the If ... Then and the End If statements. When the current character is not a space, Access skips to the Next statement because this section of the procedure does not have an Else statement.

The Select Case Statement

The Select Case statement is a variation of the If ... Then ... Else statement. After Select Case, you place the expression to be evaluated. Under this statement, you place Case and a potential value of the expression. Below Case and until the next Case or End Select, you place the statements Access performs when the value of the expression equals the value after Case. Case followed by additional statements can be created for every potential value you want to check. If you include a Case Else statement at the end of the cases, Access performs the statements between the Case Else statement and the End Select statement when the expression does not equal the values of the case statements above. The End Select statement indicates the end of the cases the Select Case statement checks for.

The Select Case statement is usually used in place of If ... Then ... Else when you have more than one situation to test. Figure 21-8 shows the same procedure function that uses the Select Case in place of the If ... Then statement. For this procedure, the Select Case checks the value of the entry in CurrentChar. When the character is a space, the three statements below Case " " are performed. For all other cases, Access performs any statements between Case Else and End Select.

The Do ... Loop and the While ... Wend Statements

To use the Do ... Loop or the While ... Wend statements, you have a condition that is tested. When Access performs the procedure, Access checks whether the condition is true, and if the condition is true, the statements between the beginning and end of these statements are performed. If the condition is false, Access skips to the statements after the Loop or Wend statement.

Using Do ... Loop and Select Case statements in a procedure

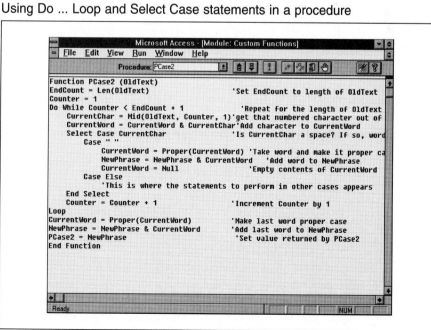

Figure 21-8 shows the Proper procedure function that uses Do ... Loop in place of the For ... Next statement. For this procedure, the variable Counter must be set and initialized. After Do While is the condition that checks whether Access has processed all of the characters in OldText. After the Do While statement are the statements you want performed each time the condition is true. At the end of these statements is the Loop statement, which tells Access the loop is finished and to test the condition again to repeat the loop if necessary. For the procedure in Figure 21-8, the statements Access repeatedly performs during each repetition of the loop are the statements between the expression that sets the value of the CurrentChar that uses the value of Counter to select which character to return, and the expression that increments the value of the Counter variable by 1.

Nesting Repetitive Statements

The procedures in Figures 21-7 and 21-8 contain two sets of repetitive processing statements. Notice how each set of repetitive processing statements is entirely placed inside one another. This is called nesting. Think of nesting as placing a set of variously sized mixing bowls inside each other. When you use multiple sets of repetitive processing statements in a procedure, they must either be sequential or nested. Sequential sets of repetitive processing statements are performed one after each other.

 Warning   Procedures cannot start a second set of repetitive processing statements with the first one ending before the second one ends. If you try doing this in one of your procedures, you will get error messages when you use the procedure that says you are missing part of a set of a repetitive processing statement.

Adding Methods to Your Modules

Methods are the means to work with the data contained in an object. Methods are like actions or statements except they only operate and are combined with specific objects. As such, you separate the method from the object variable that represents the object the method operates on with a period. An example is CreateTheSnapshot.MoveNext. MoveNext is the method that moves to the next record in the object variable represented by CreateTheSnapshot since CreateTheSnapshot is supplied as the object. Methods are like procedures in that they are provided information and possibly return some result. A method also may look like a function because methods often have arguments that are supplied after the method's name. Each of the different object variable types can have methods.

Methods have two types of behaviors. They can perform a task like a statement. These methods are entered as a statement so you might have CreateTheSnapshot.MoveNext entered on its own line in a procedure. MoveNext is the method that moves to the next record in the data represented by the CreateTheSnapshot object variable since CreateTheSnapshot is supplied as the object.

The other way methods behave is like a function. The method in this case returns a result that you want to put somewhere. The method's result can be another object or a value. An example is the statement CreateThe Snapshot=My_DB.ListTables( ). In this example, Access performs the ListTables method on the database selected by the My_DB object variable. The ListTables method creates a snapshot of the tables and queries you have in a database. A *snapshot* is a dynaset that captures the information at one point in time without updating the dynaset as the underlying data changes. This example of a method that acts as a function or function procedure stores the result of the method, a dynaset, into an object variable called CreateTheSnapshot.

Tip   To help remember whether to use an exclamation point or period to separate parts of an identifier, look at the part of the entry that appears after the exclamation point or period. If Access has determined that name, as with object properties, use a period. If you have created that name (or someone else using Microsoft Access has created it), use an exclamation point.

As an example of adding methods to a module, suppose you want to be able to enter a name and have Access, through macros and modules, tell you whether the name is the name of a table or query. First, create the form that contains a command button to perform a macro. Using a command button in a form lets you run the module that checks for the table or query name. The command button in Figure 21-9 has its On Push property set to Macro for Perform Tasks Form. When you click this

FIGURE
21-9

A command button to run a macro and the RunCode action the macro performs

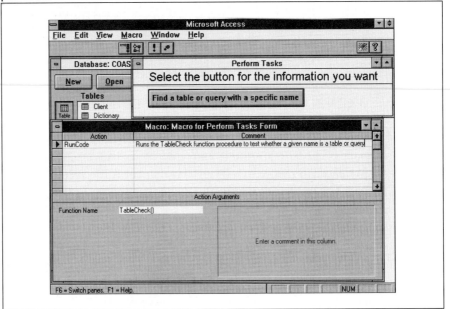

button or press ENTER, Access performs the Macro for Perform Tasks Form form. This macro is very simple since it only contains one action: the action RunCode and TableCheck() as the Function Name argument. You must enter a function procedure for the Function Name argument. When you run this macro, Access runs the TableCheck function procedure. If this TableCheck function procedure returns a value, Access will ignore it.

Now all you need are the procedures that find the table or query. These two procedures are shown in Figure 21-10. The TableCheck procedure is on the top. All this procedure does is call the IsItATable procedure. The IsItATable procedure is a sub procedure so it is entered as a statement. It does not use any arguments. The IsItATable procedure is the real workhorse of this application.

First, the Dim statement declares all of the object variables this procedure will use. Next, the Set statement sets the My_DB to represent the current database. Since you need to include the database when you

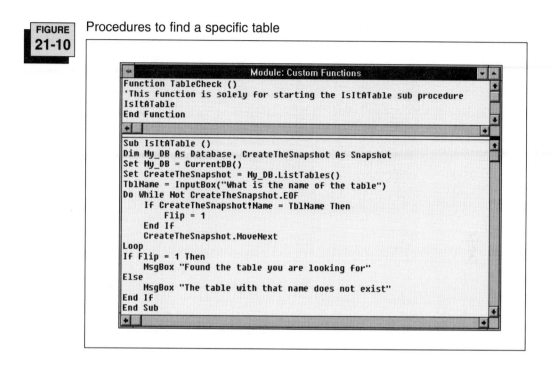

FIGURE 21-10

Procedures to find a specific table

```
                    Module: Custom Functions
Function TableCheck ()
'This function is solely for starting the IsItATable sub procedure
IsItATable
End Function

Sub IsItATable ()
Dim My_DB As Database, CreateTheSnapshot As Snapshot
Set My_DB = CurrentDB()
Set CreateTheSnapshot = My_DB.ListTables()
TblName = InputBox("What is the name of the table")
Do While Not CreateTheSnapshot.EOF
    If CreateTheSnapshot!Name = TblName Then
        Flip = 1
    End If
    CreateTheSnapshot.MoveNext
Loop
If Flip = 1 Then
    MsgBox "Found the table you are looking for"
Else
    MsgBox "The table with that name does not exist"
End If
End Sub
```

work with most of the other objects in a procedure, the Dim and the Set statements for the My_DB object variable often appear together. Next, the Set CreateTheSnapshot = My_DB.ListTables() statement creates a snapshot dynaset. This dynaset is created by the ListTables method. This method creates a snapshot dynaset that includes information about every table and query in the database. For this example, you are interested in the Name field of this data since the Name field is a Text data type that contains the names of the different tables and queries in the database. The resulting dynaset is represented in this procedure by the CreateThe Snapshot snapshot object variable.

Now, the procedure prompts for the name of the table or query that you are looking for. InputBox is a function that requires the text to appear as the prompt. When this function is performed, Access displays a dialog box like the one shown in Figure 21-11. The entry you make into this dialog box is the result of the InputBox function. This result is stored in the TblName variable. The Do While statement goes through each record in the dynaset represented by the CreateTheSnapshot object variable.

FIGURE
21-11
The dialog box displayed by InputBox function

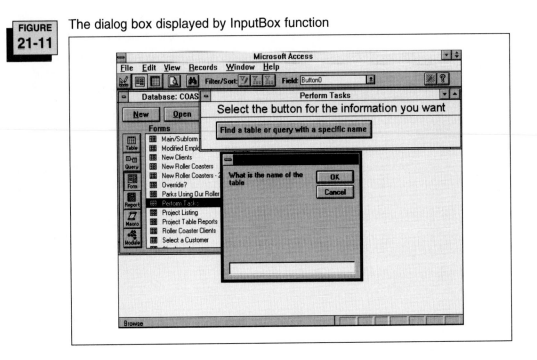

Within the Do ... Loop statements is CreateTheSnapshot. MoveNext. Snapshots as well as queries and tables have records that you can move between. When you open or create one of these objects, you are at the top record. The MoveNext method moves to the next record. For each record in the snapshot, the If ... End If statements check if the value of the Name field of the data represented by the CreateTheSnapshot object variable matches what you entered in the dialog box like the one shown in Figure 21-11. When the procedure finds an entry in the Name field that matches the entry in the TblName variable, the Flip=1 statement assigns a value to the Flip variable. This variable is *reinitialized*, or started over, every time you run the procedure.

After the procedure checks every record in the CreateTheSnapshot object variable, the second set of If ... End If statements checks the value of Flip. If Flip equals 1, the procedure has found the table name in the CreateTheSnapshot object variable during its review of every record. When Flip equals anything else, the procedure did not find the record.

In either case, the MsgBox statements display an appropriate message. Once the message is displayed and the user selects OK, Access returns to the TableCheck function procedure since it performs the End Sub statement. Since the TableCheck function procedure has only the End Function statement after the IsItATable statement, both procedures are completed. If the macro had any other actions after the RunCode action, they would be performed now. Since this macro has only the one action, Access returns to the form.

This example shows just the basics of how to use methods. You can continue to try the different methods for each of the object variable types.

Tip   Up to this point, you have seen many properties with spaces in their names. When you use property names in Access Basic, make sure that you do not include a space. For example, the Display When property appears as DisplayWhen.

Finding Mistakes in Your Procedures

While Access checks your entries as you make them, Access does not find every mistake you make. For example, the procedure in Figure 21-12 has the correct syntax for all of the statements but when you try to use

FIGURE 21-12

A procedure with a missing statement so nothing is returned

```
Module: Custom Functions
Function PCase (OldText)
EndCount = Len(OldText)
For Counter = 1 To EndCount                    'for 1 to the length of OldTe
    CurrentChar = Mid(OldText, Counter, 1)'get that numbered character
    CurrentWord = CurrentWord & CurrentChar'Add character to CurrentWor
    If CurrentChar = " " Then                  'Is CurrentChar a space? If s
        CurrentWord = Proper(CurrentWord) 'Take word and make it proper
        NewPhrase = NewPhrase & CurrentWord    'Add word to NewPhrase
        CurrentWord = Null                     'Empty contents of CurrentWor
    End If
Next
CurrentWord = Proper(CurrentWord)              'Make last word proper case
NewPhrase = NewPhrase & CurrentWord            'Add last word to NewPhrase
End Function
```

it, the function returns an empty string. Access has checked and found that none of the statements are entered incorrectly but Access has not checked that you have assigned a value to the PCase function. When you are trying to find mistakes like this, you need to be able to watch the module run so you can follow each statement as Access performs it.

Access has several features that assist you in finding errors in a module. These features include compiling the procedures, running them a step at a time, and displaying a window you can use as a scratch pad to test how a procedure is functioning.

Compiling Procedures in a Module

When you use a procedure, Access *compiles* it, which is a process that converts the statements you have entered into the instructions it internally uses to perform the procedure. You can make a procedure run faster the first time by compiling it. Also, as you work on a module, you can compile it to find any errors you have overlooked.

To compile the procedures in the active module, select Compile All from the Run menu. Access starts with the current procedure and checks each of the procedures in the module for various types of errors. If Access cannot find any errors, the compilation is finished. You will not see any message but when you look at the Run menu again, you will see that Compile All is dimmed since the module is already compiled.

If an error is found, Access displays the procedure, highlights the statement it thinks is the problem, and displays a message saying what it thinks the problem is. Figure 21-13 shows an example of this since the statement that ends the For ... Next loop is mistakenly entered as End. You can see from this example that sometimes Access does not choose the line with the problem.

Running a Procedure One Step at a Time

You often can find procedures that contain an error faster when you run the procedure a step at a time. Running a procedure one step at a time lets you watch the statements Access performs.

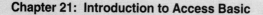

FIGURE 21-13 The message returned when a module is unsuccessfully compiled

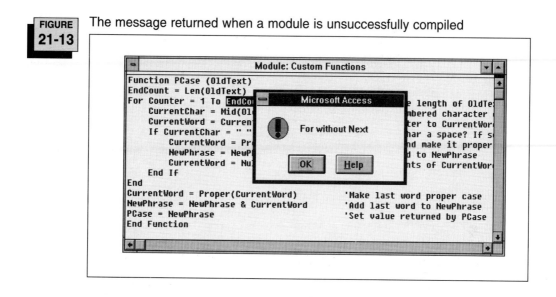

To set a procedure a step at a time, you need to add a *breakpoint*. A breakpoint is a statement that when reached, Access stops performing the procedure. You can choose to run the procedure one step at a time, restart, or continue running it. To add a breakpoint, add the Stop statement to a procedure. You also can move to a statement that you want to use as a breakpoint and choose Toggle Breakpoint from the Run menu, press F9, or, from the toolbar, click the Breakpoint button, which looks like this:

When you set a breakpoint this way, the selected statement appears bold. The difference between adding a breakpoint to a specific statement and adding the Stop statement to a procedure is the permanence of the breakpoint. When you add a Stop statement to a procedure, the breakpoint remains there until you remove it. When you add a toggle breakpoint that boldfaces a specific statement, the breakpoint only remains while the module window is open. When the module window is closed, the breakpoint is removed. Most of the time you will use temporary breakpoints and reserve Stop for when you are working with a lengthy procedure.

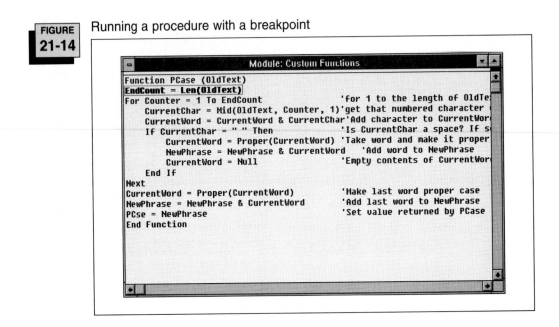

FIGURE 21-14

Running a procedure with a breakpoint

Once a procedure is set to run, the procedure runs at regular speed until Access gets to the Stop statement or the statement you have set as a breakpoint. At this point, the module window is placed on top as shown in Figure 21-14. You can see how the temporary breakpoint is boldfaced. You also can see the box around one of the statements. This box indicates the next statement Access performs. To run the next statement, choose Single Step from the Run menu, press F8, or click the Single Step button shown here:

Each time you choose Single Step from the Run menu, press F8, or click the Single Step button, Access performs the next statement. You can run the procedure at regular speed by choosing Continue in the Run menu, pressing F5, or clicking the Run button, which looks like this:

When a procedure calls another procedure, like the PCase function procedure calls the Proper function procedure in Figure 21-14, Access runs the called procedure one statement at a time as well. If you already know that the called procedure works correctly, you may want to run just the first procedure at regular speed. For example, when the PCase procedure calls the Proper procedure, you may not want to watch the Proper procedure operate one statement at a time since you know that Proper runs correctly.

You can operate a procedure you are about to call at regular speed and continue with single step viewing after the procedure is completed. To run a procedure at regular speed, when the box is around the statement that calls the other procedure, choose Procedure Step from the Run menu, press SHIFT-F8, or click the Procedure Step button shown here:

If you suddenly realize you have made a mistake in the procedure, you can fix it. For example, in the procedure in Figure 21-14, the next-to-last statement has PCase spelled as PCse. You can edit the statement and fix the error. If the statement occurs after the box, Access will use the updated statement. If the statement you change is before the statement with the box, the change made by the statement does not affect the procedure's performance but it is retained so the next time you use the procedure, the procedure will include the change.

A special feature available when you run a procedure one step at a time is that you can change which statement Access will perform next. This feature is often used when the error you have just fixed occurs before the next statement. To change which statement is next, move to that line and select Set Next Statement from the Run menu.

You also can change a procedure when you are running it one step at a time by restarting it. You might want to do this when you have just fixed an error that prevents the procedure from performing correctly. To restart a procedure, change the next statement to perform to be the one after the Function or Sub statement at the beginning. Also, you want all of the values in the procedure to be restarted as if you had not run the procedure yet. To do this, choose Reinitialize from the Run menu or click the Reinitialize button, which looks like this:

After you select the next statement to perform and reinitialize the values, you are ready to start executing the procedure. You can start the procedure at this point by clicking one of the toolbar buttons, or using the statements in the Run menu.

Using the Immediate Window

Watching Access perform a procedure one step at a time helps you spot a potential error; another especially helpful feature is being able to find the values of different variables as you run the procedure. For example, when you run the procedure in Figure 21-14, you may want to know the current values of CurrentChar and CurrentWord. Access provides you with this ability through the Immediate window. This window is put on top of the module window just like a property sheet always appears on top of the table, form, or report you are designing. You also can use the Immediate window to run procedures. You will find this especially useful with function procedures since you want to try the procedure using different values.

To display this window, choose Immediate Window from the View menu and Access adds the window like the one shown in Figure 21-15. Select this command again when you want to remove the window. This window is empty but so is any scratch pad when you start to use it. The Immediate window is used either to run procedures or to test them. Most of your entries in the window start with a ?. The question mark tells Access that you want Access to give you the value of the expression you enter. After you type the entry you want, test on a line in the Immediate window by pressing ENTER. This tells Access to process whatever is on the line. Your entry and the result remain in the window until replaced by another entry. You can always repeat one of the entries you have made in the Immediate window by moving to the line with the arrow keys and then pressing ENTER.

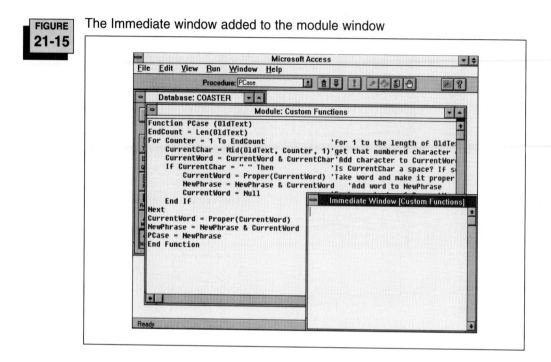

FIGURE 21-15 The Immediate window added to the module window

To run a procedure through the Immediate window, type **?** followed by the procedure name and any arguments.

Reminder Function procedures have their arguments enclosed in parentheses but sub functions do not.

To run the PCase function with the text "my new CAR", type **? PCase("my new CAR")** and press ENTER. Access performs the procedure and returns the result on the next line. If Access returns My New Car, you know the procedure is running correctly. If you do not get that as a result, the procedure has an error; you may want to add a breakpoint to the procedure to run it a step at a time.

When testing a procedure, you can test the values of the variable in the procedure through the Immediate window. Figure 21-16 shows the Immediate window while the PCase procedure is running one step at a time. In Figure 21-16, the Immediate window contains several prompts. These prompts are entered on several lines since Access does not care

The Immediate window with several requests processed

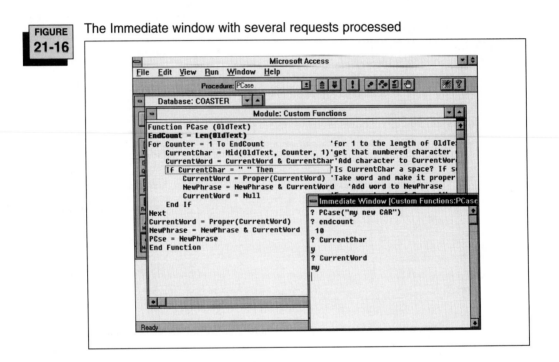

on which line in the Immediate window you make an entry. Access decides which line to process by the line that is active when you press ENTER. For the Immediate window in Figure 21-16, this feature of the Immediate window means you can constantly move to the line containing ? CurrentChar and press ENTER to repeatedly return the most up-to-date value of CurrentChar.

You also can enter one request for information while another is processing. For example, in Figure 21-16, the request for the PCase result is not complete yet other requests are prompting for variable values used to determine the PCase result.

Tip When using the Immediate window to find errors in a procedure, separate each entry you make by two or three lines. Leaving the extra lines means the entries remain on the window so you can return to them and repeat them.

Quick Reference

To Create a Module   Click the New button at the top of the database window while displaying modules, or choose New from the File menu and then Module.

To Create a Procedure   Type **Sub** or **Function** on an empty line followed by the name of the procedure and any arguments the procedure uses enclosed in parentheses. You can also choose New Procedure from the Edit menu, type the name of the function, and select OK.

To Change the Procedure Displayed   Display the previous procedure by pressing CTRL-UP ARROW, clicking the Previous Procedure button in the toolbar, and choosing Previous Procedure in the View menu. Display the next procedure by pressing CTRL-DOWN ARROW, clicking the Next Procedure button in the toolbar, and choosing Next Procedure in the View menu. An additional method of selecting which procedure you are viewing is to choose Procedures from the View menu or press F2 and then select the procedure you want to see.

To Print a Module   Choose Print from the File menu and select OK. You have all the same printing options you have for printing other database objects. All of the procedures and the declarations section are printed.

To Add a Breakpoint to a Module   Move to the statement that you want to be a breakpoint. Choose Toggle Breakpoint from the Run menu, press F9, or click the Breakpoint button in the toolbar.

To Display the Immediate Window   Choose Immediate Window from the View menu.

PART VII

Appendixes

APPENDIX

Installing Access

*T*he first step in using Access is to install it on your computer. In order to install all of Access, you should have about 11MB free on your hard disk. If you don't have that much space available, you can install just Access, without all of its features or ancillary applications, with only 3.7MB free on your hard disk.

1. Start Windows by typing **win** at the DOS prompt and press ENTER.

2. Select Run from the Program Manager's File menu.

3. Enter **A:\setup** in the Command Line text box, and select OK to start the Microsoft Access Setup application.

If your Access disks are in drive B, you should replace the A with a B as in B:\setup. After the initial screen, you are prompted to enter your name and company in the Name and Company text boxes. Select Continue, and then select Yes to confirm that the name and company you have entered is correct. If Access was previously installed on a system using the same disks, you will see a dialog box telling you that this is a copyrighted program, and warning you about copyright liabilities if you are installing it on a second machine. Select Continue to continue setting up Access, or select Cancel Setup to abort setup.

4. A dialog box indicating that older versions of .DLL files exist in the \WINDOWS\SYSTEMS directory may inform you that Access will not run unless these files are replaced. Select Replace File to continue or Abort Setup to exit the Setup program.

5. The Specify Directory dialog box opens showing the name of the directory to which Setup installs the Access program files. By default this is C:\ACCESS\. Enter the name of the directory you want the Access program installed to if it is different, and then select Continue to continue installing Access.

The setup program now examines your hard disk for available space, previously installed Access files, and how much space Access will require.

6. The Installation Options dialog box presents you with three choices for installing Access: 1. Complete installation, 2. Custom installation, and 3. Minimum installation. Complete installation installs all

Access files, and requires the most space on your hard disk (about 10.5MB). Custom installation installs only those elements of the program that you select. Minimum installation installs only those files necessary to run Access, and takes the least amount of space on your disk, about 3.7MB.

If you select the Custom Installation option, you will see the dialog box listing parts of the Microsoft Access package. Clear the check boxes of those parts that you do not want to install. The amount of space each part requires is listed beside the check boxes. Select specific ISAM drivers to install by choosing the Select button. Now you can select and clear check boxes in the opened dialog box.

7. In the Multiuser installation dialog box, you are asked if you want to join any existing workgroups. When you install Access as a multiuser application, you can use databases created by other users.

8. Access Setup prompts you for each disk as it finishes installing the preceding one. When prompted, insert the specified disk in the disk drive, and select OK.

When Microsoft Access Setup is finished installing from the disks, Access checks to see whether your AUTOEXEC.BAT file has the statement SHARE.EXE. This line in the AUTOEXEC.BAT file is required if you plan to use data from dBASE, Paradox, and Btrieve files. If you do not have SHARE.EXE in your AUTOEXEC.BAT file, Access Setup displays a dialog box asking if you want to add this line to your file. You have a choice of letting Access modify your AUTOEXEC.BAT file (and saving the original under the new name, AUTOEXEC.BAK), copying the file to a new file called AUTOEXEC.ACC and then modifying the copy, or not modifying the AUTOEXEC.BAT file at all. Choose the appropriate option and select Continue. If you select the first option, you will see a dialog box indicating that the AUTOEXEC.BAT file was successfully modified. Select OK to continue.

9. You may see a dialog box indicating that the FILES statement in AUTOEXEC.BAT is set to less than 50, and that it needs to be at

least 50 to allow DOS and Windows applications to run easily with Access loaded into memory. Select OK to continue.

10. A dialog box appears, indicating that you modified the SHARE statement in your AUTOEXEC.BAT file and therefore must restart your computer to allow the modified SHARE statement to take effect and allow you to run Access.

Installing the Open Database Connectivity (ODBC) Package

The last disk of the set you receive with Access is not required for installing Access. This disk contains another application, called the Open Database Connectivity Package, which allows you to use databases created on an SQL server. It installs various drivers, containing the information necessary to use data stored on an SQL server, and an administrative utility that associates specific files with specific drivers, so that using those files will be easier.

1. Enter **A:\setup** in the Command Line text box after selecting Run from the File menu of the Program Manager. Then select OK. If the ODBC disk is in drive B, you will want to replace the **A** with a **B** as in **B:\setup**.

2. Select Continue at the opening dialog box to install the ODBC package.

3. At the next dialog box, select or clear the appropriate check boxes. When the Install ODBC Drivers check box is selected, you can choose which drivers you want to install. When the Install ODBC Administrative Utility is selected, you install the utility that associates drivers with the databases that they access. Then select Continue.

4. The next dialog box presents the name of the directory on your hard drive into which the ODBC package will be read by Setup. By entering a new directory name in the text box, you can specify a different directory. To use the default directory, or after entering the

name of a different one, select Continue. Select Back to return to the previous dialog box.

5. If the directory specified in the previous dialog box does not exist, you are presented with a dialog box that asks if you want to create it. Select Create Directory to have it created, or select Another to choose a different directory.

6. Select the drivers that you want to install from the Available Drivers list box. Then select the Install button. These drivers are transferred to the Installed Drivers list box. If you decide you do not want to install one of the drivers in the Installed Drivers list box, select it and then select the Remove button. You can select or clear all of the drivers in the Available Drivers list box by selecting the Select All or the Clear All buttons. When finished selecting drivers to install, select Continue.

7. In the next dialog box, you can set up a new data source (or file) to install by highlighting the driver in the Installed Drivers list box, selecting Add New Name, and then selecting the file. Alternatively, select an installed data source from the Installed Data Sources (Drivers) list box and select either Configure or Remove. After installing all the data sources, select Continue.

8. Select OK, and restart your computer so that the ODBC package is available for use. Install it on your computer. The Microsoft ODBC Administrator application is added to a Microsoft ODBC group window.

APPENDIX

Glossary of Access Functions

Access has 135 functions that you can use in expressions. The expressions you use them in include validation rules for data entry, calculated entries in forms and reports, and macros and modules. This appendix lists all of the functions in alphabetical order. For each function, the text lists the syntax and a brief description of the function's results. The text in italics should be replaced by the value you want the function to use. Function arguments in brackets ([ ]) are optional and only need to be supplied when you want to use the feature the optional argument provides. The parentheses and any commas are a required part of the function.

ABS

Syntax   Abs(*number*)

Returns the absolute value of the number.

ASC

Syntax   Asc(*string expression*)

Returns the ANSI code number for the first character in a string expression.

ATN

Syntax   Atn(*number*)

Returns the arctangent of the *number*.

AVG

Syntax   Avg(*expression*)

Returns the arithmetic mean of a set of values within a specified field on a query, form, or report.

CCUR

Syntax CCur(*expression*)

Explicitly converts any valid expression to the Currency data type.

CDBL

Syntax CDbl(*expression*)

Explicitly converts any valid expression to the Double data type.

CHOOSE

Syntax Choose(*index number,variable expression*[*,variable expression*]...)

Selects and returns a value from a list of arguments.

CHR, CHR$

Syntax Chr[$](*character code*)

Returns the character for which the argument is the ANSI character code. Chr returns a Variant; Chr$ returns a string.

CINT

Syntax CInt(*expression*)

Explicitly converts any valid expression to the Integer data type.

CLNG

Syntax CLng(*expression*)

Explicitly converts any valid expression to the Long data type.

COMMAND, COMMAND$

Syntax   Command[$][()]

Returns the argument portion of the command line used to launch Access. Command returns a Variant; Command$ returns a string.

COS

Syntax   Cos(*angle*)

Returns the cosine of an angle measured in radians.

COUNT

Syntax   Count(*expression*)

Returns the number of selected records in a query, form, or report.

CSNG

Syntax   CSng(*expression*)

Explicitly converts any valid expression to the single data type.

CSTR

Syntax   CStr(*expression*)

Explicitly converts any valid expression to the string data type.

CURDIR, CURDIR$

Syntax   CurDir[$][(*drive*)]

Returns the current path for the specified drive. CurDir returns a Variant; CurDir$ returns a string.

CURRENTDB

Syntax CurrentDB()

Returns a database object for the current database.

CVAR

Syntax CVar(*expression*)

Explicitly converts any valid expression to the Variant data type.

CVDATE

Syntax CVDate(*expression*)

Converts an expression to a Variant of VarType 7 (Date).

DATE, DATE$

Syntax Date[$][()]

Returns the current system date. Date returns a Variant; Date$ returns a ten-character string.

DATEADD

Syntax DateAdd(*interval, number, date*)

Returns a Variant of VarType 7 (Date) to which a specified time interval has been added.

DATEDIFF

Syntax DateDiff(*interval, date1, date2*)

Returns a Variant that contains the number of time intervals between two specified dates.

DATEPART

Syntax   DatcPart(*interval,date*)

Returns a specified part of a given date.

DATESERIAL

Syntax   DateSerial(*year,month,day*)

Returns the date serial number for a specific year, month, and day.

DATEVALUE

Syntax   DateValue(*string expression*)

Returns the date represented by the string.

DAVG

Syntax   DAvg(*expression,domain[,criteria]*)

Returns the arithmetic mean of a set of values in the domain, a specified set of records.

DAY

Syntax   Day(*number*)

Returns an integer between 1 and 31 representing the day of the month for the number argument.

DCOUNT

Syntax   DCount(*expression,domain[,criteria]*)

Returns the number of selected records in the domain, a specified set of records.

DDB

Syntax   DDB(*cost,salvage,life,period*)

Uses the double-declining balance method to calculate the depreciation of an asset for a specific period.

DDE

Syntax   DDE(*application,topic,item*)

Initiates a dynamic-data exchange (DDE) conversation with another application, requesting an item of information from that application.

DDEINITIATE

Syntax   DDEInitiate(*application,topic*)

Begins a dynamic-data exchange (DDE) conversation with another application.

DDEREQUEST

Syntax   DDERequest(*channel number,item*)

Uses an open dynamic-data exchange (DDE) channel to request an item of information from another application.

DDESEND

Syntax   DDESend(*application,topic,item,data*)

Initiates a dynamic-data exchange (DDE) conversation with another application and sends an item of information to that application.

DFIRST

Syntax   DFirst(*expression,domain[,criteria]*)

Returns a field value from the first record in a domain, a specified set of records.

DIR, DIR$

Syntax   Dir[$][(*filespec*)]

Returns a filename that matches a specified pattern. Dir returns a Variant; Dir$ returns a string.

DLAST

Syntax   DLast(*expression,domain*[*,criteria*])

Returns a field value from the last record in a domain, a specified set of records.

DLOOKUP

Syntax   DLookup(*expression,domain*[*,criteria*])

Returns a field value in a domain, a specified set of records.

DMAX

Syntax   DMax(*expression,domain*[*,criteria*])

Returns the maximum of a set of values in a domain, a specified set of records.

DMIN

Syntax   DMin(*expression,domain*[*,criteria*])

Returns the minimum of a set of values in a domain, a specified set of records.

DSTDEV

Syntax   DStDev(*expression,domain*[*,criteria*])

Returns estimates of the standard deviation for a population sample, represented as a set of values in a domain, a specified set of records.

DSTDEVP

Syntax DStDevP(*expression,domain[,criteria]*)

Returns estimates of the standard deviation for a population represented as a set of values in a domain, a specified set of records.

DSUM

Syntax DSum(*expression,domain[,criteria]*)

Returns the sum of a set of values in a domain, a specified set of records.

DVAR

Syntax DVar(*expression,domain[,criteria]*)

Returns estimates of the variance for a population sample represented by a set of values in a domain, a specified set of records.

DVARP

Syntax DVarP(*expression,domain[,criteria]*)

Returns estimates of variance for a population represented by a set of values in a domain, a specified set of records.

ENVIRON, ENVIRON$

Syntax Environ[$](*environment string*)

Environ[$](*n*)

Returns the string associated with an operating system environment variable. Environ returns a Variant; Environ$ returns a string.

EOF

Syntax EOF(*filenumber*)

Returns a value during file input that indicates whether or not the end of a file has been reached.

ERL

Syntax   Erl

Returns the line number of the line in which the error occurred, or the closest preceding line as an Integer.

ERR

Syntax   Err

Returns a run-time error code identifying the error as an Integer.

ERROR, ERROR$

Syntax   Error[$][(*error code*)]

Returns the error message that corresponds to a given error code. Error returns a Variant; Error$ returns a string.

EVAL

Syntax   Eval(*string expression*)

Returns the value of the evaluated expression.

EXP

Syntax   Exp(*number*)

Returns the base of natural logarithms (*e*) raised to a power.

FILEATTR

Syntax   FileAttr(*filenumber,attribute*)

Returns file mode or operating system file handle information about an open file.

FIRST

Syntax   First(*expression*)

Returns a field value from the first record in a query, form, or report.

FIX

Syntax   Fix(*number*)

Returns the integer portion of a number.

FORMAT, FORMAT$

Syntax   Format[$](*expression*[,*format*])

Formats a number, date, time, or string according to instructions contained in *format.* Format returns a Variant; Format$ returns a string.

FREEFILE

Syntax   FreeFile[()]

Returns the next valid unused file number.

FV

Syntax   FV(*rate,numperiods,payment,pvalue,due*)

Returns the future value of an annuity based on periodic, constant payments and a constant interest rate.

HEX, HEX$

Syntax   Hex[$](*number*)

Returns a string that represents a hexadecimal value of a decimal argument. Hex returns a Variant; Hex$ returns a string.

HOUR

Syntax   Hour(*number*)

Returns an integer between 0 and 23 that represents the hour of the day corresponding to the time serial number provided as *number*.

IIF

Syntax   IIf(*expression,truepart,falsepart*)

Returns one of two arguments depending on the evaluation of expression.

INPUT, INPUT$

Syntax   Input[$](*n,*[#] *filenumber*)

Returns characters read from a sequential file. Input returns a Variant; Input$ returns a string.

INPUTBOX, INPUTBOX$

Syntax   InputBox[$](*prompt*[,[*title*][,[*default*][,*xpos,ypos*]]])

Displays a dialog box with a prompt. Waits for text to be input or a button chosen, and returns the contents of the edit box. InputBox returns a Variant; InputBox$ returns a string.

INSTR

Syntax   InStr([*start,*]*string expression 1,string expression 2*)

InStr(*start,string expression 1,string expression 2,compare*)

Returns the position of the first occurrence of a string within another string.

INT

Syntax   Int(*number*)

Returns the integer portion of a number.

IPMT

Syntax   IPmt(*rate,period,numperiod,pvalue, fvalue,due*)

Returns the interest payment for a given period of an annuity based on periodic, constant payments and a constant interest rate.

IRR

Syntax   IRR(*valuearray(),guess*)

Returns the internal rate of return for a series of periodic cash flows.

ISDATE

Syntax   IsDate(*Variant*)

Returns a value indicating whether or not a Variant argument can be converted to a date.

ISEMPTY

Syntax   IsEmpty(*Variant*)

Returns a value indicating whether a Variant variable has been initialized.

ISNULL

Syntax   IsNull(*Variant*)

Returns a value that indicates whether a Variant contains the NULL value.

ISNUMERIC

Syntax   IsNumeric(*Variant*)

Returns a value indicating whether a Variant variable can be converted to a Number data type.

LAST

Syntax Last(*expression*)

Returns a field value from the last record in a query, form, or report.

LBOUND

Syntax LBound(*array*[,*dimension*])

Returns the smallest available subscript for the indicated dimension of an array.

LCASE, LCASE$

Syntax LCase[$](*string expression*)

Returns a string in which all letters of the argument are converted to lowercase. LCase returns a variant; LCase$ returns a string.

LEFT, LEFT$

Syntax Left[$](*string expression,n*)

Returns the leftmost *n* characters of a String argument. Left returns a Variant; Left$ returns a string.

LEN

Syntax Len(*string expression*)
Len(*variable name*)

Returns the number of characters in a string expression, or the number of bytes required to store a variable.

LOC

Syntax Loc(*file number*)

Returns the current position within an open file.

LOF

Syntax   LOF(*file number*)

Returns the size of an open file, measured in bytes.

LOG

Syntax   Log(*number*)

Returns the natural logarithm of a number.

LTRIM, LTRIM$

Syntax   LTrim[$](*string expression*)

Returns a copy of a string with the leading spaces removed. LTrim returns a Variant; LTrim$ returns a string.

MAX

Syntax   Max(*expression*)

Returns the maximum of a set of values contained in a specified field on a query, form, or report.

MID, MID$

Syntax   Mid[$](*string expression,start*[,*length*])

Returns a string that is part of another string. Mid returns a Variant; Mid$ returns a string.

MIN

Syntax   Min(*expression*)

Returns the minimum of a set of values contained in a specified field on a query, form, or report.

MINUTE

Syntax   Minute(*number*)

Returns an integer between 1 and 59 that represents the minute of the hour corresponding to the time serial number provided as an argument.

MIRR

Syntax   Mirr(*value array(), finance rate, reinvest rate*)

Returns the modified internal rate of return for a series of periodic cash flows.

MONTH

Syntax   Month(*number*)

Returns an integer between 1 and 12 that represents the month of the year for a date serial number argument.

MSGBOX

Syntax   MsgBox(*message*[;*type*[,title]])

Displays a message in a message box and returns a number depending on how the user leaves the message box.

NOW

Syntax   Now[()]

Returns a date that represents the current date and time according to the computer's system date and time settings.

NPER

Syntax   NPer(*rate,pmt,pvalue,fvalue,due*)

Returns the number of periods for an annuity based on periodic, constant payments and a constant rate of interest.

NPV

Syntax   NPV(*rate,value array()*)

Returns the net present value of an investment based on a series of periodic cash flows and a discount rate.

OCT, OCT$

Syntax   Oct[$](*number*)

Returns text that represents the octal value of the decimal argument. Oct returns a variant; Oct$ returns a string.

OPENDATABASE

Syntax   OpenDatabase(*database*[,*exclusive*[,*read-only*]])

Opens a specified database, and returns a database object for it.

PARTITION

Syntax   Partition(*number,start,stop,interval*)

Returns a string indicating where a number occurs within a calculated series of ranges.

PMT

Syntax   Pmt(*rate,numperiod,pvalue,fvalue,due*)

Returns the payment for an annuity based on periodic, constant payments and a constant interest rate.

PPMT

Syntax   PPmt(*rate,period,numperiod,pvalue,fvalue,due*)

Returns the principal payment for a given period of an annuity based on periodic, constant payments and a constant interest rate.

PV

Syntax   PV(*rate,numperiod,payment,fvalue,due*)

Returns the present value of an annuity based on periodic, constant payments to be paid in the future and a constant interest rate.

QBCOLOR

Syntax   QBColor(*qbcolor*)

Returns the RGB code for the selected color.

RATE

Syntax   Rate(*numperiod,payment,pvalue,fvalue,due,guess*)

Returns the interest rate per period for an annuity.

RGB

Syntax   RGB[(*red,green,blue*)]

Returns the RGB code for the color with the red, green, and blue amounts.

RIGHT, RIGHT$

Syntax   Right[$](*string expression,n*)

Returns the rightmost *n* characters of the string expression.

RND

Syntax   Rnd[(*number*)]

Returns a random number.

RTRIM, RTRIM$

Syntax RTrim[$](*String expression*)

Returns a copy of a string with the trailing spaces removed. RTrim returns a Variant; RTrim$ returns a string.

SECOND

Syntax Second(*number*)

Returns an integer between 0 and 59 that represents the second of the minute from the time number argument.

SEEK

Syntax Seek(*file number*)

Returns the current file position.

SGN

Syntax Sgn(*number*)

Returns a value that indicates the sign of a number.

SHELL

Syntax Shell(*command string*[,*window style*])

Runs an executable program.

SIN

Syntax Sin(*angle*)

Returns the sine of an angle measured in radians.

SLN

Syntax   SLN(*cost,salvage,life*)

Returns the straight-line depreciation of an asset for a single period.

SPACE, SPACE$

Syntax   Space[$](*number*)

Returns a string consisting of a specified number of spaces. Space returns a Variant; Space$ returns a string.

SPC

Syntax   Spc(*number*)

Skips a specified number of spaces in a Print# statement or a Print method.

SQR

Syntax   Sqr(*number*)

Returns the square root of a number.

STDEV

Syntax   StDev(*expression*)

Returns an estimate of the standard deviation for a population sample represented as a set of values in a specified field on a query, form, or report.

STDEVP

Syntax   StDevP(*expression*)

Returns an estimate of the standard deviation for a population represented as a set of values in a specified field on a query, form, or report.

STR, STR$

Syntax   Str[$](*number*)

Returns a string representation of a value of a numeric expression. Str returns a variant; Str$ returns a string.

STRCOMP

Syntax   StrComp(*stringexp1,stringexp2[,compare)]*)

Returns a value indicating how well tub strings compare.

STRING, STRING$

Syntax   string[$](*number,character code*)

string[$](*number,string*)

Returns a string of identical characters specified as the ANSI character or the first character in a string.

SUM

Syntax   Sum(*expression*)

Returns the sum of a set of values contained in a specified field on a query, form, or report.

SWITCH

Syntax   Switch(*variable expression 1,variable 1[,variable expression 2, variable 2...[,variable expression 7, variable 7]]*)

Evaluates a list of expressions and returns a value or an expression associated with the first expression that is true.

SYD

Syntax   SYD(*cost,salvage,life,period*)

Returns the sum-of-year's digits depreciation of an asset for a specified period.

TAB

Syntax   Tab(*column*)

Moves to the position at which the next character prints when used with the Print# statement or the Print method.

TAN

Syntax   Tan(*angle*)

Returns the tangent of an angle measured in radians.

TIME, TIME$

Syntax   Time[$][()]

Returns the computer's current system time. Time returns a variant; Time$ returns a string.

TIMER

Syntax   Timer[()]

Returns the number of seconds that have elapsed since 12:00 A.M., according to the system time.

TIMESERIAL

Syntax   TimeSerial(*hour,minute,second*)

Returns the time serial for a specific time.

TIMEVALUE

Syntax   TimeValue(*string expression*)

Returns the time represented by *string expression.*

TRIM, TRIM$

Syntax   Trim[$](*string expression*)

Returns a copy of a string with the leading and trailing spaces removed. Trim returns a Variant; Trim$ returns a string.

UBOUND

Syntax   UBound(*array,*[*dimension*])

Returns the largest available subscript for the indicated dimension of an array.

UCASE, UCASE$

Syntax   UCase[$](*string expression*)

Returns a string in which all letters of string expression are converted to uppercase. UCase returns a variant: UCase$ returns a string.

USER

Syntax   User()

Returns the name of the current user.

VAL

Syntax   Val(*string expression*)

Returns the numeric value of a string of characters that contains numeric characters.

VAR

Syntax   Var(*expression*)

Returns an estimate of the Variance for a population sample represented as a set of values contained within a specified field of a query, form, or report.

VARP

Syntax   VarP(*expression*)

Returns an estimate of the Variance for a population represented as a set of values contained in a specified field of a query, form, or report.

VARTYPE

Syntax   VarType(*Variant*)

Returns a value that indicates how a Variant is stored internally by Access Basic.

WEEKDAY

Syntax   Weekday(*number*)

Returns an integer between 1 and 7 that represents the day of the week for a date serial number argument.

YEAR

Syntax   Year(*number*)

Returns an integer between 100 and 9999 that represents the year of a date argument.

APPENDIX

Sample Database Tables

*T*he examples in this book use the five tables introduced in Chapter 1. If you want to try creating some of these examples yourself, you will want to enter the tables. In the following pages are the tables this book uses. At the beginning of each table is the definition for the table that includes field name, data type, description, and other table properties the fields use. Following the table definition is the data contained in each table.

Client Table

Table Definition

Field Name	Data Type	Description	Size	Default Value	Indexed
City	Text		50		No
Client Id	Counter	Unique client identification number			Yes
Client Name	Text	Name of the amusement park	50		No
Contact	Text	Contact individual	50		No
Mailing Address	Text	P.O. Box or other mailing address	50		No
Park Desc	Memo	Park description and information on other park coasters and planned projects			No
Park Location	Text	Location of park rather than mailing address	50		No
Phone	Number		Double	0	No
State	Text		50		No
Total Invoices	Currency			0	No
Total Payments	Currency			0	No
YTD Invoices	Currency			0	No
YTD Payments	Currency			0	No
Zip Code	Text		50		No

Client Id	Client Name Contact Park Location	Mailing Address City, State, Zip Code Phone	YTD Invoices	YTD Payments	Total Invoices	Total Payments
1	Family Fun Land Jeff Jackson Isle Royale	P.O. Box 345 Houghton, MI 49312 6162239999	$2,500,000	$2,300,000	$2,500,000	$2,300,00

Park Desc: Large amusement park that has been popular for over 50 years. Only access to the park is by ferry. Three different adult's and two children's coasters are already operational

2	Teen Land Mary Morris Ashtabula Park	P.O. Box 786 Ashtabula, OH 44321 2169999090	$3,900,000	$1,900,000	$7,100,900	$5,100,90

Park Desc: Turn of the century amusement park with many family riders and some superb coasters

3	Amusement Technolo Mark Willia Panacea on the	P.O. Box 5346 Panacea on the Beach, FL 33012 8144444578	$4,100,000	$2,000,000	11,800,000	$9,700,00

Park Desc: This coastal amusement park combines the charm of the Florida landscape with the thrills of its amusement rides.

4	Arden Entertainment Jerry McCell Indianapolis	100 Federal Avenue Indianapolis, IN 67821	$198,000		$198,000	

Park Desc:

1

Client Id	Client Name Contact Park Location	Mailing Address City, State, Zip Code Phone	YTD Invoices	YTD Payments	Total Invoices	Total Payments
5	Family Amusements	P.O. Box 123548 Stanton, PA 78378	$1,500,000	$1,500,000	$1,500,000	$1,500,00
	Stanton					
Park Desc:						
6	Playland Consortium	P.O. Box 5839 Wheeling, WV 45678	$1,800,000	$1,800,000	$3,200,000	$3,200,00
	Wheeling					
Park Desc:						
7	Island Waterplay Inc.	1 Waterplay Lane Raleigh, NC 12378	$0	$0	$3,100,000	$2,600,00
	Raleigh					
Park Desc:						
8	Entertainment Plus	P.O. Box 4892368 Jersey City, NJ 08767				
	Jersey City					
Park Desc:						

Employee Table

Table Definition

Field Name	Data Type	Description	Size	Format	Caption	Default Value	Indexed
Bill Rate	Currency	Hourly client billing rate		Currency		10	No
City	Text		20				No
Date of Hire	Date/Time			Medium Date			No
Department	Text		12				No
Employee Id	Counter	Employee Identification Number					Yes
Extension	Number		Double	000	Office Ext.		No
First Name	Text		15	>			No
Home Phone	Text		50				No
Job Class	Number	Two digit job class code	Integer	General Number		0	Yes
Last Name	Text		20	>			No
Middle Initial	Text		1	>			No
Pay Rate	Currency	Hourly pay rate		Currency		0	No
Picture	OLE Object				Photo		No
State	Text		2			OH	No
Street Address	Text		50				No
Zip Code	Text		10				No

Field Name: Bill Rate
Validation Rule [Bill Rate]>=[Pay Rate]*1.1
Validation Text: To make a profit the billing rate must be at least 10% more than the pay rate

Field Name: Extension
Validation Rule [Extension]>0 And [Extension]<3500
Validation Text: Valid Phone extensions are between 1 and 3499

Field Name: Job Class
Validation Rule [Job Class]>9 And [Job Class]<51
Validation Text: Job Class must be between 10 and 50

Field Name: Pay Rate
Validation Rule [Pay Rate]>4.24 And [Pay Rate]<35.0
Validation Text: The pay rate must be between minimum wage and $35 hr.

Employee Id	First Name, Middle Initial, Last Name Street Address City, State, Zip Code Home Phone			Pay Rate	Bill Rate	Date of Hire	Job Class	Department	Office Ext.
1	William 111 Cedar Ave. Cleveland, OH 44123 (216)413-2222	W.	Wild	$35.00	$60.00	15-Mar-92	11	Design	234
2	Dan 51 Mentor Ave. Mentor, OH 44231 (216)591-1111	D.	Danger	$30.00	$50.00	17-Jan-87	41	Testing	1703

Employee Id	First Name, Middle Initial, Last Name Street Address City, State, Zip Code Home Phone			Pay Rate	Bill Rate	Date of Hire	Job Class	Department	Office Ext.
3	Rodger 886 Larch Street Cleveland, OH 43212 (216)765-9999	R.	Rolling	$33.00	$55.00	15-Apr-90	22	Design	876
4	Sandra 1232 Hillside Rd Gates Mills, OH 44040 (216)889-8888	S.	Scary	$31.00	$50.00	01-Feb-92	21	Design	567
5	Harry 321 Wood Ave. Mayfield, OH 44120 (216)765-7777	H.	Higher	$6.50	$10.00	16-May-90	32	Construction	3499
6	Tommy 213 25th St. Cleveland, OH 44037 (216)444-5555	T.	Thrill	$7.00	$10.00	07-Jun-88	33	Construction	543
7	Richard 45 Eagle Lane Solon, OH 44019 (216)333-1111	R.	Rock	$8.00	$10.00	03-Apr-89	31	Construction	876
8	Donna 111 Weaver Ave Columbus, OH 43514 (614)555-6666	D.	Dare	$35.00	$75.00	05-Mar-91	12	Design	321
9	Johnny 78 Fordham Dri Austinburg, OH 42124 (216)777-2222	J.	Jump	$6.50	$10.00	06-Nov-90	31	Construction	1098
10	Brenda 21 Circle Drive Gates Mills, OH 44040 (216)999-9999	B.	Brave	$32.00	$55.00	06-Dec-87	41	Testing	1230

William Wild's picture is a copy of Andrew Fuller's picture in the NWind sample database.
Harry Higher's picture is a copy of Michael Suyama's picture in the NWind sample database.

Employee Time Log

Table Definition

Field Name	Data Type	Description	Size	Indexed
Date	Date	First day of the week		Yes
Employee Id	Number	Matches up with Employee Id in the Employee table	Long Integer	Yes
Hours	Number	Number of hours spent on project	Integer	No
Project Number	Number	Matches up with Coaster Id in the Project table	Long Integer	Yes

Date	Employee Id	Project Number	Hours	Date	Employee Id	Project Number	Hours
6/12/92	1	1	20	6/19/92	1	1	4
6/12/92	1	4	12	6/19/92	1	5	36
6/12/92	1	7	8	6/19/92	2	2	28
6/12/92	2	2	35	6/19/92	2	7	12
6/12/92	2	3	5	6/19/92	3	5	40
6/12/92	3	5	40	6/19/92	4	5	20
6/12/92	4	5	40	6/19/92	4	6	20
6/12/92	5	3	18	6/19/92	5	2	30
6/12/92	5	4	6	6/19/92	5	8	10
6/12/92	5	8	13	6/19/92	6	4	40
6/12/92	6	4	2	6/19/92	7	2	40
6/12/92	6	5	38	6/19/92	8	6	40
6/12/92	7	2	40	6/19/92	9	2	40
6/12/92	8	5	15	6/19/92	10	2	40
6/12/92	8	6	25				
6/12/92	9	2	40				
6/12/92	10	2	40				

Invoice Register Table

Table Definition

Field Name	Data Type	Description	Size	Default Value	Indexed
Invoice Amount	Currency			0	No
Invoice Date	Date/Time				No
Invoice Number	Number		Double	0	Yes
Payment Amount	Currency			0	No
Payment Date	Date/Time				No
Project Id	Number	Matches up with Coaster Id in the Project table	Long Integer	0	Yes

Invoice Number	Invoice Date	Invoice Amount	Payment Amount	Payment Date	Project Id
975	1/31/89	$500,000	$500,000	3/12/89	9
986	3/31/89	$2,000,000	$2,000,000	6/1/89	9
1001	10/31/89	$500,000	$500,000	2/18/90	9
1005	3/30/90	$1,500,000	$1,500,000	4/15/90	8
1012	6/30/90	$200,900	$200,900	7/28/90	9
1018	10/31/90	$1,100,000	$1,100,000	3/16/91	8
1021	12/31/90	$250,000	$250,000	2/16/91	3
1030	3/31/91	$400,000	$400,000	5/15/91	7
1056	6/30/91	$500,000	$0		8
1057	6/30/91	$500,000	$500,000	7/28/91	1
1058	7/30/91	$2,750,000	$2,750,000	9/7/91	3
1059	8/30/91	$1,000,000	$1,000,000	9/26/91	7
1062	10/31/91	$1,200,000	$1,200,000	12/20/91	1
1063	10/31/91	$3,000,000	$3,000,000	12/21/91	3
1068	1/31/92	$400,000	$400,000	2/13/92	4
1070	1/31/92	$350,000	$350,000	4/4/92	6
1071	1/31/92	$300,000	$300,000	2/20/92	4
1072	2/29/92	$200,000	$0		4
1073	2/29/92	$400,000	$400,000	6/1/92	2
1074	2/29/92	$1,600,000	$1,600,000	4/5/92	4
1078	3/31/92	$1,700,000	$1,700,000	5/3/92	1
1085	4/30/92	$1,150,000	$1,150,000	7/18/92	6
1092	5/31/92	$600,000	$300,000	7/15/92	1
1093	5/31/92	$198,000	$0		5
1094	5/31/92	$1,500,000	$1,500,000	7/17/92	2
2005	6/30/92	$1,800,000	$0		3
2006	6/30/92	$1,800,000	$1,800,000	7/29/92	7
2011	7/31/92	$2,000,000	$0		2

Project Table

Table Description

Field Name	Data Type	Description	Size	Default Value	Indexed
Actual Cost	Currency	Actual labor and material costs		0	No
Angle	Number	Greatest angle of descent	Double	0	No
Capacity	Number	Maximum number of riders in 1 hour	Double	0	No
Client Id	Number	Number from client table	Long Integer	0	Yes
Coaster Id	Counter	Unique coaster identification number			Yes
Coaster Name	Text	Name of coaster ride	50		No
Completed	Yes/No	Completed project		No	No
Drop	Number	Maximum drop	Double	0	No
Est Cost	Currency	Projected out of pocket cost for labor and material		0	No
Features	Memo	Unique features of the ride			No
Height	Number	Maximum height	Double	0	No
Operational	Date/Time	Projected or actual operational date			No
Picture	OLE Object	Picture of model or operational ride			No
Speed	Number	Greatest speed in mph	Double	0	No
Time	Number	Length of ride in minutes	Double	0	No
Track	Number	Length of ride track	Double	0	No
Vehicles	Number	Total number of vehicles	Double	0	No

The Format property of the Completed field is Yes/No

Coaster Id: 1   **Coaster Name:** Scream Machine   **Client Id:**   3

Completed: No   **Operational:** 10/4/93   **Est Cost:** $7,800,000.00   **Actual Cost** $4,000,000.00

Track: 5780   **Time:** 2.8   **Picture:**
Height: 168   **Speed:** 70
Drop: 160   **Capacity:** 1800
Angle: 54   **Vehicles:** 3
Features: All wood coaster with steep drops and many curves. Each train holds 28 passengers

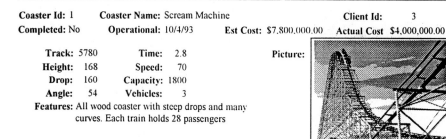

Coaster Id: 2   **Coaster Name:** Blue Arrow   **Client Id:**   2

Completed: No   **Operational:** 8/20/92   **Est Cost:** $4,000,000.00   **Actual Cost** $3,900,000.00

Track: 5200   **Time:** 2   **Picture:**
Height: 205   **Speed:** 73
Drop: 182   **Capacity:** 2300
Angle: 60   **Vehicles:** 6
Features: Steep 60 degree first hill drop on this steel tubular track coaster with fiberglass cars each holding 36 passengers

Coaster Id: 3   **Coaster Name:** Astro Transport   **Client Id:**   3
Completed: Yes   **Operational:** 5/21/92   **Est Cost:** $7,500,000.00   **Actual Cost** $7,800,000.00

Track: 2000	**Time:** 2	**Picture:**
Height: 68	**Speed:** 50	
Drop: 30	**Capacity:** 1900	
Angle: 58	**Vehicles:** 5	

Features: Special effects are the highlight of this space
age transport

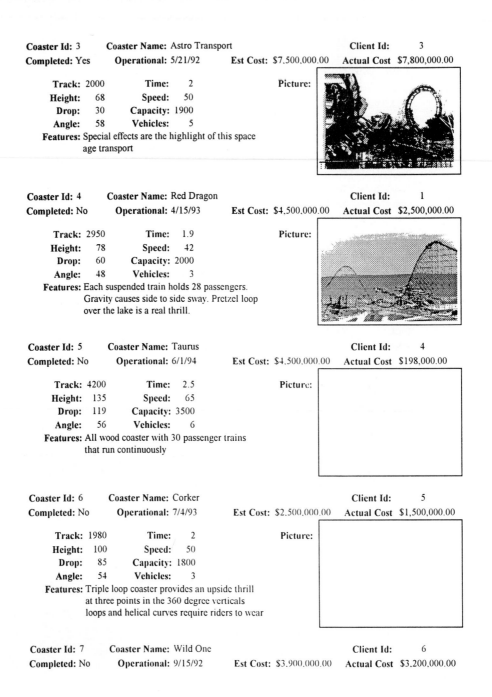

Coaster Id: 4   **Coaster Name:** Red Dragon   **Client Id:**   1
Completed: No   **Operational:** 4/15/93   **Est Cost:** $4,500,000.00   **Actual Cost** $2,500,000.00

Track: 2950	**Time:** 1.9	**Picture:**
Height: 78	**Speed:** 42	
Drop: 60	**Capacity:** 2000	
Angle: 48	**Vehicles:** 3	

Features: Each suspended train holds 28 passengers.
Gravity causes side to side sway. Pretzel loop
over the lake is a real thrill.

Coaster Id: 5   **Coaster Name:** Taurus   **Client Id:**   4
Completed: No   **Operational:** 6/1/94   **Est Cost:** $4,500,000.00   **Actual Cost** $198,000.00

Track: 4200	**Time:** 2.5	**Picture:**
Height: 135	**Speed:** 65	
Drop: 119	**Capacity:** 3500	
Angle: 56	**Vehicles:** 6	

Features: All wood coaster with 30 passenger trains
that run continuously

Coaster Id: 6   **Coaster Name:** Corker   **Client Id:**   5
Completed: No   **Operational:** 7/4/93   **Est Cost:** $2,500,000.00   **Actual Cost** $1,500,000.00

Track: 1980	**Time:** 2	**Picture:**
Height: 100	**Speed:** 50	
Drop: 85	**Capacity:** 1800	
Angle: 54	**Vehicles:** 3	

Features: Triple loop coaster provides an upside thrill
at three points in the 360 degree verticals
loops and helical curves require riders to wear

Coaster Id: 7   **Coaster Name:** Wild One   **Client Id:**   6
Completed: No   **Operational:** 9/15/92   **Est Cost:** $3,900,000.00   **Actual Cost** $3,200,000.00

Track: 1895   **Time:** 1.5   **Picture:**
Height: 100   **Speed:** 50
Drop: 87   **Capacity:** 1000
Angle: 52   **Vehicles:** 7
Features: The four passenger trains can move quickly through sharp turns accentuating speed and turn sensations

Coaster Id: 8   **Coaster Name:** White Lightnin   **Client Id:** 7
Completed: Yes   **Operational:** 2/15/91   **Est Cost:** $2,800,000.00   **Actual Cost** $3,100,000.00

Track: 2600   **Time:** 2.8   **Picture:**
Height: 68   **Speed:** 50
Drop: 60   **Capacity:** 2500
Angle: 48   **Vehicles:** 5
Features: Sharp spiral turns and splashing water make this ride popular

Coaster Id: 9   **Coaster Name:** The Runaway   **Client Id:** 2
Completed: Yes   **Operational:** 3/28/90   **Est Cost:** $3,215,000.00   **Actual Cost** $3,200,900.00

Track: 2675   **Time:** 1.75   **Picture:**
Height: 120   **Speed:** 46
Drop: 100   **Capacity:** 1350
Angle: 53   **Vehicles:** 2
Features: Twenty four passengers experience negative G force through exciting dips

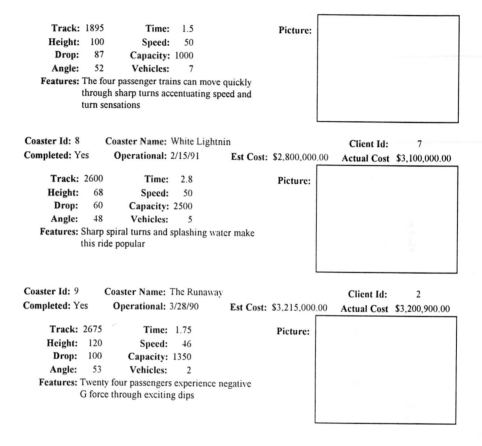

APPENDIX

Notes for SQL Users

SQL, or Structured Query Language, is a language that is designed to work with relational databases similar to Access. SQL queries data, updates data, and manages the data in a database. Whether or not you realize it, you have used SQL every time you created a query. Other database management products also can use SQL. Access supports a subset of SQL statements that you will find adequate for many tasks.

Microsoft has an SQL server that you can use to store your databases. SQL databases are relational databases that let you access the data over several platforms. You can use the tables you store in the SQL server by attaching the SQL tables to an Access database. For example, you might have an SQL server to store your database and use Microsoft Access to work with the data.

SQL in Access

Microsoft Access can use SQL statements in several locations. SQL statements are used in queries to describe the data the query presents. SQL statements can be used to select the items that appear in list boxes and combo boxes. You can use SQL statements that choose the data that appears in forms and reports. You can run SQL statements in macros as well as use parts of SQL statements for other actions in a macro. Modules also use SQL statements although the features they provide are beyond the introduction to programming presented in Chapter 21.

SQL Statements in Queries

The SQL statement Microsoft Access uses in a query is a statement that defines the data the query uses and the results this query presents. You do not have to create this SQL statement because Access does it for you. Access takes the query design you create in the query design window and creates an SQL statement that represents the results you want the query to present. You can see this SQL statement by selecting SQL from the Uiew menu when looking at a query's design. A sample SQL statement might look like this:

```
SELECT  DISTINCTROW [Employee Time Log].Date, [Employee Time
Log].[Employee Id], [Employee Time Log].[Project Number],
[Employee Time Log].Hours, Employee.[First Name], Em-
ployee.[Last Name], Employee.[Bill Rate]
FROM Employee, [Employee Time Log],
Employee INNER JOIN [Employee Time Log] ON Employee.[Employee
Id] = [Employee Time Log].[Employee Id]
WHERE ((([Employee Time Log].Date=#06/12/92#))
WITH OWNERACCESS OPTION;
```

This particular SQL statement is for the Employee Names and Hours query shown in Chapter 7 as an example of using two tables in a query. When looking at the SQL query, you can copy it by pressing CTRL-INS just as you would copy other entries that you edit. You may want to copy the SQL statement so you can use it to select the items that appear in a list or combo box control of a report. You can change the SQL statement and Access will modify the query design to match any changes you have made. If you are not familiar with SQL, use the query design window to design the query that lets Access make the conversion between the query design and the SQL statement that defines the query.

Most of the queries you create use the SELECT SQL statement, which is described in the last section in this appendix. The append, delete, and update action queries use other SQL statements. These SQL statements are INSERT INTO for append queries, DELETE for delete queries, and UPDATE for update queries.

SQL Statements in List and Combo Box Controls

List box and combo box controls can use SQL statements to select the items that Access presents in the list boxes and controls. To use an SQL statement for a list box and combo box control, supply the SQL statement for the Row Source property of the list box and combo box control either by typing the SQL statement directly or copying the statement from the Clipboard. Often you will copy the SQL statement from a query and then paste it into a form's list box or combo box control's Row Source property. The results of the SQL statement are the contents in the list of the list box or combo box control. An example of an SQL statement provided for the Row Source property is SELECT Client.[Client Name], Client.[Client Id] from Client; with the Row Source Type property set to Table/Query. This sample SQL statement includes the client names and numbers from the Client table in the list box.

Using SQL Statements for a Form or Report

Forms and reports can use an SQL statement as the Record Source property of the form or report. When you use an SQL statement as the Record Source property, the form or report includes the records the SQL statement selects. You can use the SQL statement from a query as the Record Source property, and the results are the same as if you created a query that uses the same SQL statement and used that query as the Record Source property of the form or report.

Using SQL Statements in a Macro

Macros can include SQL statements as actions or arguments. To run an SQL statement in a macro, use the RunSQL action. This action has a single argument, the SQL statement the RunSQL action performs. An example of an SQL statement entered for this purpose is SELECT Client.[Client Name], Client.[Client Id], Client.Contact INTO [Temporary Client] FROM Client; this creates a new table named Temporary Client that contains the values from three fields from each of the records.

Several macro actions use part of SQL statements for their Where Condition action argument. The information for the argument is an expression—the same expression an SQL SELECT statement uses to choose which records the statement chooses. The SQL statement for an ApplyFilter action's Where Condition argument selects the records the filter displays. An SQL statement for an OpenForm or OpenReport action's Where Condition argument selects the records included in the form or report.

SQL Statements in Modules

SQL statements in modules usually are for advanced features beyond the basics of modules presented in Chapter 21. Procedures use SQL statements for various reasons. Here are several:

☐ The CreateSnapshot method for databases, record sets, or QueryDef objects can use SQL statements to choose the data that appears in the snapshot object this method creates.

☐ The Filter property of dynaset and snapshot objects can be set to part of an SQL statement. This is just like the parts of SQL statements the Where Condition argument uses for various macro actions. When you use part of an SQL statement for the Filter property of these objects, you are selecting which records in these objects are selected.

☐ The SQL property of QueryDef objects uses SQL statements to set the records selected by a query definition object.

The SELECT SQL Statement

The real powerhouse behind SQL is the SELECT statement. This is the SQL statement most frequently used by Access. The SELECT statement chooses the data to present and how the data is presented. The WHERE part of this statement is the same part of the SQL statement used when you supply the Where Condition argument of a macro action. Using a SELECT SQL statement lets you access any database Access can open. You can use the SELECT statement to reference data that is not in the current database.

Like all SQL statements, the SELECT statement ends with a semicolon. Using this character to end statements means you can use multiple lines in a single statement. Access knows that it has reached the end of the statement when it finds the semicolon.

After SELECT is the data you want to return. For each field to appear in the data returned, supply the table or query name (in brackets if the name includes spaces) and a period. Then enter the name of the field, enclosed in brackets if the field name includes spaces. An example is Employee.[First Name]. These field names are separated by commas. If you want a field renamed, follow the field description with the word AS and the new field name, enclosed in brackets if it includes spaces.

You may see DISTINCTROW in the SELECT statements before the field names. DISTINCTROW is a reserved word (a word that has a special meaning to SQL and that you cannot use for other purposes). By including this word in a SELECT statement, you make the data in more types of query results updatable.

Next, the SELECT statement describes the source of the data by the word FROM and the tables or query names that provide the source of data. These table and query names are separated by commas, and the names must be enclosed in brackets when the name includes spaces. You can use an asterisk (*) in place of a field name when you want to include all fields from the chosen table. If the database containing the tables is not the current database, enter **IN** followed by the database name to include data from the outside database in the results of the SQL statement.

In the example just given, Access included the INNER JOIN to link the tables. Following INNER JOIN is the name of one of the tables or queries, and then ON followed by the expression that links the two tables or queries. In the example, the records from the two tables are joined by the Employee ID fields of the Employee table and the Employee Time Log table.

The WHERE part of a SELECT statement selects the records from the tables that appear in the statement's results. WHERE is followed by an expression that chooses the records you want to see. The information after the WHERE is similar to the entries in the Criteria rows in the QBE grid. Since everything needed for a query is explicitly provided in the SQL SELECT statement, you will see ANDS to indicate the parts of the criteria that are located on the same line and ORS to indicate the parts of the criteria that are located on separate lines in the QBE grid.

GROUP BY creates groups of records according to the common values of the fields you place after GROUP BY. ORDER BY indicates how the records the SELECT statement chooses are organized. The ORDER BY clause provides the information that appears in the Sort row of the QBE grid.

APPENDIX

Toolbar Reference

Access has many buttons on its toolbar that you will use. This appendix shows the different Access environments and the buttons that appear on the toolbar. Next to each button is a description of the function the button performs. Buttons that appear in multiple toolbars are explained only in the first toolbar in which that button appears.

Database Window

Button	Button Name	Description
	Print Preview button	Shows how the datasheet, form, or report will appear when printed
	New Query button	Creates a new query based on the query or table selected in the database window if one is selected
	New Form button	Creates a new form based on the query or table selected in the database window if one is selected
	New Report button	Creates a new report based on the query or table selected in the database window if one is selected
	Undo button	Undoes your most recent action
	Help button	Opens Microsoft Access Help

Design View (Tables)

Button	Button Name	Description
	Design View button	Switches you to the design view of a table, query, or form
	Datasheet View button	Switches you to the datasheet view of a table, query, or form
	Properties button	Displays or conceals the property sheet for the selected control, section, or database object
	Primary Key button	Makes the selected field or fields the primary key for the table

Design View (Queries)

Button	Button Name	Description
Σ	Totals button	Displays or conceals the Totals row in the QBE grid
!	Run button	Runs a query, or, in a macro window, a macro

Datasheet View (Tables and Queries)

Button	Button Name	Description
🔍	Find button	Opens the Find dialog box, allowing you to search the active table or dynaset for the data you specify
Field: Description	Field box	Moves you to the field you select

Design View (Forms Window)

Button	Button Name	Description
📋	Form View button	Switches you to the form view of a form
🖼	Field List button	Conceals or displays a window listing all fields in the underlying table or query
🎨	Palette button	Displays or conceals the palette
MS Sans Serif	Font box	Selects the font for the selected control
8	Font-size box	Selects the size of the font for the selected control

Button	Button Name	Description
B	Bold button	Makes the text in the selected control bold
I	Italic button	Makes the text in the selected control italic
<u>U</u>	Underline button	Makes the text in the selected control underline
≡	Align-Left button	Left-aligns the text in the selected control
≡	Center button	Centers the text in the selected control
≡	Align-Right button	Right-aligns the text in the selected control
ABC 789	General Alignment button	Aligns the text in the selected control to the left, and the numbers to the right

Datasheet and Form View (Forms Window)

Button	Button Name	Description
Edit Filter/Sort	Edit Filter/Sort	Opens the Filter window to create or edit a filter
Apply Filter	Apply/Sort Filter button	Applies the current filter
Show All	Show All Records button	Displays all records in underlying table by removing any applied filters

Report Window

Button	Button Name	Description
🔲	Sorting and Grouping button	Conceals or displays the Sorting and Grouping window to let you select how you want to sort and group data for your report

Macro Window

Button	Button Name	Description
🔲	Macro Names button	Displays or conceals the Macro Name column used to designate macro names within a macro group
🔲	Conditions button	Displays or conceals the Condition column used to enter conditions that determine whether an action is performed in a macro

Button	Button Name	Description
🔲	Single Step button	Executes a macro or Access Basic procedure one step (an action or statement) at a time

Module Window

Button	Button Name	Description
Procedure: PCase	Procedure box	Selects the procedure or declarations section displayed in the module window
🔲	Previous Procedure button	Displays the previous Access Basic procedure in the module window
🔲	Next Procedure button	Displays the next Access Basic procedure in the module window
🔲	Procedure Step button	Moves you through the Access Basic code one procedure at a time
🔲	Reinitialize button	Stops execution of Access Basic procedures and clears all variables
🔲	Breakpoint button	Sets or clears a breakpoint on the current line of code

Print Preview and Sample Preview Window

| Print... | Setup... | Zoom | Cancel | | ? |

Button	Button Name	Description
Print...	Print button	Prints the datasheet, form, or report
Setup...	Setup button	Displays the Print Setup dialog box
Zoom	Zoom button	Switches between showing a magnified portion of the page or the entire page
Cancel	Cancel button	Exits Print Preview

Index

Q

Some of Access's function key assignments are global, which means that these function keys do the same thing all the time. Other function keys are specific to views or windows. These keys may not be used in all views or windows, or they may have a different purpose in one window than they do in another. Therefore, the function keys are listed in four sections. The first section explains the global function key assignments, the second explains the function keys used in the design view, the third explains the function keys used in the datasheet and in the form view, and the fourth explains the function keys used in the Module window.

Global Function Keys

Press	To
F1	Display Help with information about the selected command, dialog box, property, control, action, Access Basic keyword, or window.
F11	Bring the Database window to the front.
F12	Open the Save As dialog box.
SHIFT-F1	Display the question mark pointer instead of the normal mouse pointer. Click the question mark pointer on a screen object for which you want more information.
SHIFT-F12	Save a database object.
CTRL-F4	Close the active window.
CTRL-F6	Cycle between open windows.
ALT-F1	Bring the Database window to the front.
ALT-F2	Open the Save As dialog box.
ALT-F4	Close a dialog box or quit Access.
ALT-SHIFT-F2	Save a database object.

Design View Function Keys

Press	To
F2	Toggle between showing an insertion point and selecting the field in the design view of tables, queries, and macros.
F6	Toggle between the top and bottom portions of the window in the design view of tables and queries and the Filter window.
SHIFT-F2	Open the Zoom box to enter text more conveniently into small input areas.

Datasheet and Form View Function Keys

Press	To
F2	Toggle between showing an insertion point and selecting a field.
F4	Open a combo or list box.

Press	To
F5	Move to the Record Number box. Enter the record number you want to move to and press ENTER.
F6	In form view, cycle forward through the header, detail section, and footer of a form.
F7	Open the Find dialog box.
F8	Activate Extend mode. Keep pressing this key to extend the selection to the word, field, record, and all records.
F9	Recalculate the fields in the window.
SHIFT-F4	Find the next occurrence of the text you specified without reopening the Find or Replace dialog box.
SHIFT-F5	Save a record.
SHIFT-F6	In form view, cycle backward through the header, detail, and footer sections of a form.
SHIFT-F7	Open the Replace dialog box.
SHIFT-F8	Reverse the selection made with F8. To cancel Extend mode completely, press ESC.
SHIFT-F9	Requery the underlying tables. In a subform, only the tables underlying the subform are requeried.

Module Window Function Keys

Press	To
F2	View procedures.
F3	Find the next occurrence of the text you specified without reopening the Find or Replace dialog box.
F5	Continue execution.
F6	Toggle between the upper and lower panes when the window has been split.
F7	Open the Find dialog box.
F8	Run in single step mode.
F9	Toggle a breakpoint at the selected line.
SHIFT-F2	Go to the selected procedures definition.
SHIFT-F3	Find the previous occurrence of the text you specified without reopening the Find or Replace dialog box.
SHIFT-F7	Open the Replace dialog box.
SHIFT-F8	Procedure step.